O-Parts HUNTER

SEISHI KISHIMOTO

7

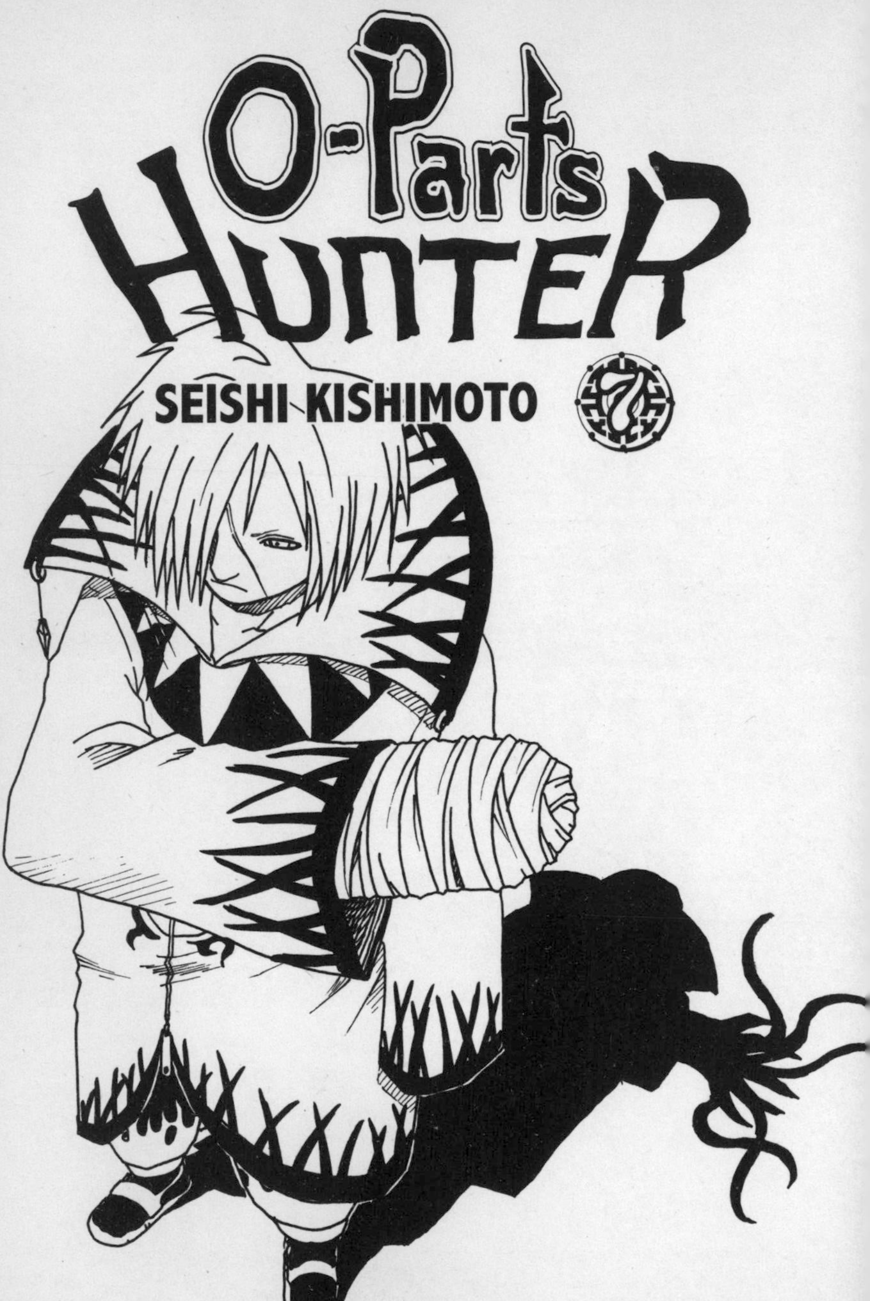

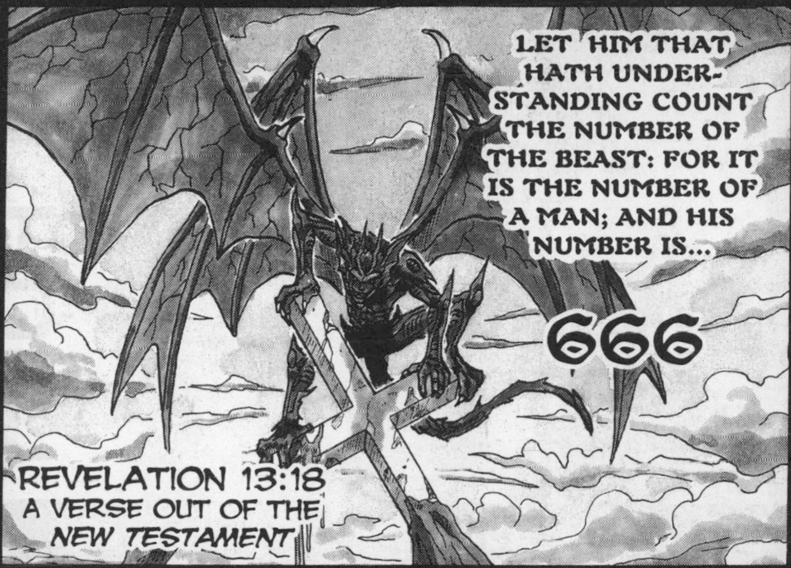
LET HIM THAT HATH UNDER-STANDING COUNT THE NUMBER OF THE BEAST: FOR IT IS THE NUMBER OF A MAN; AND HIS NUMBER IS...
666
REVELATION 13:18
A VERSE OUT OF THE *NEW TESTAMENT*

O-Parts Hunter

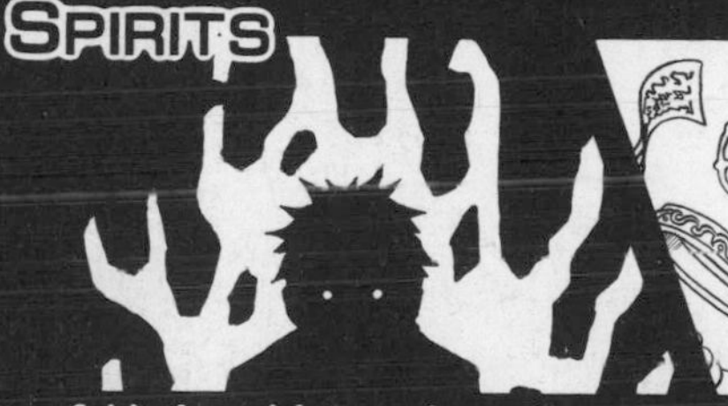
SPIRITS

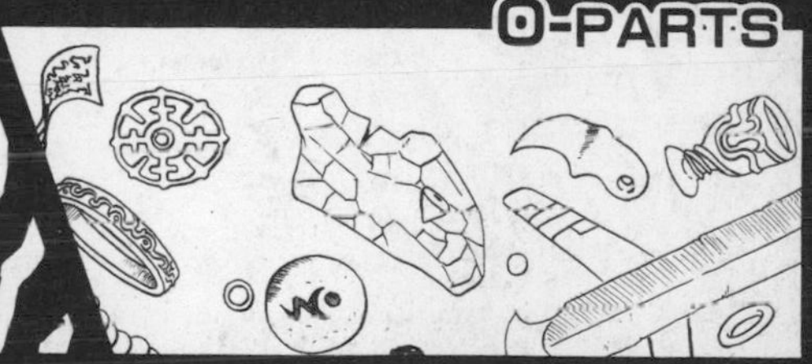
O-PARTS

Spirit: A special energy force which only the O.P.T.s have. The amount of Spirit they have within them determines how strong of an O.P.T. they are.

O-Parts: Amazing artifacts with mystical powers left from an ancient civilization. They have been excavated from various ruins around the world. Depending on their Effects, O-Parts are given a rank from E to SS within a seven-tiered system.

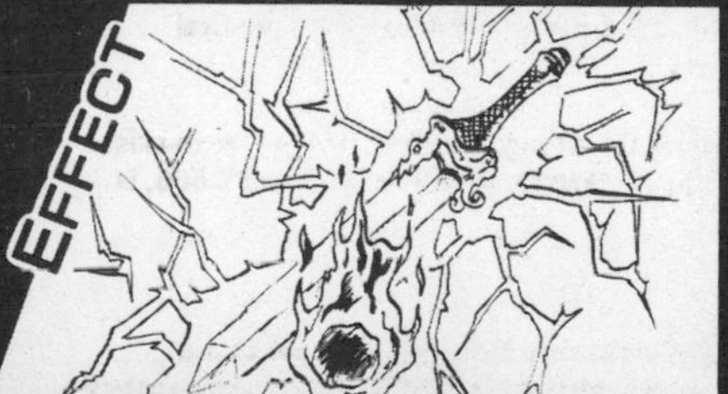
EFFECT

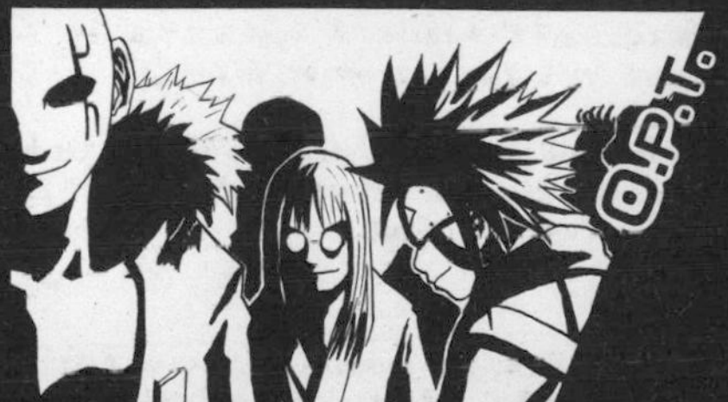
O.P.T.

Effect: The special energy (power) the O-Parts possess. It can only be used when an O.P.T. sends his Spirit into an O-Part.

O.P.T.: One who has the ability to release and use the powers of the O-Parts. The name O.P.T. is an abbreviated form of O-Part Tactician.

CHARACTERS

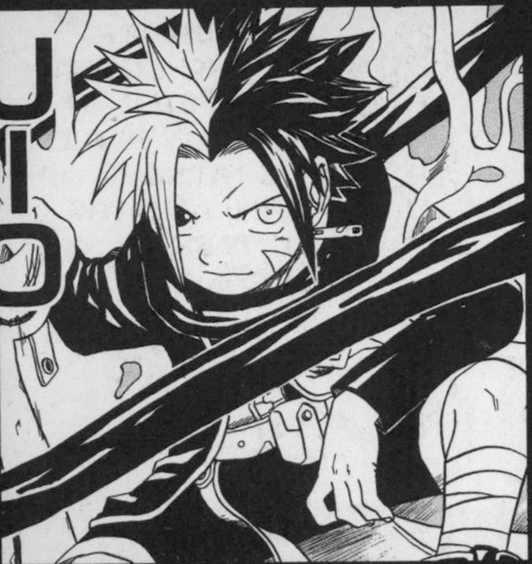
JIO

Jio Freed
A wild O.P.T. boy whose dream is world domination! He has been emotionally damaged by his experiences in the past, but is still gung-ho about his new adventures! O-Part: New Zero-shiki (Rank B)
Effect: Triple (Increasing power by a factor of three)

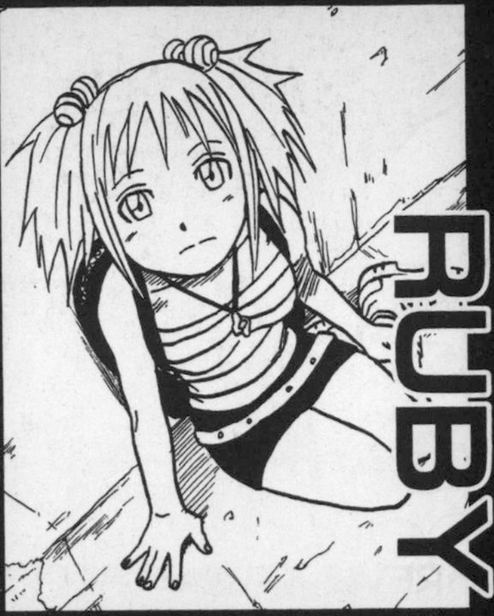
RUBY

Ruby
A treasure hunter who can decipher ancient texts. She meets Jio during her search for a legendary O-Part.

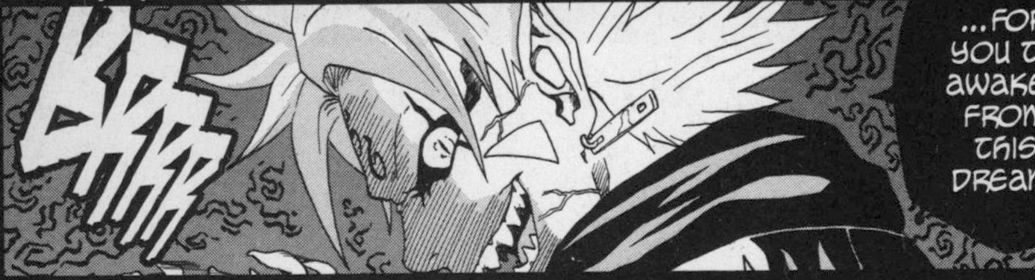
...FOR YOU TO AWAKEN FROM THIS DREAM.

Satan
This demon is thought to be a mutated form of Jio. It is a creature shrouded in mystery with earth-shattering powers.

STORY

Ascald: a world where people fight amongst themselves in order to get their hands on mystical objects left behind by an ancient civilization...the O-Parts.

In that world, a monster that strikes fear into the hearts of the strongest of men is rumored to exist. Those who have seen the monster all tell of the same thing – that the number of the beast, 666, is engraved on its forehead.

***

Jio, an O.P.T. boy who wants to rule the world, travels the globe with Ruby, a girl in search of a legendary O-Part and her missing father. Jio was separated from Ruby in Entotsu City, a town crushed under the heel of its own government, but he gained a new traveling companion along the way—a novice O.P.T. named Ball. Together, they discovered the source of the town's woes: Mexis, an O-Part of mass destruction! Jio managed to destroy Mexis, free the townspeople and reunite with Ruby...but his victory may have cost him his soul. Because Mexis has already activated the spirit of Satan within Jio... and bit by bit, it is taking him over...

O-Parts HunteR

7

Table of Contents

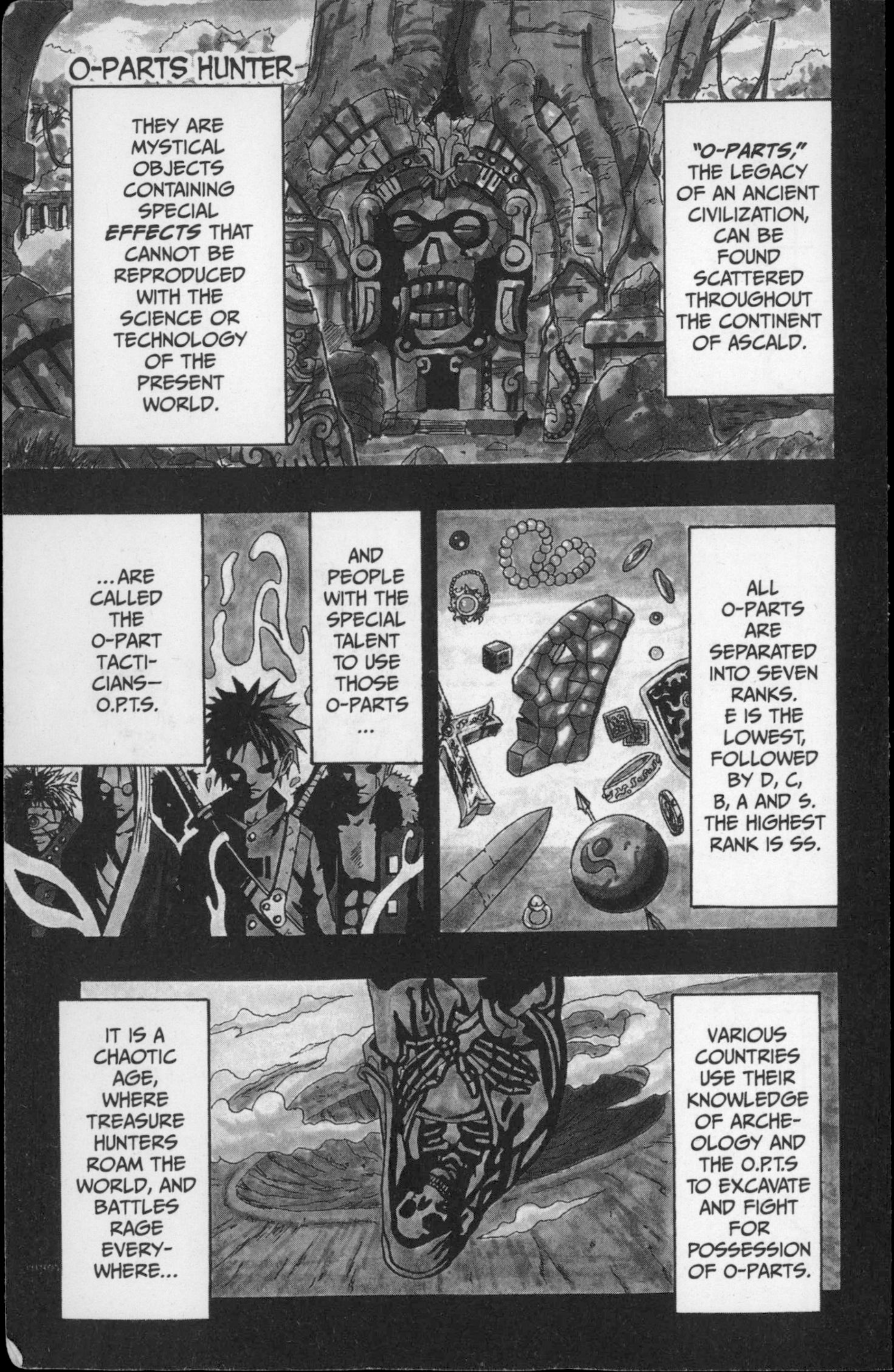
O-PARTS HUNTER
"O-PARTS," THE LEGACY OF AN ANCIENT CIVILIZATION, CAN BE FOUND SCATTERED THROUGHOUT THE CONTINENT OF ASCALD.
THEY ARE MYSTICAL OBJECTS CONTAINING SPECIAL EFFECTS THAT CANNOT BE REPRODUCED WITH THE SCIENCE OR TECHNOLOGY OF THE PRESENT WORLD.
ALL O-PARTS ARE SEPARATED INTO SEVEN RANKS. E IS THE LOWEST, FOLLOWED BY D, C, B, A AND S. THE HIGHEST RANK IS SS.
AND PEOPLE WITH THE SPECIAL TALENT TO USE THOSE O-PARTS ...
...ARE CALLED THE O-PART TACTI-CIANS— O.P.T.S.
VARIOUS COUNTRIES USE THEIR KNOWLEDGE OF ARCHE-OLOGY AND THE O.P.T.S TO EXCAVATE AND FIGHT FOR POSSESSION OF O-PARTS.
IT IS A CHAOTIC AGE, WHERE TREASURE HUNTERS ROAM THE WORLD, AND BATTLES RAGE EVERY-WHERE...

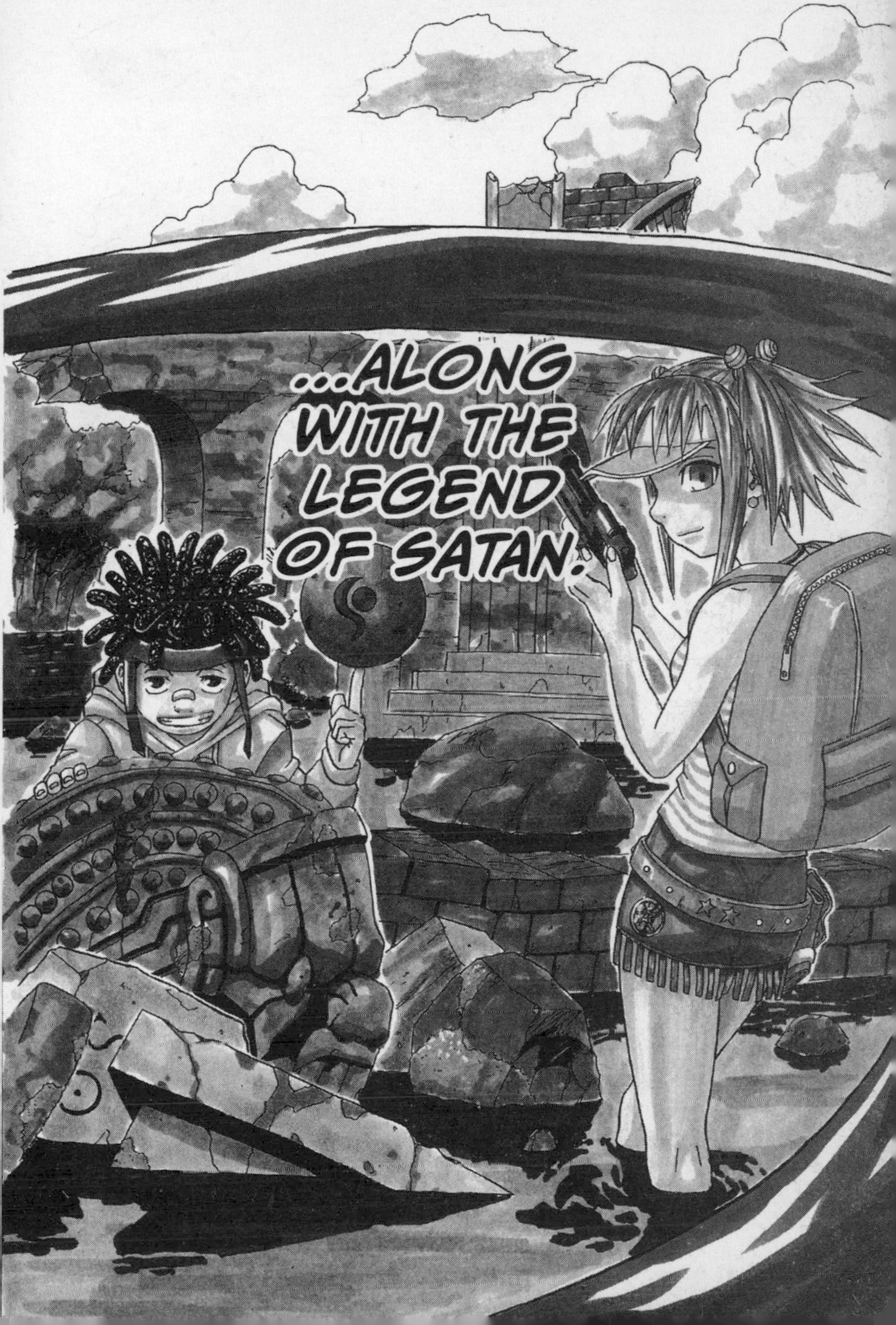
...ALONG WITH THE LEGEND OF SATAN.

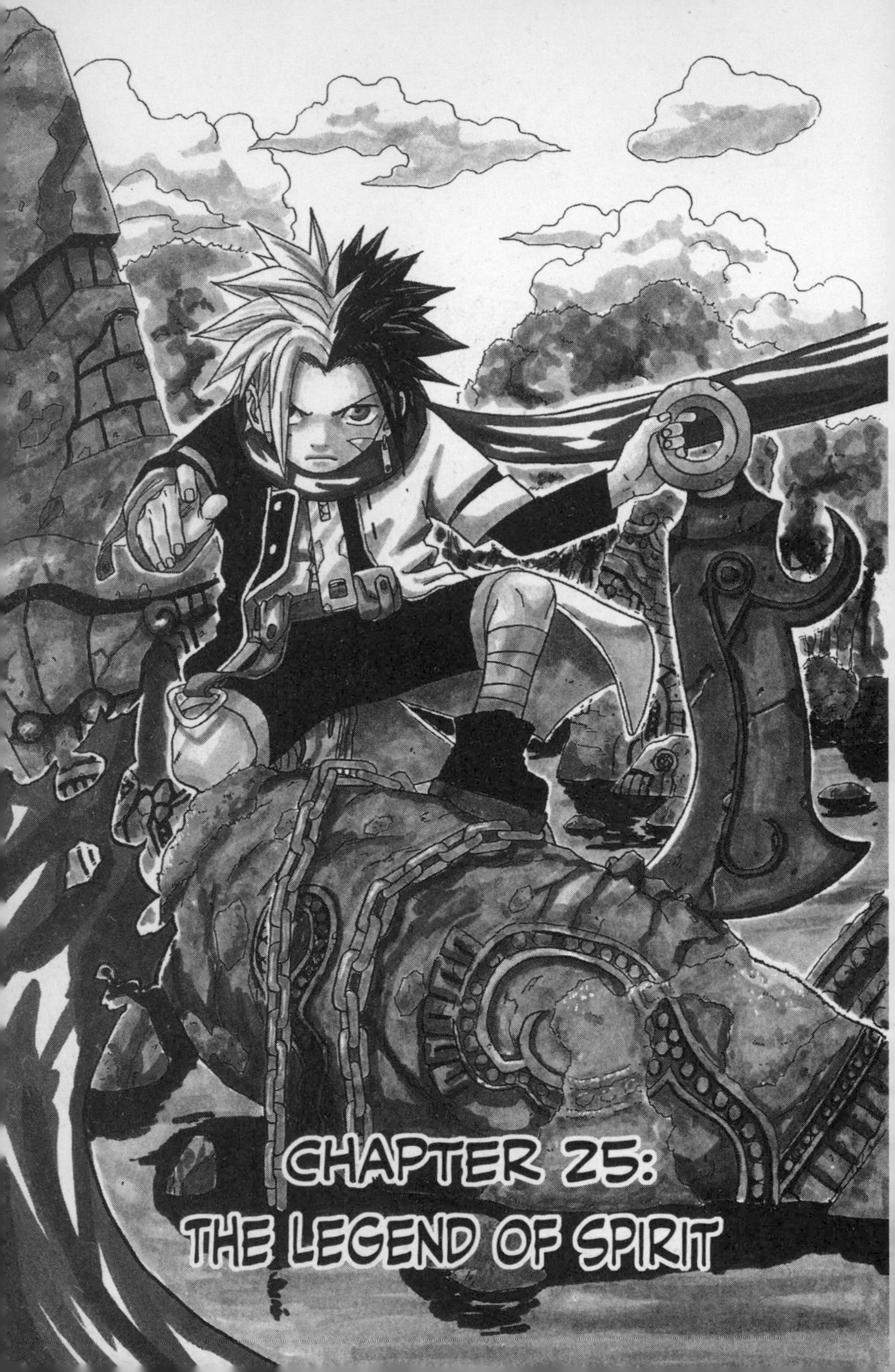
CHAPTER 25:
THE LEGEND OF SPIRIT

SEISHI AND BAMBOO

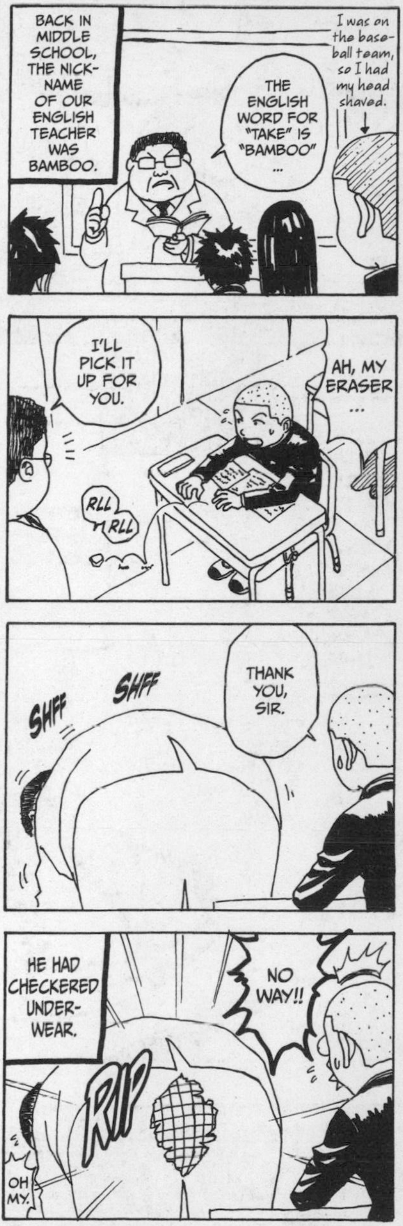
I was on the baseball team, so I had my head shaved.
THE ENGLISH WORD FOR "TAKE" IS "BAMBOO" ...
BACK IN MIDDLE SCHOOL, THE NICKNAME OF OUR ENGLISH TEACHER WAS BAMBOO.
AH, MY ERASER ...
I'LL PICK IT UP FOR YOU.
RLL RLL
THANK YOU, SIR.
SHFF
SHFF
NO WAY!!
HE HAD CHECKERED UNDERWEAR.
RIP
OH MY.

SEISHI AND INSECT CATCHING

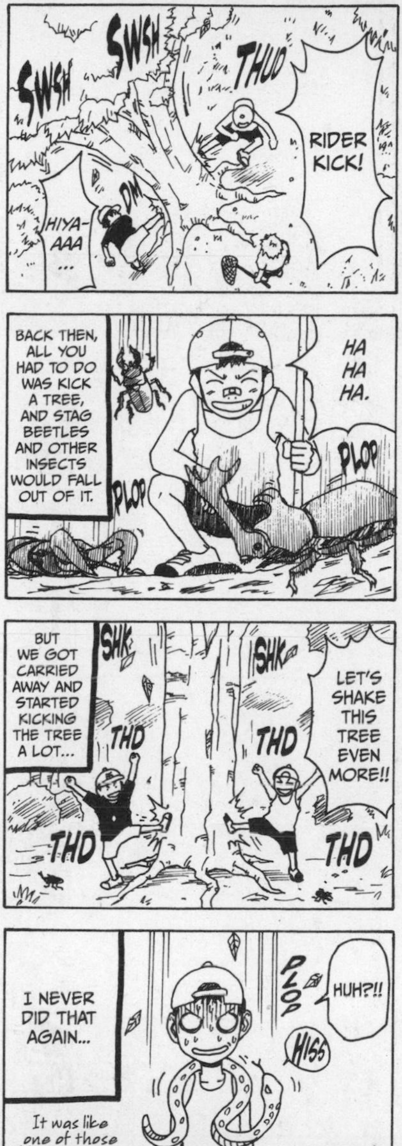
RIDER KICK!
THUD
SWSH
SWSH
DM
HIYA-AAA ...
HA HA HA.
BACK THEN, ALL YOU HAD TO DO WAS KICK A TREE, AND STAG BEETLES AND OTHER INSECTS WOULD FALL OUT OF IT.
PLOP
PLOP
LET'S SHAKE THIS TREE EVEN MORE!!
SHK
THD
SHK
BUT WE GOT CARRIED AWAY AND STARTED KICKING THE TREE A LOT...
THD
THD
THD
HUH?!!
PLOP
HISS
I NEVER DID THAT AGAIN...
It was like one of those TV shows where they search for mythical creatures...

※ These four-panel manga are nonfiction.

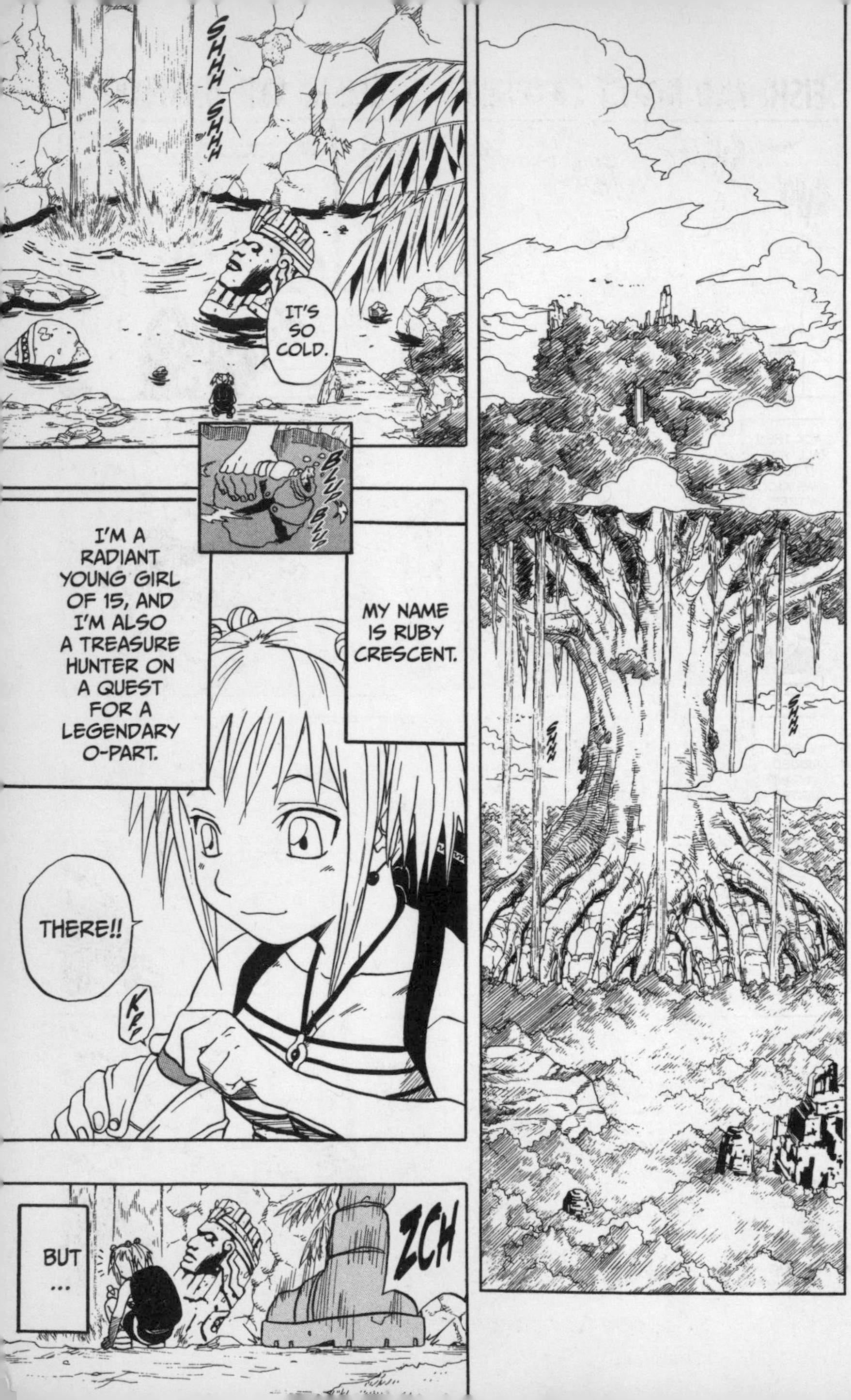
SHHH
SHHH
SHHH SHHH
IT'S SO COLD.
BLUB BLUB
MY NAME IS RUBY CRESCENT.
I'M A RADIANT YOUNG GIRL OF 15, AND I'M ALSO A TREASURE HUNTER ON A QUEST FOR A LEGENDARY O-PART.
THERE!!
KF
ZCH
BUT ...

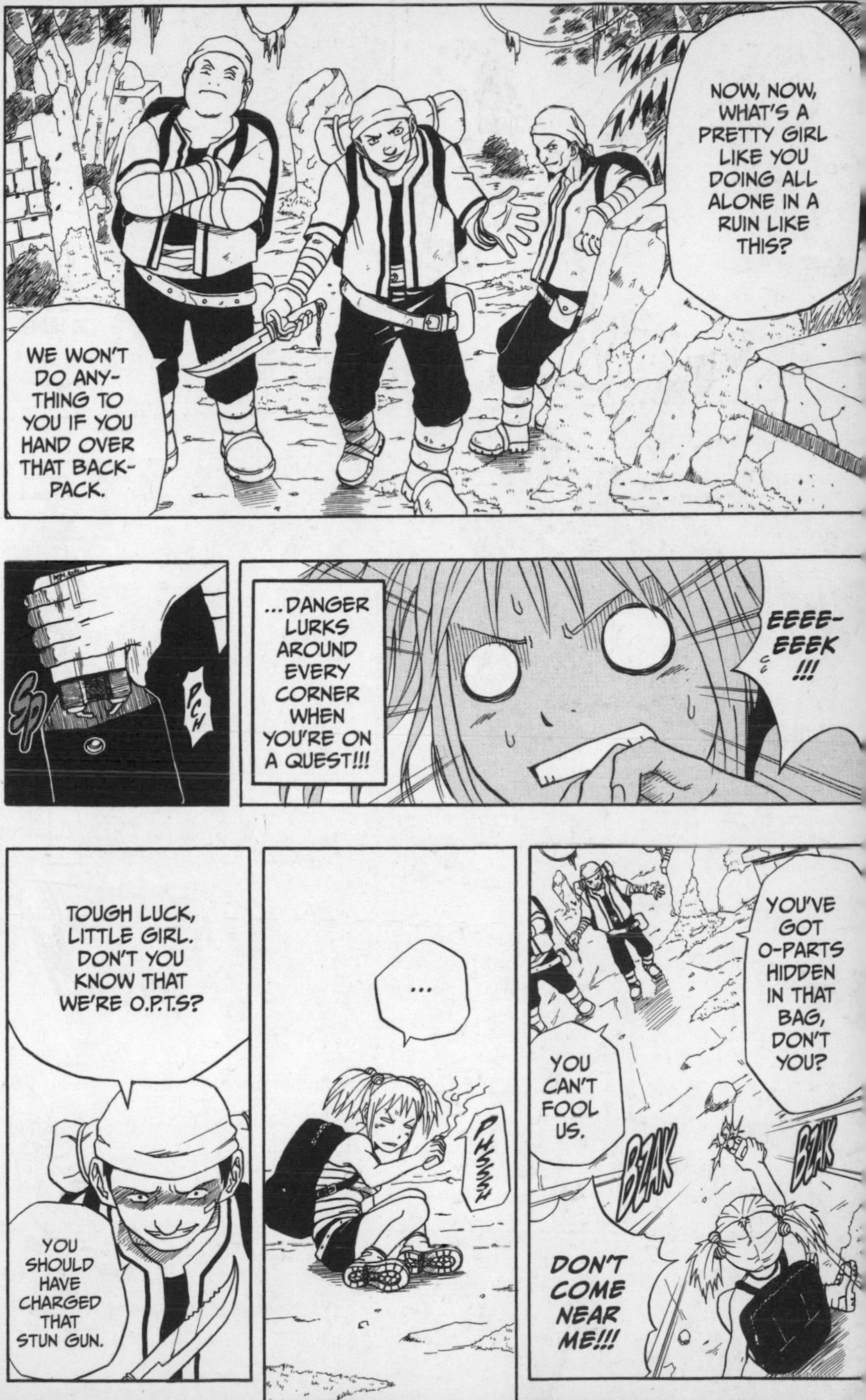
NOW, NOW, WHAT'S A PRETTY GIRL LIKE YOU DOING ALL ALONE IN A RUIN LIKE THIS?
WE WON'T DO ANY-THING TO YOU IF YOU HAND OVER THAT BACK-PACK.
EEEE-EEEK!!!
...DANGER LURKS AROUND EVERY CORNER WHEN YOU'RE ON A QUEST!!!
SP
PCH
YOU'VE GOT O-PARTS HIDDEN IN THAT BAG, DON'T YOU?
YOU CAN'T FOOL US.
BZAK
BZAK
DON'T COME NEAR ME!!!
...
PHSSSH
TOUGH LUCK, LITTLE GIRL. DON'T YOU KNOW THAT WE'RE O.P.T.S?
YOU SHOULD HAVE CHARGED THAT STUN GUN.

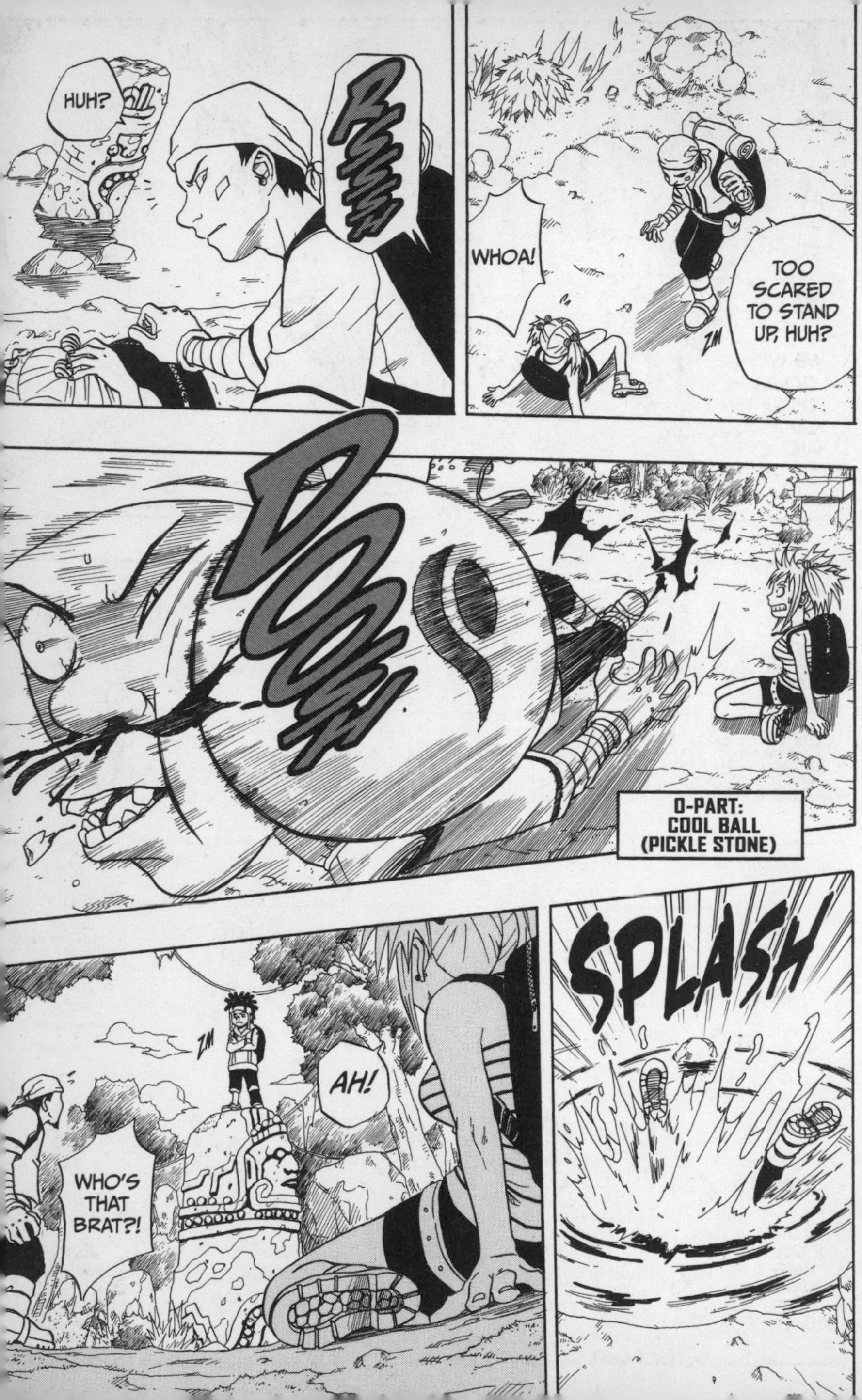
TOO SCARED TO STAND UP, HUH?
ZM
WHOA!
HUH?
O-PART: COOL BALL (PICKLE STONE)
SPLASH
AH!
ZM
WHO'S THAT BRAT?!

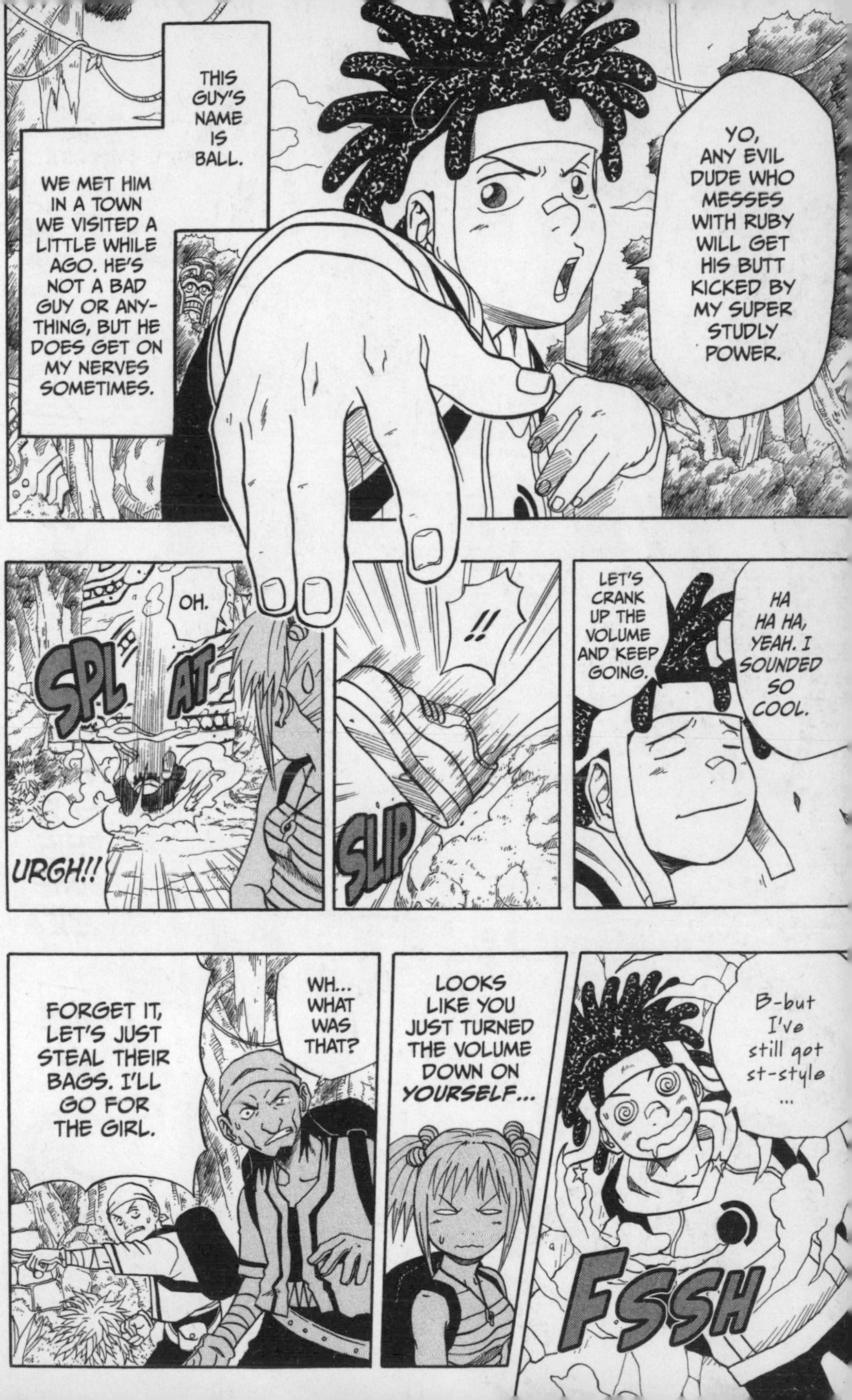
YO, ANY EVIL DUDE WHO MESSES WITH RUBY WILL GET HIS BUTT KICKED BY MY SUPER STUDLY POWER.
THIS GUY'S NAME IS BALL.
WE MET HIM IN A TOWN WE VISITED A LITTLE WHILE AGO. HE'S NOT A BAD GUY OR ANY-THING, BUT HE DOES GET ON MY NERVES SOMETIMES.
HA HA HA, YEAH. I SOUNDED SO COOL.
LET'S CRANK UP THE VOLUME AND KEEP GOING.
!!
SLIP
OH.
SPLAT
URGH!!
B-but I've still got st-style ...
FSSH
LOOKS LIKE YOU JUST TURNED THE VOLUME DOWN ON *YOURSELF*...
WH... WHAT WAS THAT?
FORGET IT, LET'S JUST STEAL THEIR BAGS. I'LL GO FOR THE GIRL.

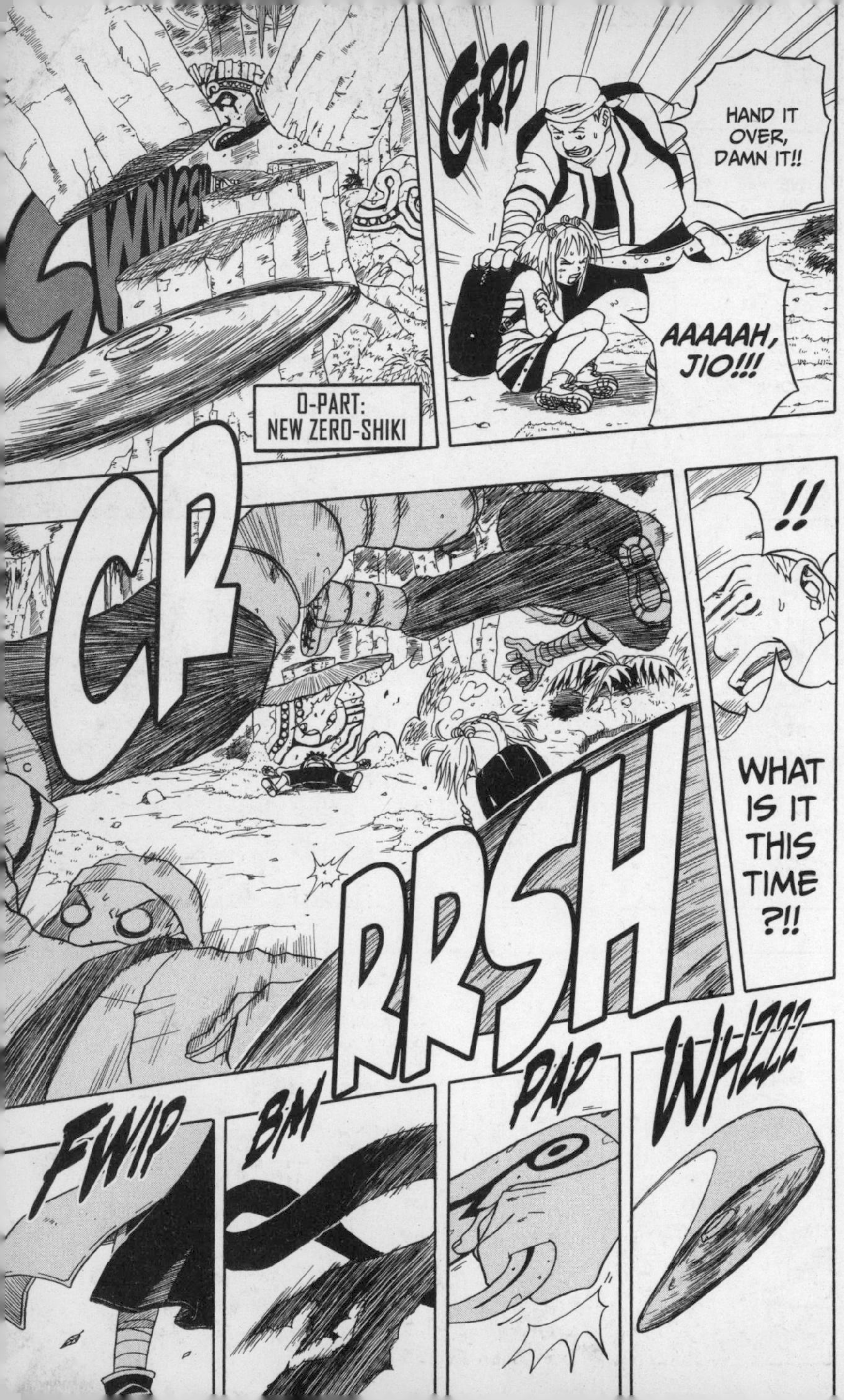
GRP
HAND IT OVER, DAMN IT!!
AAAAAH, JIO!!!
SWNSS!
O-PART: NEW ZERO-SHIKI
!!
WHAT IS IT THIS TIME ?!!
CR
RRSH
WHZZZ
DAP
BAM
FWIP

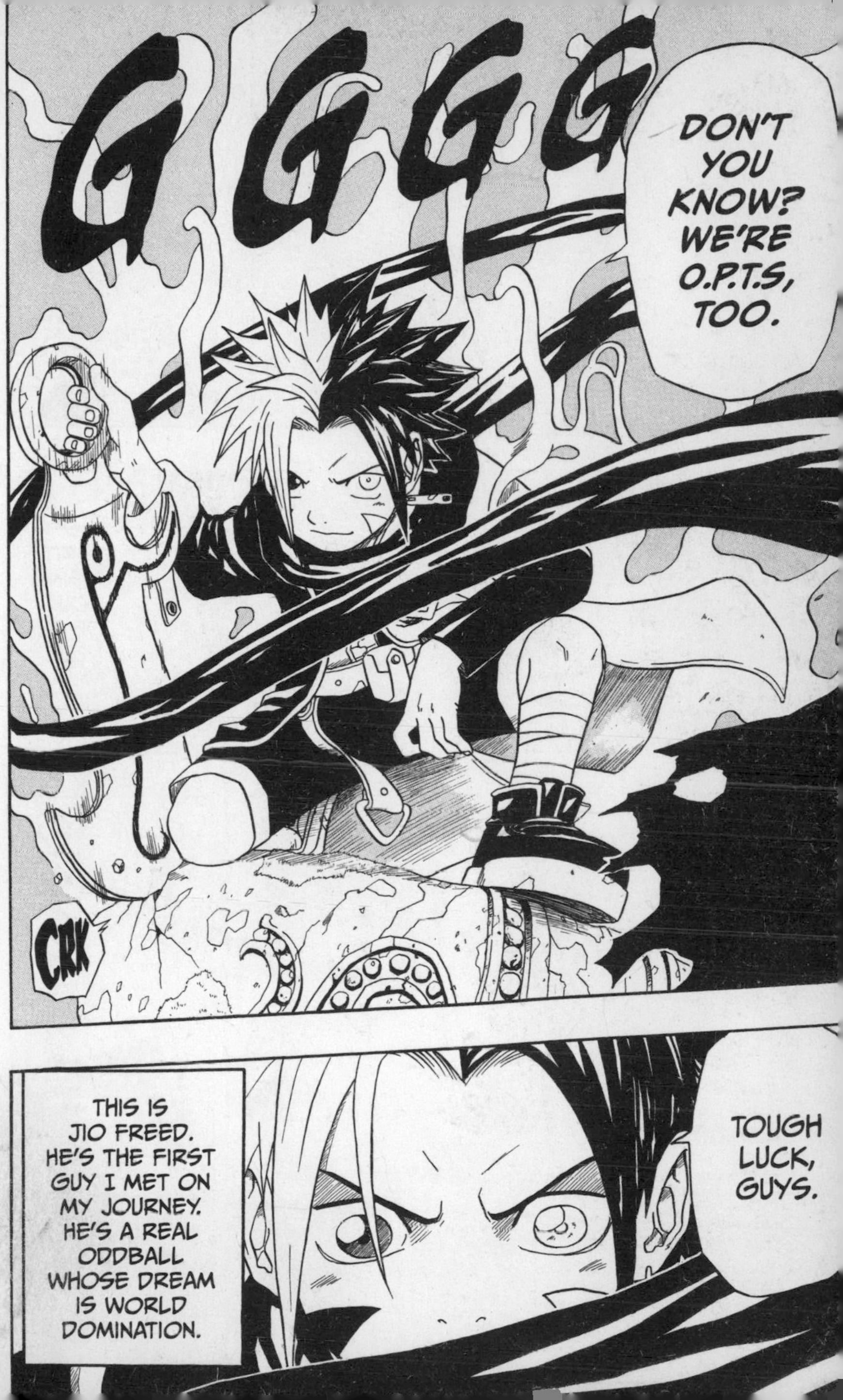
GGGG
DON'T YOU KNOW? WE'RE O.P.T.S, TOO.
CRK
TOUGH LUCK, GUYS.
THIS IS JIO FREED. HE'S THE FIRST GUY I MET ON MY JOURNEY. HE'S A REAL ODDBALL WHOSE DREAM IS WORLD DOMINATION.

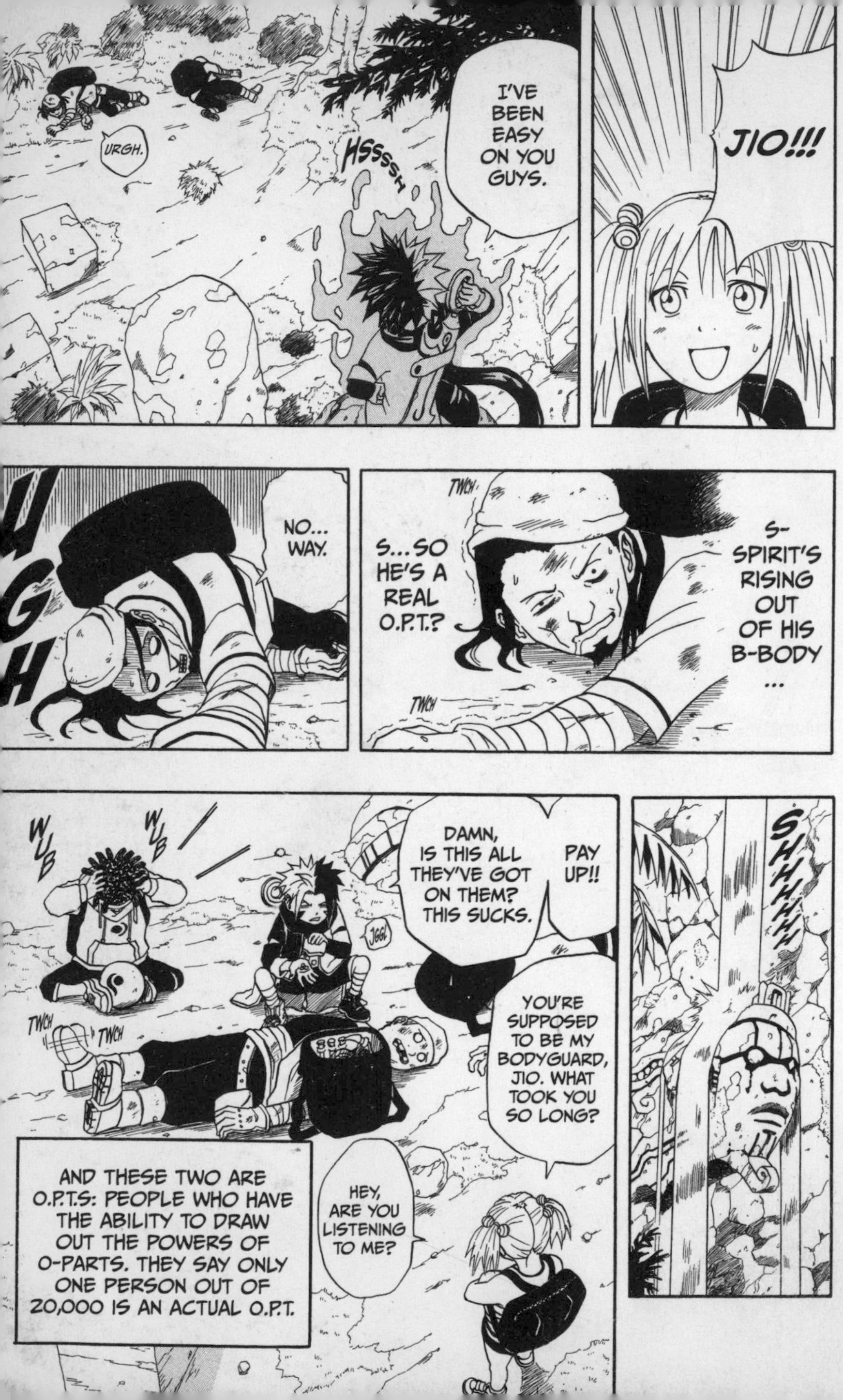
JIO!!!
I'VE BEEN EASY ON YOU GUYS.
HSSSSSH
URGH.
S-SPIRIT'S RISING OUT OF HIS B-BODY...
S...SO HE'S A REAL O.P.T.?
TWCH
TWCH
NO... WAY.
SHHHHHH
PAY UP!!
DAMN, IS THIS ALL THEY'VE GOT ON THEM? THIS SUCKS.
WUB
WUB
JGGL
TWCH TWCH
YOU'RE SUPPOSED TO BE MY BODYGUARD, JIO. WHAT TOOK YOU SO LONG?
HEY, ARE YOU LISTENING TO ME?
AND THESE TWO ARE O.P.T.S: PEOPLE WHO HAVE THE ABILITY TO DRAW OUT THE POWERS OF O-PARTS. THEY SAY ONLY ONE PERSON OUT OF 20,000 IS AN ACTUAL O.P.T.

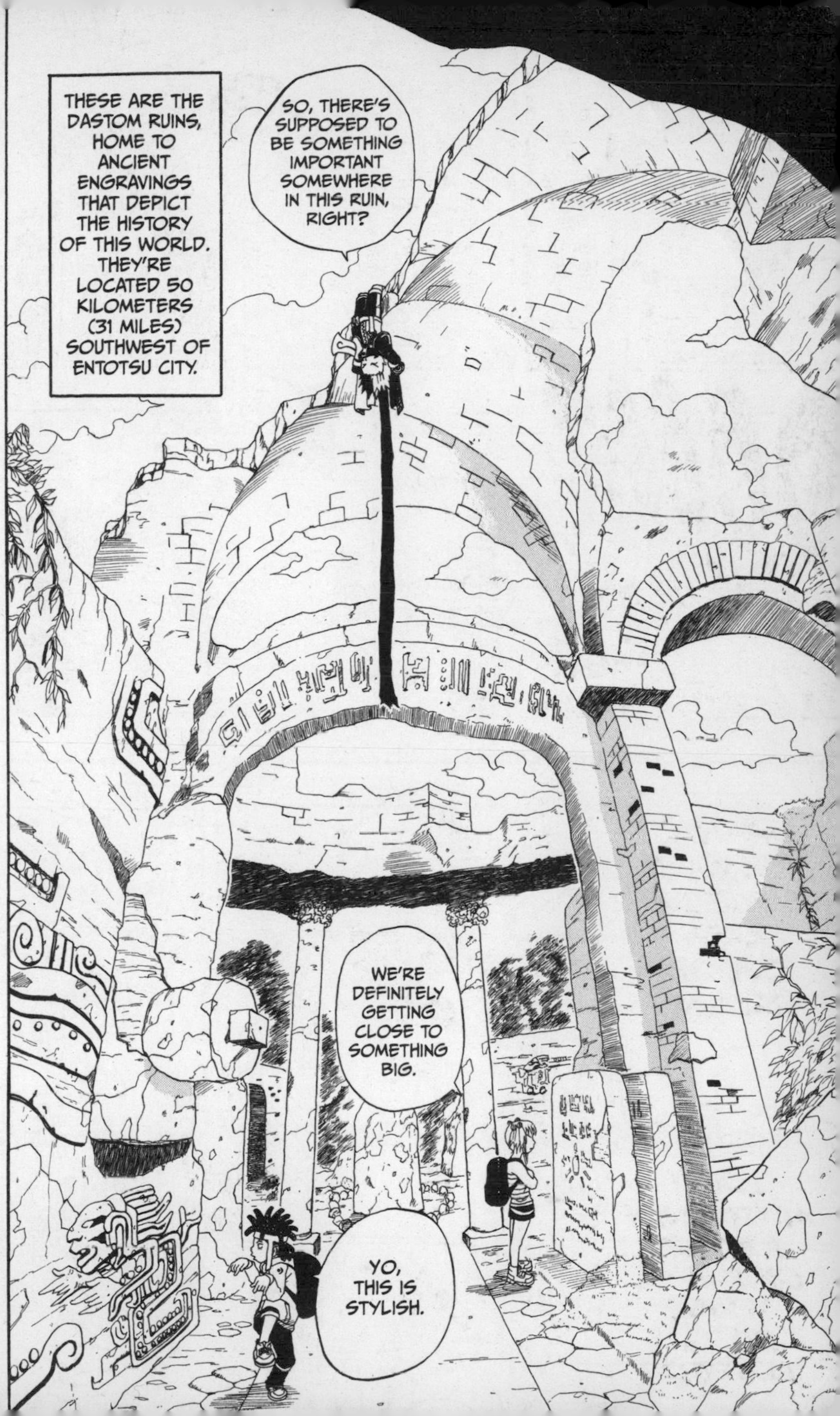
THESE ARE THE DASTOM RUINS, HOME TO ANCIENT ENGRAVINGS THAT DEPICT THE HISTORY OF THIS WORLD. THEY'RE LOCATED 50 KILOMETERS (31 MILES) SOUTHWEST OF ENTOTSU CITY.
SO, THERE'S SUPPOSED TO BE SOMETHING IMPORTANT SOMEWHERE IN THIS RUIN, RIGHT?
WE'RE DEFINITELY GETTING CLOSE TO SOMETHING BIG.
YO, THIS IS STYLISH.

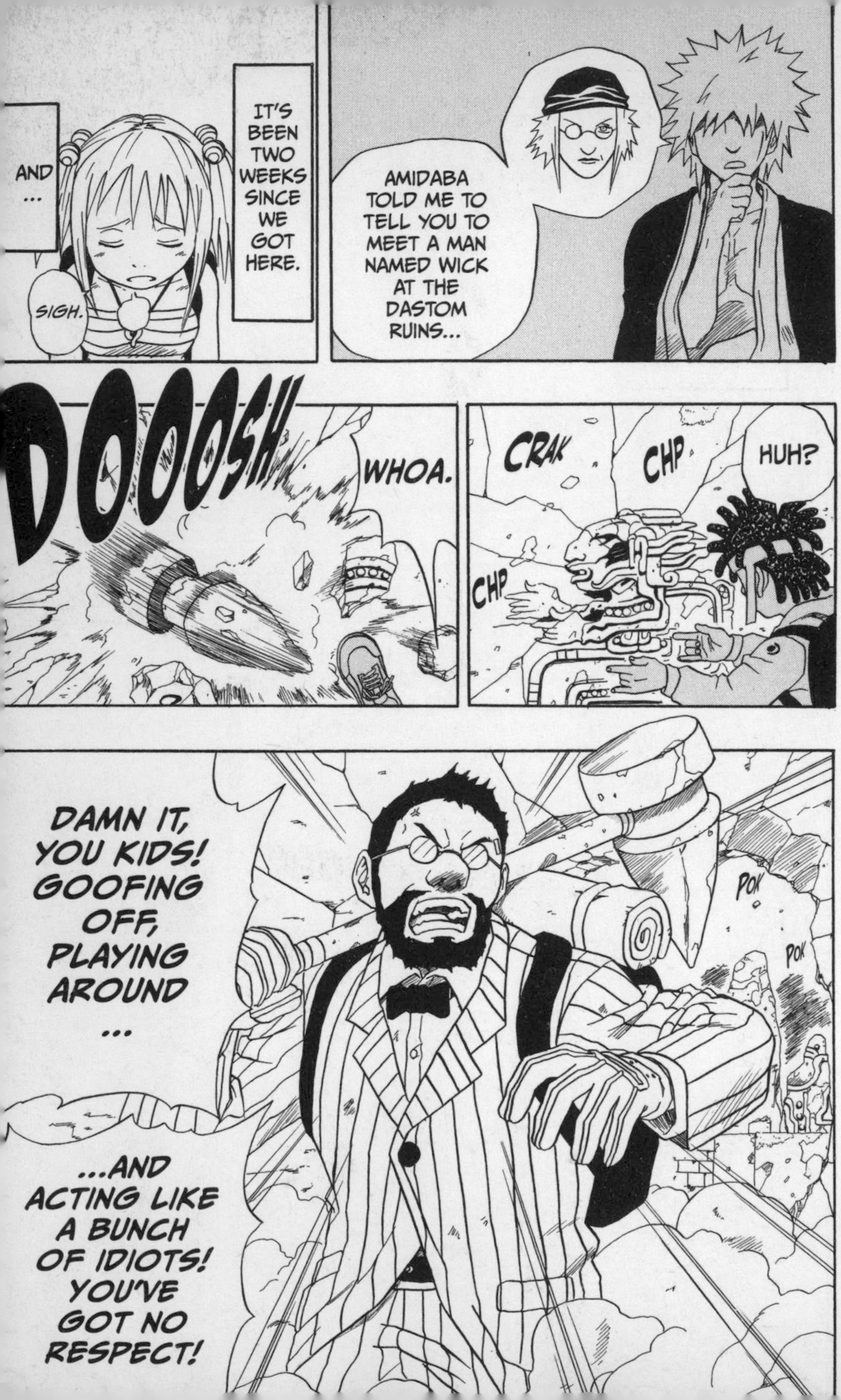
AMIDABA TOLD ME TO TELL YOU TO MEET A MAN NAMED WICK AT THE DASTOM RUINS...
IT'S BEEN TWO WEEKS SINCE WE GOT HERE.
AND ...
SIGH.
HUH?
CHP
CRAK
CHP
WHOA.
DOOOSH
POK
POK
DAMN IT, YOU KIDS! GOOFING OFF, PLAYING AROUND ...
...AND ACTING LIKE A BUNCH OF IDIOTS! YOU'VE GOT NO RESPECT!

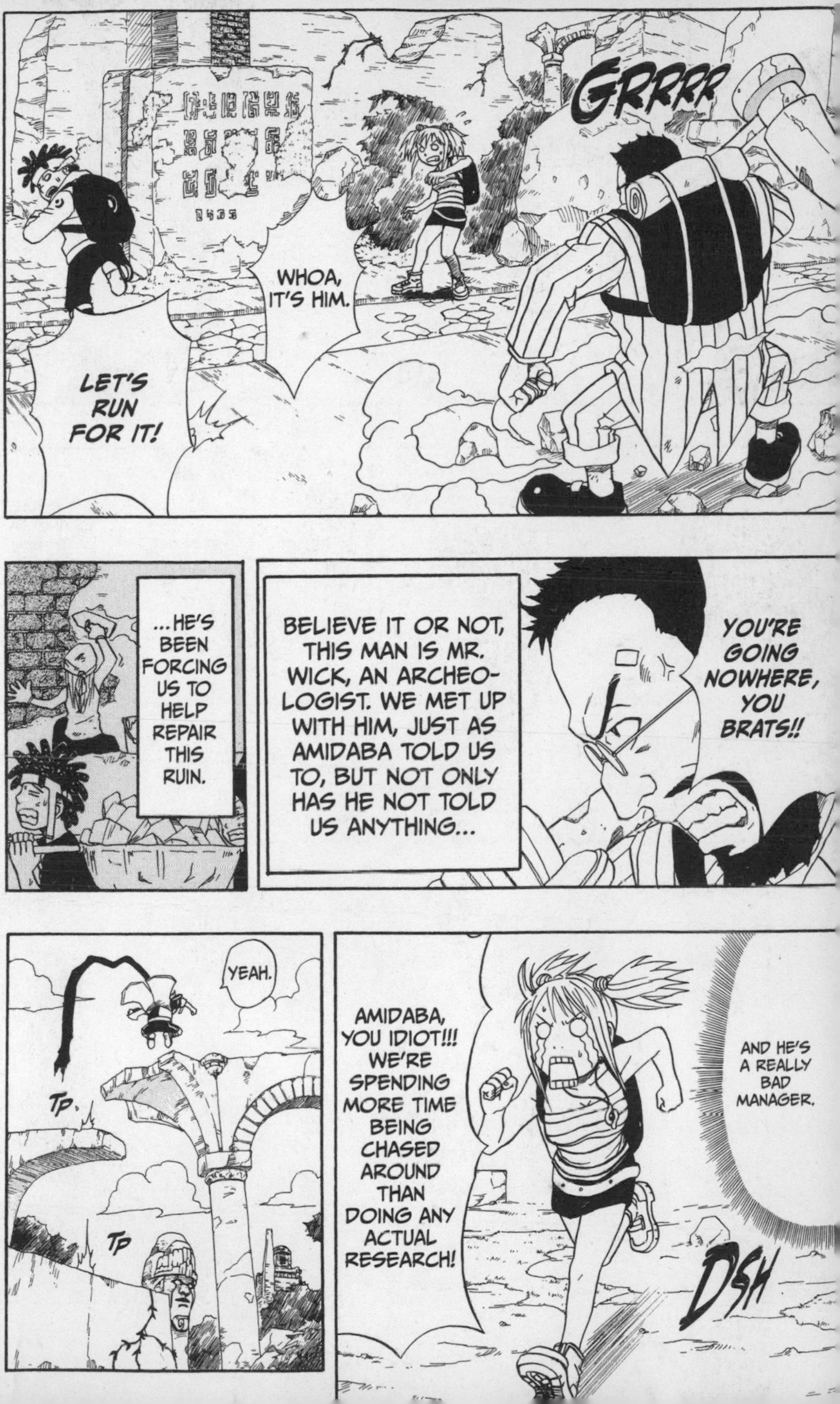
GRRRR
WHOA, IT'S HIM.
LET'S RUN FOR IT!
YOU'RE GOING NOWHERE, YOU BRATS!!
BELIEVE IT OR NOT, THIS MAN IS MR. WICK, AN ARCHEO-LOGIST. WE MET UP WITH HIM, JUST AS AMIDABA TOLD US TO, BUT NOT ONLY HAS HE NOT TOLD US ANYTHING...
...HE'S BEEN FORCING US TO HELP REPAIR THIS RUIN.
AND HE'S A REALLY BAD MANAGER.
AMIDABA, YOU IDIOT!!! WE'RE SPENDING MORE TIME BEING CHASED AROUND THAN DOING ANY ACTUAL RESEARCH!
DSH
YEAH.
TP.
TP

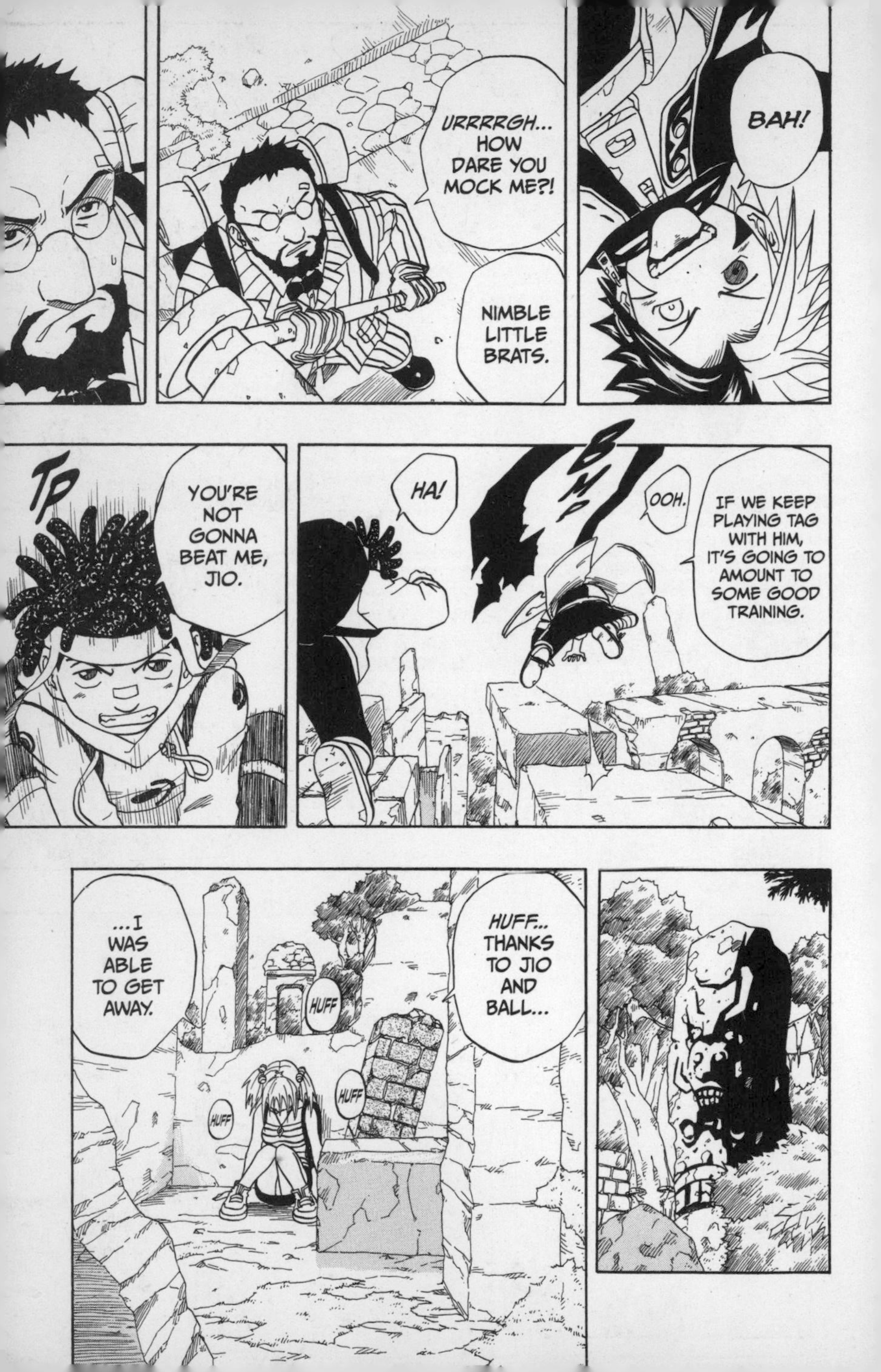
BAH!
URRRRGH... HOW DARE YOU MOCK ME?!
NIMBLE LITTLE BRATS.
IF WE KEEP PLAYING TAG WITH HIM, IT'S GOING TO AMOUNT TO SOME GOOD TRAINING.
OOH.
BMP
HA!
YOU'RE NOT GONNA BEAT ME, JIO.
TP
HUFF... THANKS TO JIO AND BALL...
HUFF
...I WAS ABLE TO GET AWAY.
HUFF
HUFF

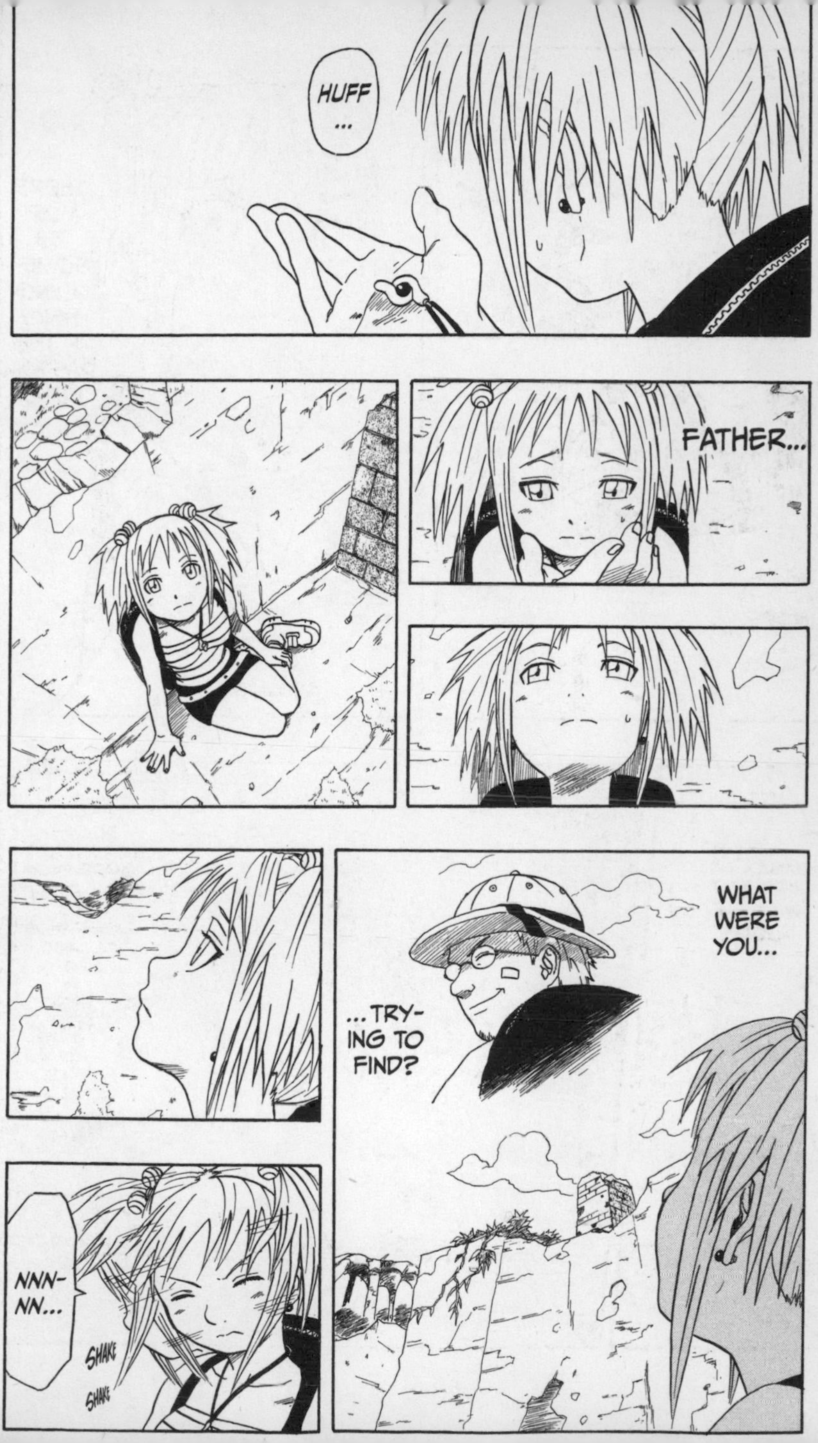
HUFF ...
FATHER...
WHAT WERE YOU...
...TRY-ING TO FIND?
NNN-NN...
SHAKE
SHAKE

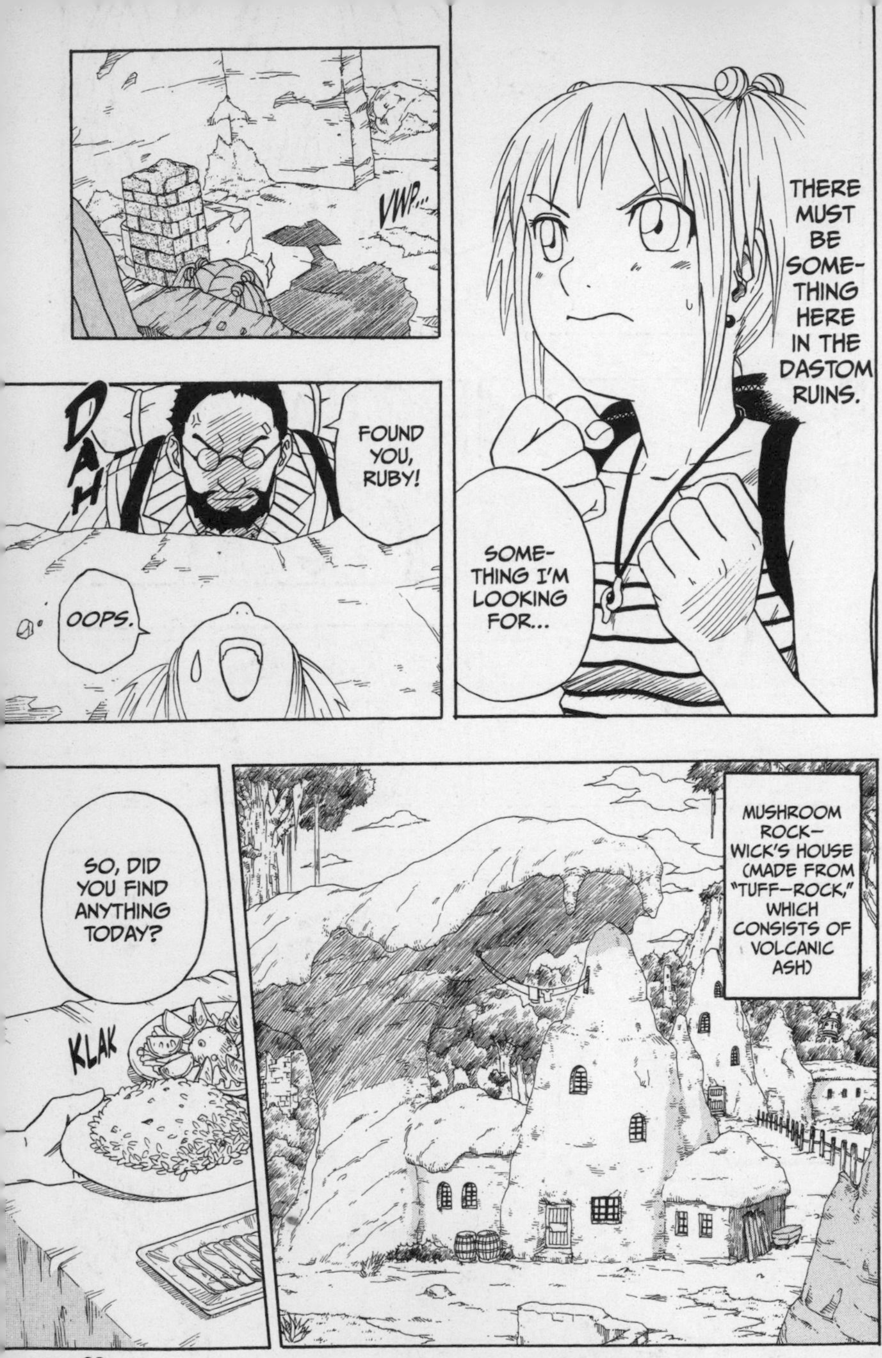
THERE MUST BE SOME-THING HERE IN THE DASTOM RUINS.
SOME-THING I'M LOOKING FOR...
VWP...
DAH
FOUND YOU, RUBY!
OOPS.
MUSHROOM ROCK—WICK'S HOUSE (MADE FROM "TUFF—ROCK," WHICH CONSISTS OF VOLCANIC ASH)
SO, DID YOU FIND ANYTHING TODAY?
KLAK

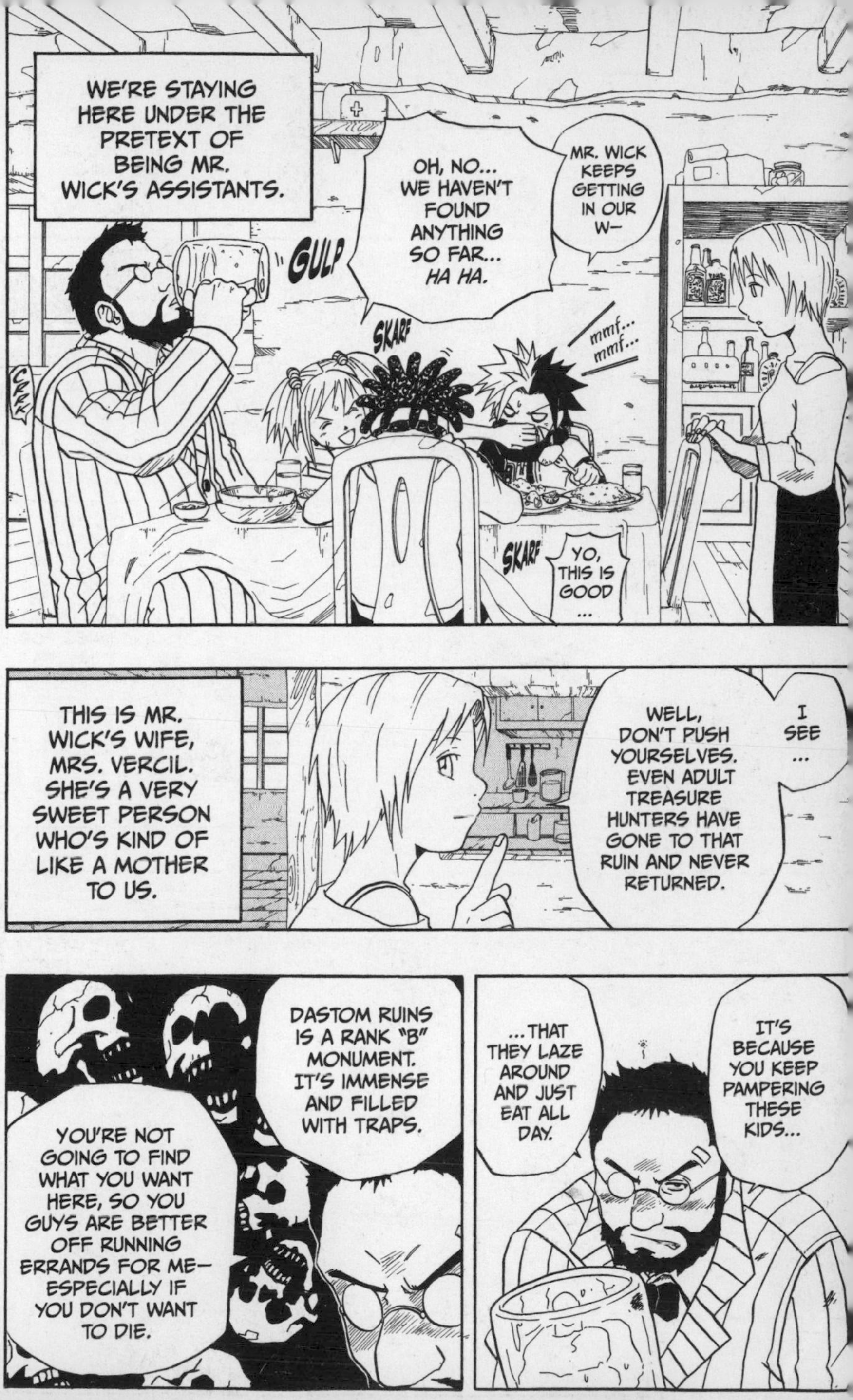
MR. WICK KEEPS GETTING IN OUR W—
OH, NO... WE HAVEN'T FOUND ANYTHING SO FAR... HA HA.
WE'RE STAYING HERE UNDER THE PRETEXT OF BEING MR. WICK'S ASSISTANTS.
GULP
mmf... mmf...
SKARF
YO, THIS IS GOOD ...
SKARF
CRRK
I SEE ...
WELL, DON'T PUSH YOURSELVES. EVEN ADULT TREASURE HUNTERS HAVE GONE TO THAT RUIN AND NEVER RETURNED.
THIS IS MR. WICK'S WIFE, MRS. VERCIL. SHE'S A VERY SWEET PERSON WHO'S KIND OF LIKE A MOTHER TO US.
IT'S BECAUSE YOU KEEP PAMPERING THESE KIDS...
...THAT THEY LAZE AROUND AND JUST EAT ALL DAY.
DASTOM RUINS IS A RANK "B" MONUMENT. IT'S IMMENSE AND FILLED WITH TRAPS.
YOU'RE NOT GOING TO FIND WHAT YOU WANT HERE, SO YOU GUYS ARE BETTER OFF RUNNING ERRANDS FOR ME—ESPECIALLY IF YOU DON'T WANT TO DIE.

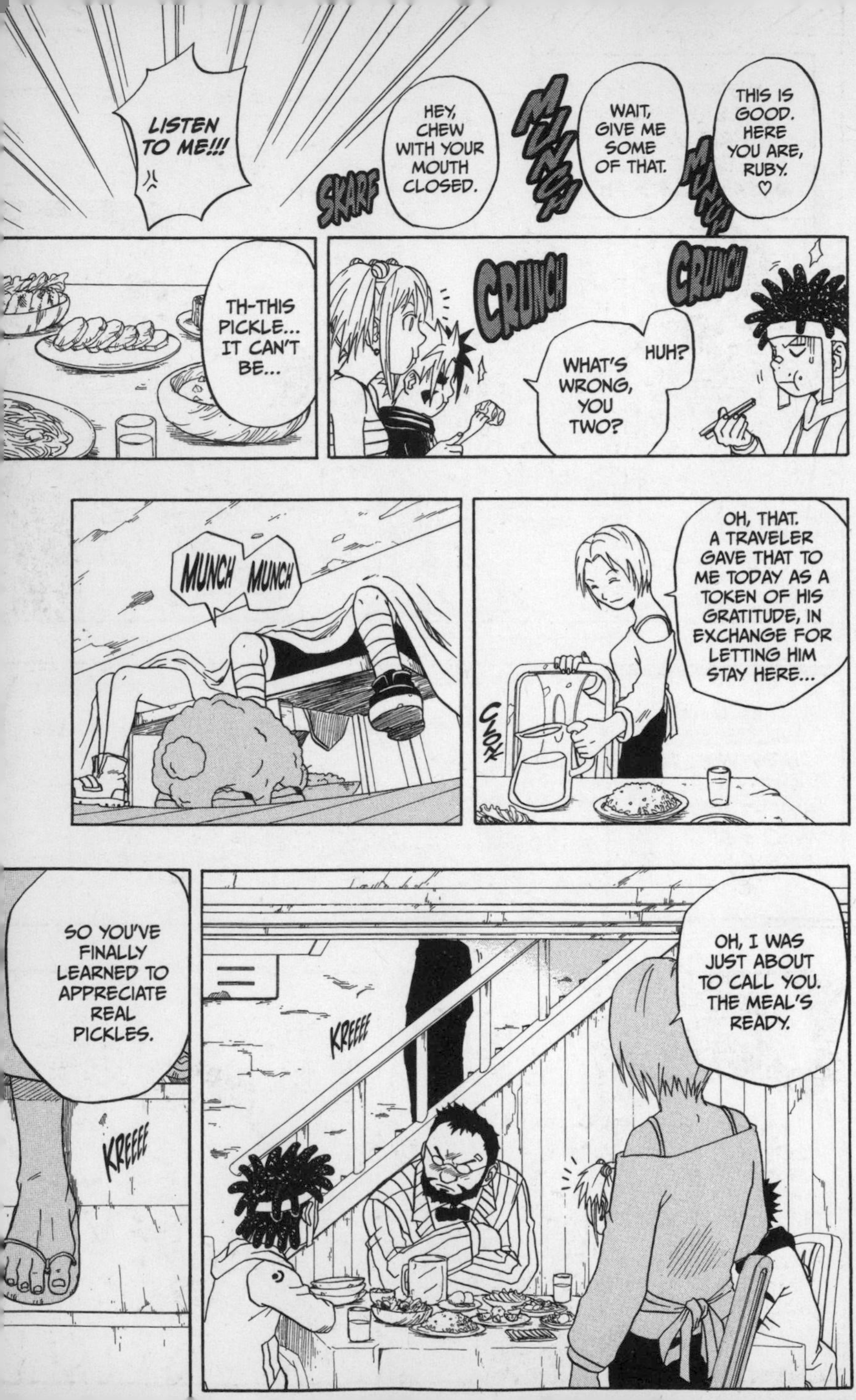
THIS IS GOOD. HERE YOU ARE, RUBY. ♡
MUNCH
WAIT, GIVE ME SOME OF THAT.
MUNCH
HEY, CHEW WITH YOUR MOUTH CLOSED.
SKARF
LISTEN TO ME!!!
CRUNCH
CRUNCH
HUH?
WHAT'S WRONG, YOU TWO?
TH-THIS PICKLE... IT CAN'T BE...
OH, THAT. A TRAVELER GAVE THAT TO ME TODAY AS A TOKEN OF HIS GRATITUDE, IN EXCHANGE FOR LETTING HIM STAY HERE...
CLOK
MUNCH
MUNCH
OH, I WAS JUST ABOUT TO CALL YOU. THE MEAL'S READY.
KREEEE
SO YOU'VE FINALLY LEARNED TO APPRECIATE REAL PICKLES.
KREEEE

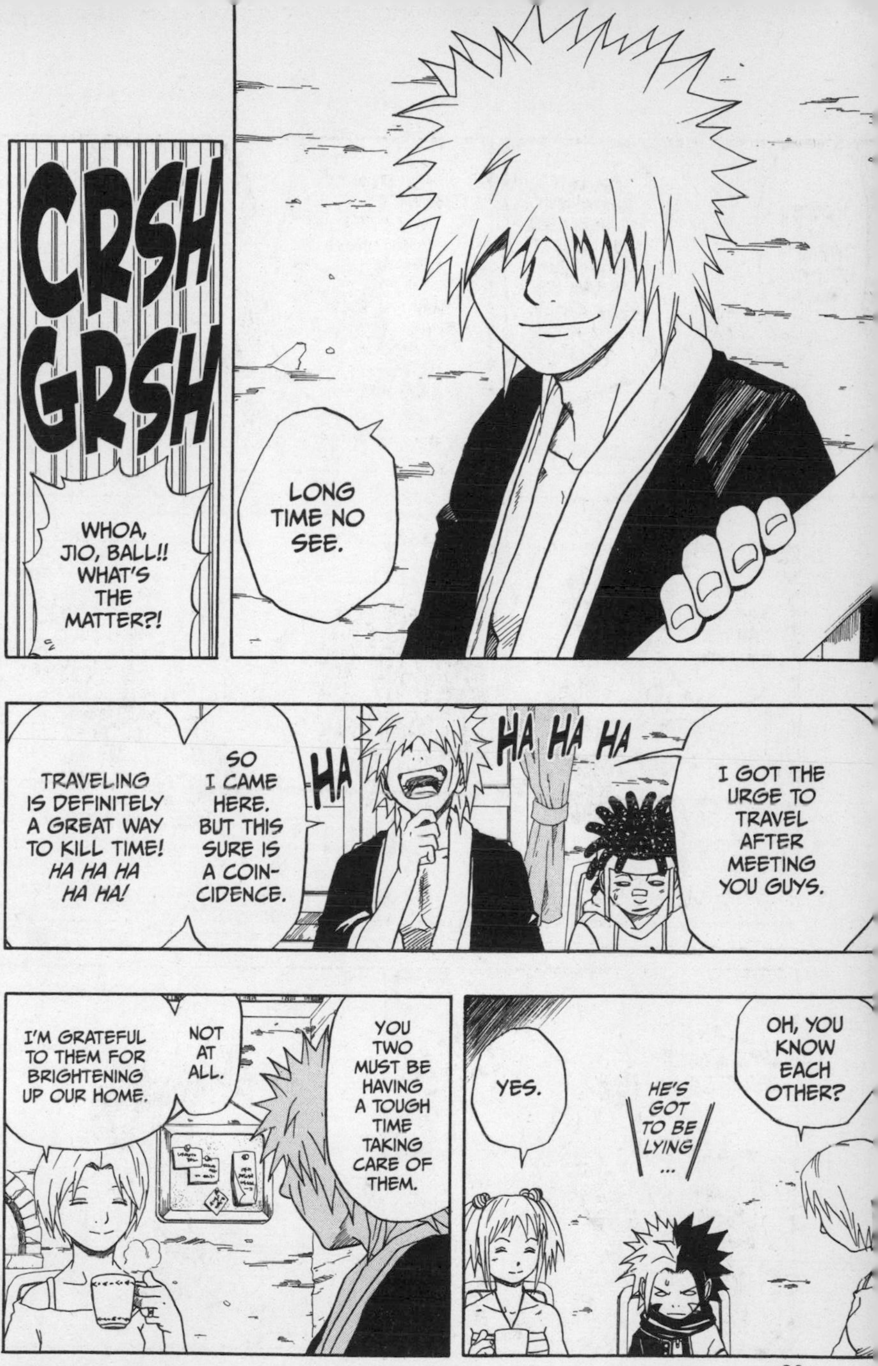
LONG TIME NO SEE.
CRSH GRSH
WHOA, JIO, BALL!! WHAT'S THE MATTER?!
I GOT THE URGE TO TRAVEL AFTER MEETING YOU GUYS.
HA HA HA
HA
SO I CAME HERE. BUT THIS SURE IS A COINCIDENCE.
TRAVELING IS DEFINITELY A GREAT WAY TO KILL TIME! *HA HA HA HA HA!*
OH, YOU KNOW EACH OTHER?
HE'S GOT TO BE LYING...
YES.
YOU TWO MUST BE HAVING A TOUGH TIME TAKING CARE OF THEM.
NOT AT ALL.
I'M GRATEFUL TO THEM FOR BRIGHTENING UP OUR HOME.

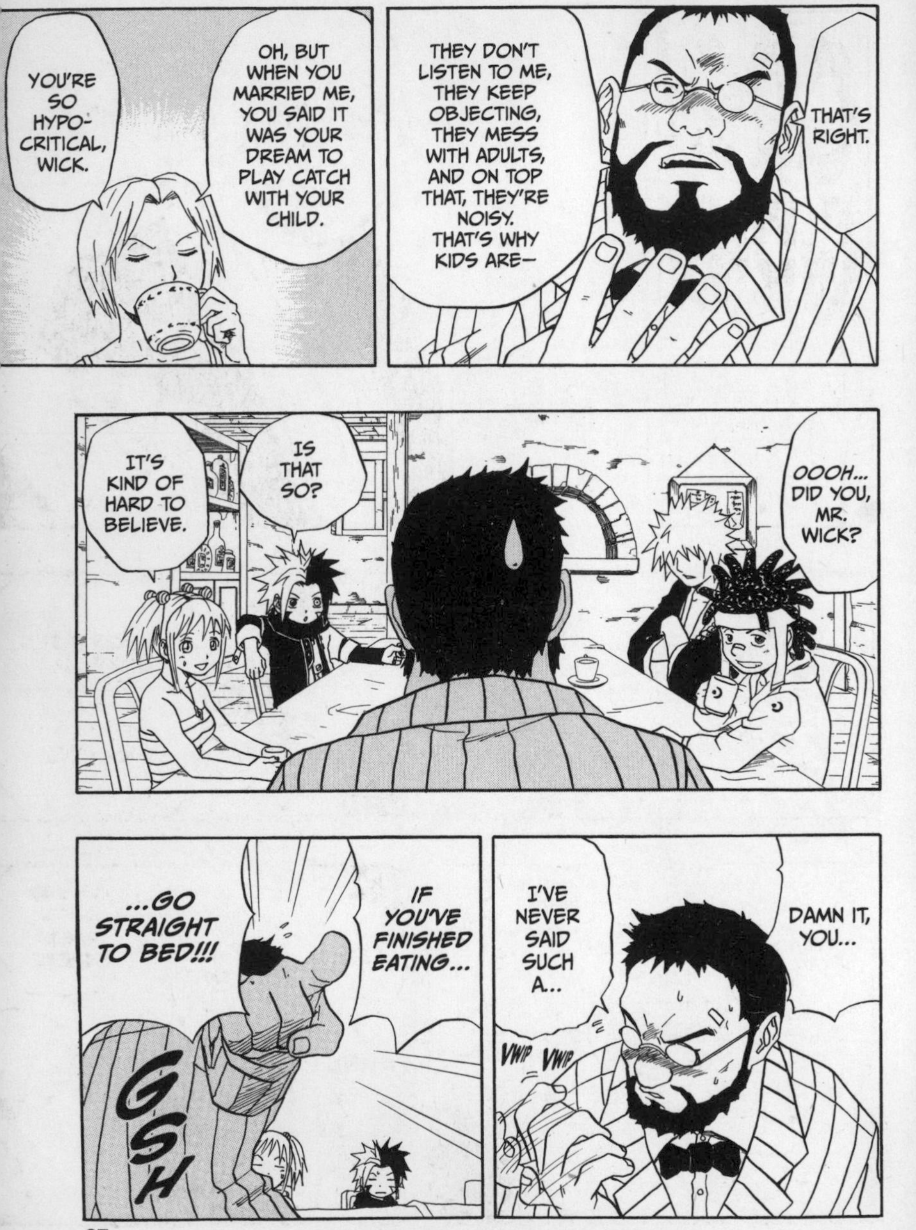
THAT'S RIGHT.
THEY DON'T LISTEN TO ME, THEY KEEP OBJECTING, THEY MESS WITH ADULTS, AND ON TOP THAT, THEY'RE NOISY. THAT'S WHY KIDS ARE—
OH, BUT WHEN YOU MARRIED ME, YOU SAID IT WAS YOUR DREAM TO PLAY CATCH WITH YOUR CHILD.
YOU'RE SO HYPO-CRITICAL, WICK.
OOOH... DID YOU, MR. WICK?
IS THAT SO?
IT'S KIND OF HARD TO BELIEVE.
DAMN IT, YOU...
I'VE NEVER SAID SUCH A...
VWIP VWIP
IF YOU'VE FINISHED EATING...
...GO STRAIGHT TO BED!!!
GSH

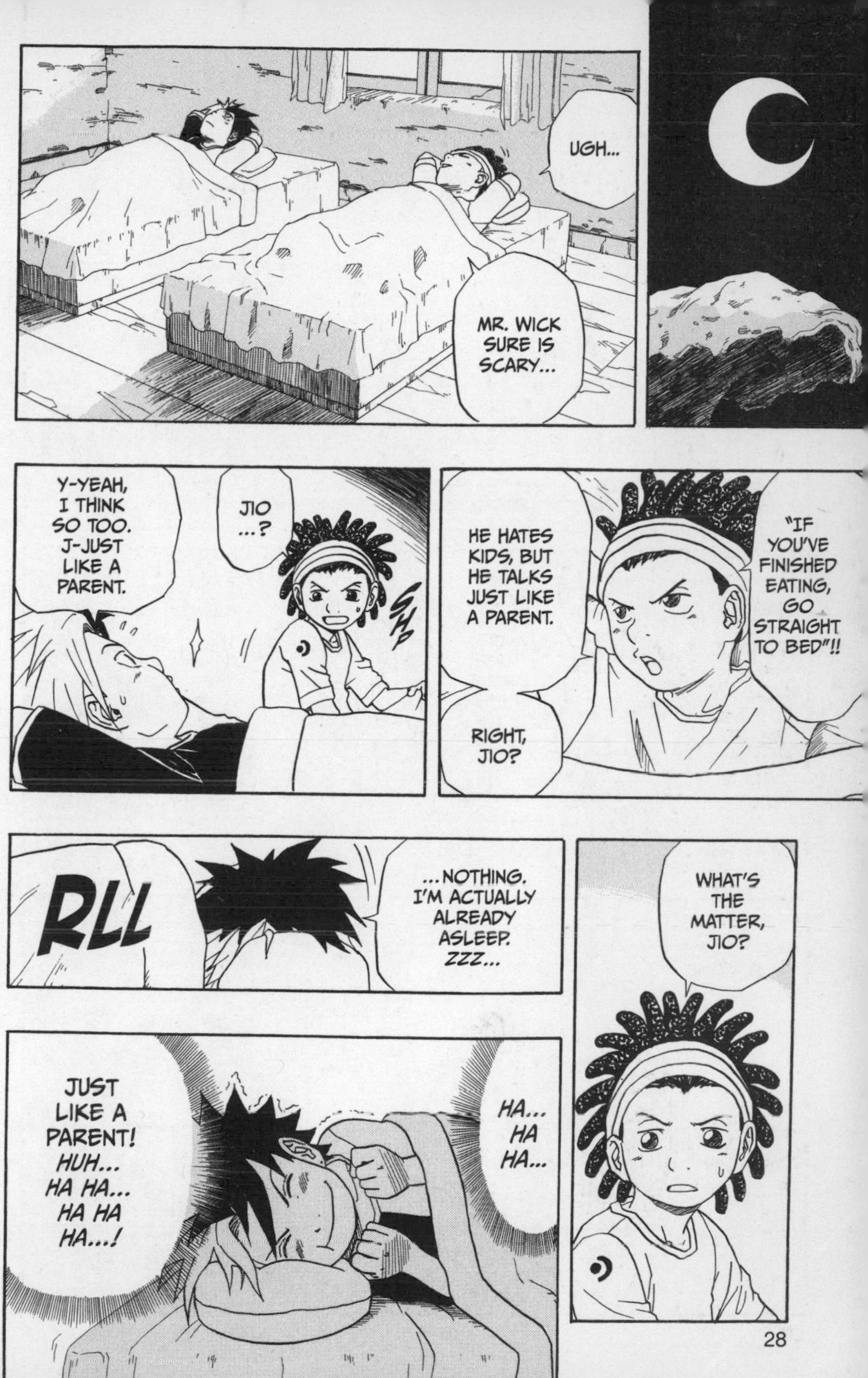
UGH...
MR. WICK SURE IS SCARY...
"IF YOU'VE FINISHED EATING, GO STRAIGHT TO BED"!!
HE HATES KIDS, BUT HE TALKS JUST LIKE A PARENT.
RIGHT, JIO?
JIO ...?
Y-YEAH, I THINK SO TOO. J-JUST LIKE A PARENT.
WHAT'S THE MATTER, JIO?
...NOTHING. I'M ACTUALLY ALREADY ASLEEP. ZZZ...
RLL
HA... HA HA...
JUST LIKE A PARENT! HUH... HA HA... HA HA HA...!

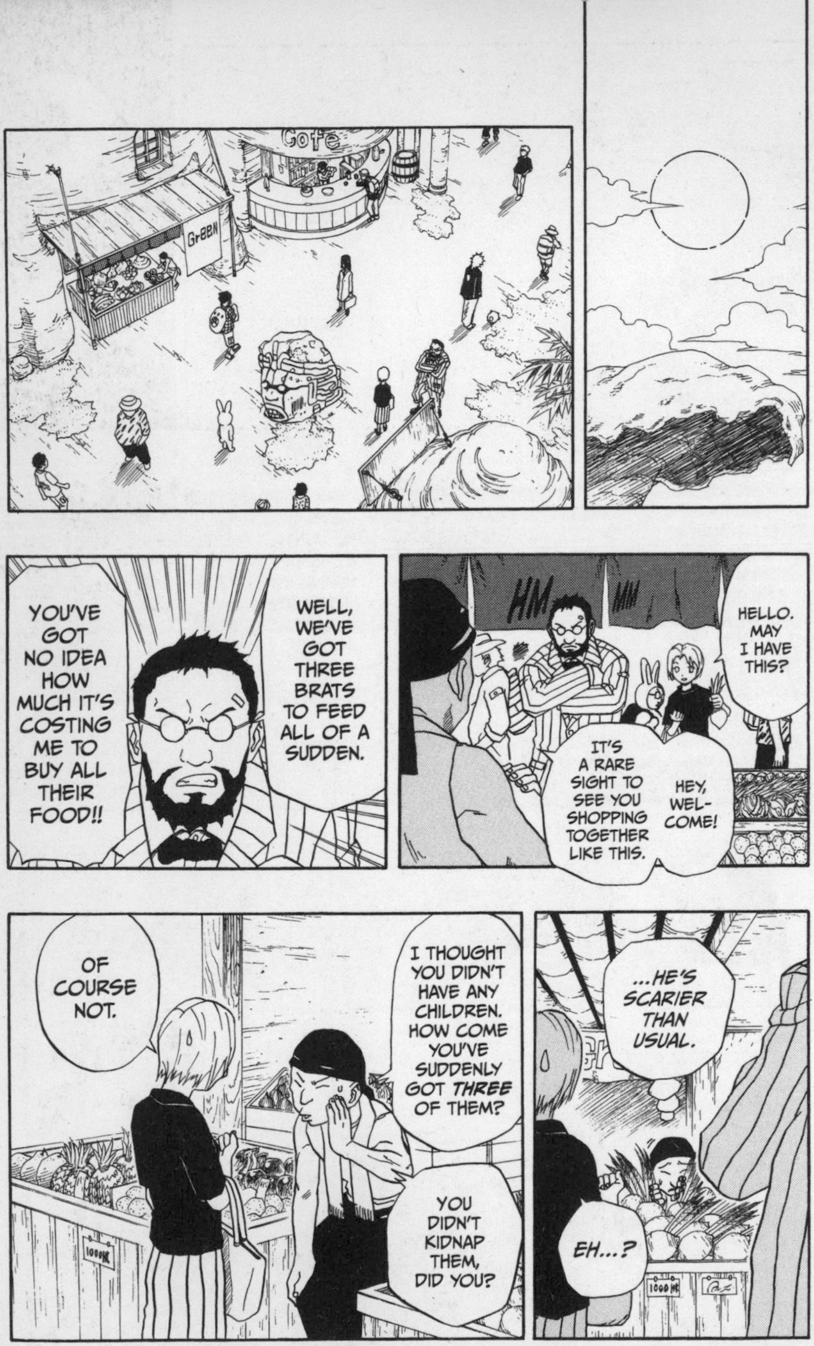
Cafe
Green
HELLO. MAY I HAVE THIS?
HM MM
HEY, WEL-COME!
IT'S A RARE SIGHT TO SEE YOU SHOPPING TOGETHER LIKE THIS.
WELL, WE'VE GOT THREE BRATS TO FEED ALL OF A SUDDEN.
YOU'VE GOT NO IDEA HOW MUCH IT'S COSTING ME TO BUY ALL THEIR FOOD!!
...HE'S SCARIER THAN USUAL.
EH...?
I THOUGHT YOU DIDN'T HAVE ANY CHILDREN. HOW COME YOU'VE SUDDENLY GOT *THREE* OF THEM?
YOU DIDN'T KIDNAP THEM, DID YOU?
OF COURSE NOT.

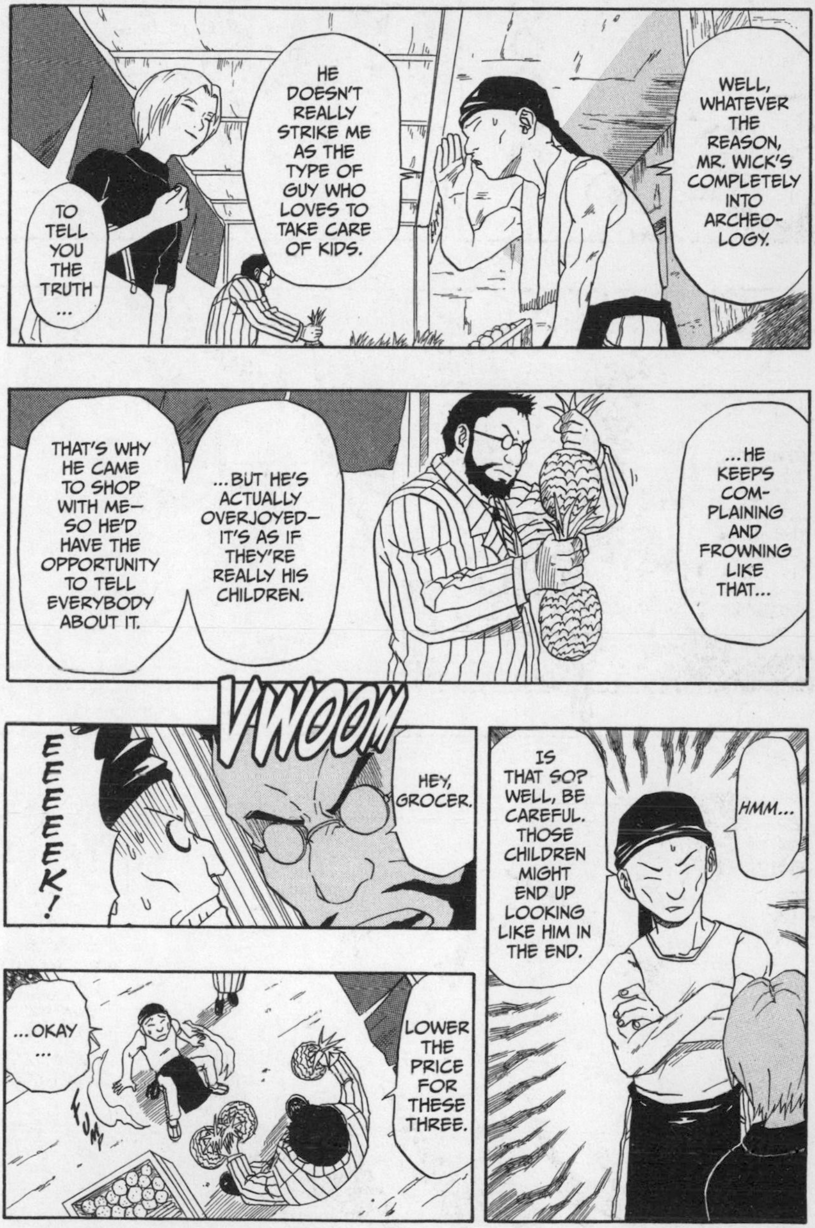
WELL, WHATEVER THE REASON, MR. WICK'S COMPLETELY INTO ARCHEO-LOGY.
HE DOESN'T REALLY STRIKE ME AS THE TYPE OF GUY WHO LOVES TO TAKE CARE OF KIDS.
TO TELL YOU THE TRUTH ...
...HE KEEPS COM-PLAINING AND FROWNING LIKE THAT...
...BUT HE'S ACTUALLY OVERJOYED— IT'S AS IF THEY'RE REALLY HIS CHILDREN.
THAT'S WHY HE CAME TO SHOP WITH ME— SO HE'D HAVE THE OPPORTUNITY TO TELL EVERYBODY ABOUT IT.
HMM...
IS THAT SO? WELL, BE CAREFUL. THOSE CHILDREN MIGHT END UP LOOKING LIKE HIM IN THE END.
VWOOM
HEY, GROCER.
EEEEEEK!
LOWER THE PRICE FOR THESE THREE.
...OKAY ...

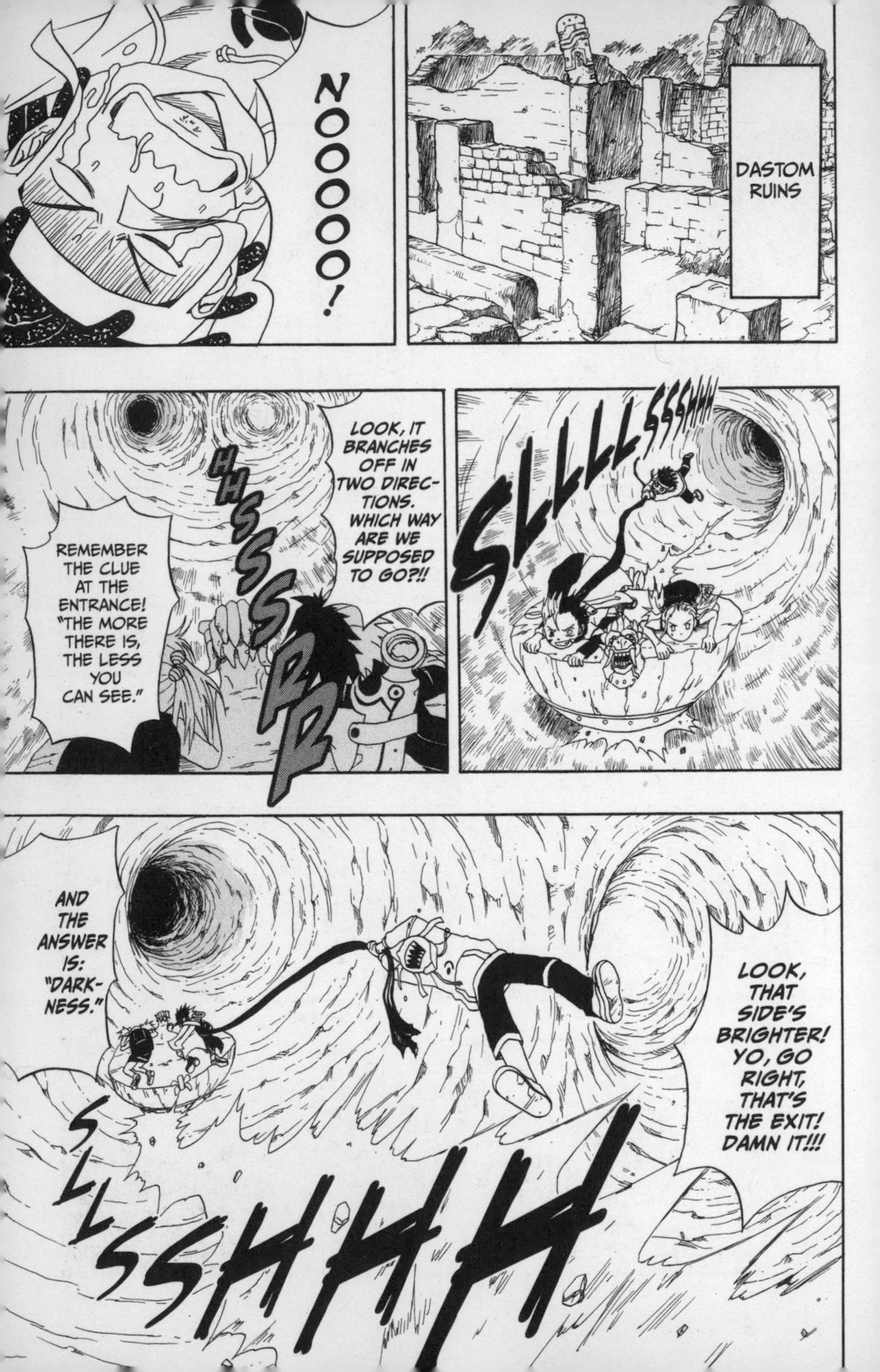
DASTOM RUINS
NOOOOOO!
SLLLLLSSSHHHH
LOOK, IT BRANCHES OFF IN TWO DIREC-TIONS. WHICH WAY ARE WE SUPPOSED TO GO?!!
REMEMBER THE CLUE AT THE ENTRANCE! "THE MORE THERE IS, THE LESS YOU CAN SEE."
LOOK, THAT SIDE'S BRIGHTER! YO, GO RIGHT, THAT'S THE EXIT! DAMN IT!!!
AND THE ANSWER IS: "DARK-NESS."
SLLSSHHHH

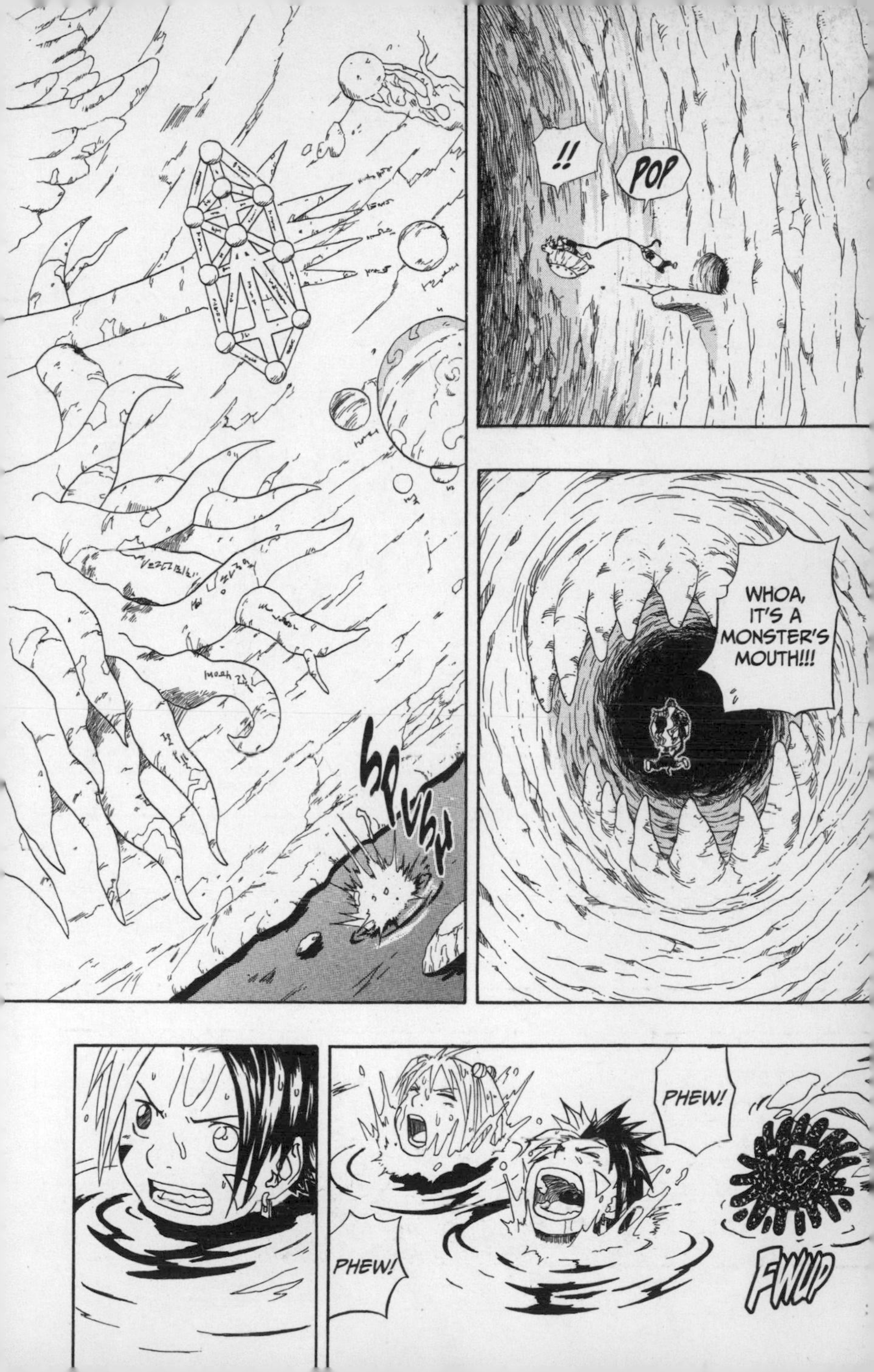
POP
!!
WHOA, IT'S A MONSTER'S MOUTH!!!
PHEW!
FWUP
PHEW!

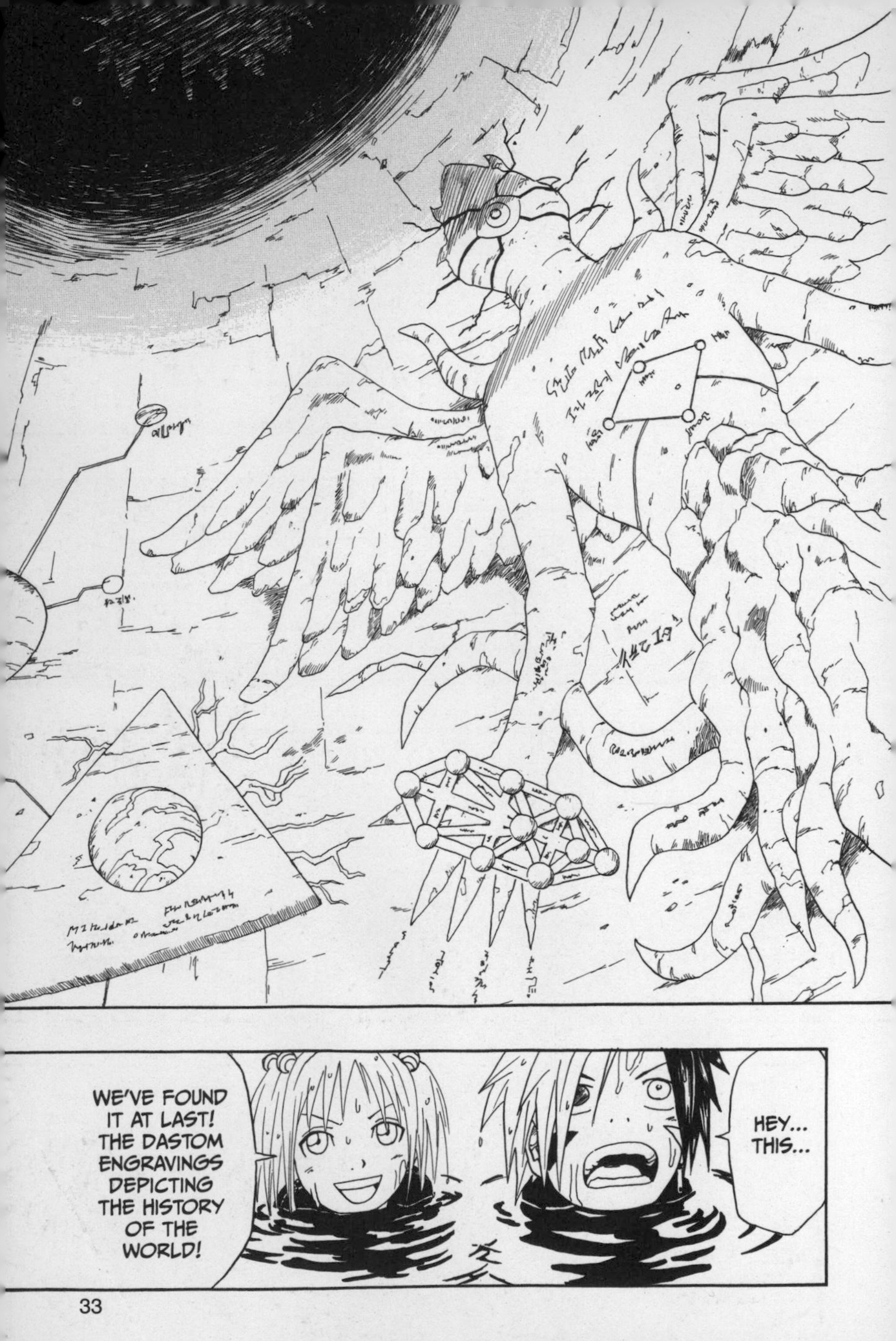
HEY... THIS...
WE'VE FOUND IT AT LAST! THE DASTOM ENGRAVINGS DEPICTING THE HISTORY OF THE WORLD!

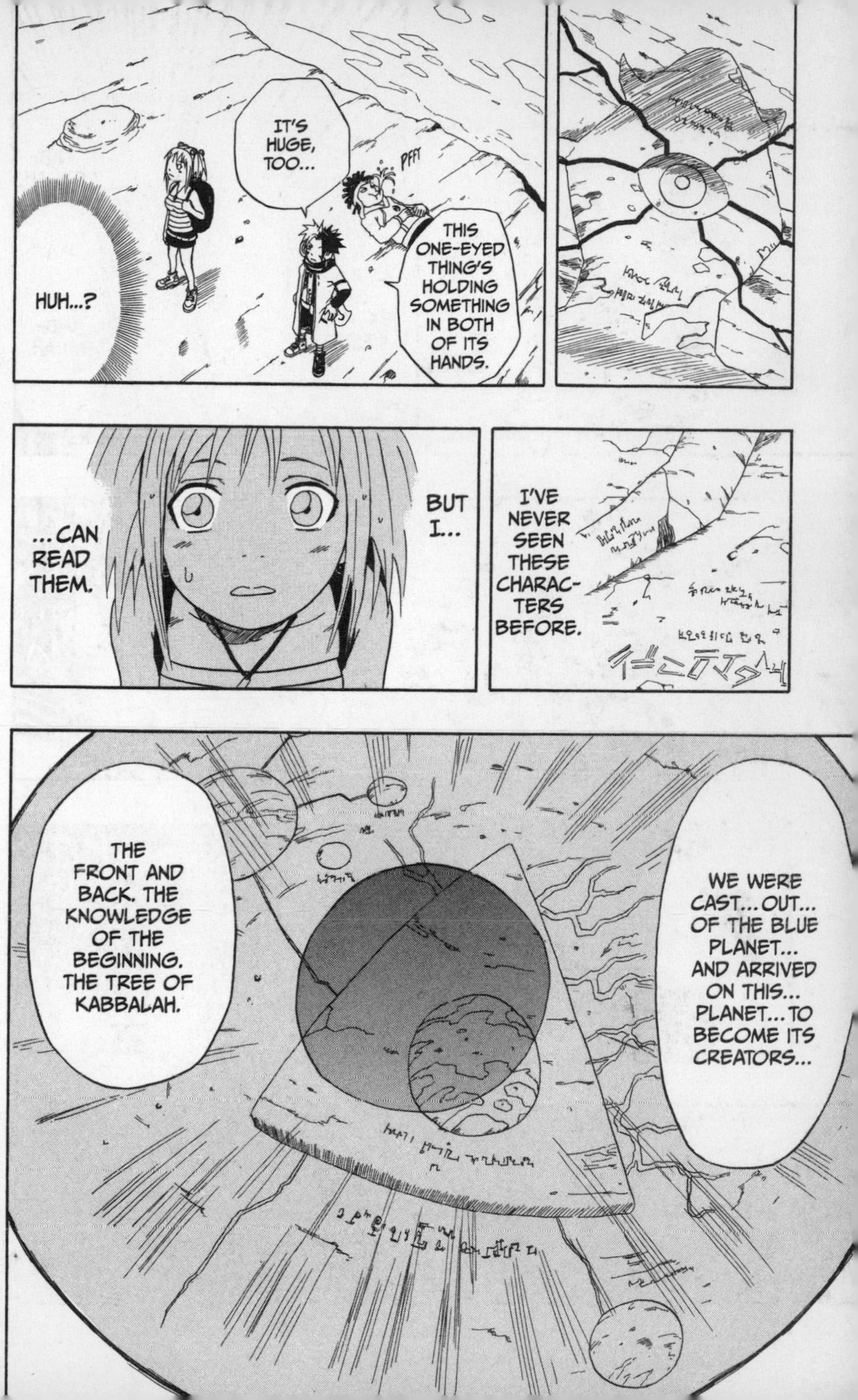
IT'S HUGE, TOO...
PFFT
THIS ONE-EYED THING'S HOLDING SOMETHING IN BOTH OF ITS HANDS.
HUH...?
I'VE NEVER SEEN THESE CHARACTERS BEFORE.
BUT I...
...CAN READ THEM.
WE WERE CAST...OUT... OF THE BLUE PLANET... AND ARRIVED ON THIS... PLANET...TO BECOME ITS CREATORS...
THE FRONT AND BACK. THE KNOWLEDGE OF THE BEGINNING. THE TREE OF KABBALAH.

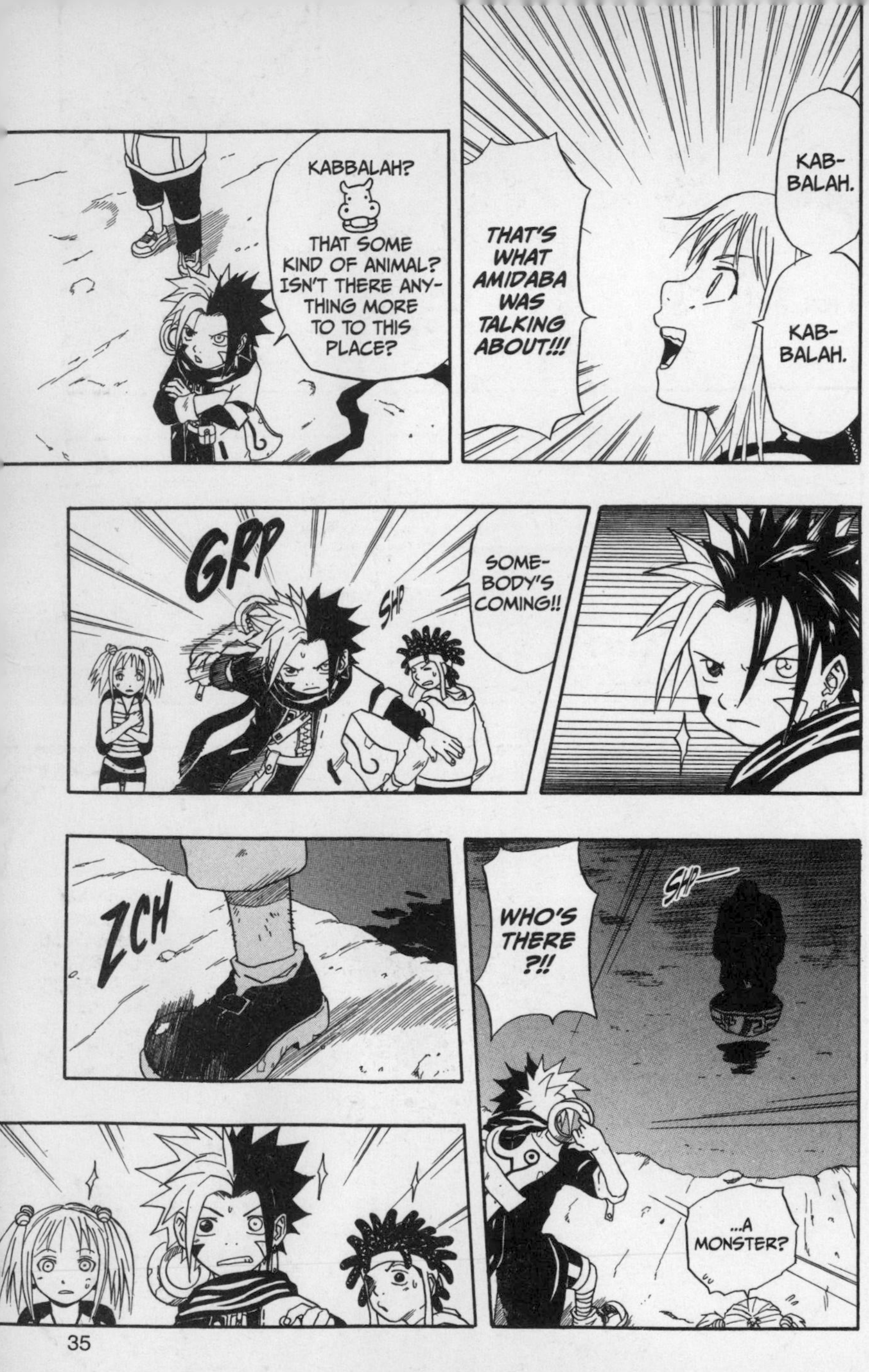
KAB-BALAH.
KAB-BALAH.
THAT'S WHAT AMIDABA WAS TALKING ABOUT!!!
KABBALAH? THAT SOME KIND OF ANIMAL? ISN'T THERE ANYTHING MORE TO TO THIS PLACE?
SOME-BODY'S COMING!!
GRP
SHP
SHP
WHO'S THERE ?!!
...A MONSTER?
ZCH

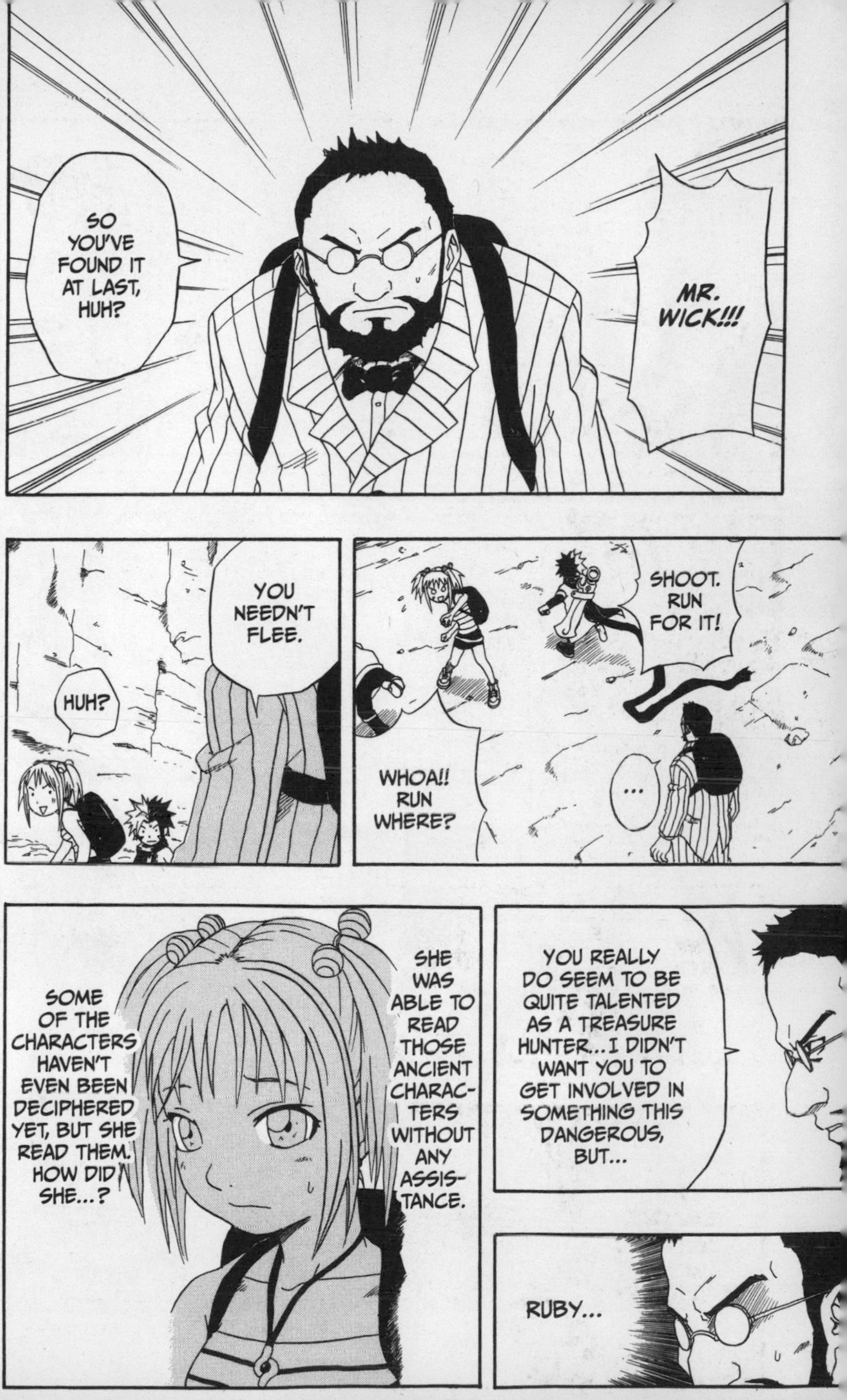
MR. WICK!!!
SO YOU'VE FOUND IT AT LAST, HUH?
SHOOT. RUN FOR IT!
WHOA!! RUN WHERE?
...
YOU NEEDN'T FLEE.
HUH?
YOU REALLY DO SEEM TO BE QUITE TALENTED AS A TREASURE HUNTER...I DIDN'T WANT YOU TO GET INVOLVED IN SOMETHING THIS DANGEROUS, BUT...
RUBY...
SHE WAS ABLE TO READ THOSE ANCIENT CHARAC-TERS WITHOUT ANY ASSIS-TANCE.
SOME OF THE CHARACTERS HAVEN'T EVEN BEEN DECIPHERED YET, BUT SHE READ THEM. HOW DID SHE...?

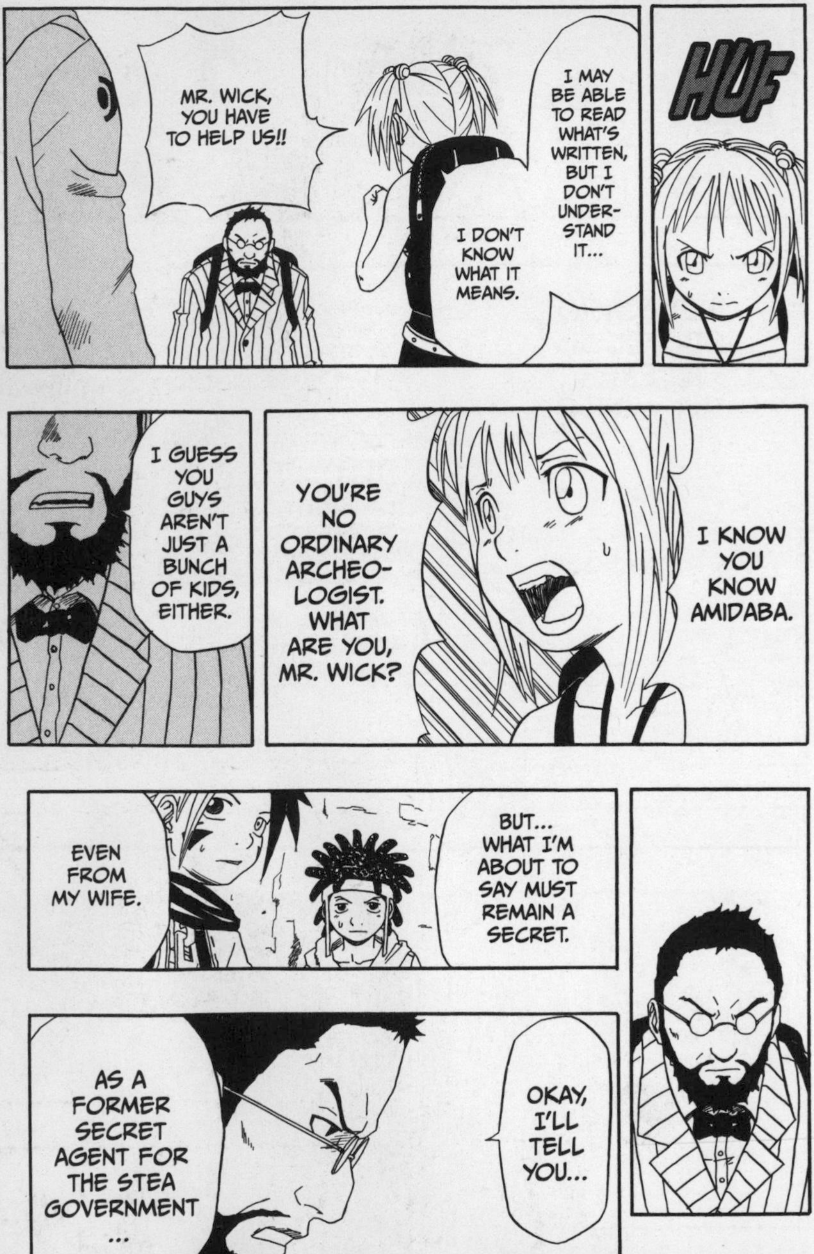
HUF
I MAY BE ABLE TO READ WHAT'S WRITTEN, BUT I DON'T UNDERSTAND IT...
I DON'T KNOW WHAT IT MEANS.
MR. WICK, YOU HAVE TO HELP US!!
I KNOW YOU KNOW AMIDABA.
YOU'RE NO ORDINARY ARCHEOLOGIST. WHAT ARE YOU, MR. WICK?
I GUESS YOU GUYS AREN'T JUST A BUNCH OF KIDS, EITHER.
BUT... WHAT I'M ABOUT TO SAY MUST REMAIN A SECRET.
EVEN FROM MY WIFE.
OKAY, I'LL TELL YOU...
AS A FORMER SECRET AGENT FOR THE STEA GOVERNMENT ...

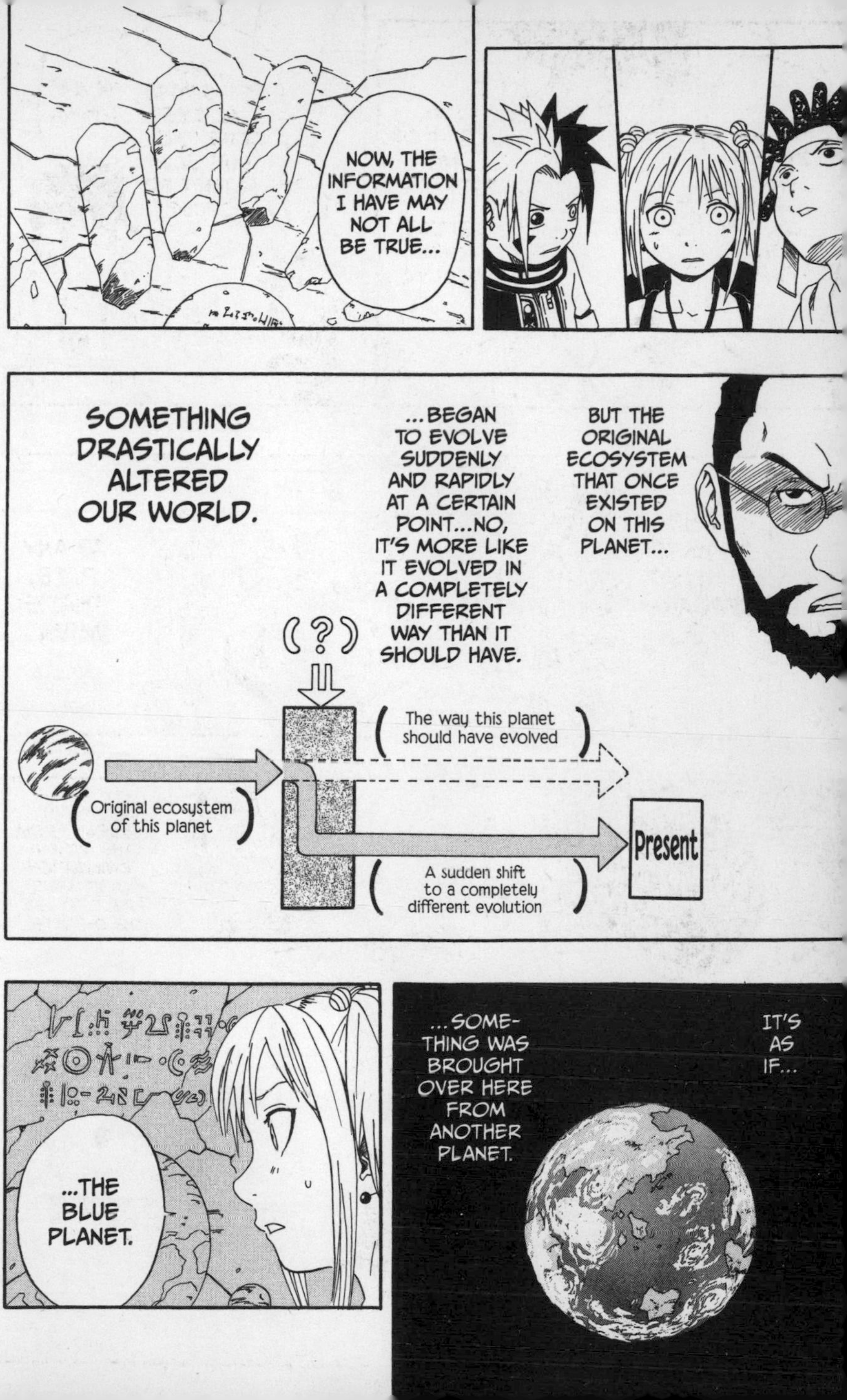
NOW, THE INFORMATION I HAVE MAY NOT ALL BE TRUE...
BUT THE ORIGINAL ECOSYSTEM THAT ONCE EXISTED ON THIS PLANET...
...BEGAN TO EVOLVE SUDDENLY AND RAPIDLY AT A CERTAIN POINT...NO, IT'S MORE LIKE IT EVOLVED IN A COMPLETELY DIFFERENT WAY THAN IT SHOULD HAVE.
SOMETHING DRASTICALLY ALTERED OUR WORLD.
(?)
The way this planet should have evolved
Original ecosystem of this planet
Present
A sudden shift to a completely different evolution
IT'S AS IF...
...SOMETHING WAS BROUGHT OVER HERE FROM ANOTHER PLANET.
...THE BLUE PLANET.

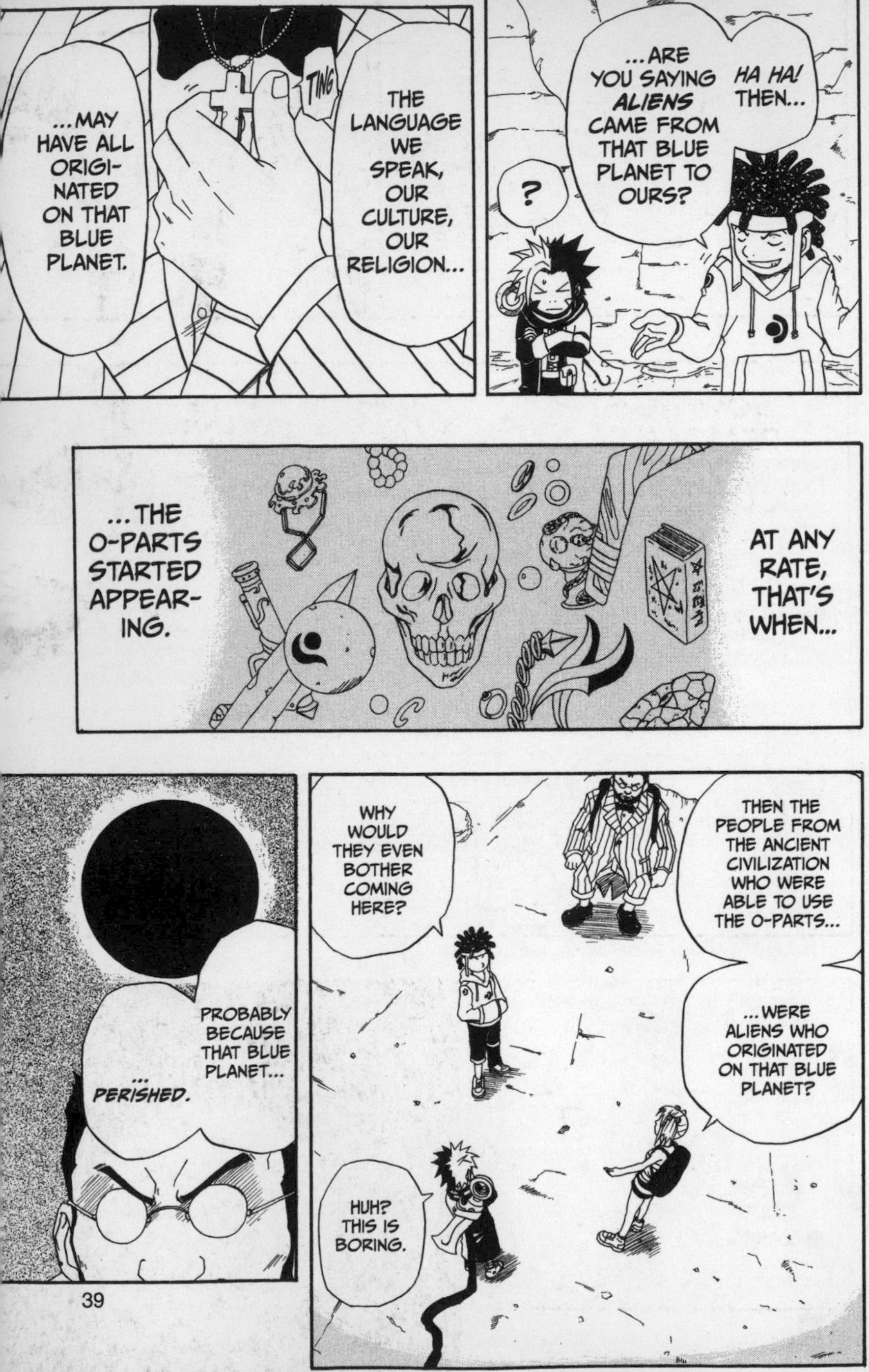
HA HA! THEN...
...ARE YOU SAYING *ALIENS* CAME FROM THAT BLUE PLANET TO OURS?
?
THE LANGUAGE WE SPEAK, OUR CULTURE, OUR RELIGION...
TING
...MAY HAVE ALL ORIGINATED ON THAT BLUE PLANET.
AT ANY RATE, THAT'S WHEN...
...THE O-PARTS STARTED APPEARING.
THEN THE PEOPLE FROM THE ANCIENT CIVILIZATION WHO WERE ABLE TO USE THE O-PARTS...
...WERE ALIENS WHO ORIGINATED ON THAT BLUE PLANET?
WHY WOULD THEY EVEN BOTHER COMING HERE?
HUH? THIS IS BORING.
PROBABLY BECAUSE THAT BLUE PLANET...
...*PERISHED.*

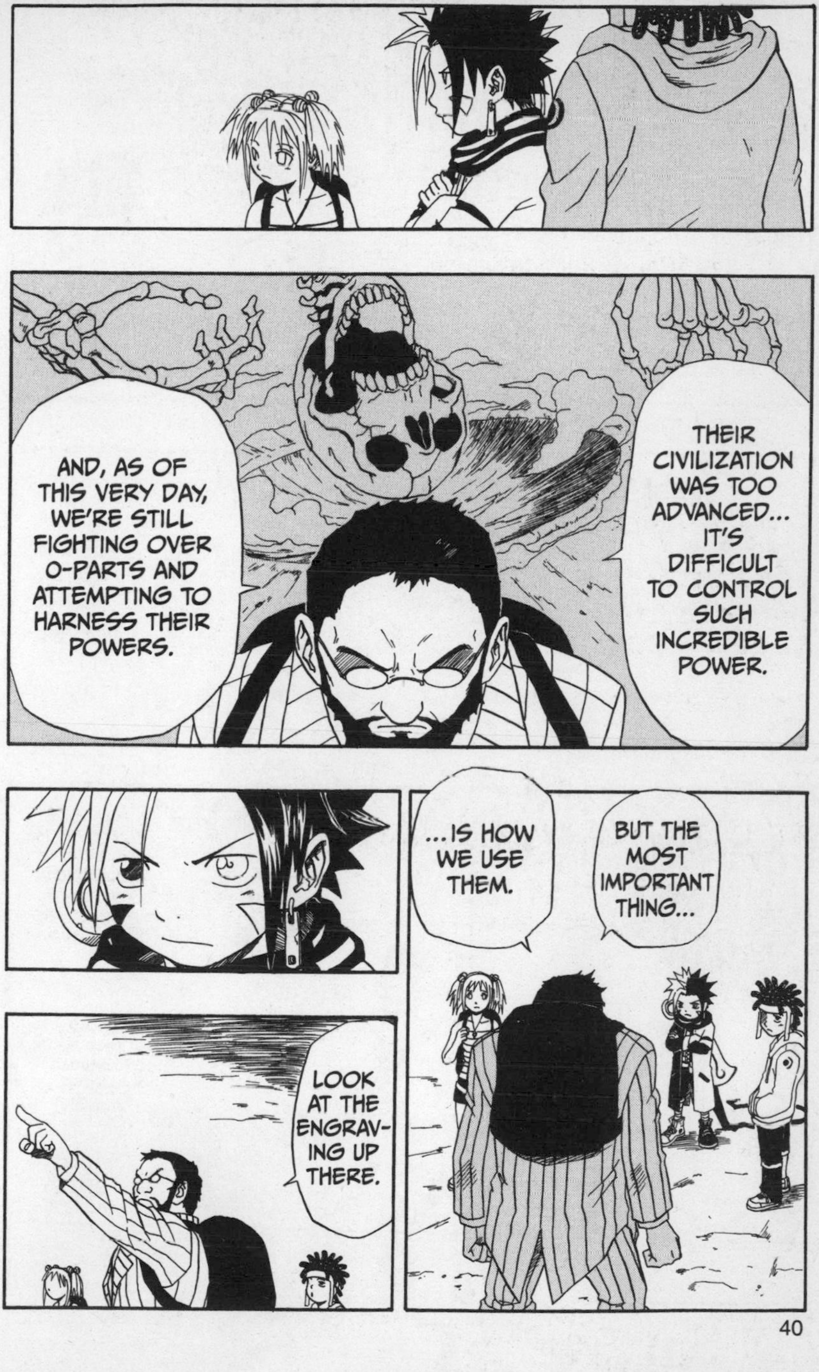
THEIR CIVILIZATION WAS TOO ADVANCED... IT'S DIFFICULT TO CONTROL SUCH INCREDIBLE POWER.
AND, AS OF THIS VERY DAY, WE'RE STILL FIGHTING OVER O-PARTS AND ATTEMPTING TO HARNESS THEIR POWERS.
BUT THE MOST IMPORTANT THING...
...IS HOW WE USE THEM.
LOOK AT THE ENGRAV-ING UP THERE.

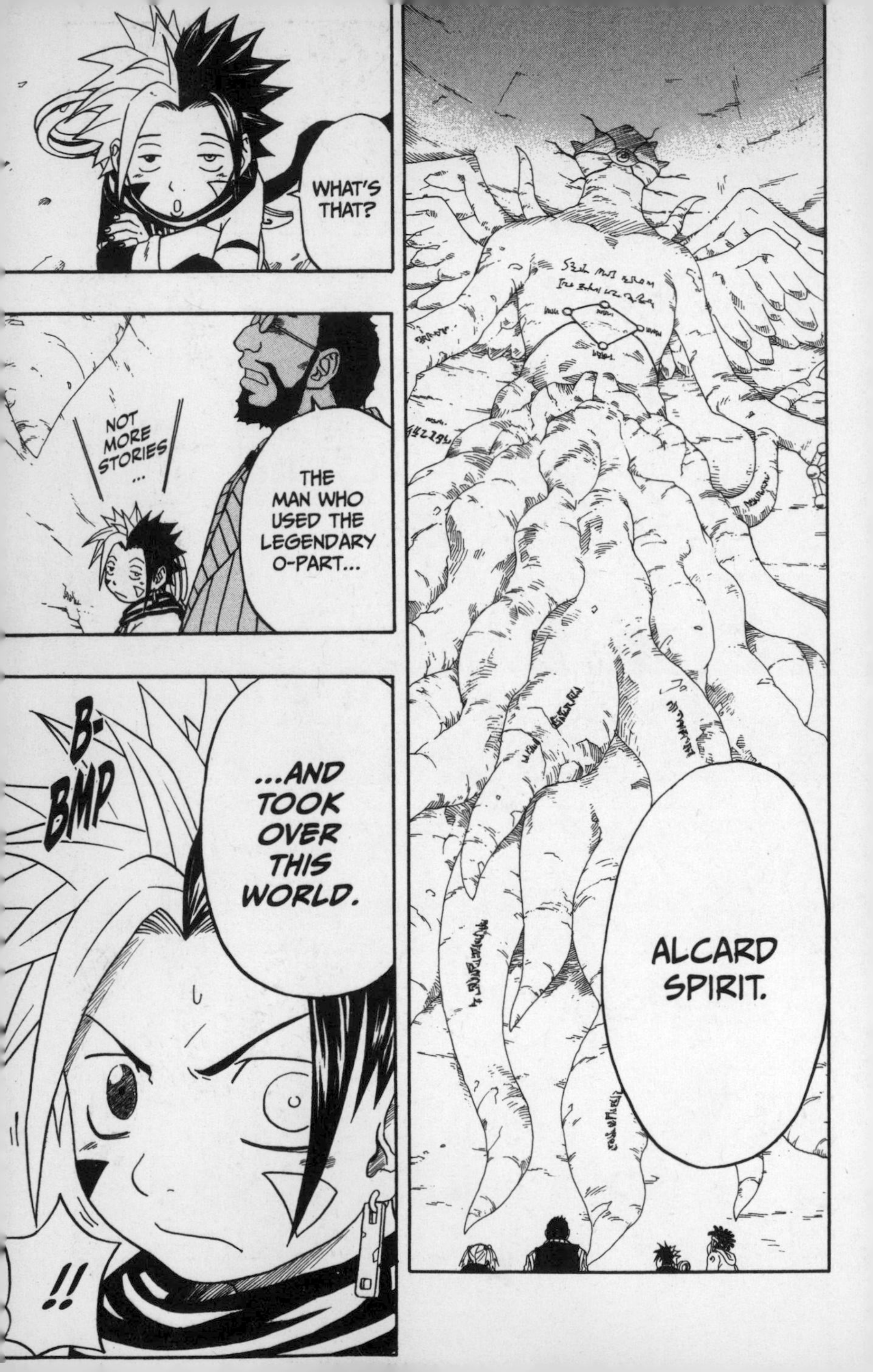
ALCARD SPIRIT.
WHAT'S THAT?
THE MAN WHO USED THE LEGENDARY O-PART...
NOT MORE STORIES ...
...AND TOOK OVER THIS WORLD.
B-BMP
!!

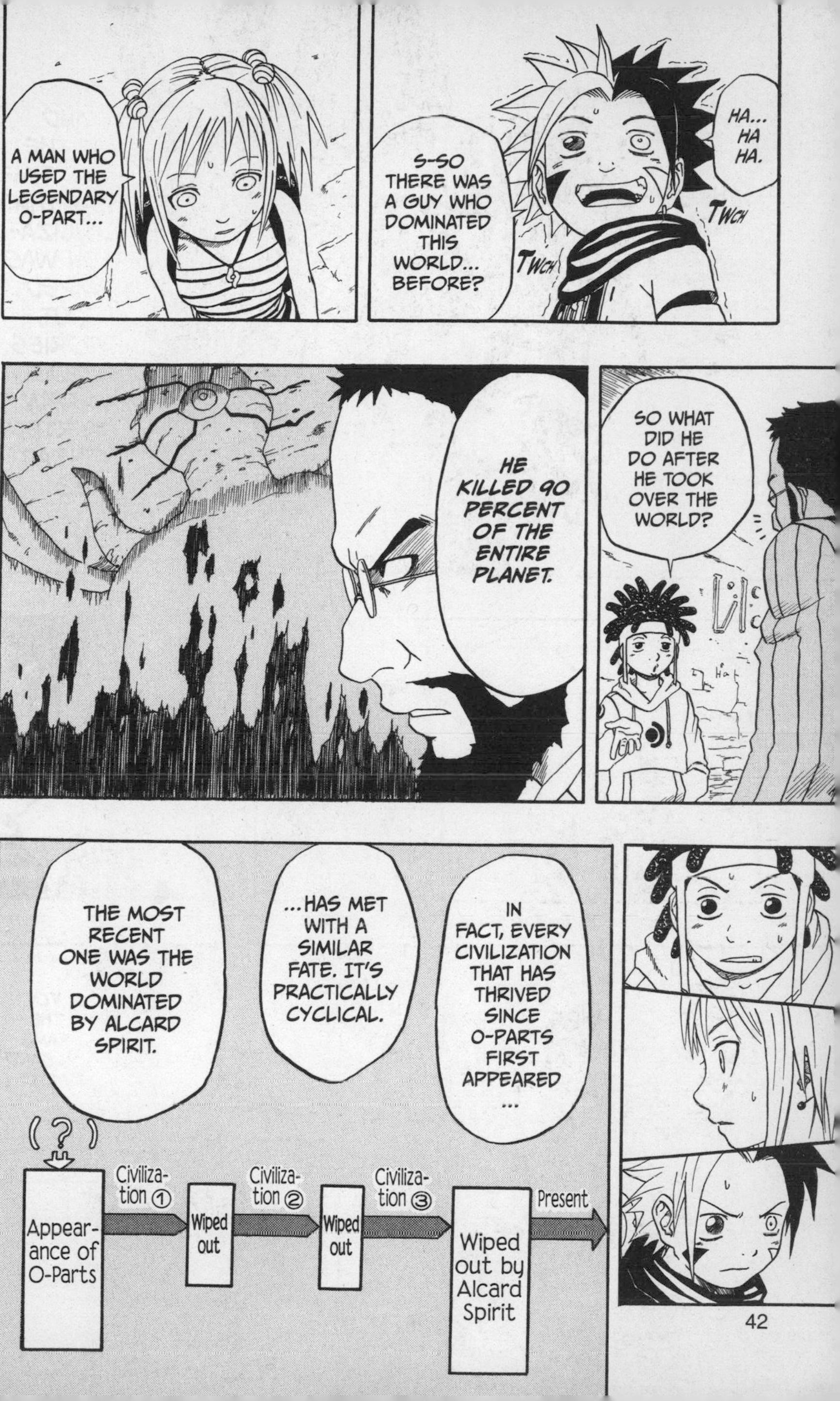
HA... HA HA.
TWCH
S-SO THERE WAS A GUY WHO DOMINATED THIS WORLD... BEFORE?
TWCH
A MAN WHO USED THE LEGENDARY O-PART...
SO WHAT DID HE DO AFTER HE TOOK OVER THE WORLD?
HE KILLED 90 PERCENT OF THE ENTIRE PLANET.
IN FACT, EVERY CIVILIZATION THAT HAS THRIVED SINCE O-PARTS FIRST APPEARED...
...HAS MET WITH A SIMILAR FATE. IT'S PRACTICALLY CYCLICAL.
THE MOST RECENT ONE WAS THE WORLD DOMINATED BY ALCARD SPIRIT.
(?)
Appearance of O-Parts
Civilization ①
Wiped out
Civilization ②
Wiped out
Civilization ③
Wiped out by Alcard Spirit
Present

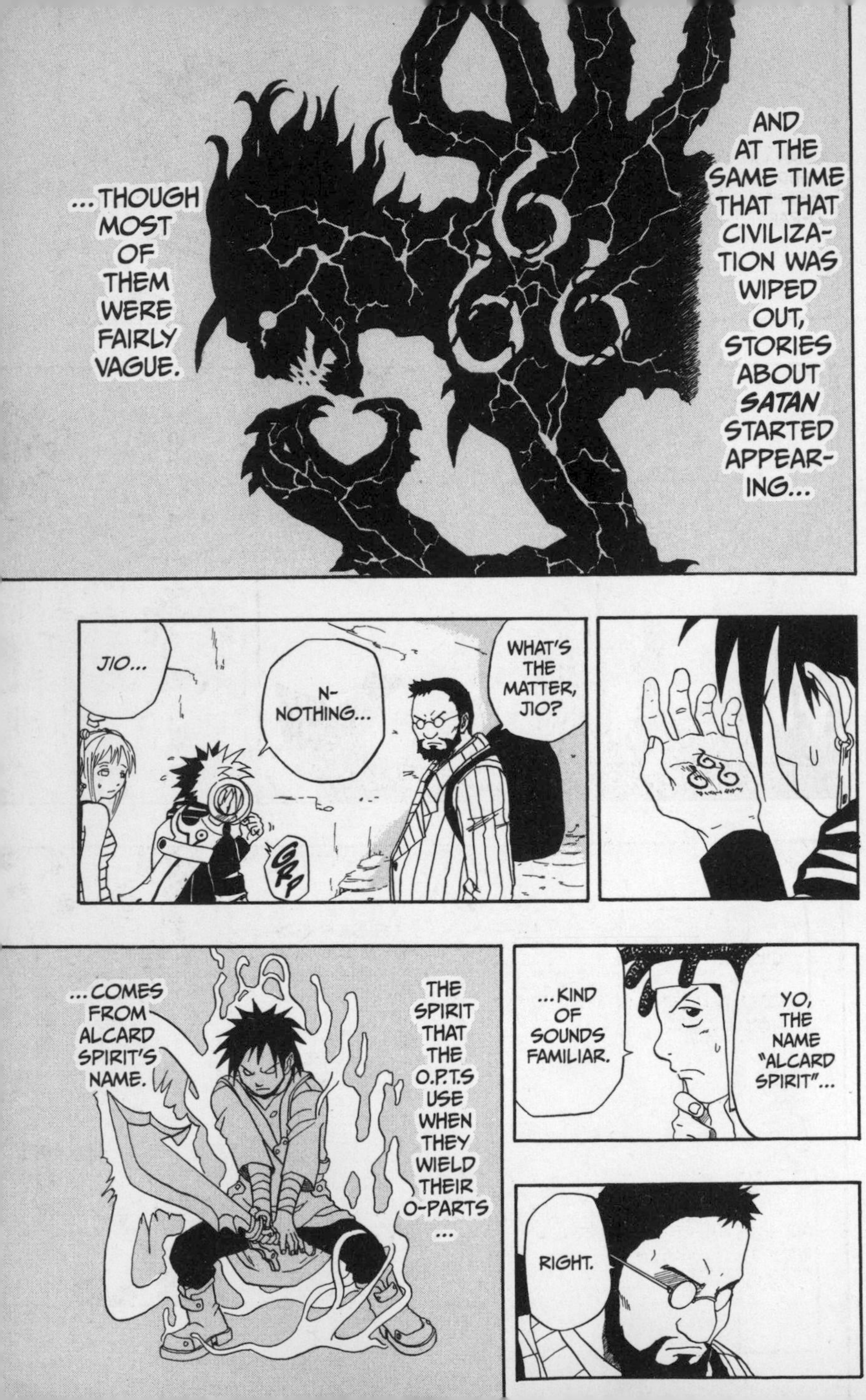
AND AT THE SAME TIME THAT THAT CIVILIZATION WAS WIPED OUT, STORIES ABOUT *SATAN* STARTED APPEARING...
...THOUGH MOST OF THEM WERE FAIRLY VAGUE.
WHAT'S THE MATTER, JIO?
N-NOTHING...
JIO...
GRR
YO, THE NAME "ALCARD SPIRIT"...
...KIND OF SOUNDS FAMILIAR.
RIGHT.
THE SPIRIT THAT THE O.P.T.S USE WHEN THEY WIELD THEIR O-PARTS...
...COMES FROM ALCARD SPIRIT'S NAME.

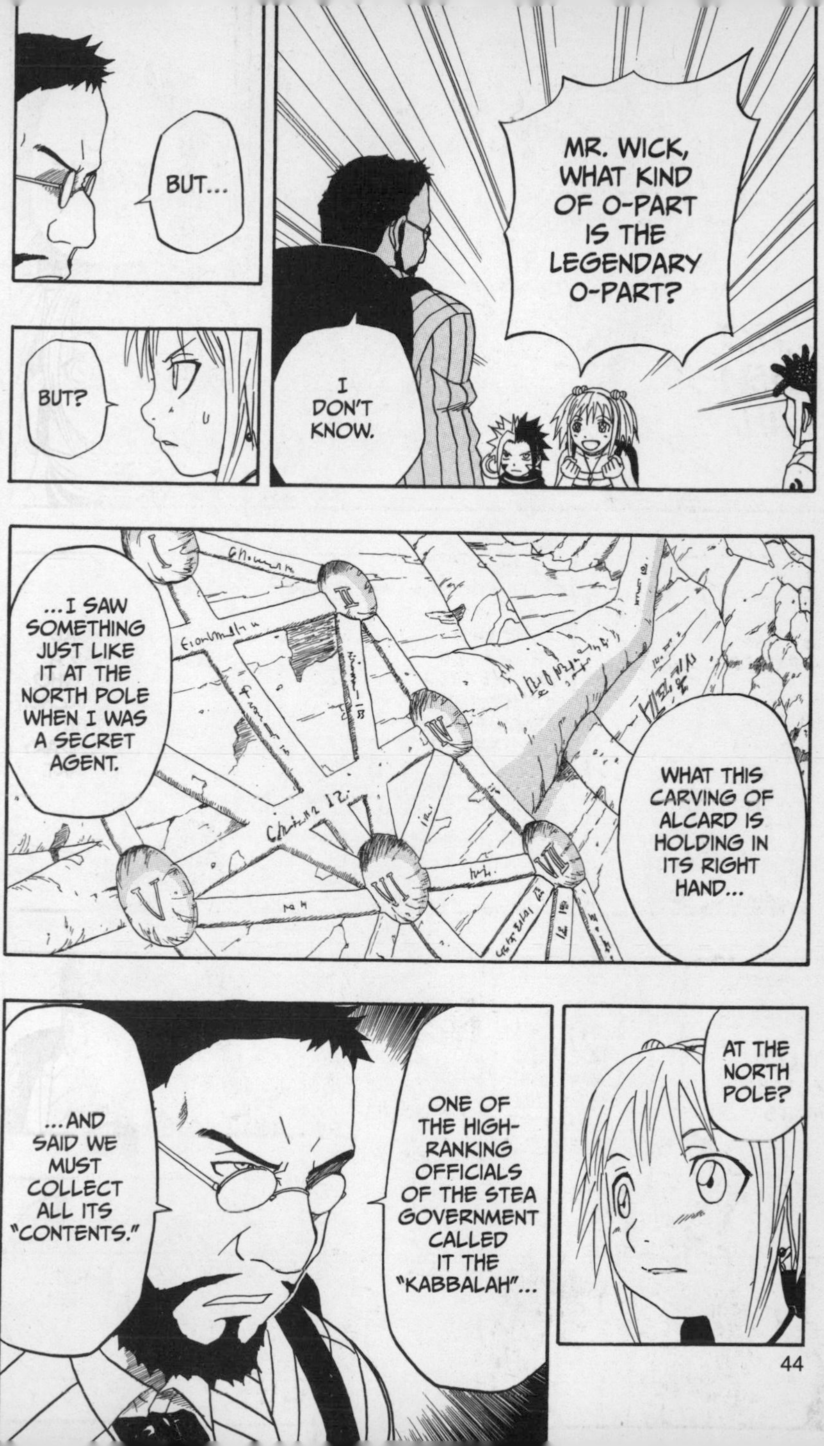
MR. WICK, WHAT KIND OF O-PART IS THE LEGENDARY O-PART?
I DON'T KNOW.
BUT...
BUT?
WHAT THIS CARVING OF ALCARD IS HOLDING IN ITS RIGHT HAND...
...I SAW SOMETHING JUST LIKE IT AT THE NORTH POLE WHEN I WAS A SECRET AGENT.
AT THE NORTH POLE?
ONE OF THE HIGH-RANKING OFFICIALS OF THE STEA GOVERNMENT CALLED IT THE "KABBALAH"...
...AND SAID WE MUST COLLECT ALL ITS "CONTENTS."

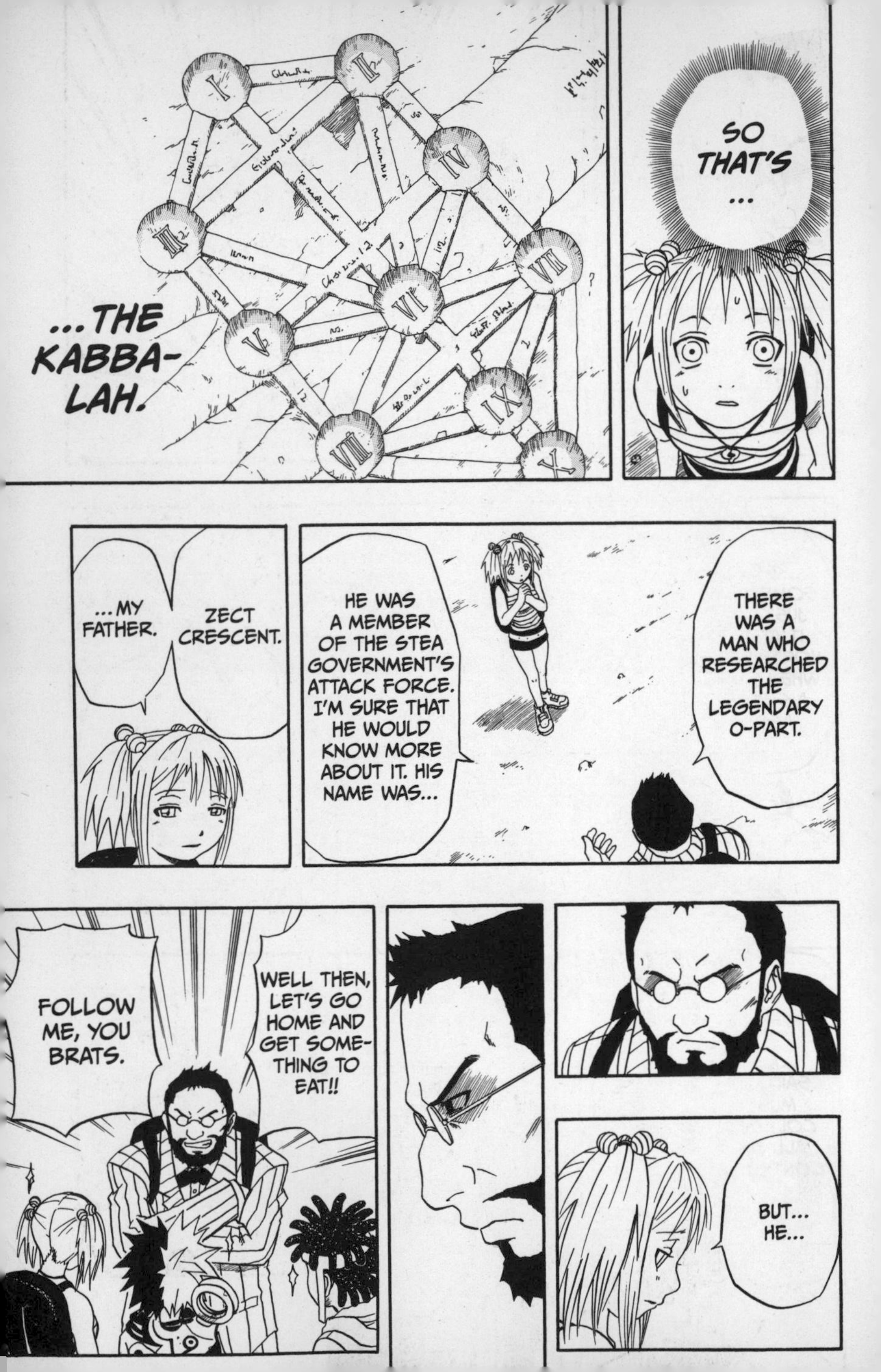
SO THAT'S ...
...THE KABBA-LAH.
THERE WAS A MAN WHO RESEARCHED THE LEGENDARY O-PART.
HE WAS A MEMBER OF THE STEA GOVERNMENT'S ATTACK FORCE. I'M SURE THAT HE WOULD KNOW MORE ABOUT IT. HIS NAME WAS...
ZECT CRESCENT.
...MY FATHER.
BUT... HE...
WELL THEN, LET'S GO HOME AND GET SOME-THING TO EAT!!
FOLLOW ME, YOU BRATS.

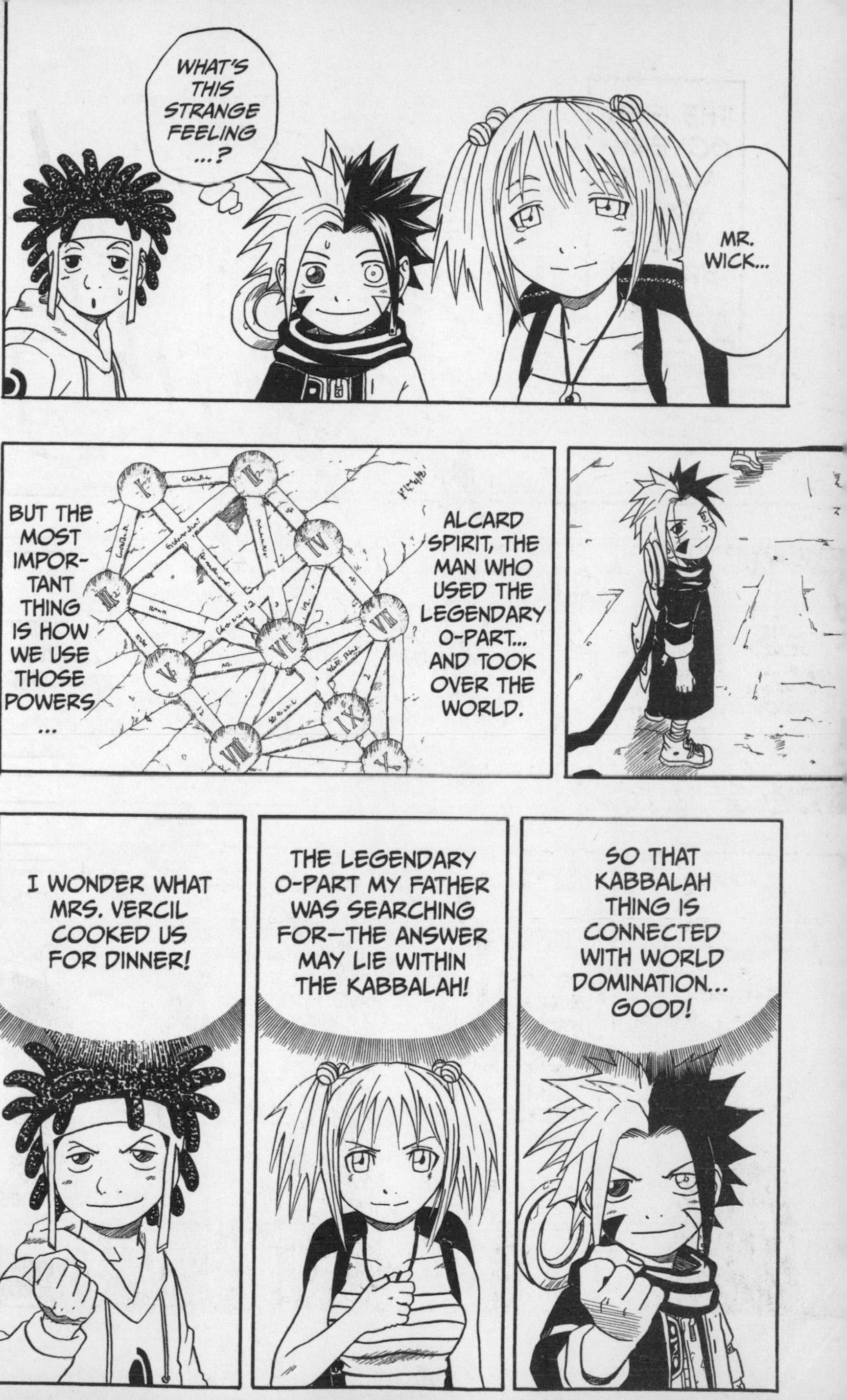
MR. WICK...
WHAT'S THIS STRANGE FEELING ...?
ALCARD SPIRIT, THE MAN WHO USED THE LEGENDARY O-PART... AND TOOK OVER THE WORLD.
BUT THE MOST IMPOR-TANT THING IS HOW WE USE THOSE POWERS ...
SO THAT KABBALAH THING IS CONNECTED WITH WORLD DOMINATION... GOOD!
THE LEGENDARY O-PART MY FATHER WAS SEARCHING FOR—THE ANSWER MAY LIE WITHIN THE KABBALAH!
I WONDER WHAT MRS. VERCIL COOKED US FOR DINNER!

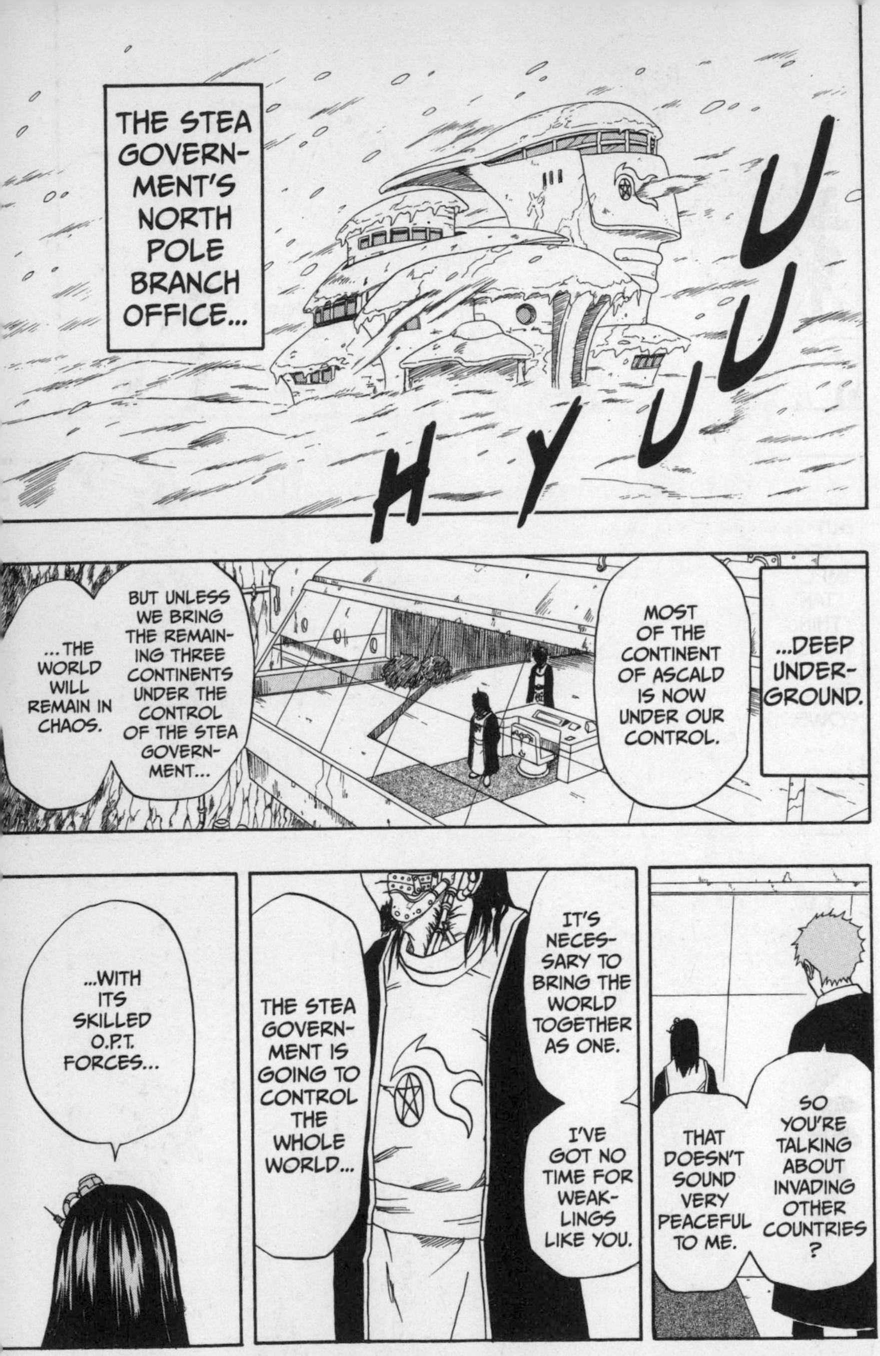
THE STEA GOVERNMENT'S NORTH POLE BRANCH OFFICE...
HYUUUU
...DEEP UNDERGROUND.
MOST OF THE CONTINENT OF ASCALD IS NOW UNDER OUR CONTROL.
BUT UNLESS WE BRING THE REMAINING THREE CONTINENTS UNDER THE CONTROL OF THE STEA GOVERNMENT...
...THE WORLD WILL REMAIN IN CHAOS.
SO YOU'RE TALKING ABOUT INVADING OTHER COUNTRIES?
THAT DOESN'T SOUND VERY PEACEFUL TO ME.
IT'S NECESSARY TO BRING THE WORLD TOGETHER AS ONE.
I'VE GOT NO TIME FOR WEAKLINGS LIKE YOU.
THE STEA GOVERNMENT IS GOING TO CONTROL THE WHOLE WORLD...
...WITH ITS SKILLED O.P.T. FORCES...

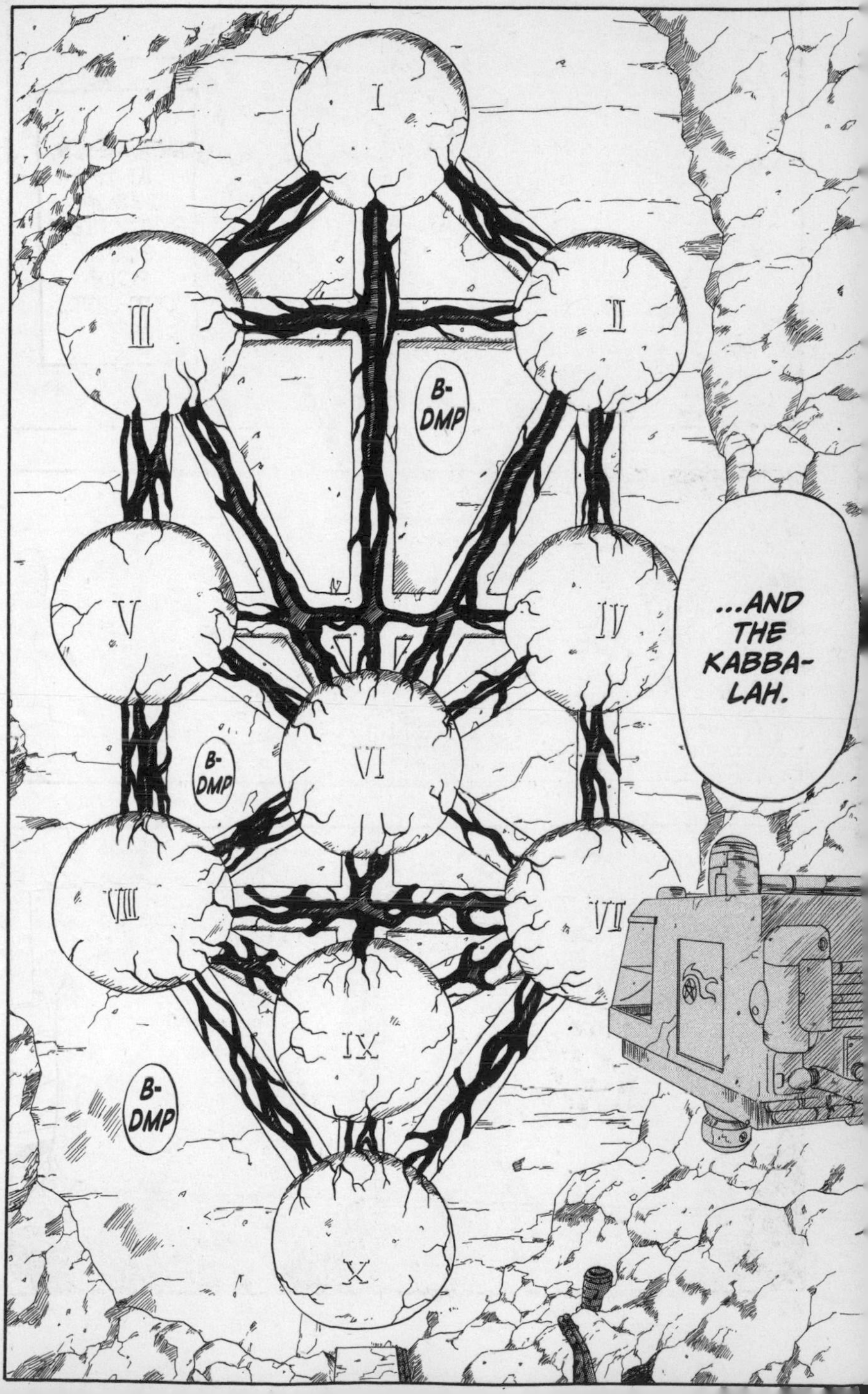
...AND THE KABBALAH.
B-DMP
B-DMP
B-DMP

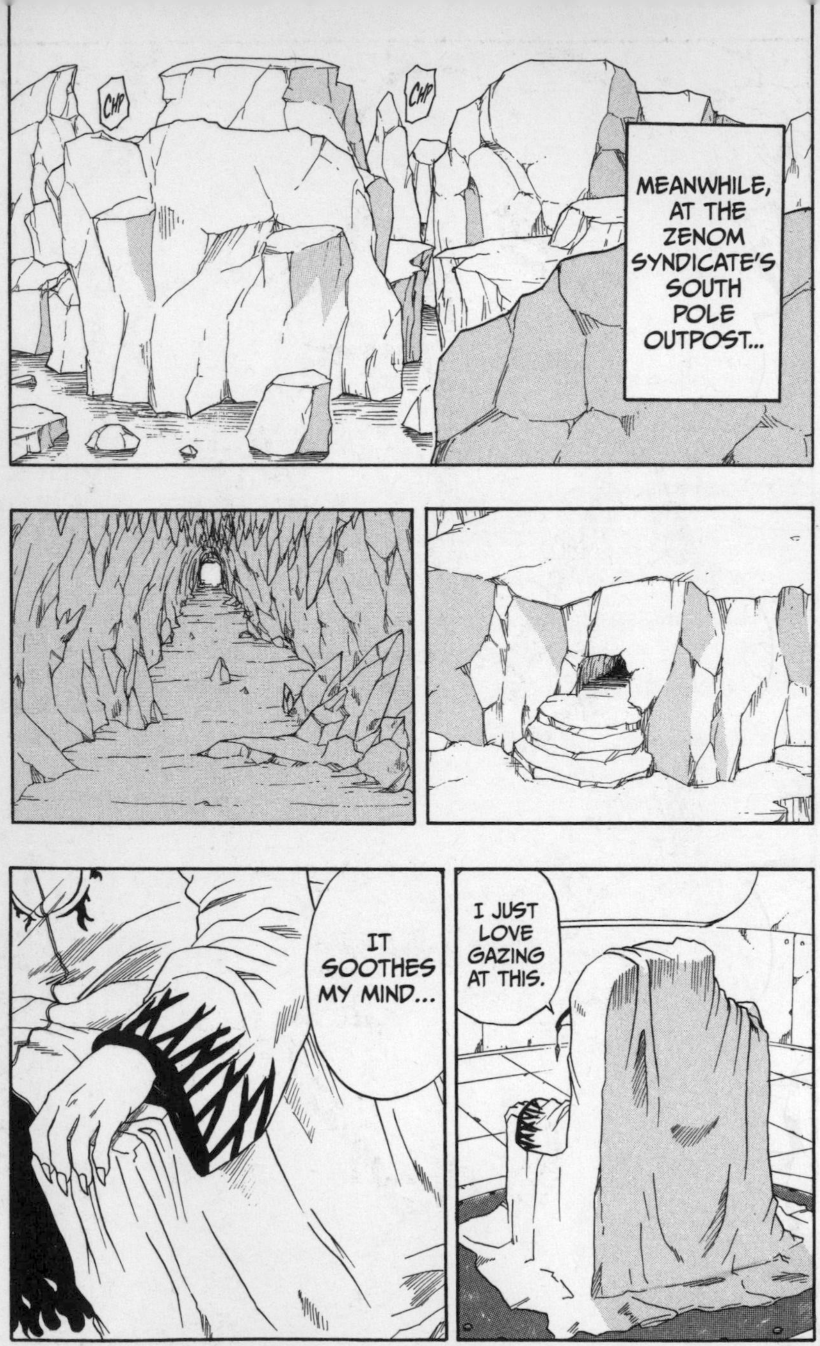
CHP
CHP
MEANWHILE, AT THE ZENOM SYNDICATE'S SOUTH POLE OUTPOST...
I JUST LOVE GAZING AT THIS.
IT SOOTHES MY MIND...

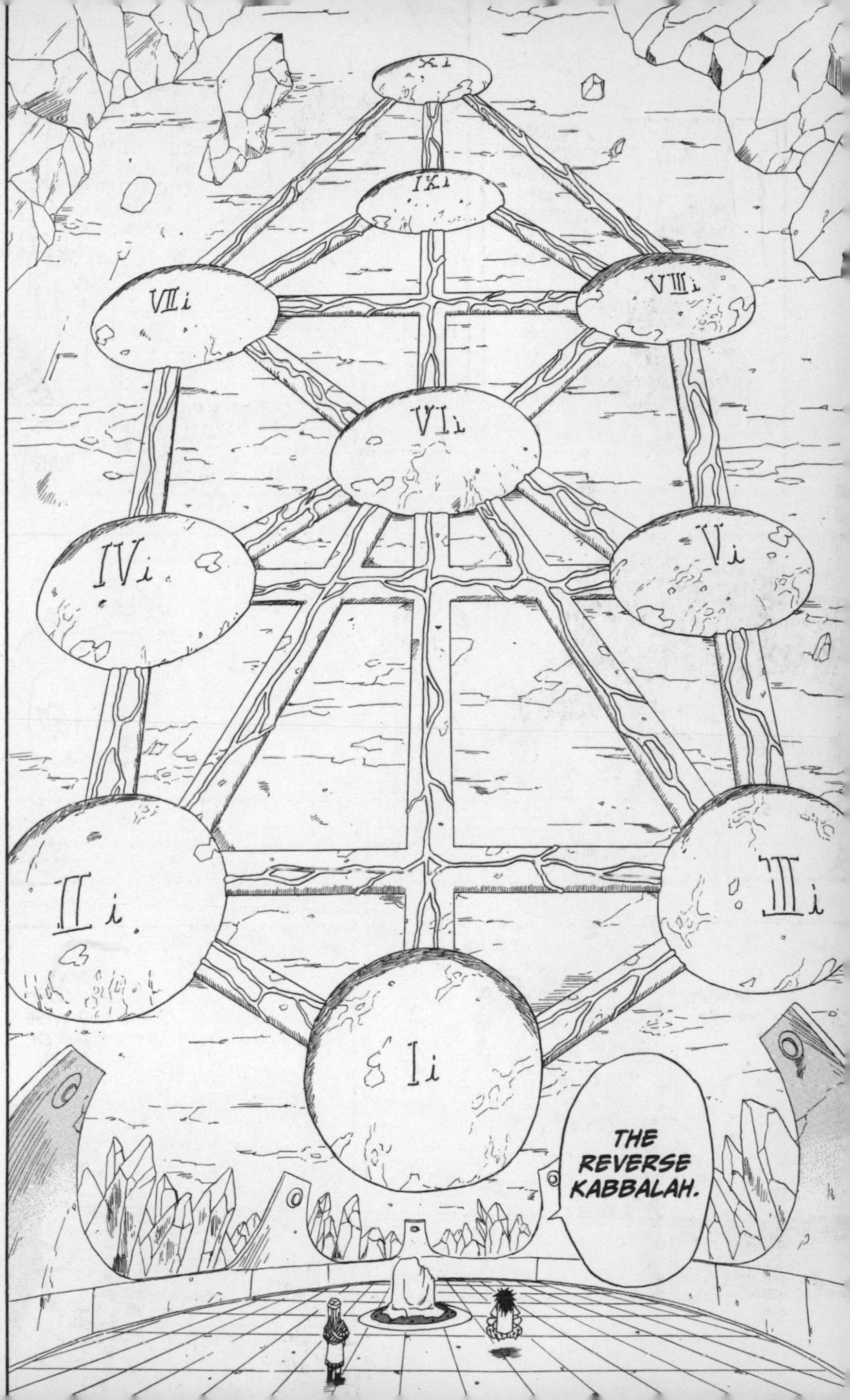
THE REVERSE KABBALAH.

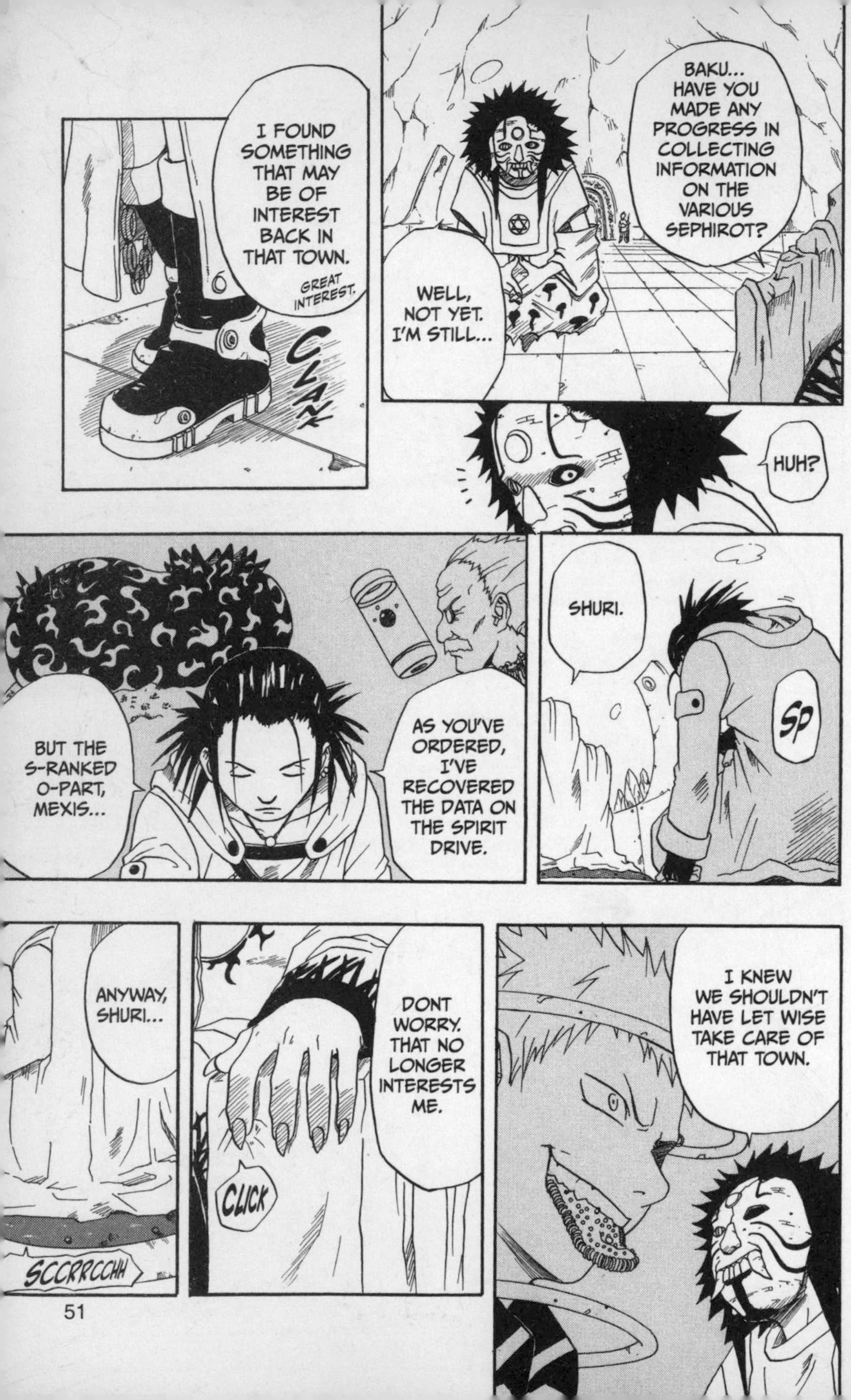
BAKU... HAVE YOU MADE ANY PROGRESS IN COLLECTING INFORMATION ON THE VARIOUS SEPHIROT?
WELL, NOT YET. I'M STILL...
HUH?
I FOUND SOMETHING THAT MAY BE OF INTEREST BACK IN THAT TOWN.
GREAT INTEREST.
CLANK
SHURI.
Sp
AS YOU'VE ORDERED, I'VE RECOVERED THE DATA ON THE SPIRIT DRIVE.
BUT THE S-RANKED O-PART, MEXIS...
I KNEW WE SHOULDN'T HAVE LET WISE TAKE CARE OF THAT TOWN.
DONT WORRY. THAT NO LONGER INTERESTS ME.
CLICK
ANYWAY, SHURI...
SCCRRCCHH

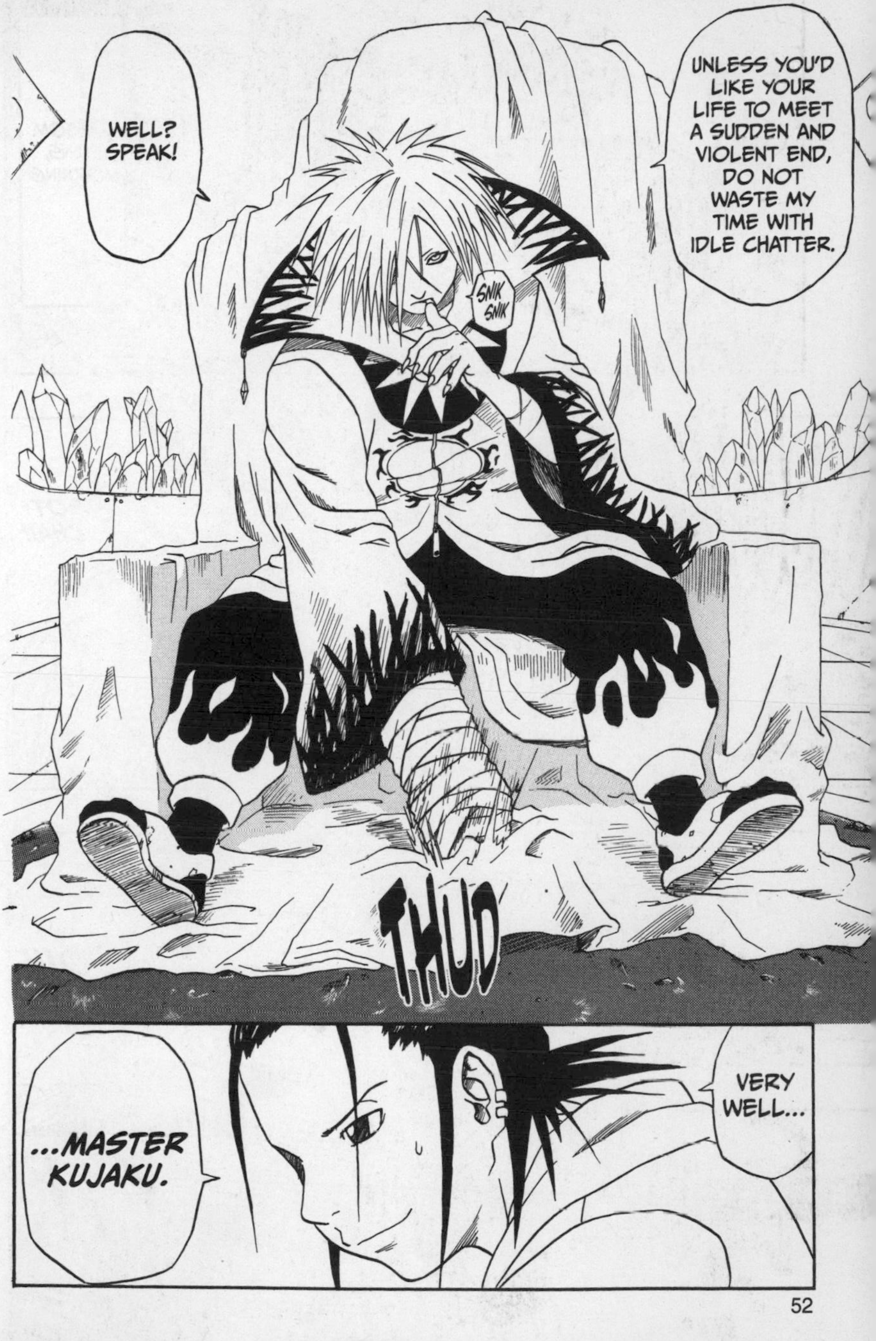
UNLESS YOU'D LIKE YOUR LIFE TO MEET A SUDDEN AND VIOLENT END, DO NOT WASTE MY TIME WITH IDLE CHATTER.
SNIK SNIK
WELL? SPEAK!
THUD
VERY WELL...
...MASTER KUJAKU.

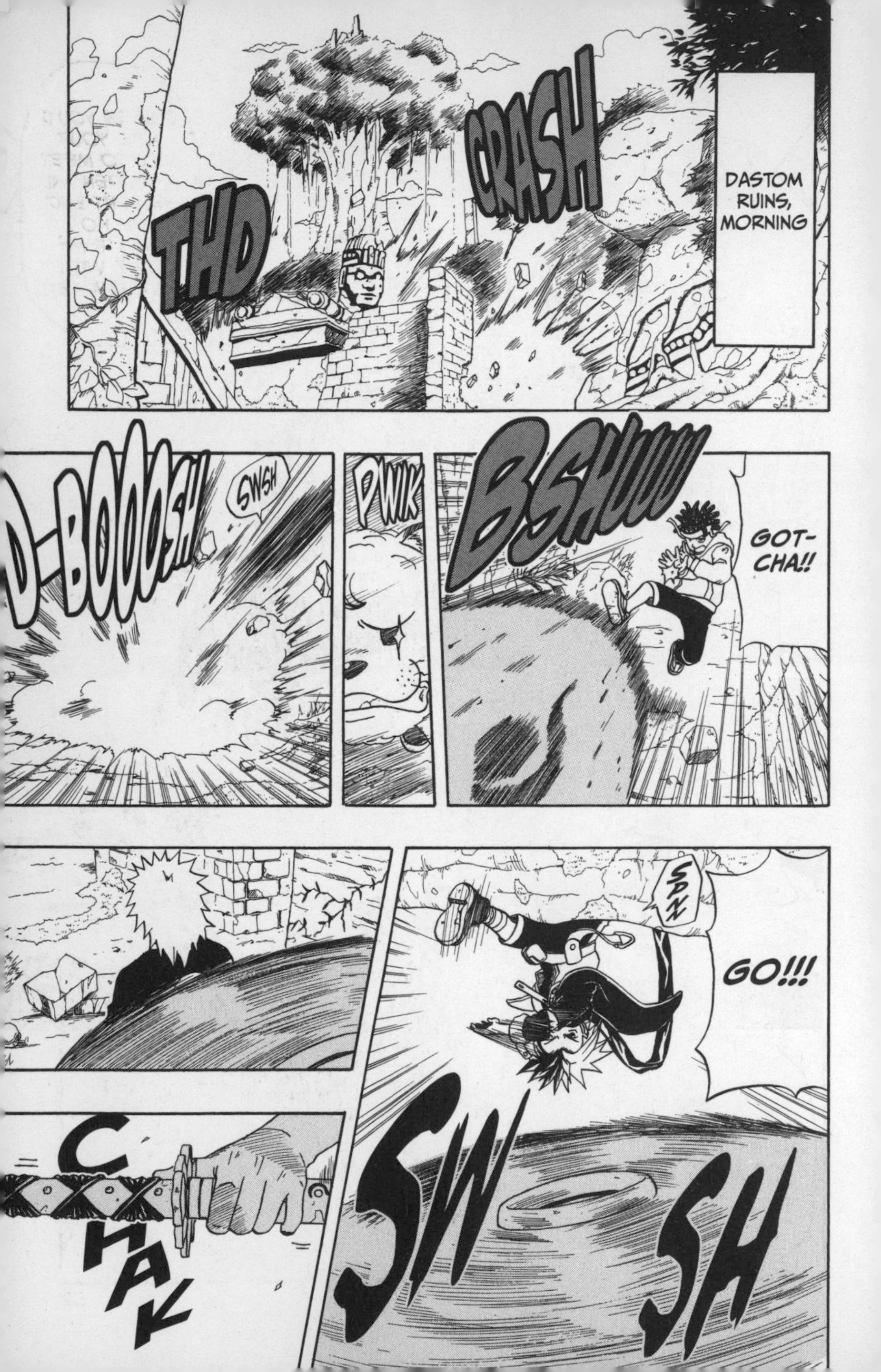
DASTOM RUINS, MORNING
CRASH
THD
GOT-CHA!!
BSHUUU
PWIK
SWSH
D-BOOOSH
SPNN
GO!!!
SWSH
CHAK

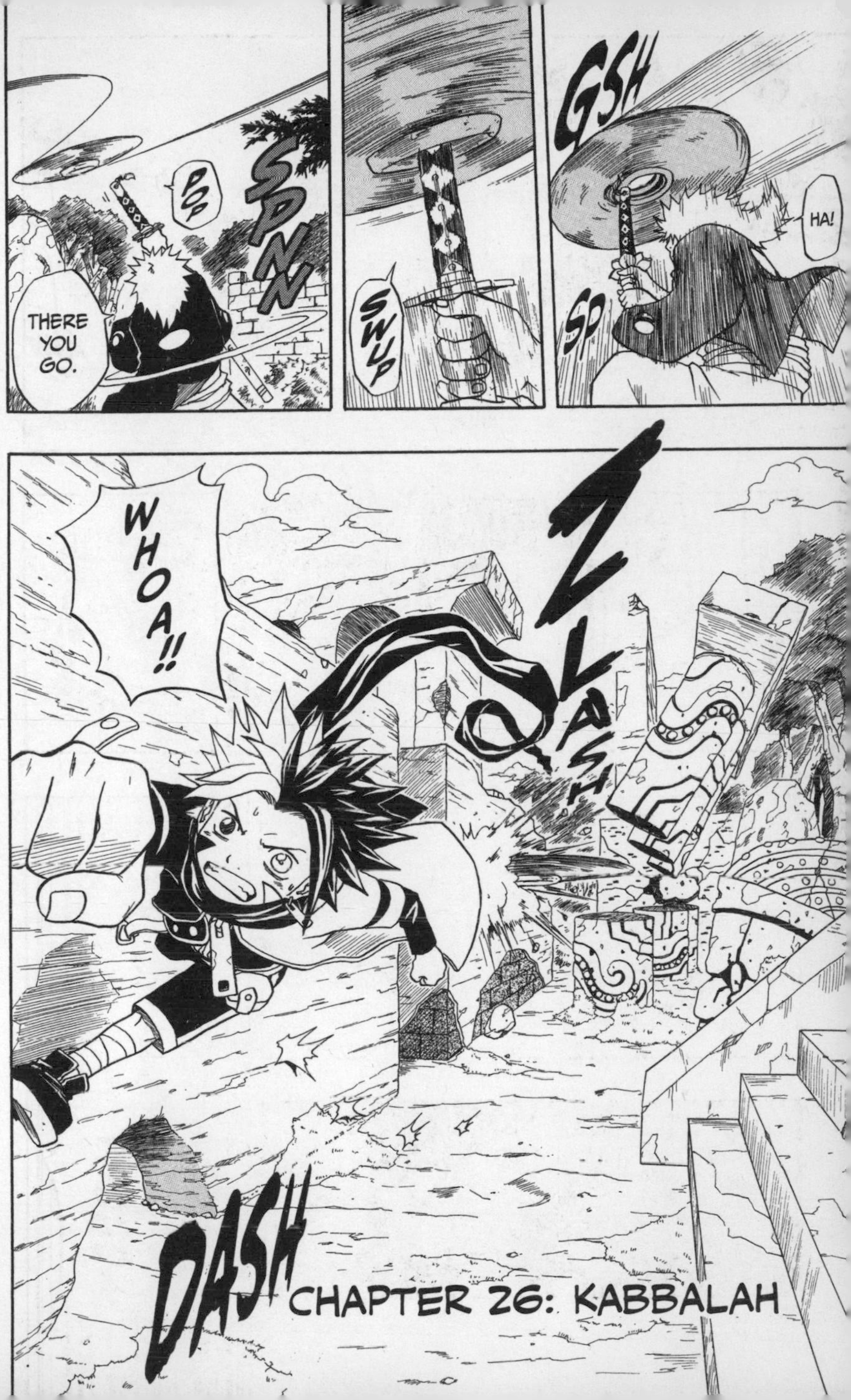
GSH
HA!
SP
SWUP
SPNN
POP
THERE YOU GO.
WHOA!!
VASH
DASH

CHAPTER 26: KABBALAH

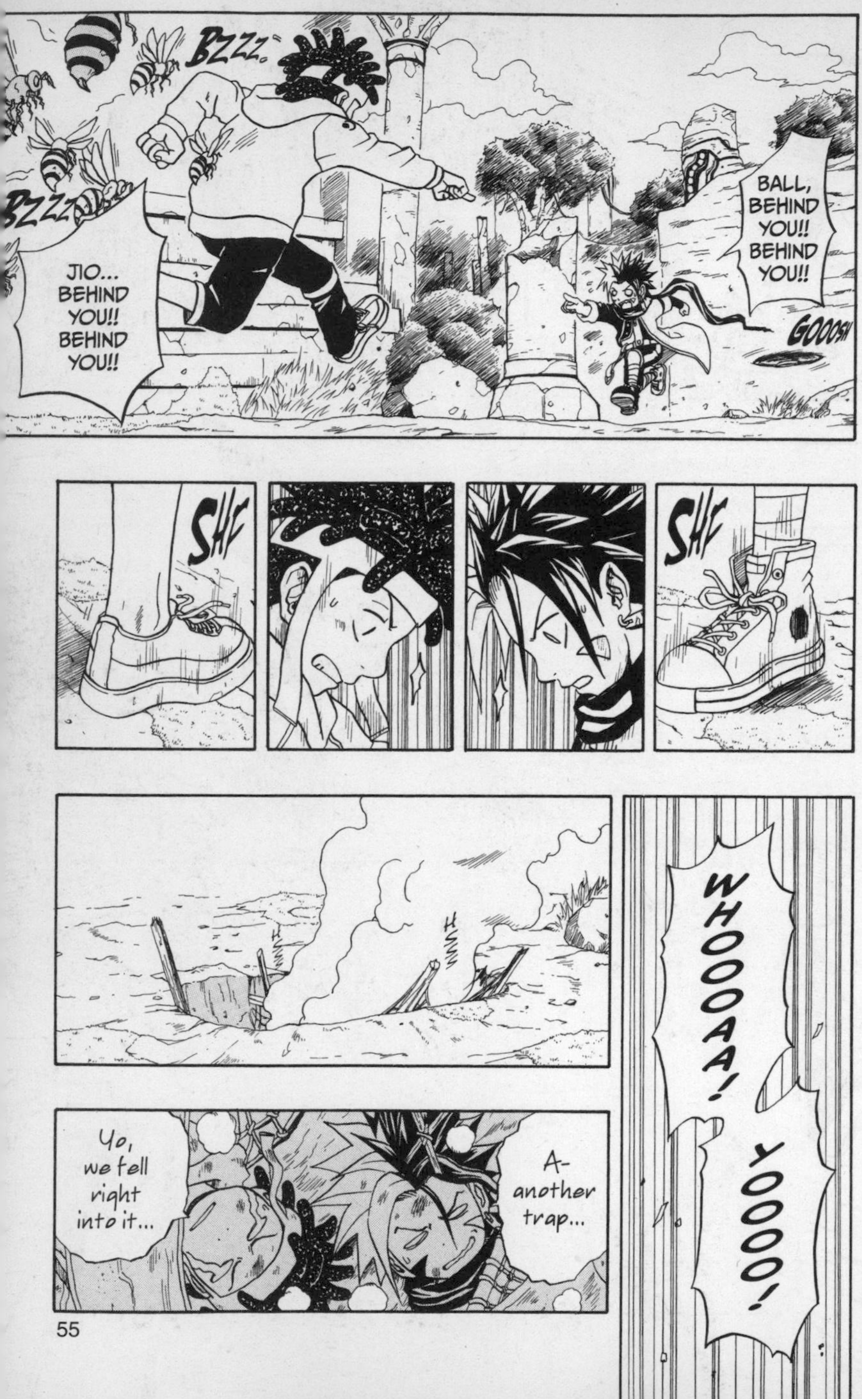
BALL, BEHIND YOU!! BEHIND YOU!!
GOOSH
BZZZ
JIO... BEHIND YOU!! BEHIND YOU!!
BZZZ
SHF
SHF
WHOOOAA! YOOOOO!
HSSS
HSSS
A- another trap...
Yo, we fell right into it...

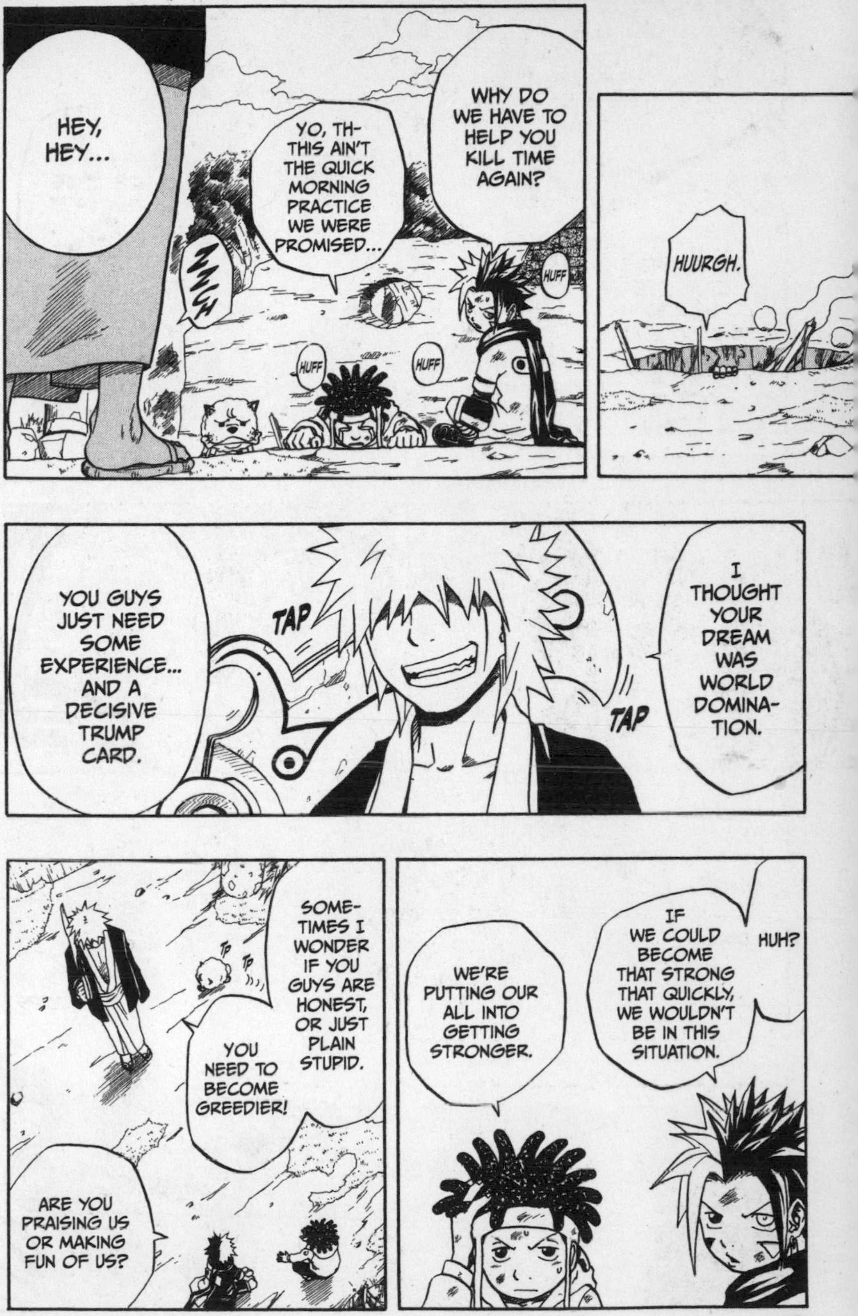
HUURGH.
WHY DO WE HAVE TO HELP YOU KILL TIME AGAIN?
HUFF
YO, TH- THIS AIN'T THE QUICK MORNING PRACTICE WE WERE PROMISED...
HUFF
HUFF
HEY, HEY...
I THOUGHT YOUR DREAM WAS WORLD DOMINA- TION.
TAP
TAP
YOU GUYS JUST NEED SOME EXPERIENCE... AND A DECISIVE TRUMP CARD.
HUH?
IF WE COULD BECOME THAT STRONG THAT QUICKLY, WE WOULDN'T BE IN THIS SITUATION.
WE'RE PUTTING OUR ALL INTO GETTING STRONGER.
SOME- TIMES I WONDER IF YOU GUYS ARE HONEST, OR JUST PLAIN STUPID.
YOU NEED TO BECOME GREEDIER!
ARE YOU PRAISING US OR MAKING FUN OF US?

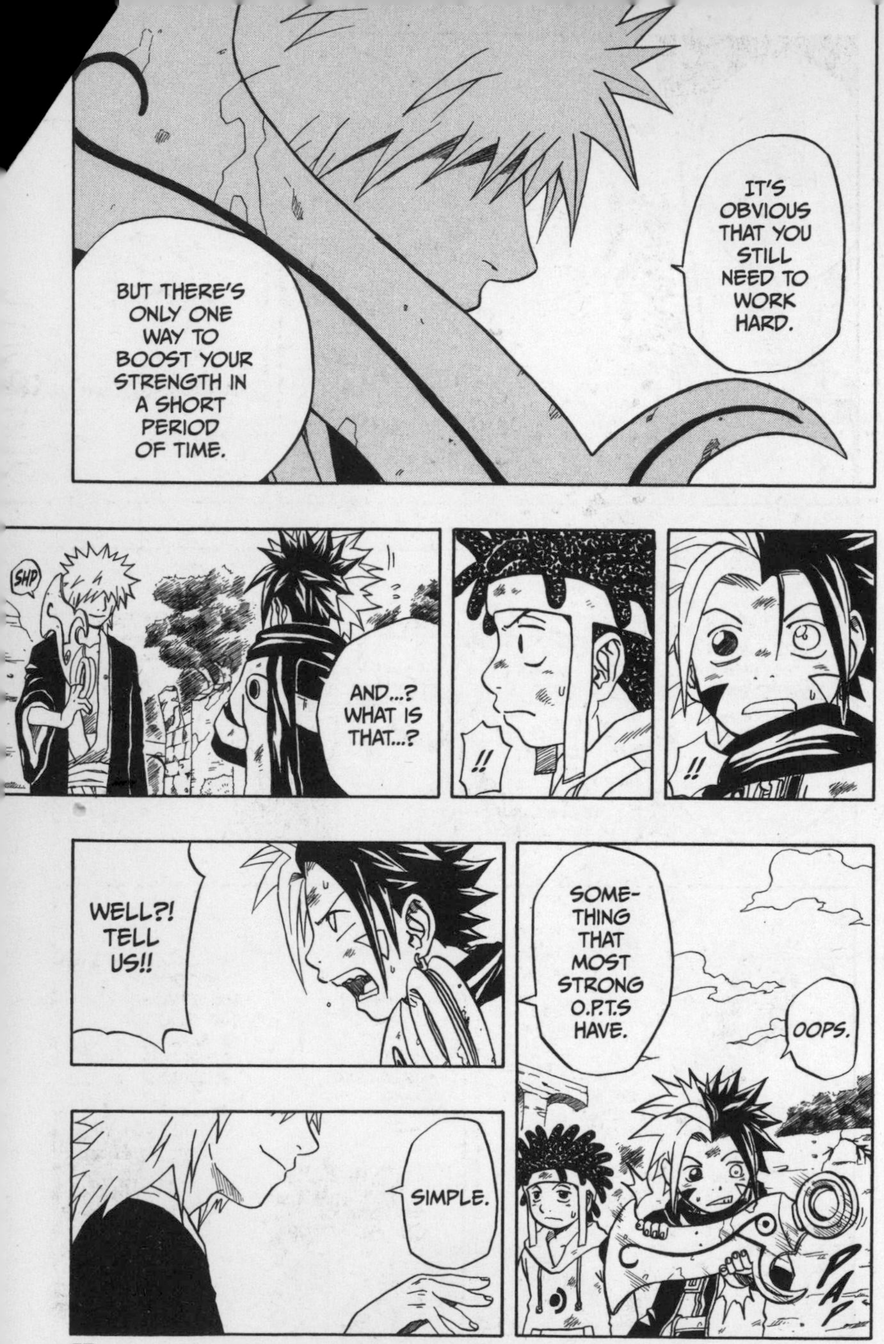
IT'S OBVIOUS THAT YOU STILL NEED TO WORK HARD.
BUT THERE'S ONLY ONE WAY TO BOOST YOUR STRENGTH IN A SHORT PERIOD OF TIME.
!!
!!
AND...? WHAT IS THAT...?
SHP
SOME-THING THAT MOST STRONG O.P.T.S HAVE.
OOPS.
PAP
WELL?! TELL US!!
SIMPLE.

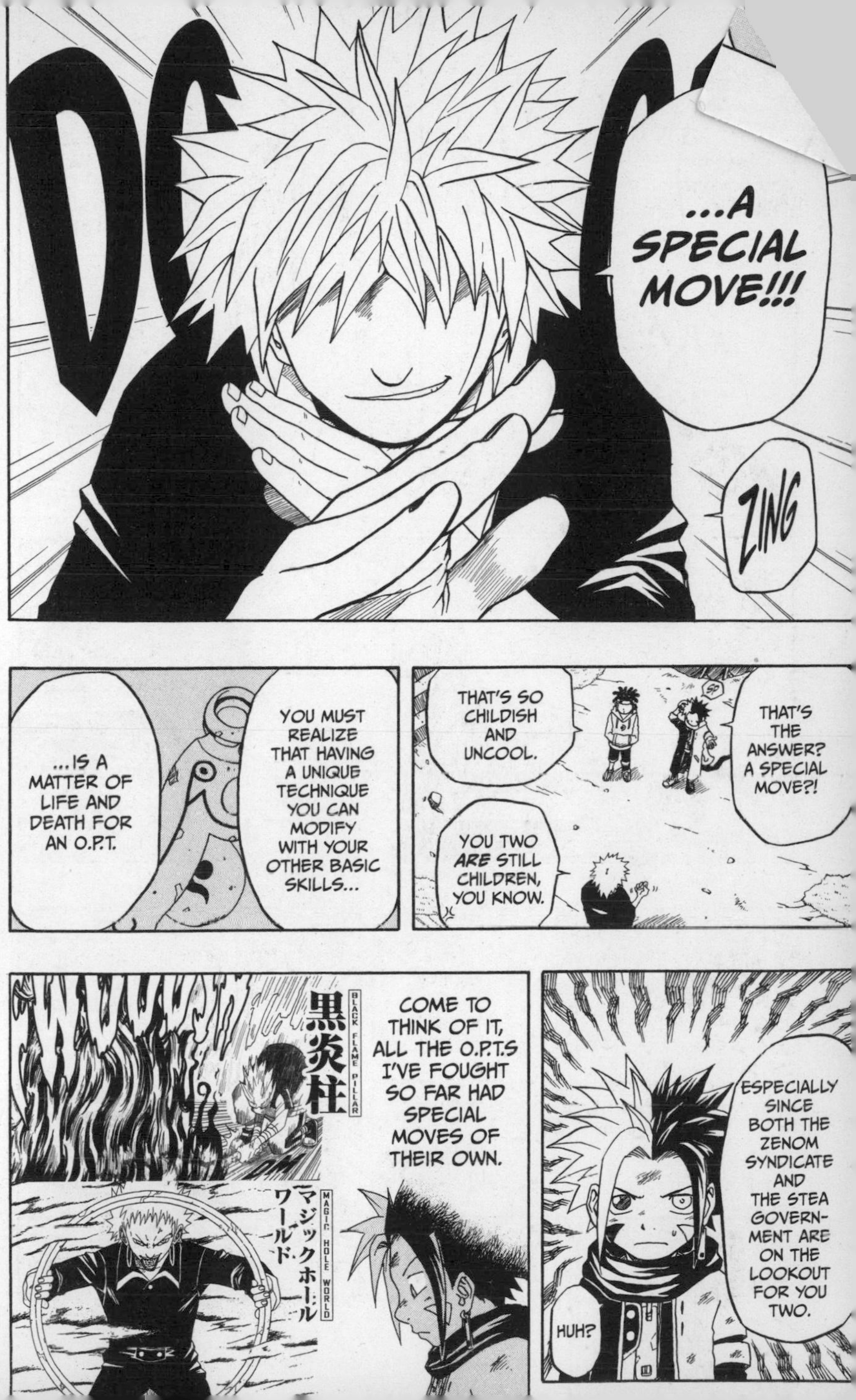
...A SPECIAL MOVE!!!
ZING
THAT'S THE ANSWER? A SPECIAL MOVE?!
SP
THAT'S SO CHILDISH AND UNCOOL.
YOU TWO ARE STILL CHILDREN, YOU KNOW.
YOU MUST REALIZE THAT HAVING A UNIQUE TECHNIQUE YOU CAN MODIFY WITH YOUR OTHER BASIC SKILLS...
...IS A MATTER OF LIFE AND DEATH FOR AN O.P.T.
ESPECIALLY SINCE BOTH THE ZENOM SYNDICATE AND THE STEA GOVERNMENT ARE ON THE LOOKOUT FOR YOU TWO.
HUH?
COME TO THINK OF IT, ALL THE O.P.T.S I'VE FOUGHT SO FAR HAD SPECIAL MOVES OF THEIR OWN.
黒炎柱 BLACK FLAME PILLAR
マジックホールワールド MAGIC HOLE WORLD

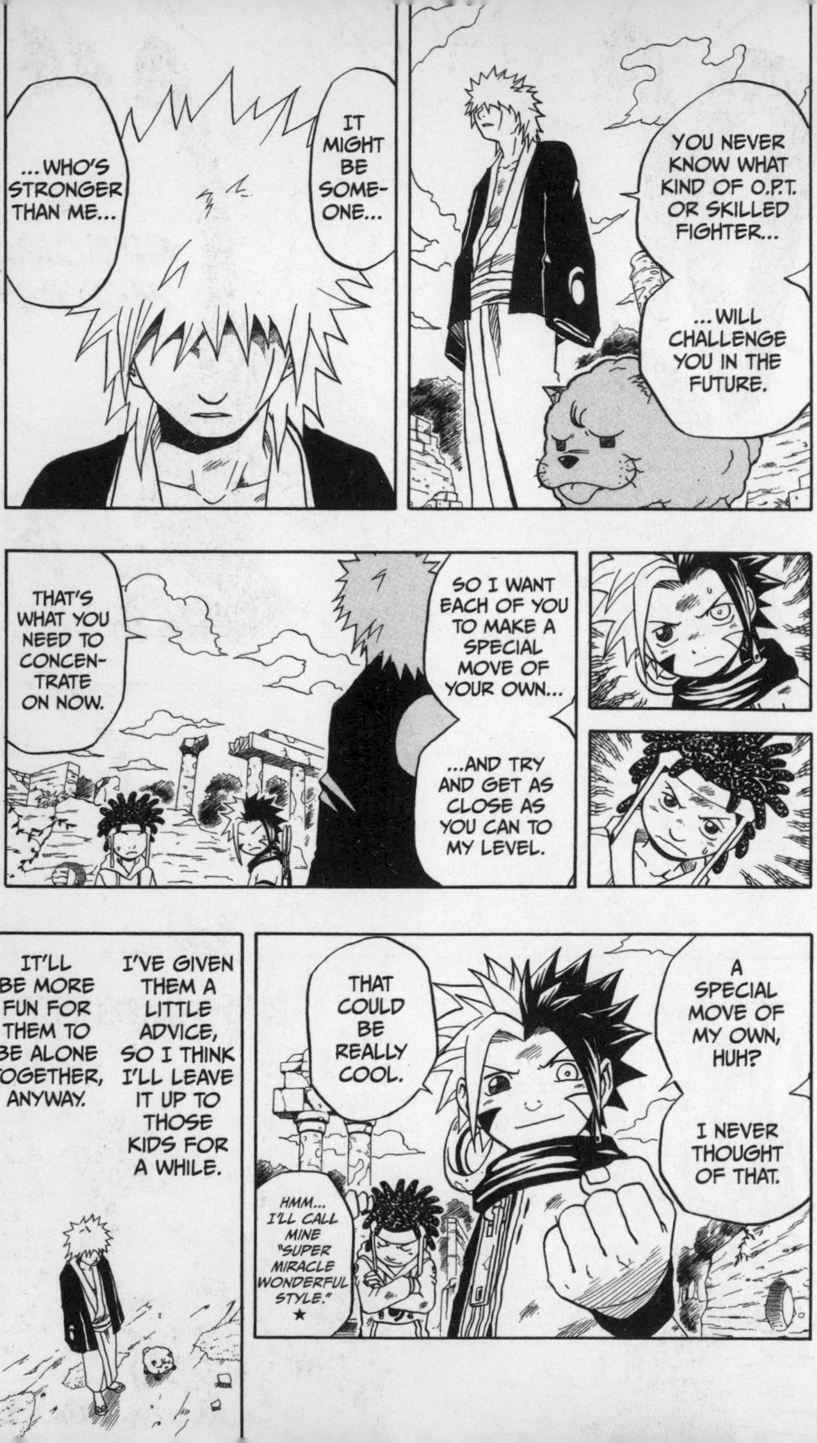
YOU NEVER KNOW WHAT KIND OF O.P.T. OR SKILLED FIGHTER...
...WILL CHALLENGE YOU IN THE FUTURE.
IT MIGHT BE SOME-ONE...
...WHO'S STRONGER THAN ME...
SO I WANT EACH OF YOU TO MAKE A SPECIAL MOVE OF YOUR OWN...
...AND TRY AND GET AS CLOSE AS YOU CAN TO MY LEVEL.
THAT'S WHAT YOU NEED TO CONCEN-TRATE ON NOW.
A SPECIAL MOVE OF MY OWN, HUH?
I NEVER THOUGHT OF THAT.
THAT COULD BE REALLY COOL.
HMM... I'LL CALL MINE "SUPER MIRACLE WONDERFUL STYLE." ★
I'VE GIVEN THEM A LITTLE ADVICE, SO I THINK I'LL LEAVE IT UP TO THOSE KIDS FOR A WHILE.
IT'LL BE MORE FUN FOR THEM TO BE ALONE TOGETHER, ANYWAY.

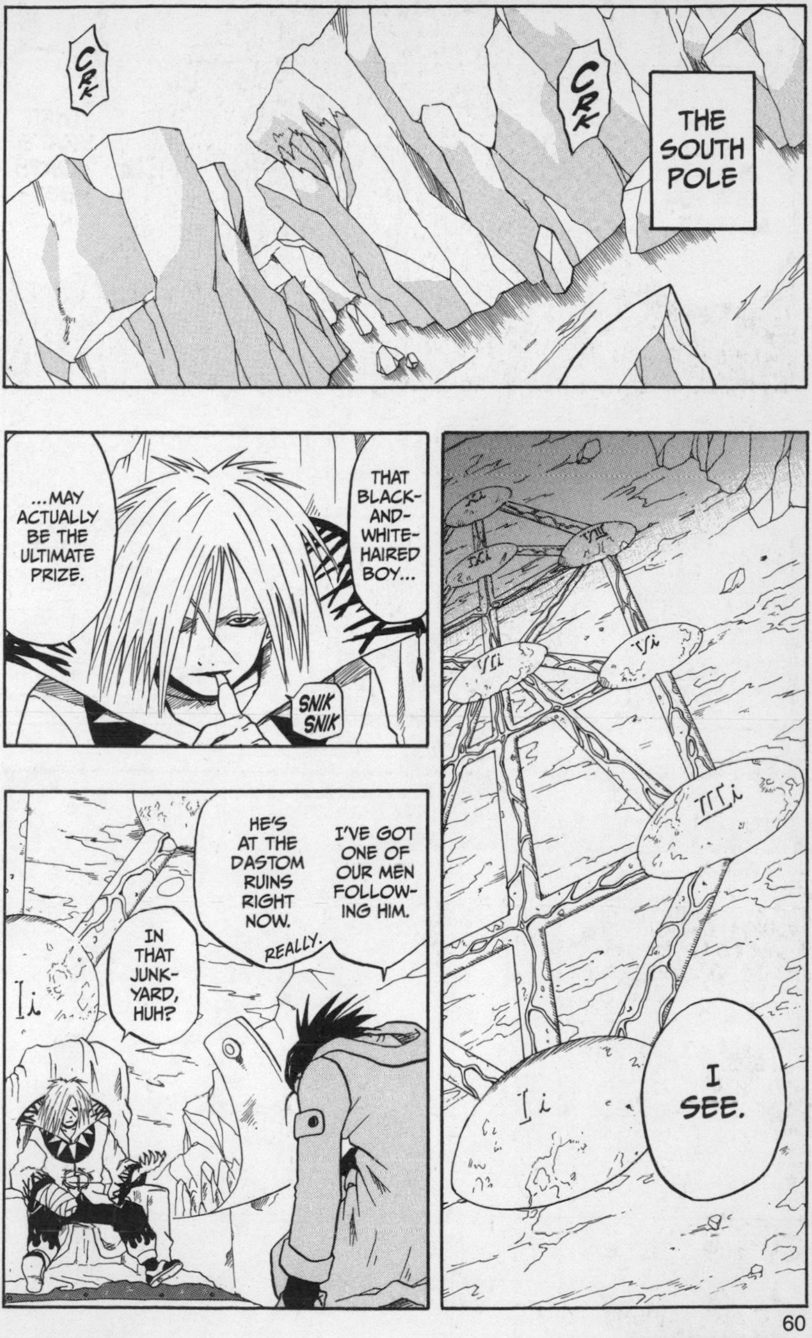
THE SOUTH POLE
CRK
CRK
I SEE.
THAT BLACK-AND-WHITE-HAIRED BOY...
...MAY ACTUALLY BE THE ULTIMATE PRIZE.
SNIK SNIK
I'VE GOT ONE OF OUR MEN FOLLOW-ING HIM.
HE'S AT THE DASTOM RUINS RIGHT NOW.
REALLY.
IN THAT JUNK-YARD, HUH?

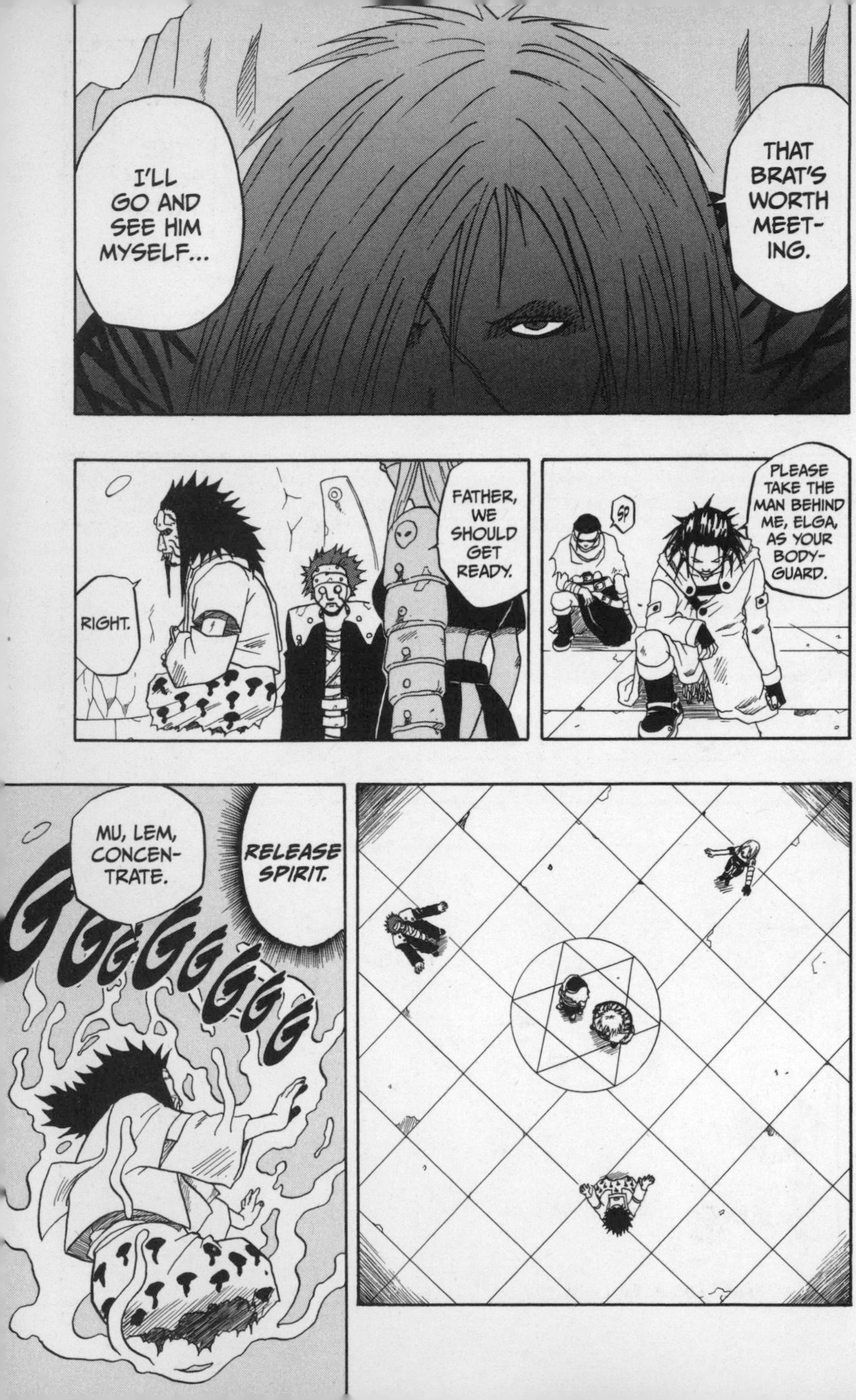
THAT BRAT'S WORTH MEET-ING.
I'LL GO AND SEE HIM MYSELF...
SP
PLEASE TAKE THE MAN BEHIND ME, ELGA, AS YOUR BODY-GUARD.
FATHER, WE SHOULD GET READY.
RIGHT.
RELEASE SPIRIT.
MU, LEM, CONCEN-TRATE.
GGGGGGGGGG

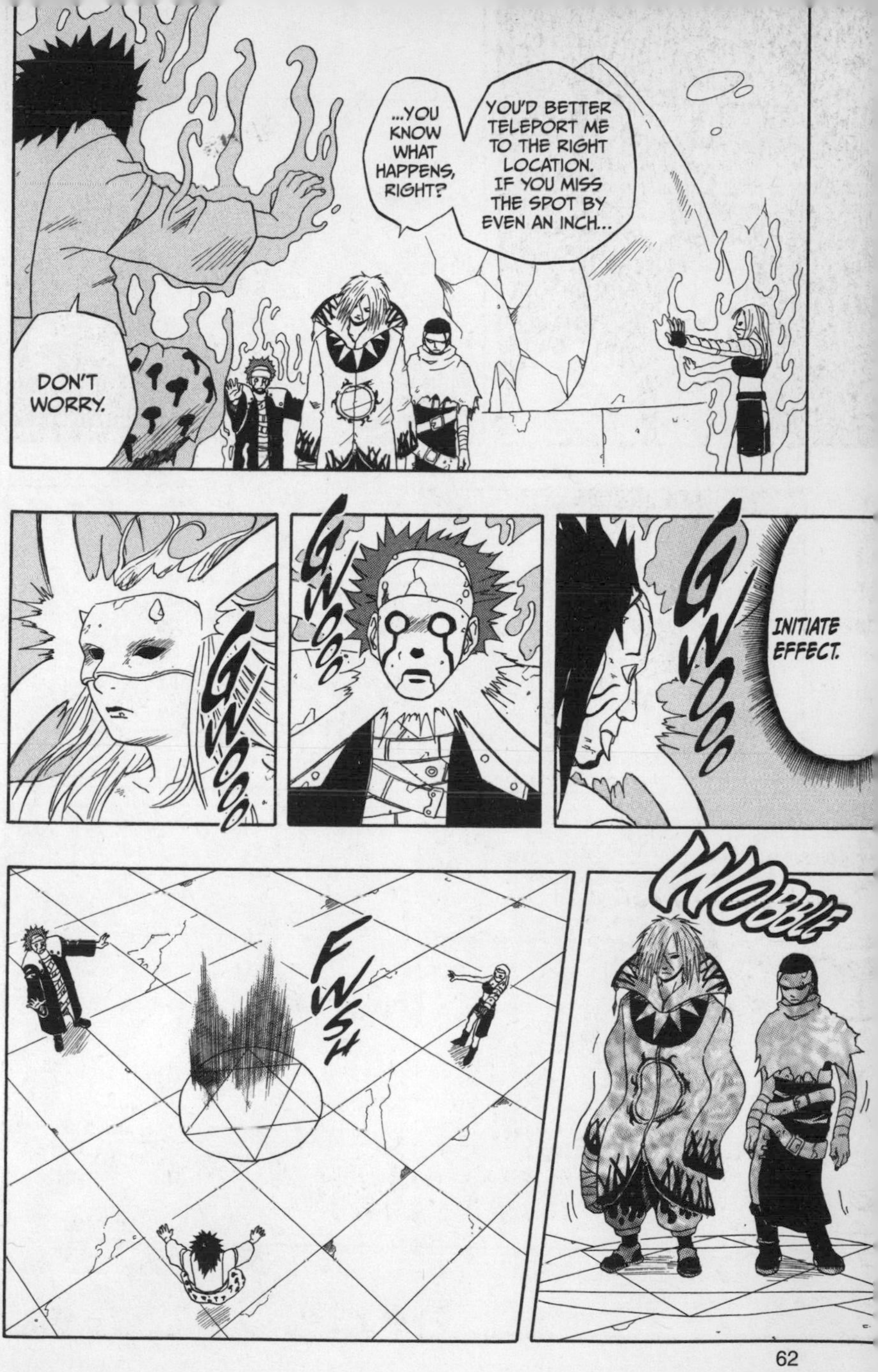
YOU'D BETTER TELEPORT ME TO THE RIGHT LOCATION. IF YOU MISS THE SPOT BY EVEN AN INCH...
...YOU KNOW WHAT HAPPENS, RIGHT?
DON'T WORRY.
INITIATE EFFECT.
GWOOO
GWOOO
GWOOO
WOBBLE
FWSH

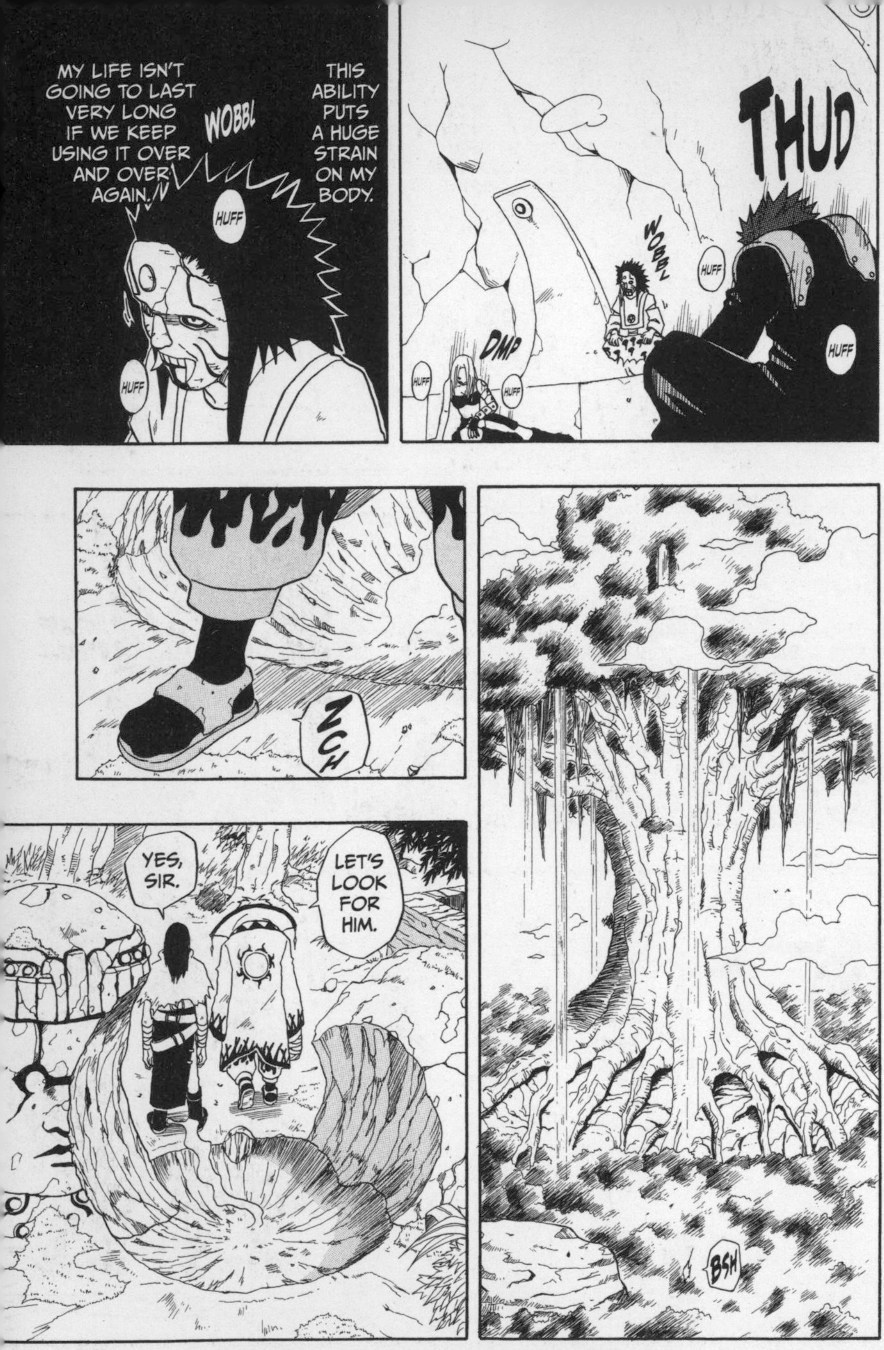
THUD
WOBBL
HUFF
HUFF
DMP
HUFF
HUFF
THIS ABILITY PUTS A HUGE STRAIN ON MY BODY.
MY LIFE ISN'T GOING TO LAST VERY LONG IF WE KEEP USING IT OVER AND OVER AGAIN.
WOBBL
HUFF
HUFF
BSH
NCH
LET'S LOOK FOR HIM.
YES, SIR.

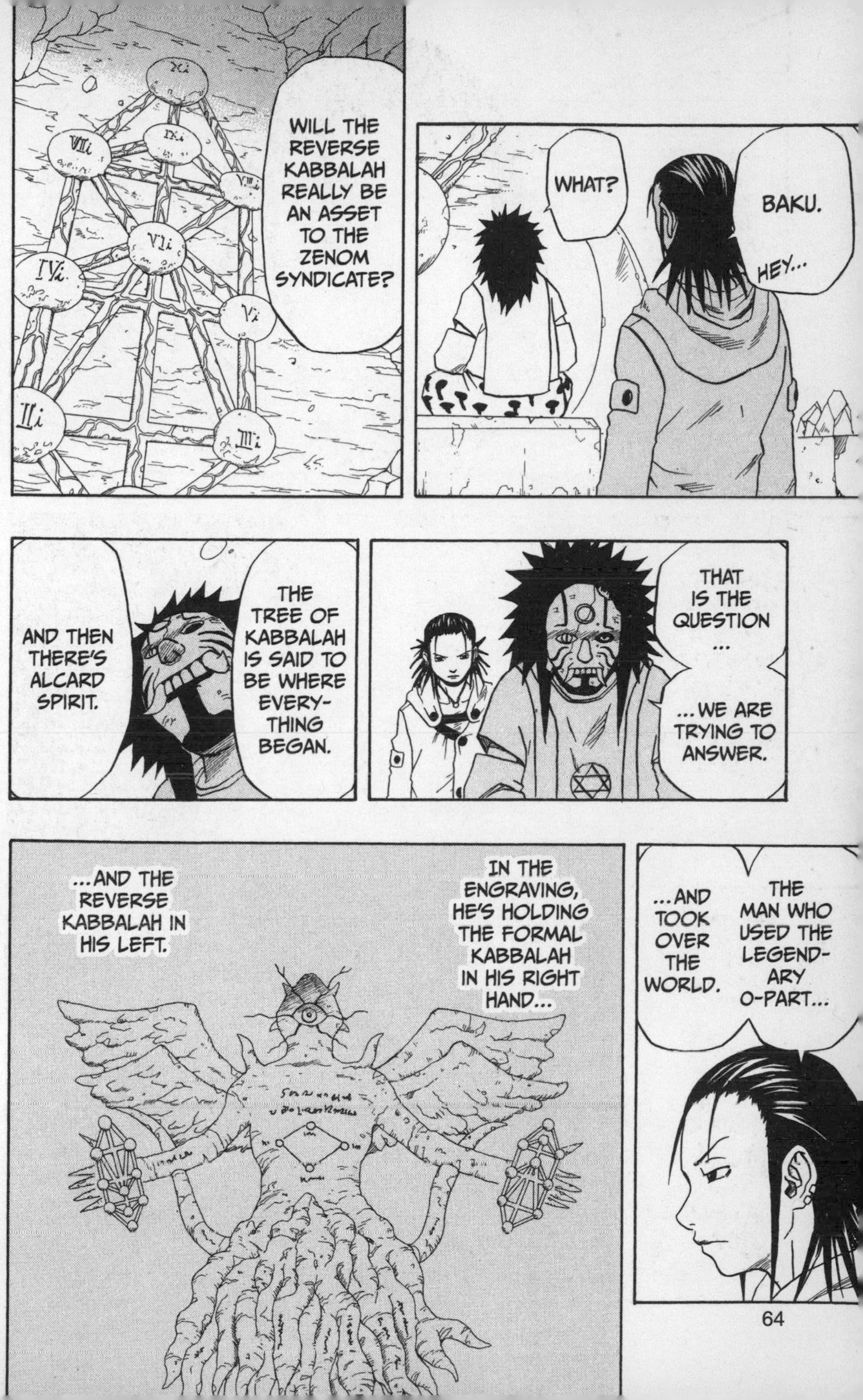
BAKU.
HEY...
WHAT?
WILL THE REVERSE KABBALAH REALLY BE AN ASSET TO THE ZENOM SYNDICATE?
THAT IS THE QUESTION ...
...WE ARE TRYING TO ANSWER.
THE TREE OF KABBALAH IS SAID TO BE WHERE EVERYTHING BEGAN.
AND THEN THERE'S ALCARD SPIRIT.
THE MAN WHO USED THE LEGENDARY O-PART...
...AND TOOK OVER THE WORLD.
IN THE ENGRAVING, HE'S HOLDING THE FORMAL KABBALAH IN HIS RIGHT HAND...
...AND THE REVERSE KABBALAH IN HIS LEFT.

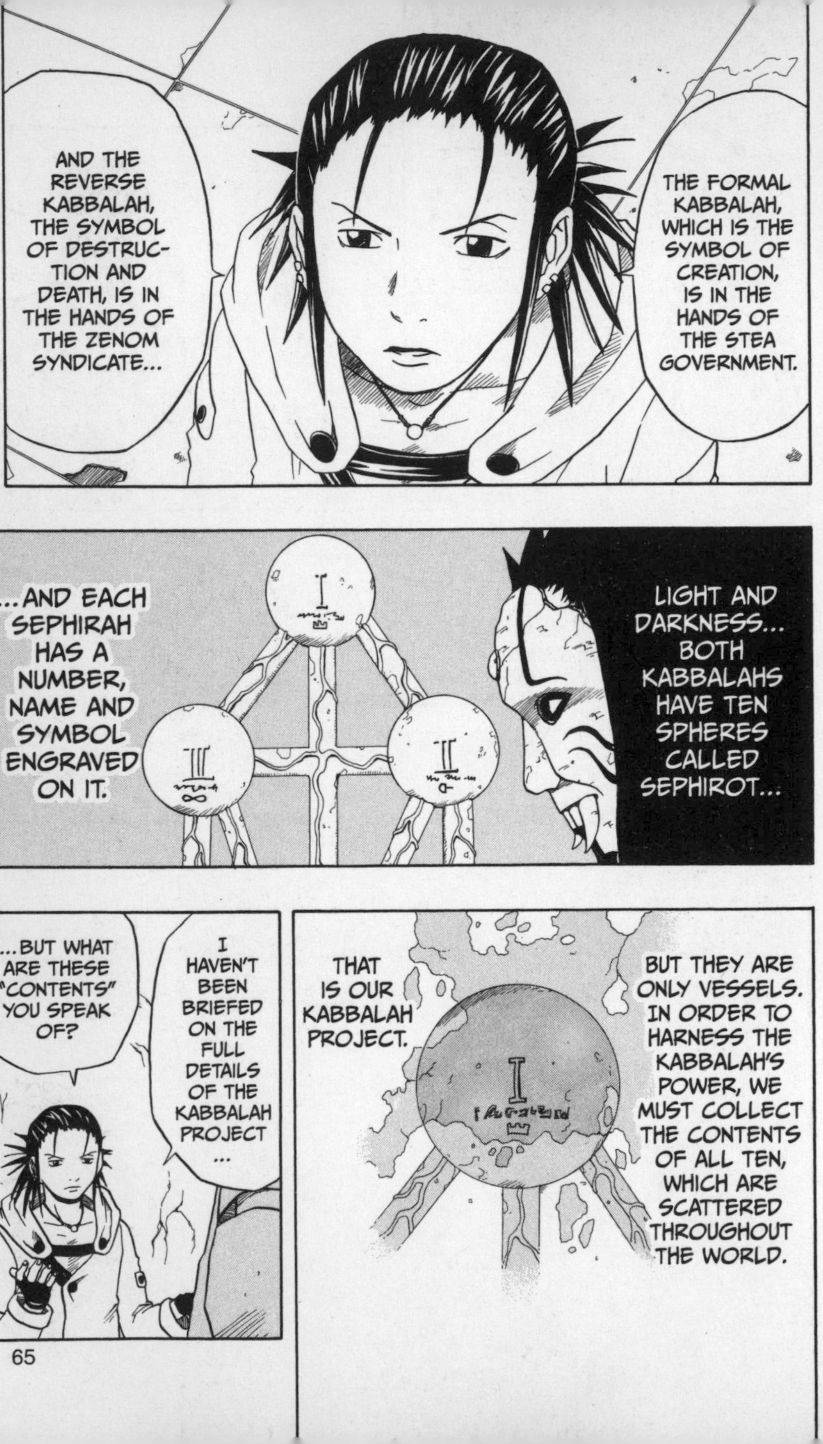
THE FORMAL KABBALAH, WHICH IS THE SYMBOL OF CREATION, IS IN THE HANDS OF THE STEA GOVERNMENT.
AND THE REVERSE KABBALAH, THE SYMBOL OF DESTRUCTION AND DEATH, IS IN THE HANDS OF THE ZENOM SYNDICATE...
LIGHT AND DARKNESS... BOTH KABBALAHS HAVE TEN SPHERES CALLED SEPHIROT...
...AND EACH SEPHIRAH HAS A NUMBER, NAME AND SYMBOL ENGRAVED ON IT.
BUT THEY ARE ONLY VESSELS. IN ORDER TO HARNESS THE KABBALAH'S POWER, WE MUST COLLECT THE CONTENTS OF ALL TEN, WHICH ARE SCATTERED THROUGHOUT THE WORLD.
THAT IS OUR KABBALAH PROJECT.
I HAVEN'T BEEN BRIEFED ON THE FULL DETAILS OF THE KABBALAH PROJECT ...
...BUT WHAT ARE THESE "CONTENTS" YOU SPEAK OF?

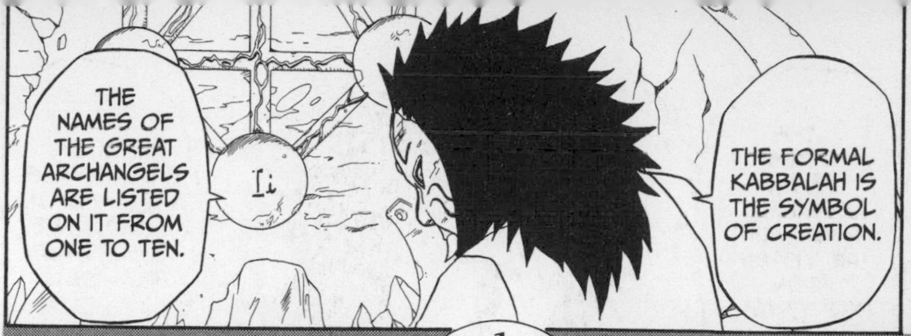
THE FORMAL KABBALAH IS THE SYMBOL OF CREATION.
THE NAMES OF THE GREAT ARCHANGELS ARE LISTED ON IT FROM ONE TO TEN.

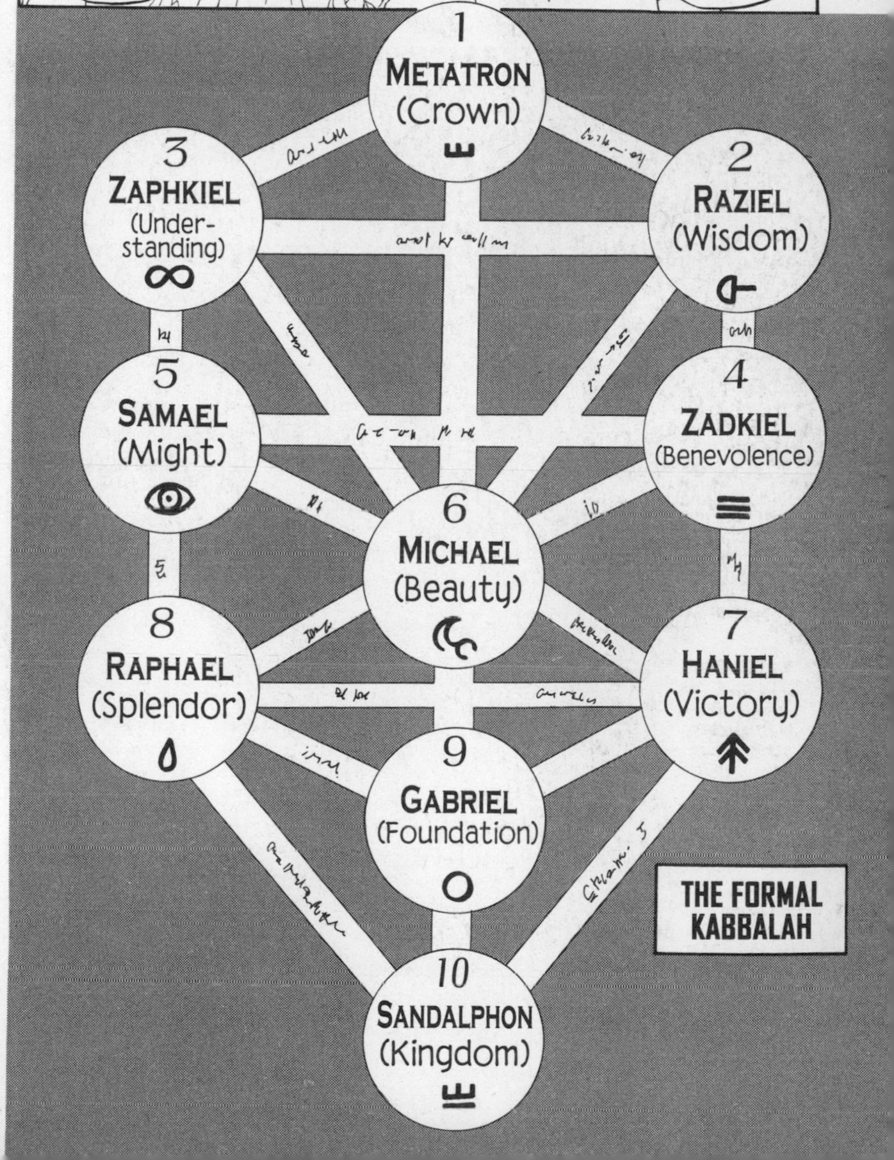
1 METATRON (Crown)
2 RAZIEL (Wisdom)
3 ZAPHKIEL (Under-standing)
4 ZADKIEL (Benevolence)
5 SAMAEL (Might)
6 MICHAEL (Beauty)
7 HANIEL (Victory)
8 RAPHAEL (Splendor)
9 GABRIEL (Foundation)
10 SANDALPHON (Kingdom)
THE FORMAL KABBALAH

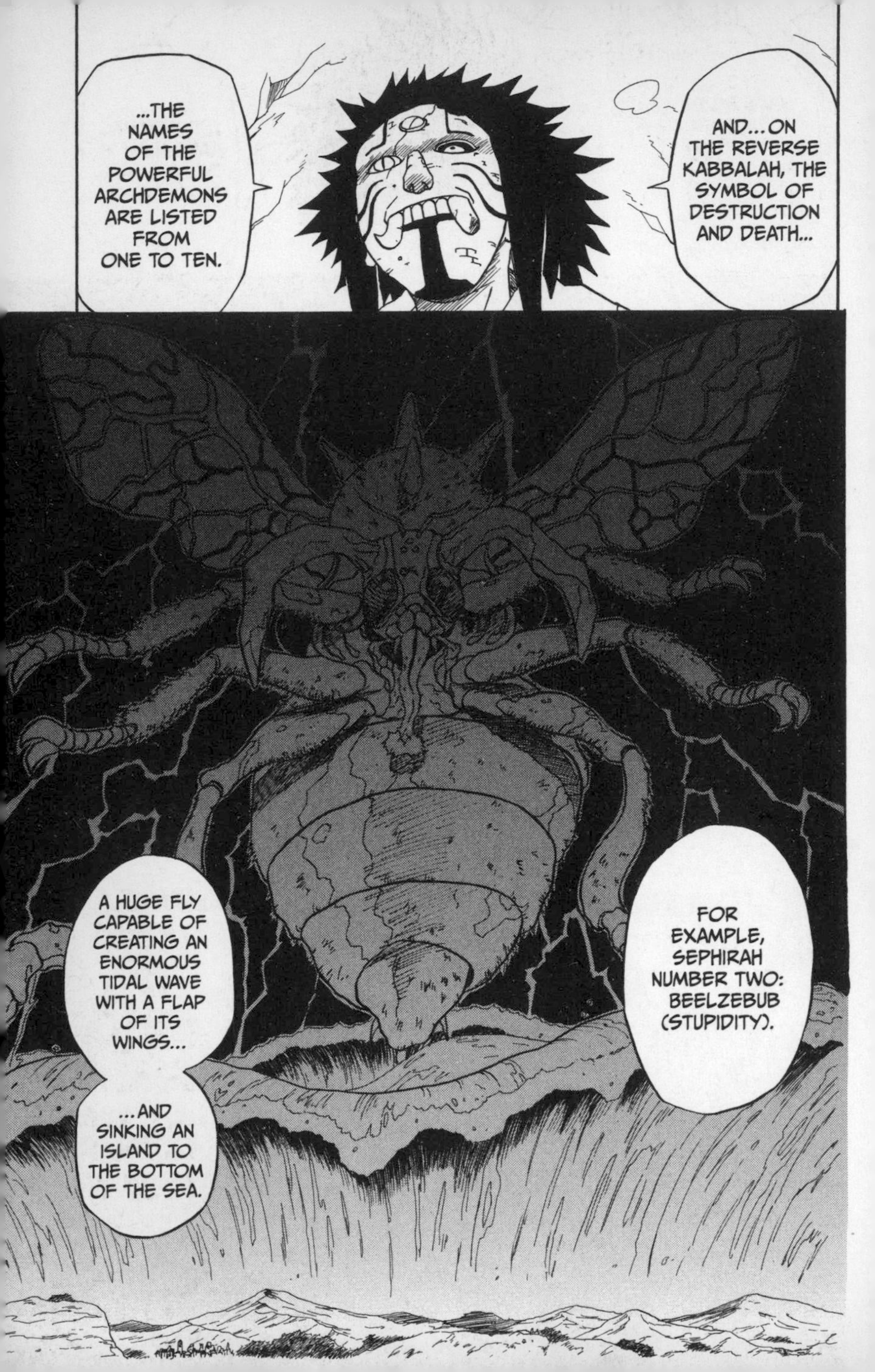
AND...ON THE REVERSE KABBALAH, THE SYMBOL OF DESTRUCTION AND DEATH...
...THE NAMES OF THE POWERFUL ARCHDEMONS ARE LISTED FROM ONE TO TEN.
FOR EXAMPLE, SEPHIRAH NUMBER TWO: BEELZEBUB (STUPIDITY).
A HUGE FLY CAPABLE OF CREATING AN ENORMOUS TIDAL WAVE WITH A FLAP OF ITS WINGS...
...AND SINKING AN ISLAND TO THE BOTTOM OF THE SEA.

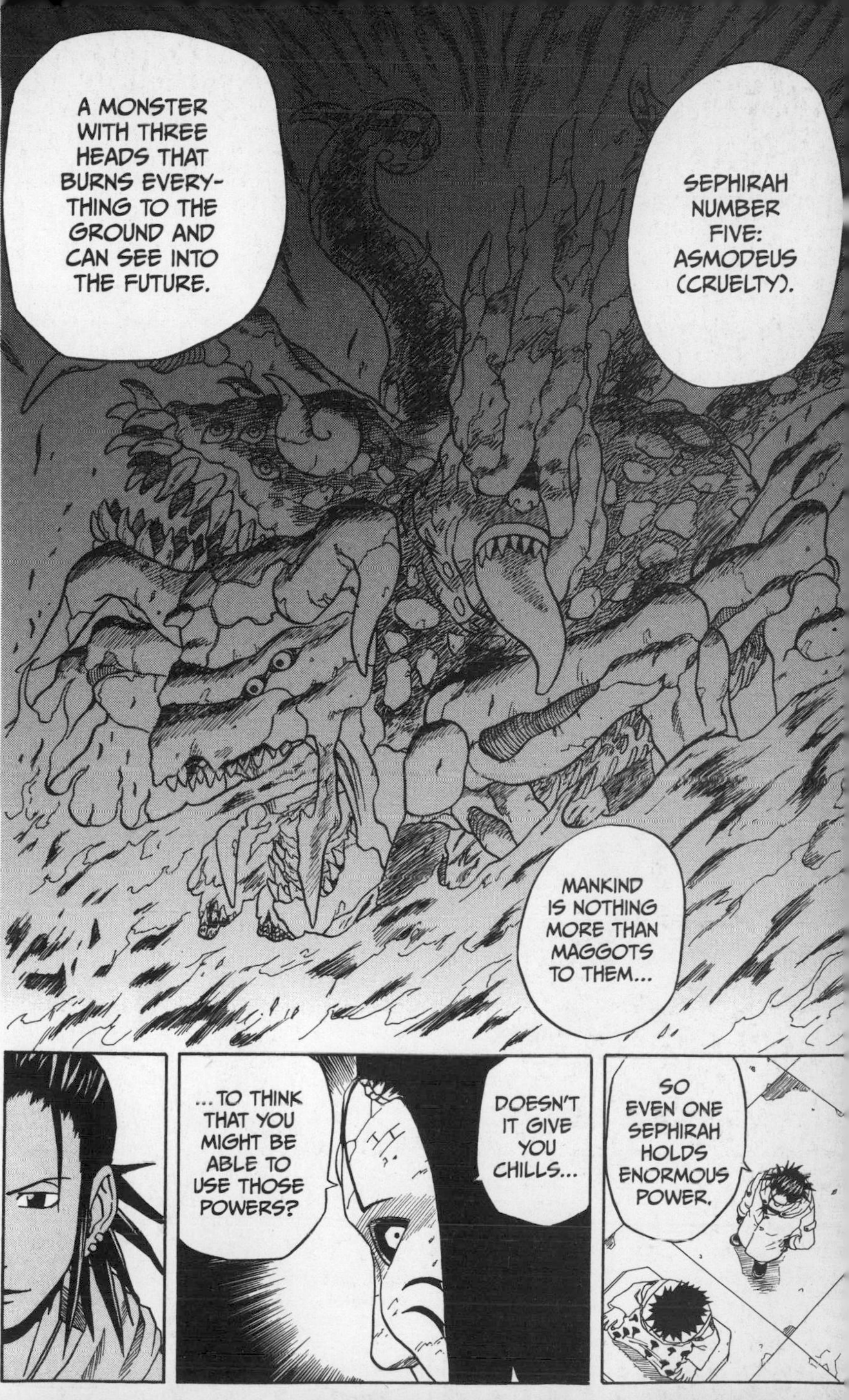
SEPHIRAH NUMBER FIVE: ASMODEUS (CRUELTY).
A MONSTER WITH THREE HEADS THAT BURNS EVERY-THING TO THE GROUND AND CAN SEE INTO THE FUTURE.
MANKIND IS NOTHING MORE THAN MAGGOTS TO THEM...
SO EVEN ONE SEPHIRAH HOLDS ENORMOUS POWER.
DOESN'T IT GIVE YOU CHILLS...
...TO THINK THAT YOU MIGHT BE ABLE TO USE THOSE POWERS?

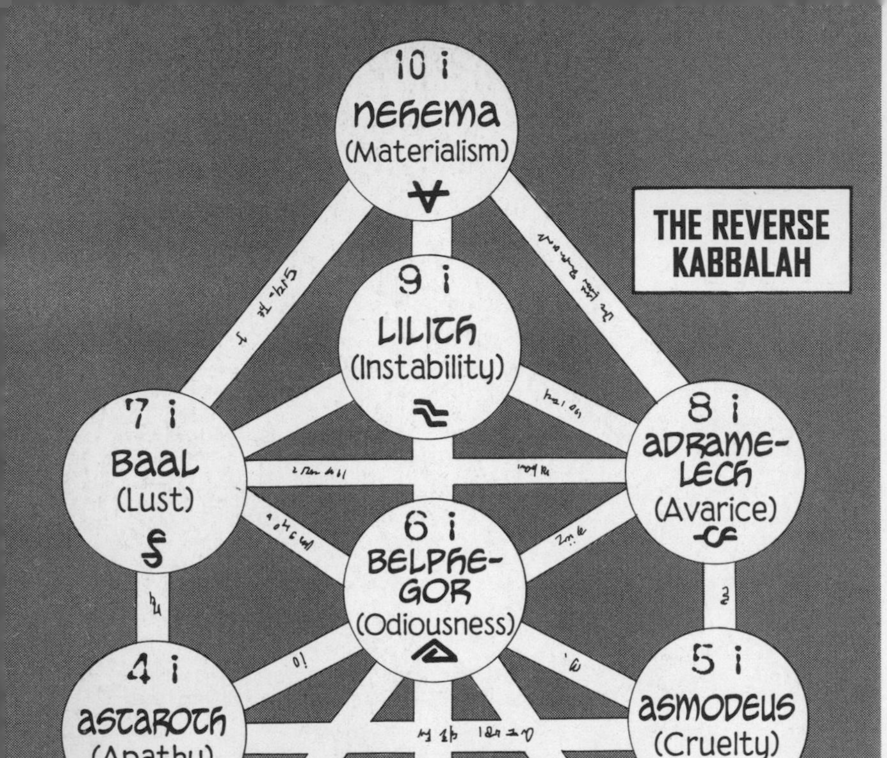
THE REVERSE KABBALAH
10 i
NEHEMA
(Materialism)
9 i
LILITH
(Instability)
8 i
ADRAME-
LECH
(Avarice)
7 i
BAAL
(Lust)
6 i
BELPHE-
GOR
(Odiousness)
5 i
ASMODEUS
(Cruelty)
4 i
ASTAROTH
(Apathy)
3 i
LUCIFUGE
(Rejection)
2 i
BEELZEBUB
(Stupidity)
1 i

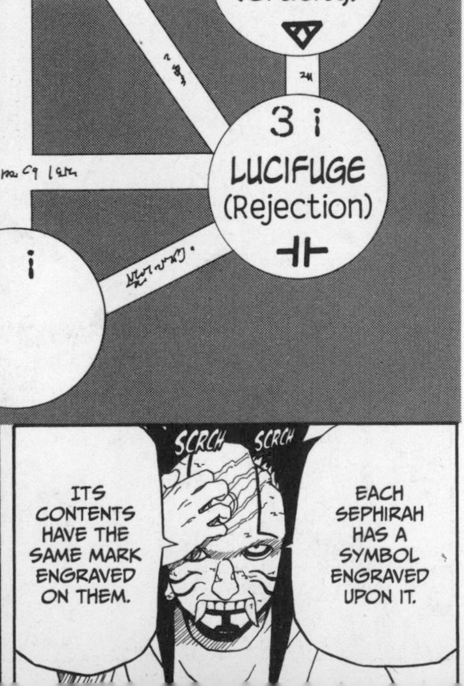
SCRCH
SCRCH
EACH SEPHIRAH HAS A SYMBOL ENGRAVED UPON IT.
ITS CONTENTS HAVE THE SAME MARK ENGRAVED ON THEM.

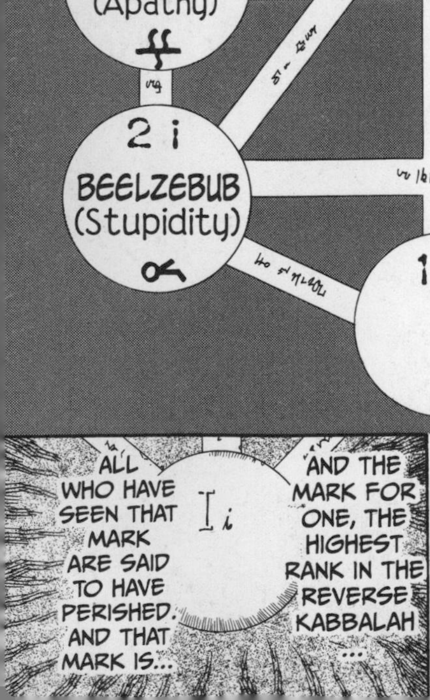
AND THE MARK FOR ONE, THE HIGHEST RANK IN THE REVERSE KABBALAH...
I i
ALL WHO HAVE SEEN THAT MARK ARE SAID TO HAVE PERISHED. AND THAT MARK IS...

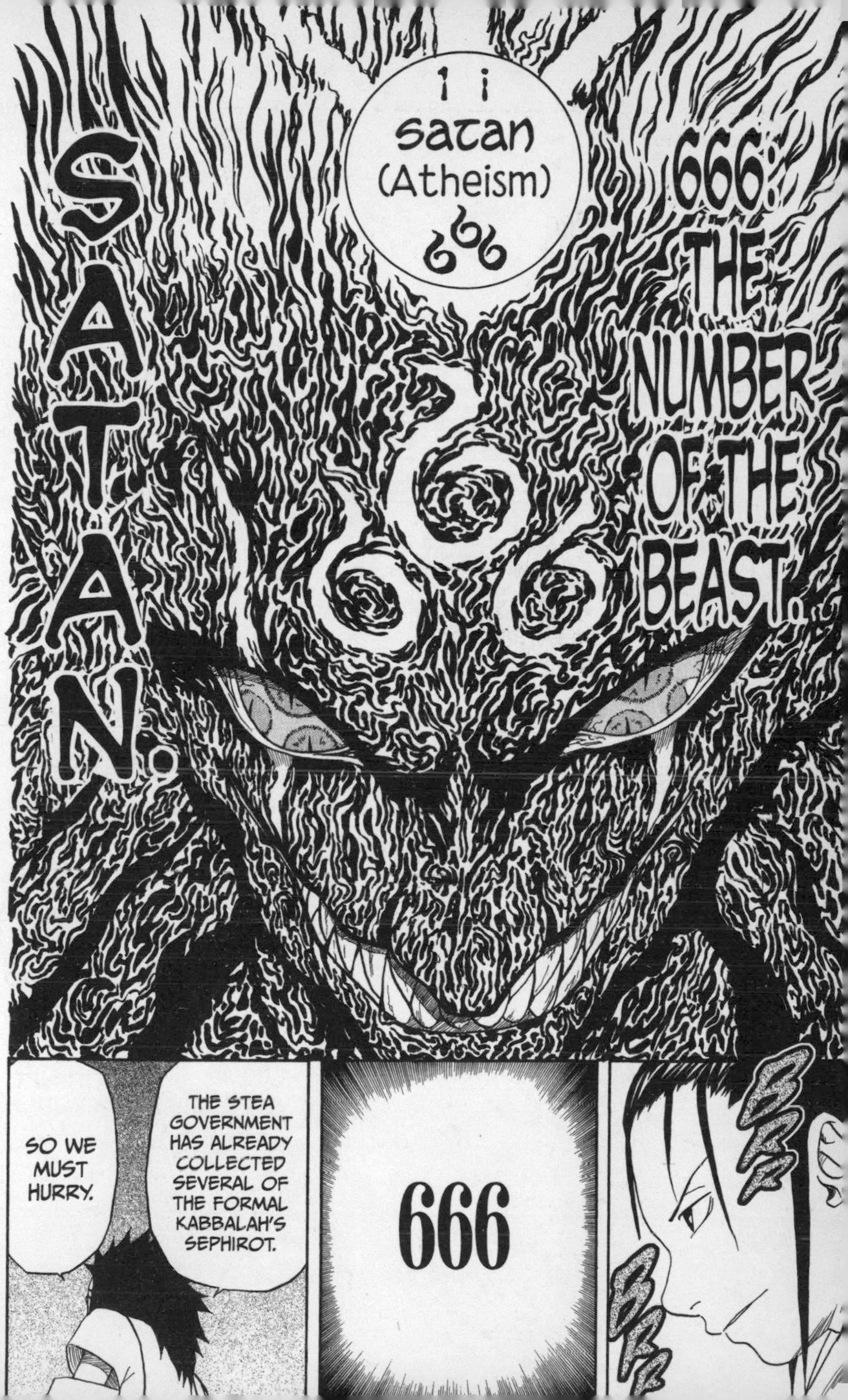
satan
(Atheism)
666
666: THE NUMBER OF THE BEAST.
SATAN.
666
THE STEA GOVERNMENT HAS ALREADY COLLECTED SEVERAL OF THE FORMAL KABBALAH'S SEPHIROT.
SO WE MUST HURRY.

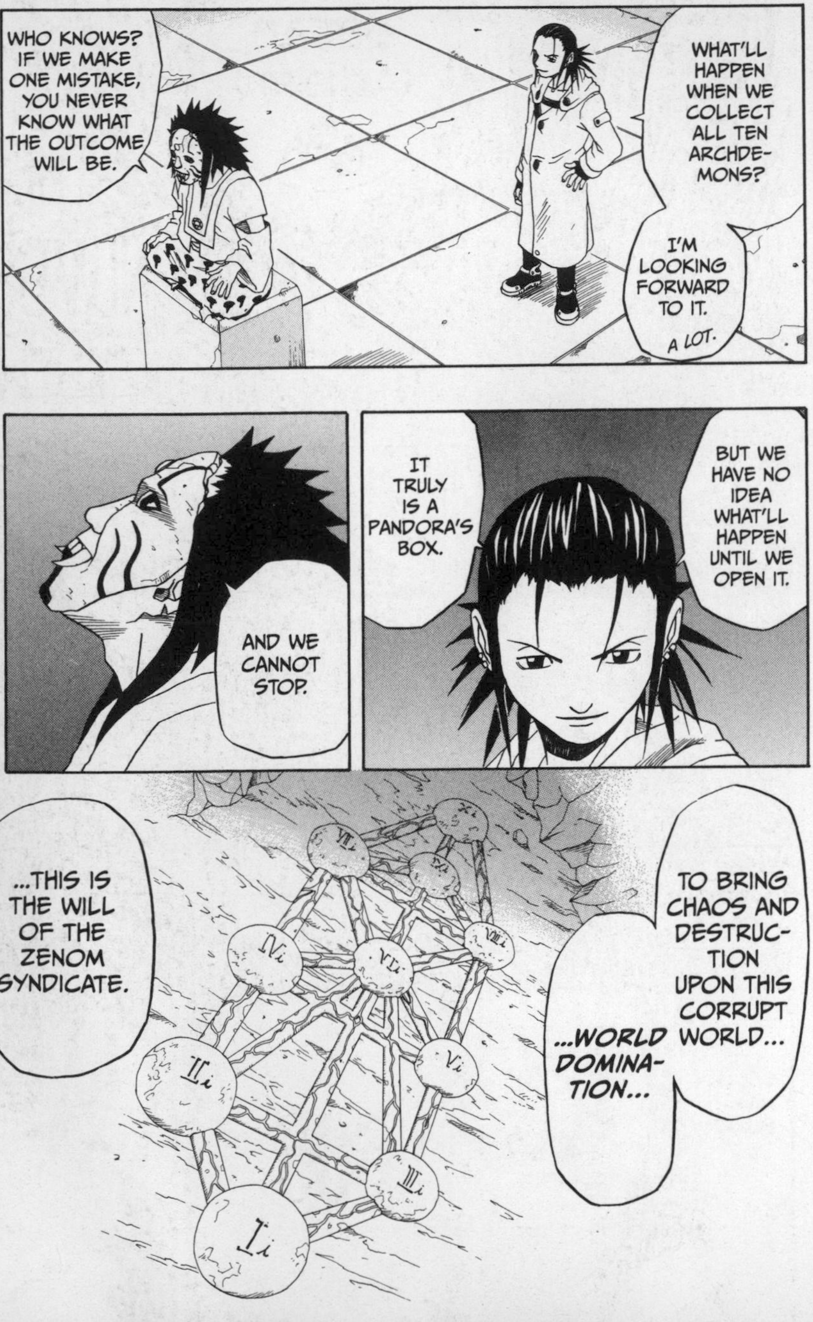
WHAT'LL HAPPEN WHEN WE COLLECT ALL TEN ARCHDEMONS?
I'M LOOKING FORWARD TO IT.
A LOT.
WHO KNOWS? IF WE MAKE ONE MISTAKE, YOU NEVER KNOW WHAT THE OUTCOME WILL BE.
BUT WE HAVE NO IDEA WHAT'LL HAPPEN UNTIL WE OPEN IT.
IT TRULY IS A PANDORA'S BOX.
AND WE CANNOT STOP.
TO BRING CHAOS AND DESTRUCTION UPON THIS CORRUPT WORLD...
...WORLD DOMINATION...
...THIS IS THE WILL OF THE ZENOM SYNDICATE.

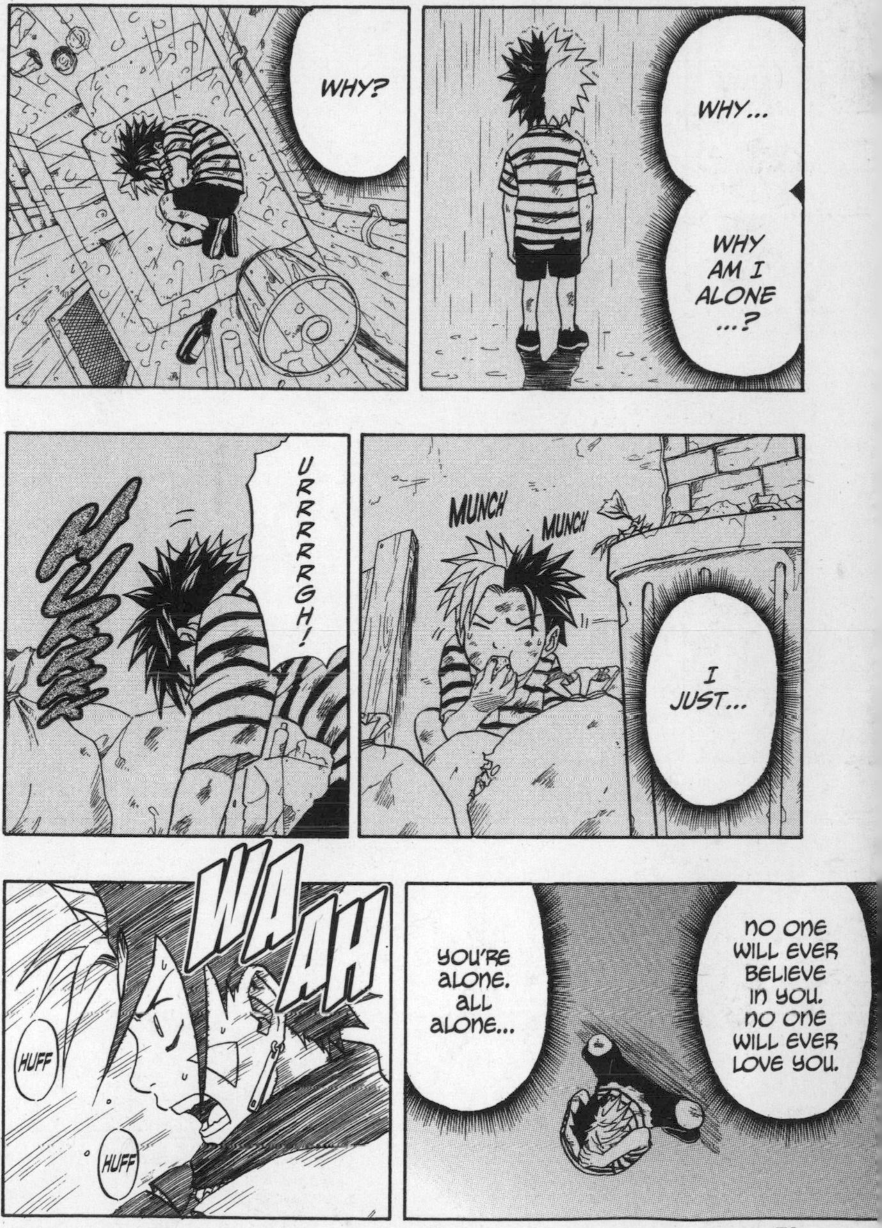
WHY...
WHY AM I ALONE ...?
WHY?
MUNCH
MUNCH
I JUST...
URRRRRGH!
NO ONE WILL EVER BELIEVE IN YOU. NO ONE WILL EVER LOVE YOU.
YOU'RE ALONE. ALL ALONE...
WAAH
HUFF
HUFF

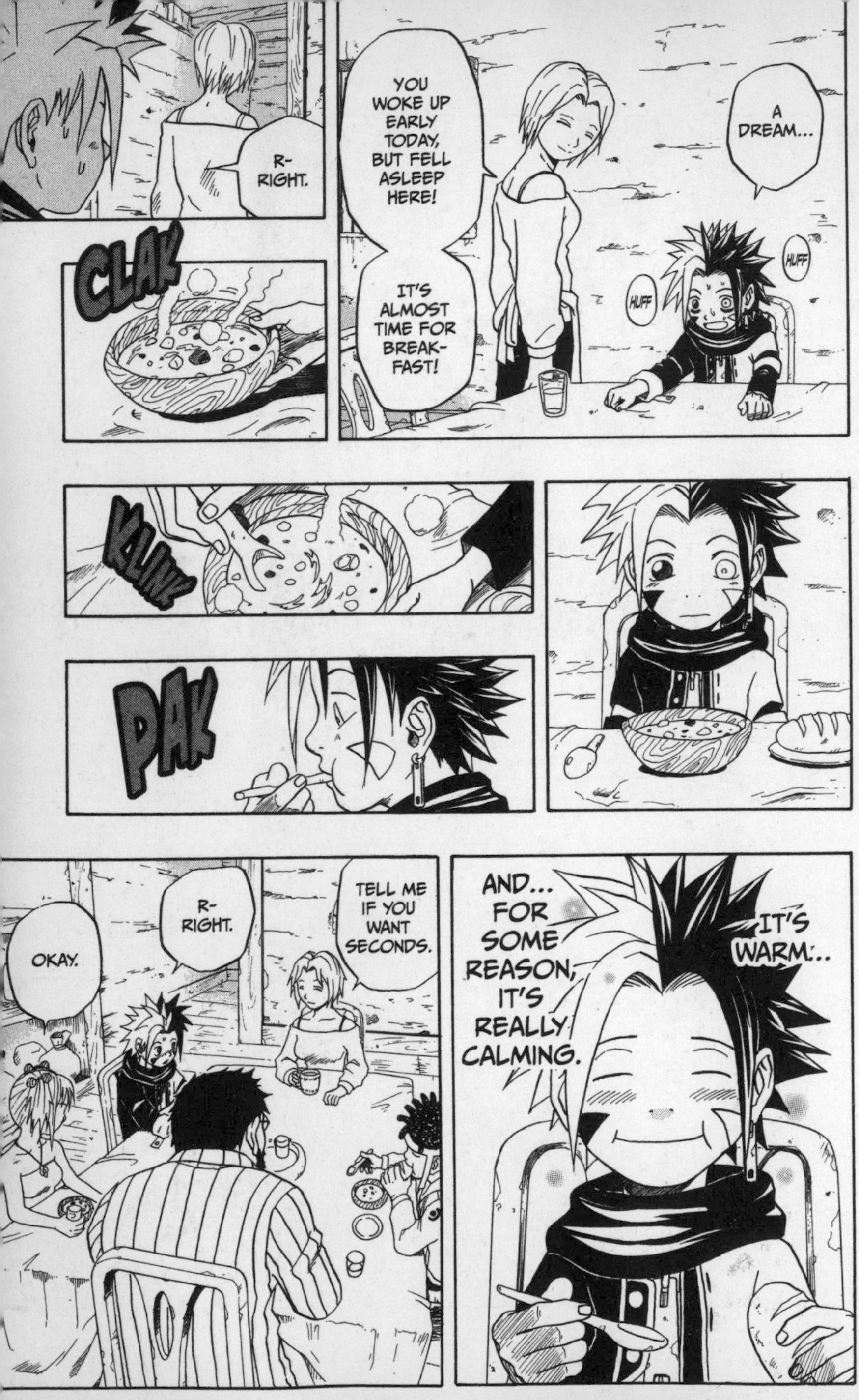
A DREAM...
HUFF
HUFF
YOU WOKE UP EARLY TODAY, BUT FELL ASLEEP HERE!
IT'S ALMOST TIME FOR BREAK-FAST!
R-RIGHT.
CLAK
KLINK
PAK
IT'S WARM...
AND... FOR SOME REASON, IT'S REALLY CALMING.
TELL ME IF YOU WANT SECONDS.
R-RIGHT.
OKAY.

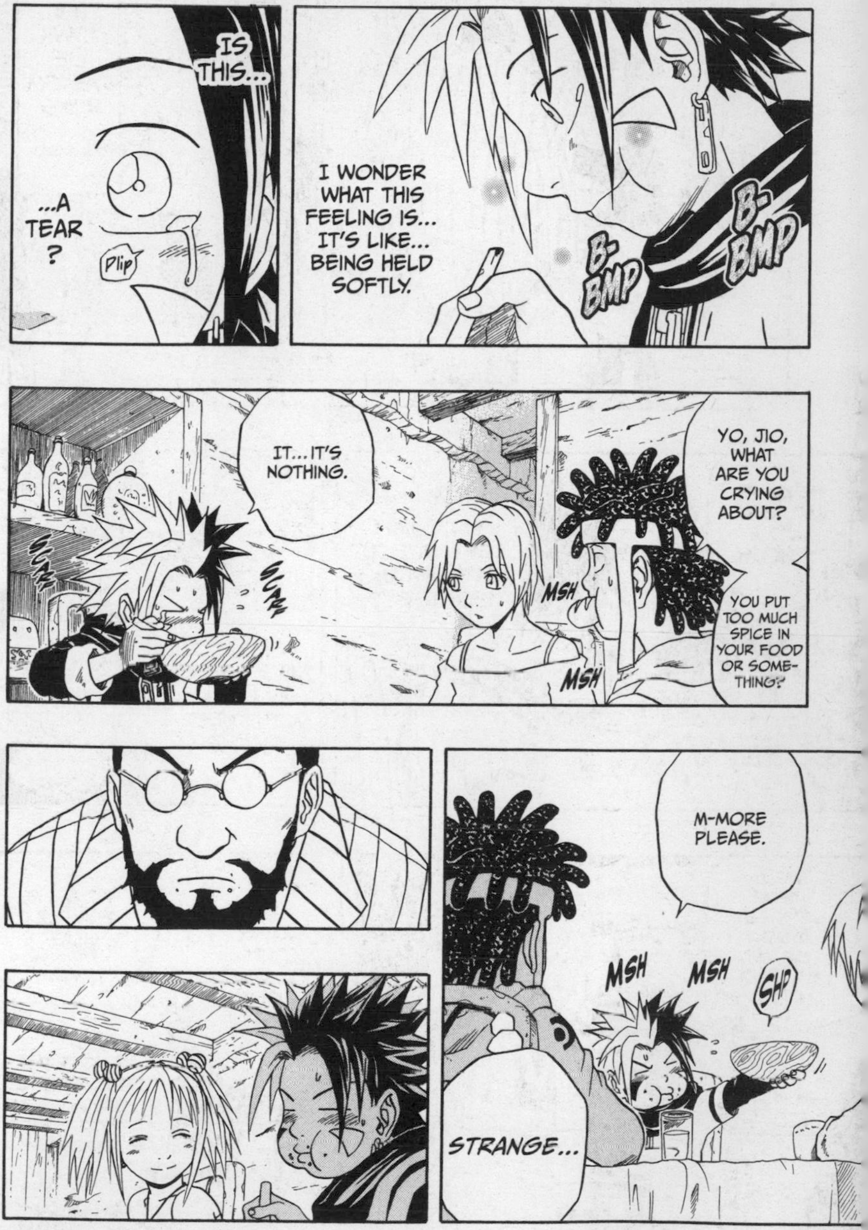
I WONDER WHAT THIS FEELING IS... IT'S LIKE... BEING HELD SOFTLY.
B-BMP
B-BMP
IS THIS...
...A TEAR?
Plip
YO, JIO, WHAT ARE YOU CRYING ABOUT?
YOU PUT TOO MUCH SPICE IN YOUR FOOD OR SOME-THING?
MSH
MSH
IT...IT'S NOTHING.
M-MORE PLEASE.
MSH
MSH
SHP
STRANGE...

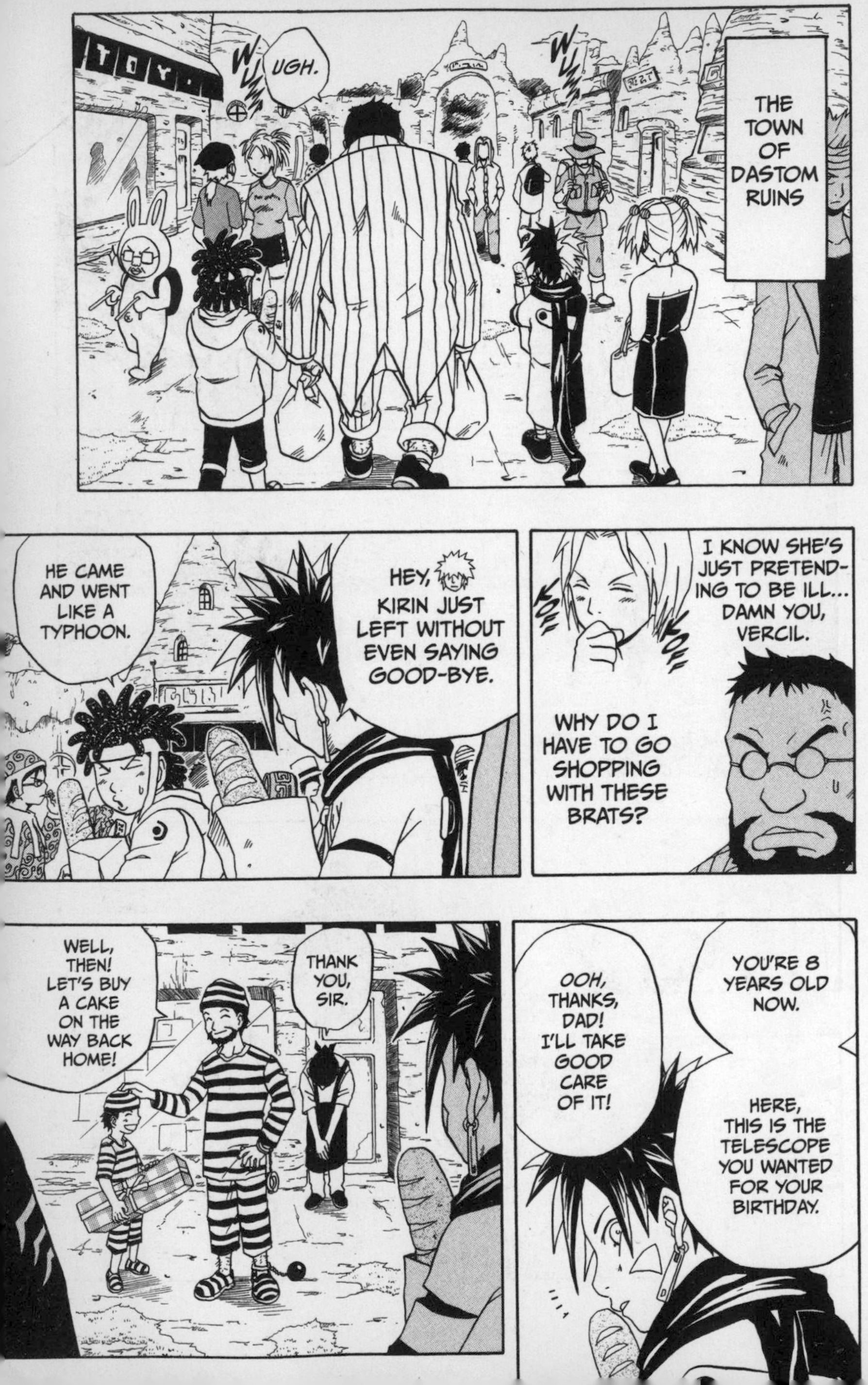
THE TOWN OF DASTOM RUINS
UGH.
I KNOW SHE'S JUST PRETENDING TO BE ILL... DAMN YOU, VERCIL.
WHY DO I HAVE TO GO SHOPPING WITH THESE BRATS?
HEY, KIRIN JUST LEFT WITHOUT EVEN SAYING GOOD-BYE.
HE CAME AND WENT LIKE A TYPHOON.
YOU'RE 8 YEARS OLD NOW.
HERE, THIS IS THE TELESCOPE YOU WANTED FOR YOUR BIRTHDAY.
OOH, THANKS, DAD! I'LL TAKE GOOD CARE OF IT!
THANK YOU, SIR.
WELL, THEN! LET'S BUY A CAKE ON THE WAY BACK HOME!

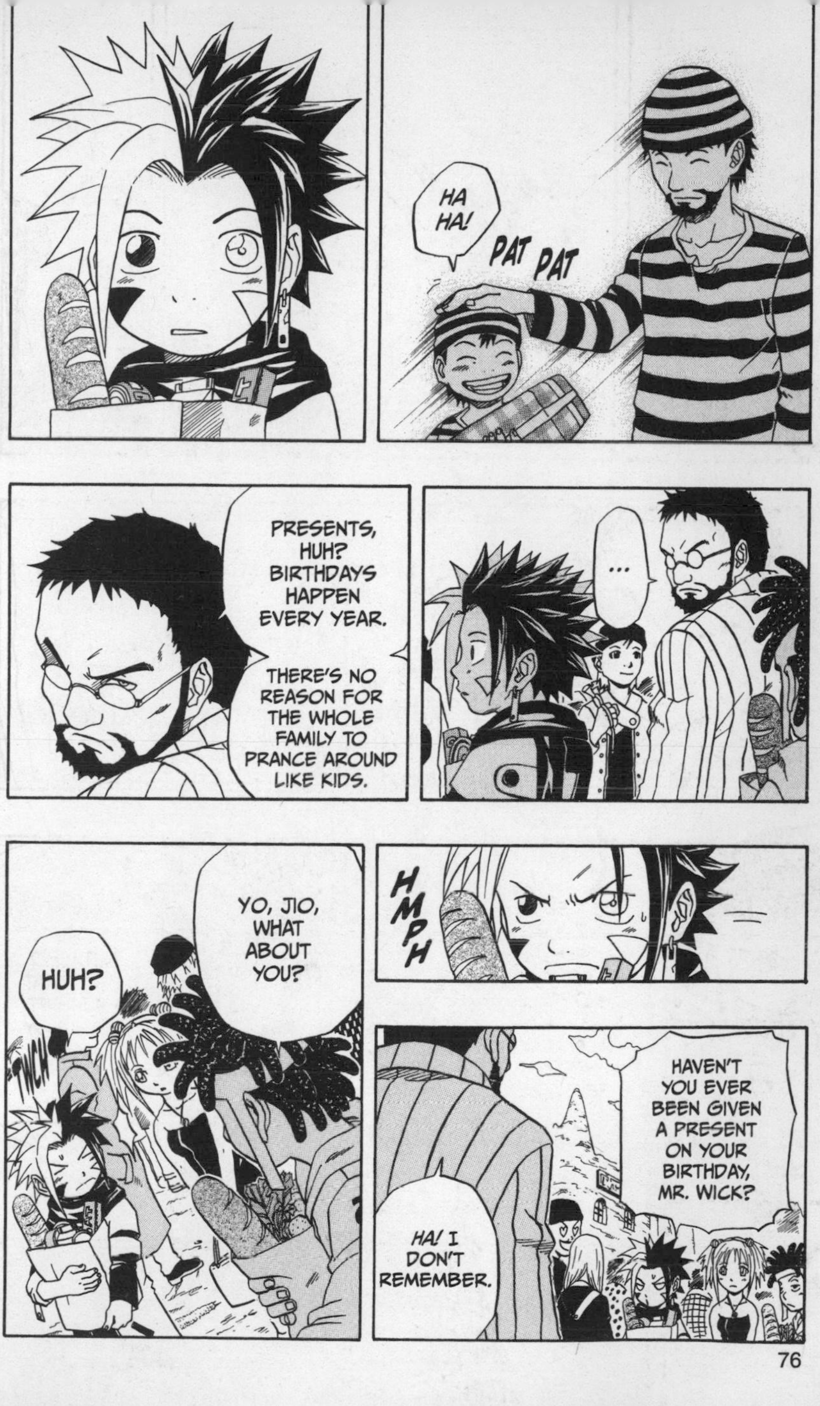
HA HA!
PAT PAT
...
PRESENTS, HUH? BIRTHDAYS HAPPEN EVERY YEAR.
THERE'S NO REASON FOR THE WHOLE FAMILY TO PRANCE AROUND LIKE KIDS.
HMPH
HAVEN'T YOU EVER BEEN GIVEN A PRESENT ON YOUR BIRTHDAY, MR. WICK?
HA! I DON'T REMEMBER.
YO, JIO, WHAT ABOUT YOU?
HUH?
TWICH

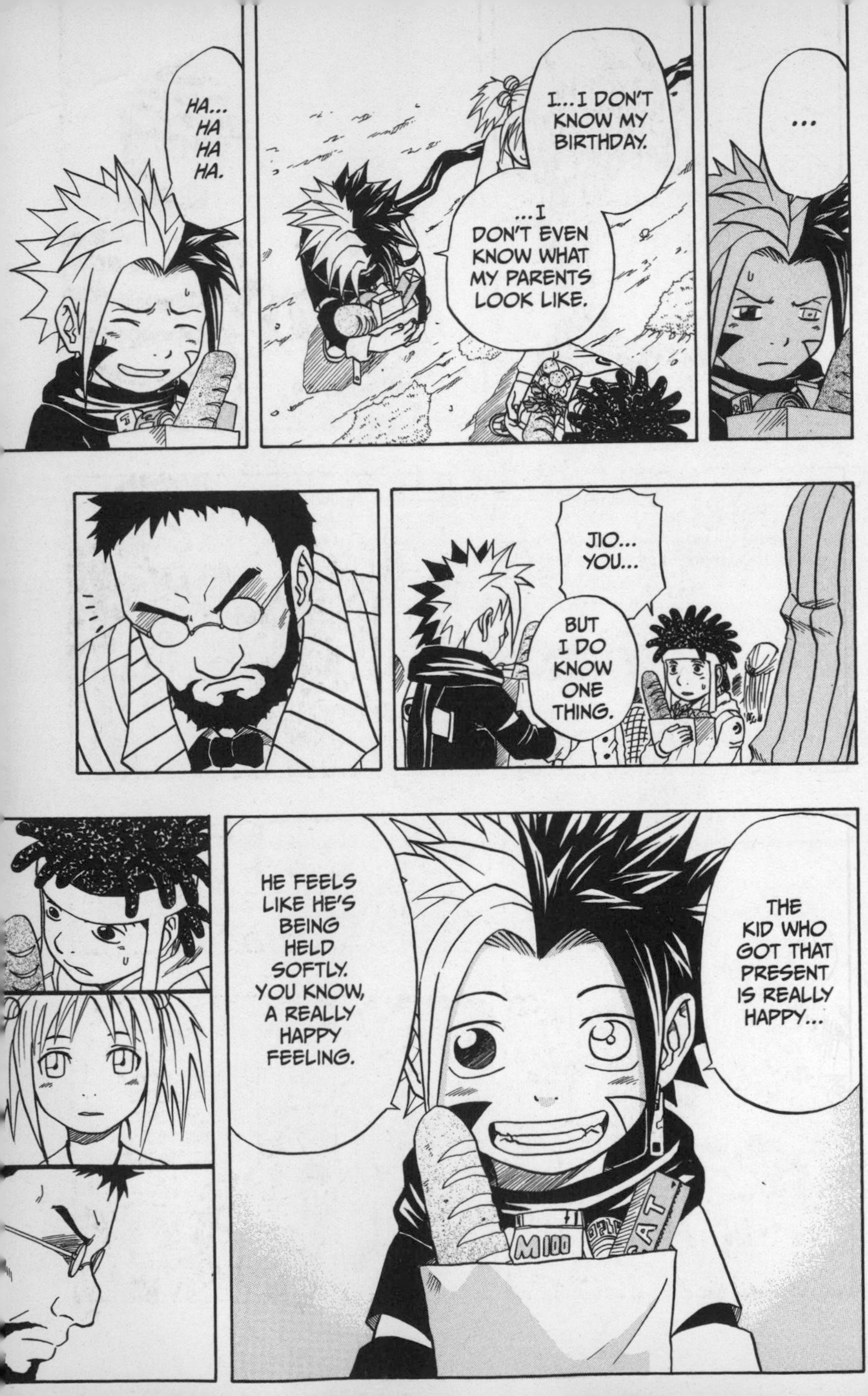
...
I...I DON'T KNOW MY BIRTHDAY.
...I DON'T EVEN KNOW WHAT MY PARENTS LOOK LIKE.
HA... HA HA HA.
JIO... YOU...
BUT I DO KNOW ONE THING.
THE KID WHO GOT THAT PRESENT IS REALLY HAPPY...
HE FEELS LIKE HE'S BEING HELD SOFTLY. YOU KNOW, A REALLY HAPPY FEELING.

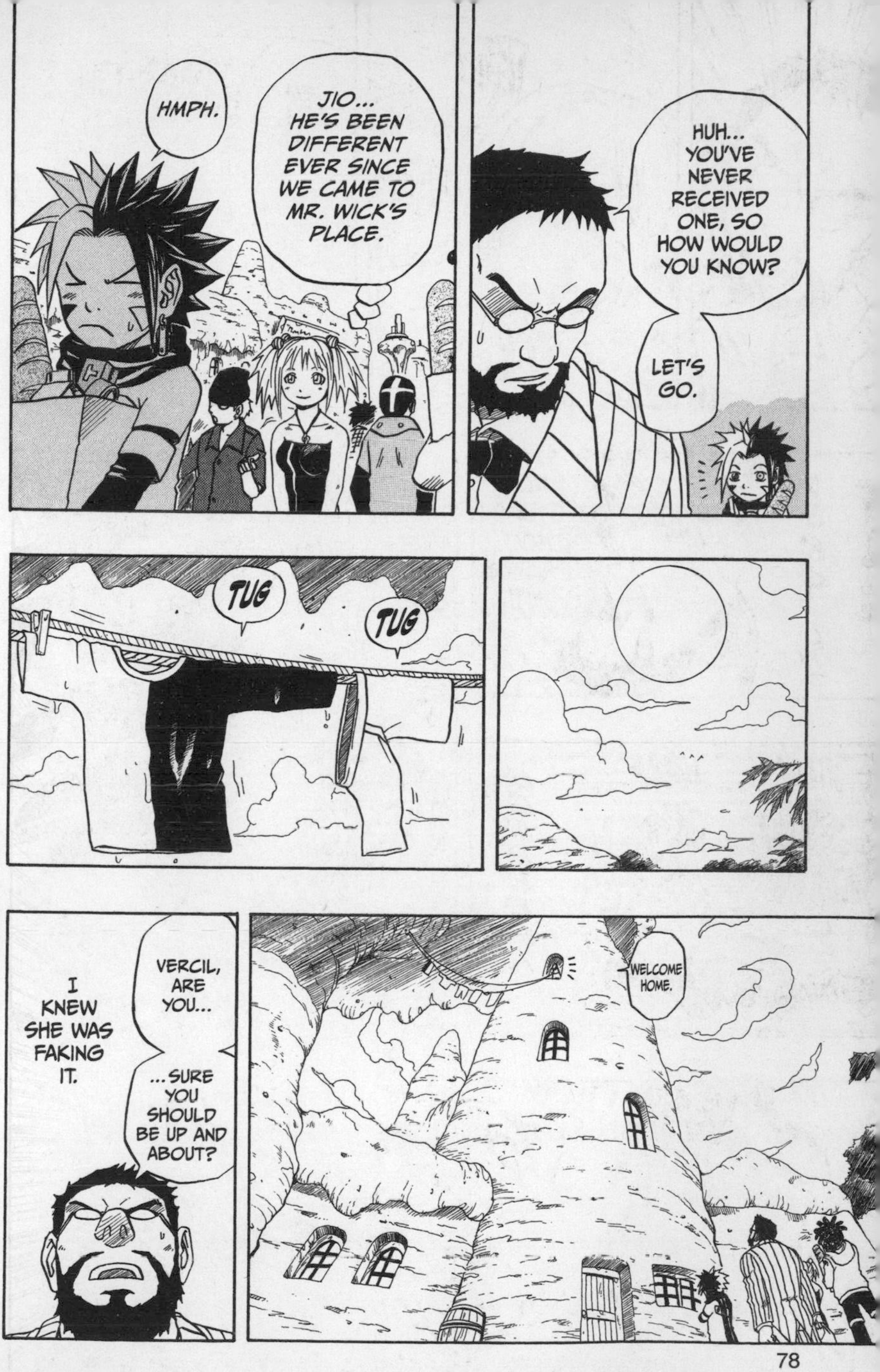
HUH... YOU'VE NEVER RECEIVED ONE, SO HOW WOULD YOU KNOW?
LET'S GO.
JIO... HE'S BEEN DIFFERENT EVER SINCE WE CAME TO MR. WICK'S PLACE.
HMPH.
TUG
TUG
WELCOME HOME.
VERCIL, ARE YOU...
...SURE YOU SHOULD BE UP AND ABOUT?
I KNEW SHE WAS FAKING IT.

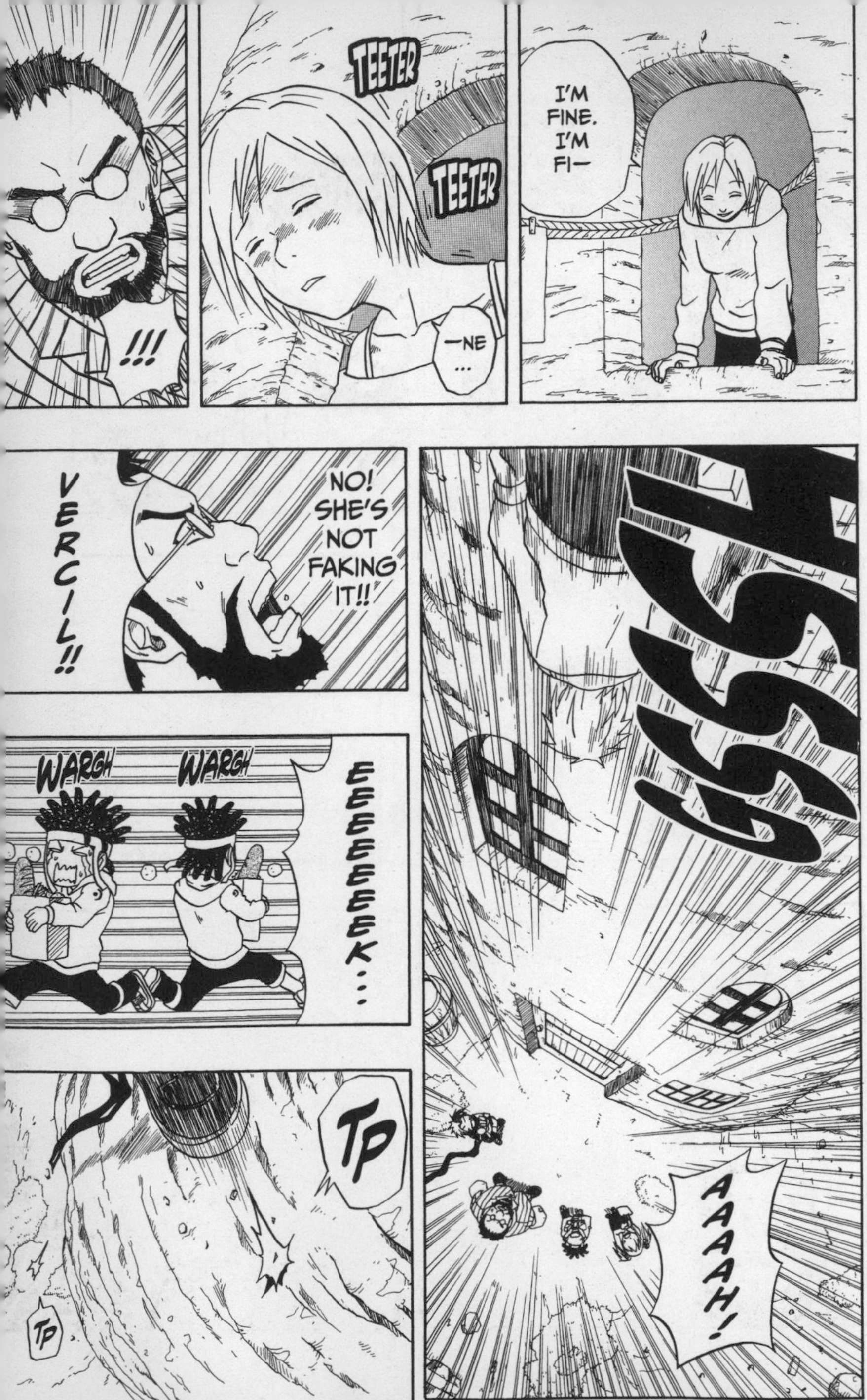
I'M FINE. I'M FI—
TEETER
TEETER
—NE ...
!!!
AAAAH!
NO! SHE'S NOT FAKING IT!!
VERCIL!!
EEEEEEEEK...
WARGH
WARGH
TP
TP

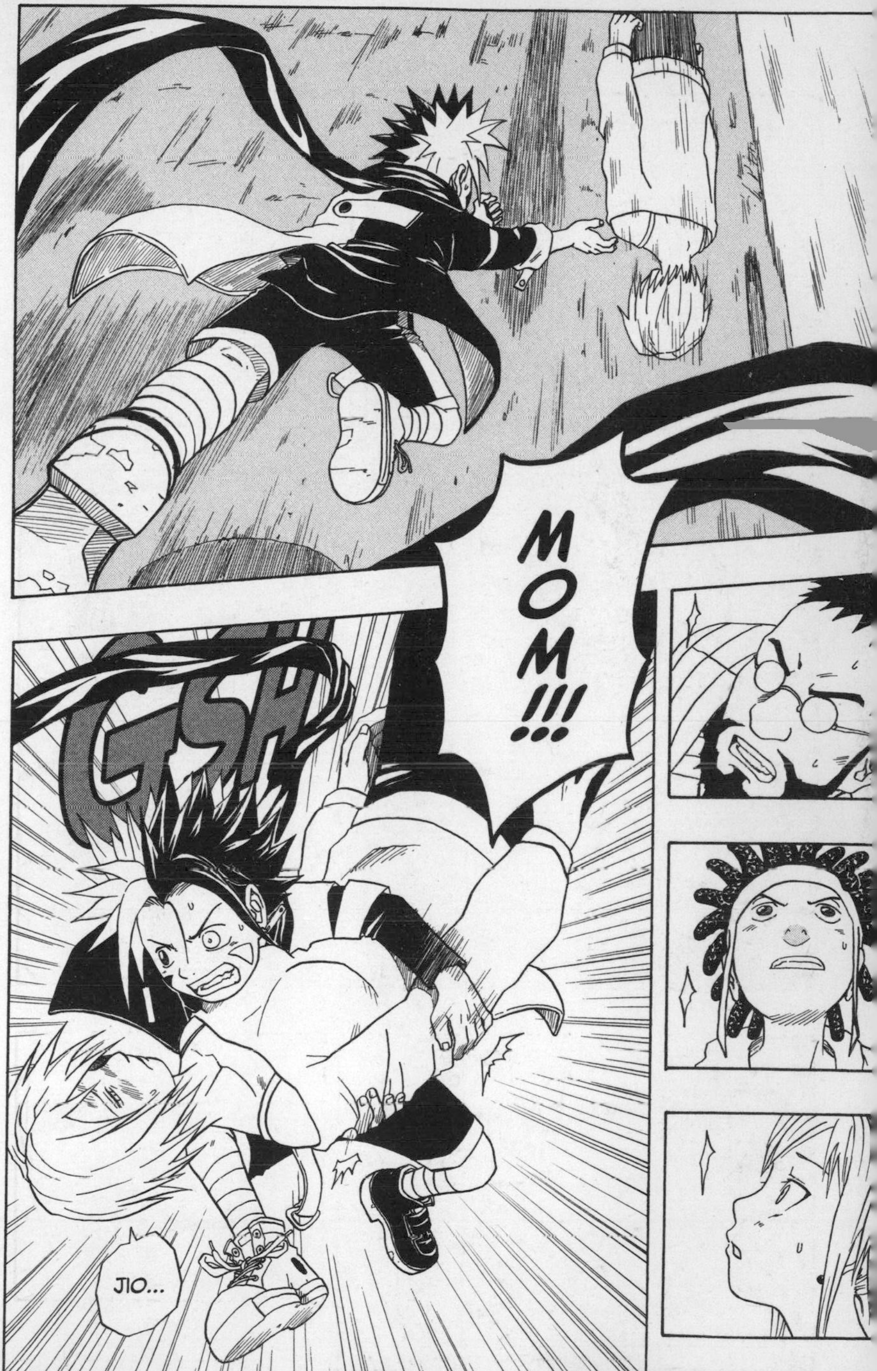
MOM!!!
GSH
JIO...

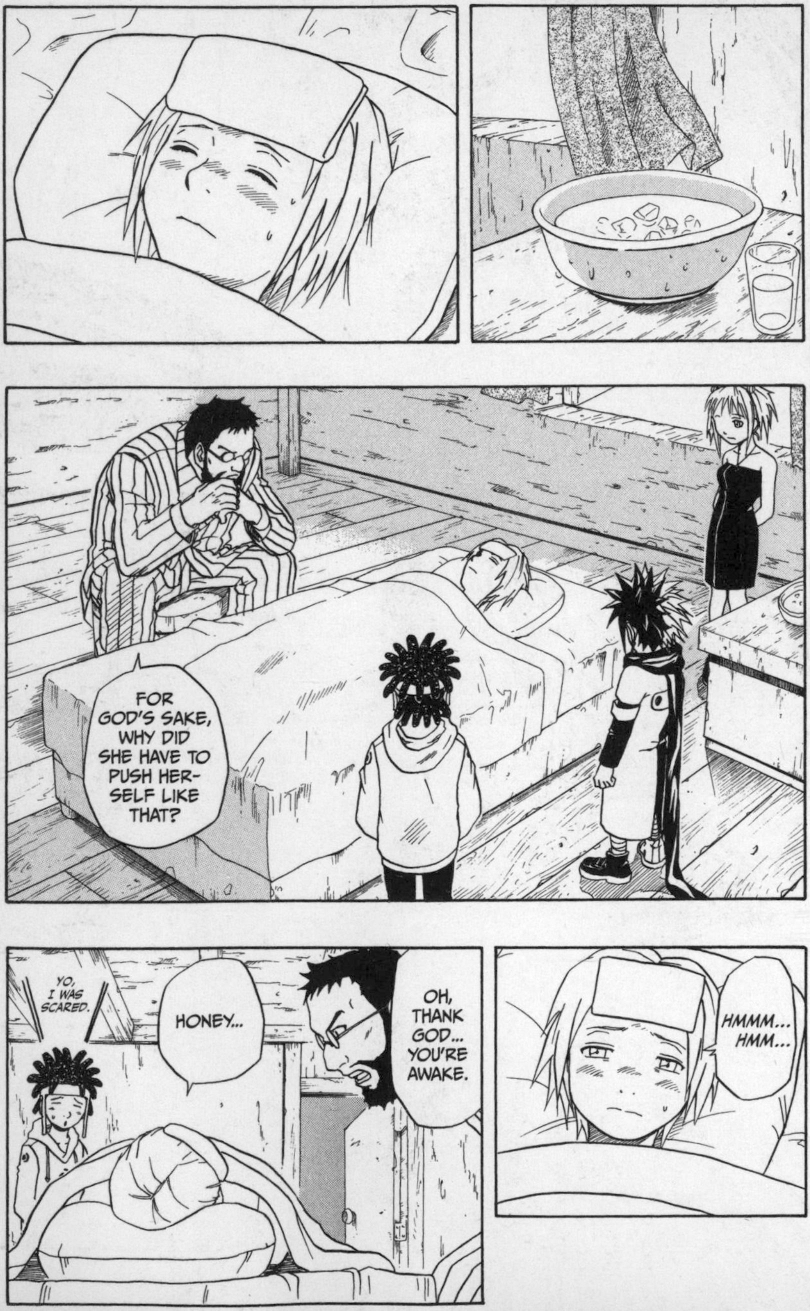
FOR GOD'S SAKE, WHY DID SHE HAVE TO PUSH HER-SELF LIKE THAT?
HMMM... HMM...
OH, THANK GOD... YOU'RE AWAKE.
HONEY...
YO, I WAS SCARED.

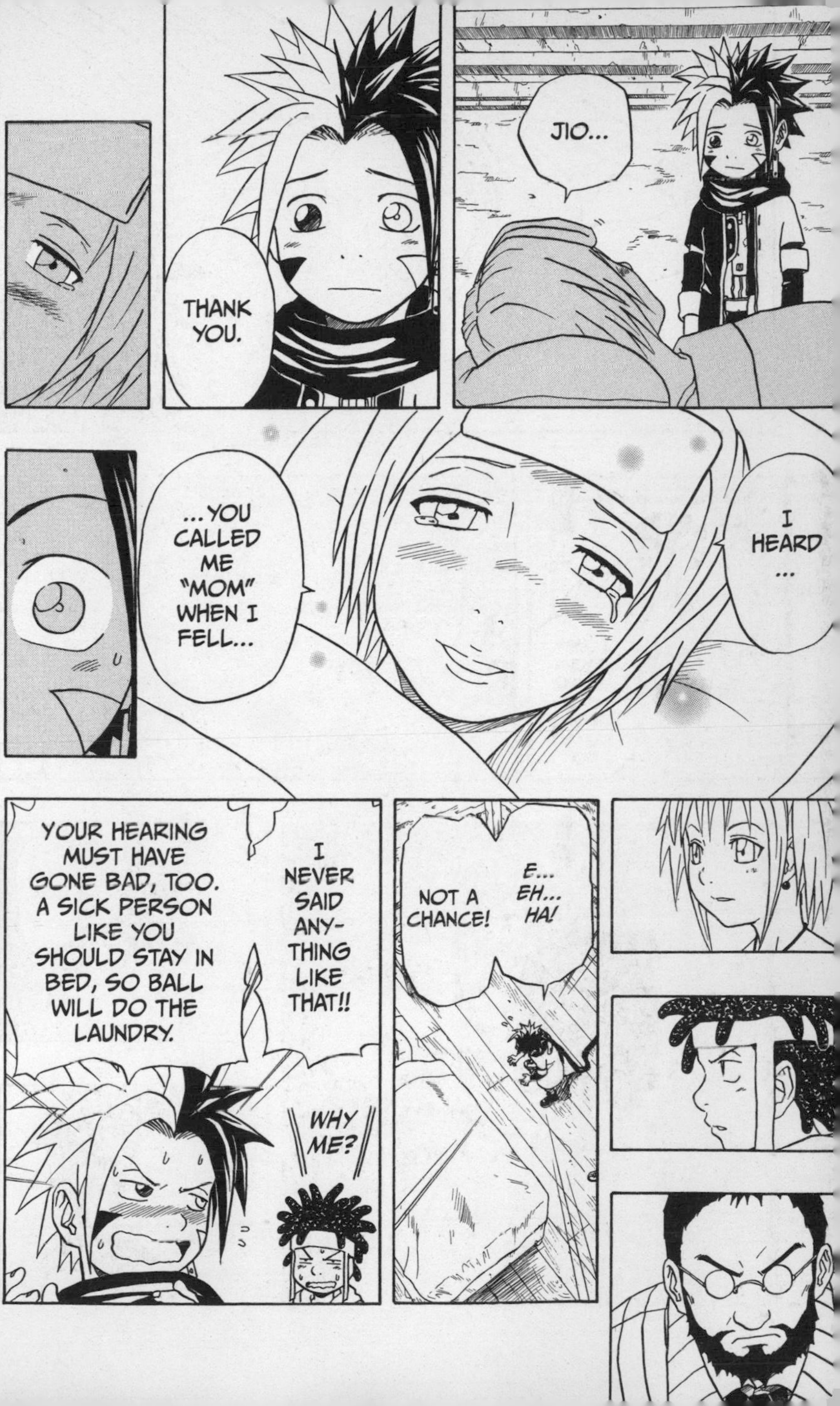
JIO...
THANK YOU.
I HEARD ...
...YOU CALLED ME "MOM" WHEN I FELL...
E... EH... HA!
NOT A CHANCE!
I NEVER SAID ANY-THING LIKE THAT!!
YOUR HEARING MUST HAVE GONE BAD, TOO. A SICK PERSON LIKE YOU SHOULD STAY IN BED, SO BALL WILL DO THE LAUNDRY.
WHY ME?

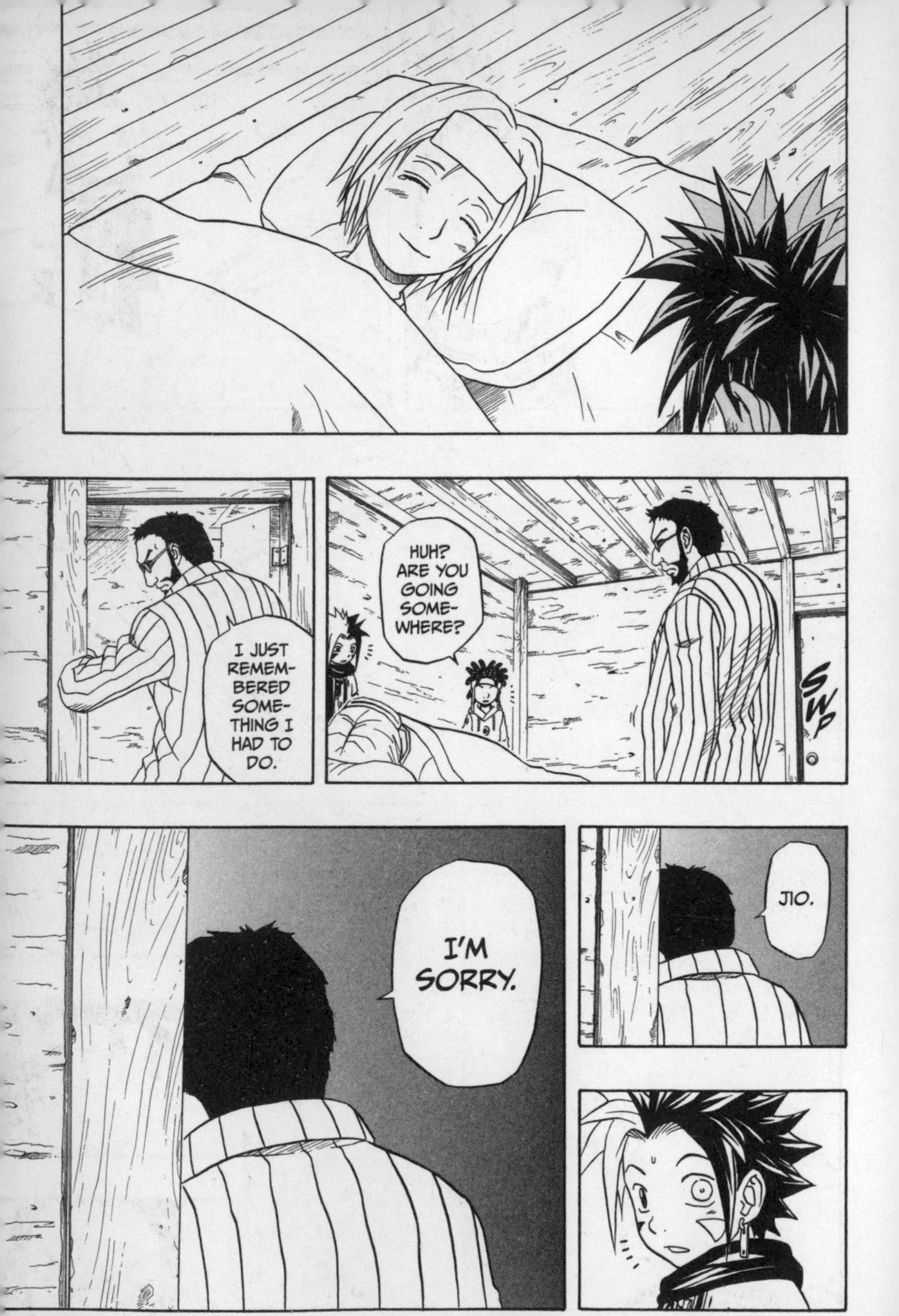
HUH? ARE YOU GOING SOME-WHERE?
SWP
I JUST REMEMBERED SOMETHING I HAD TO DO.
JIO.
I'M SORRY.

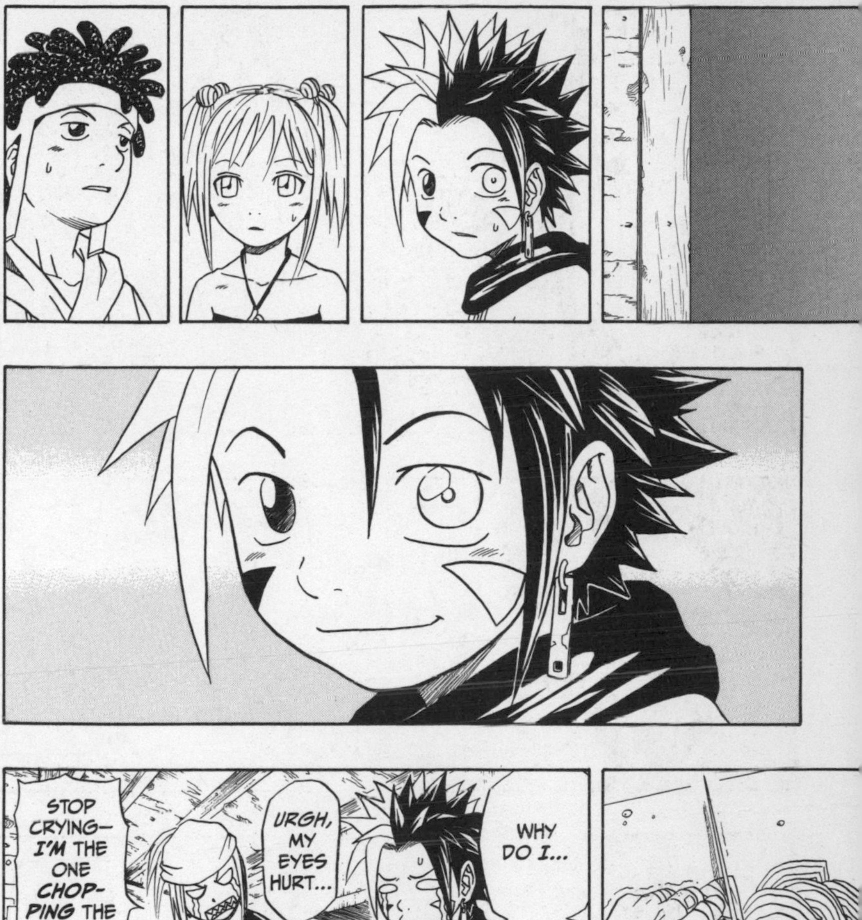
SHAKE
SHAKE
WHY DO I...
...HAVE TO PEEL THE SKIN OFF THE ONIONS?
URGH, MY EYES HURT...
SHUK
STOP CRYING—I'M THE ONE CHOPPING THE ONIONS, YOU KNOW!!!

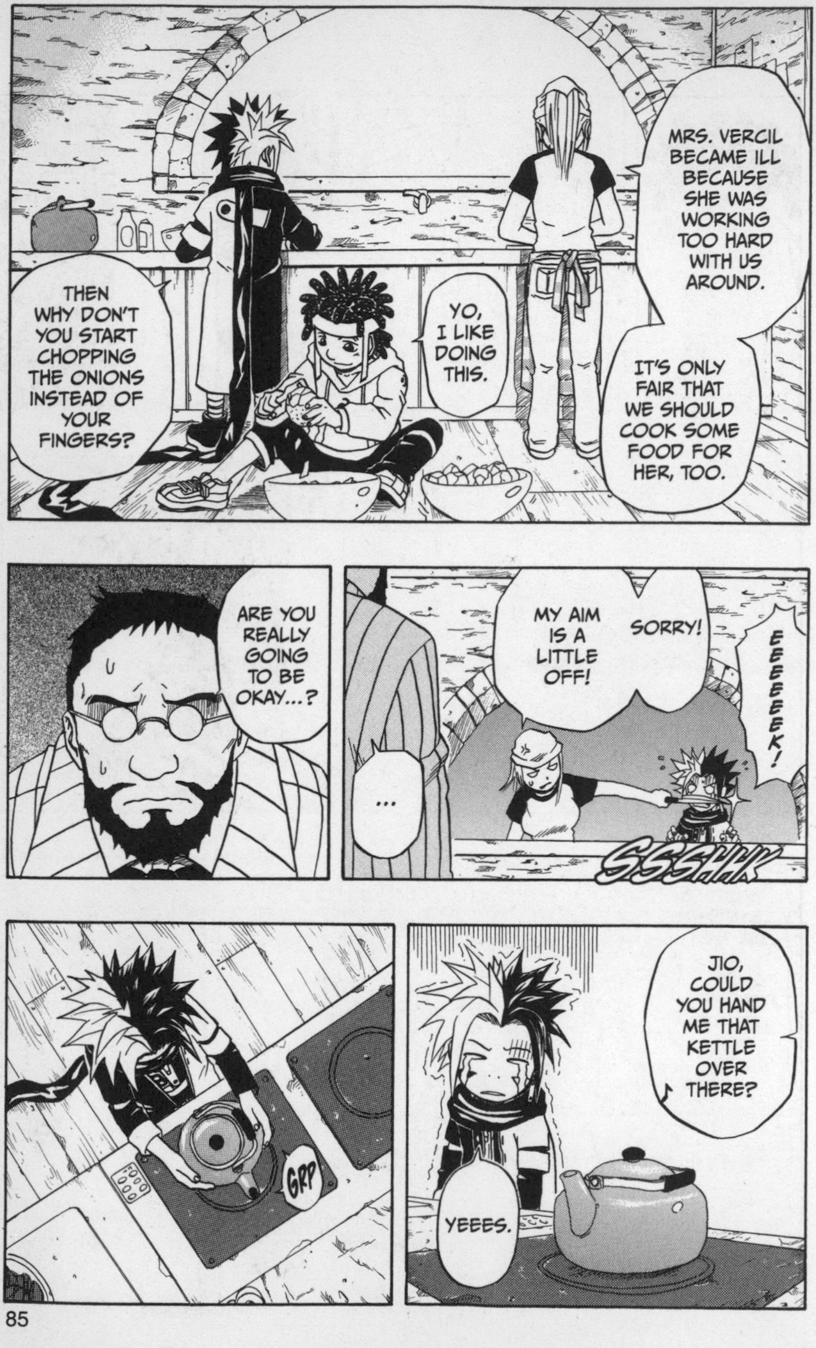
MRS. VERCIL BECAME ILL BECAUSE SHE WAS WORKING TOO HARD WITH US AROUND.
IT'S ONLY FAIR THAT WE SHOULD COOK SOME FOOD FOR HER, TOO.
YO, I LIKE DOING THIS.
THEN WHY DON'T YOU START CHOPPING THE ONIONS INSTEAD OF YOUR FINGERS?
EEEEEEEK!
SORRY!
MY AIM IS A LITTLE OFF!
...
SSSHHK
ARE YOU REALLY GOING TO BE OKAY...?
JIO, COULD YOU HAND ME THAT KETTLE OVER THERE?
YEEES.
GRP

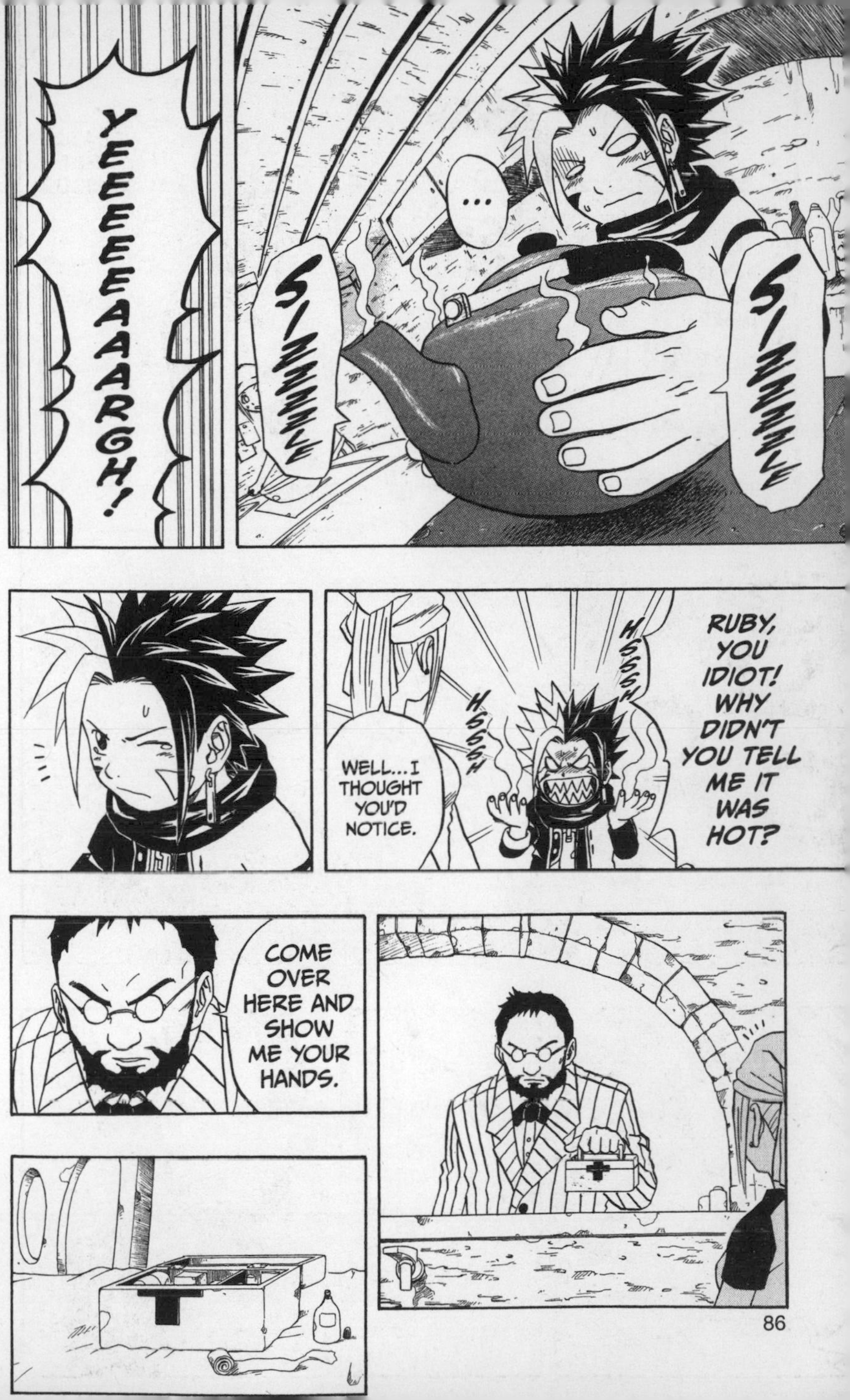
SIZZZZZLE
...
SIZZZZZLE
YEEEEEAAARGH!
RUBY, YOU IDIOT! WHY DIDN'T YOU TELL ME IT WAS HOT?
HSSSH
HSSSH
WELL... I THOUGHT YOU'D NOTICE.
COME OVER HERE AND SHOW ME YOUR HANDS.

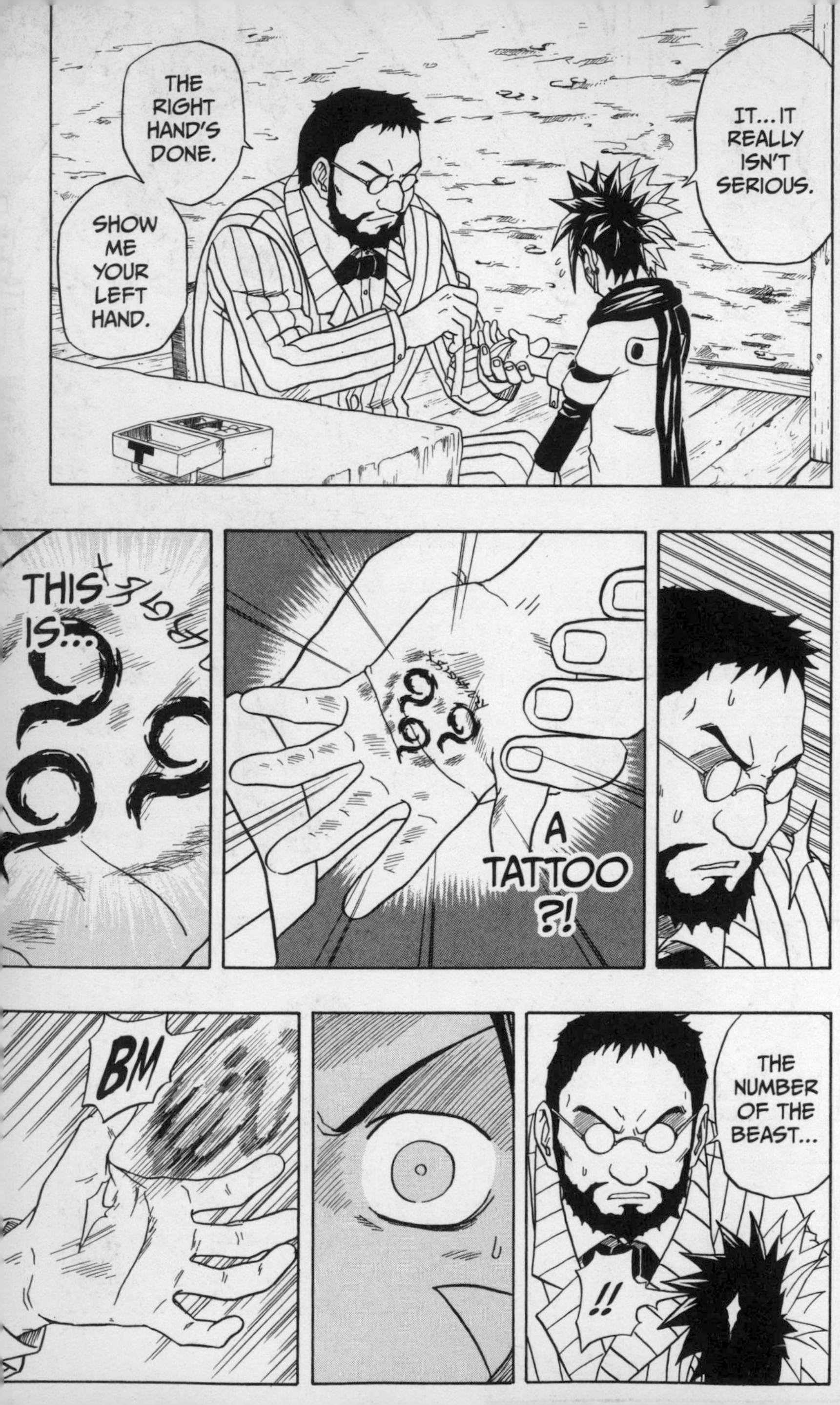
IT... IT REALLY ISN'T SERIOUS.
THE RIGHT HAND'S DONE.
SHOW ME YOUR LEFT HAND.
A TATTOO ?!
THIS IS...
THE NUMBER OF THE BEAST...
!!
BM

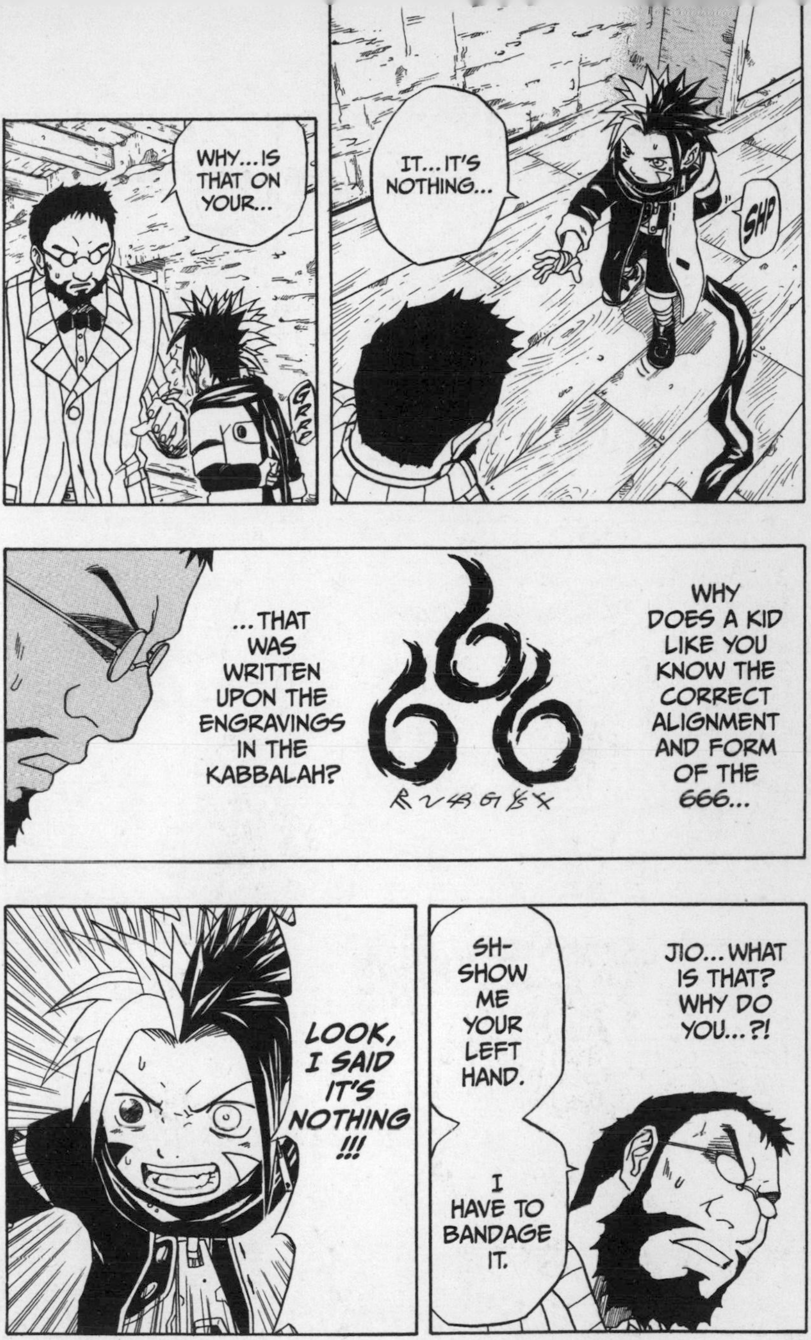
IT... IT'S NOTHING...
SHP
WHY... IS THAT ON YOUR...
GRRR
WHY DOES A KID LIKE YOU KNOW THE CORRECT ALIGNMENT AND FORM OF THE 666...
...THAT WAS WRITTEN UPON THE ENGRAVINGS IN THE KABBALAH?
JIO... WHAT IS THAT? WHY DO YOU...?!
SH-SHOW ME YOUR LEFT HAND.
I HAVE TO BANDAGE IT.
LOOK, I SAID IT'S NOTHING!!!

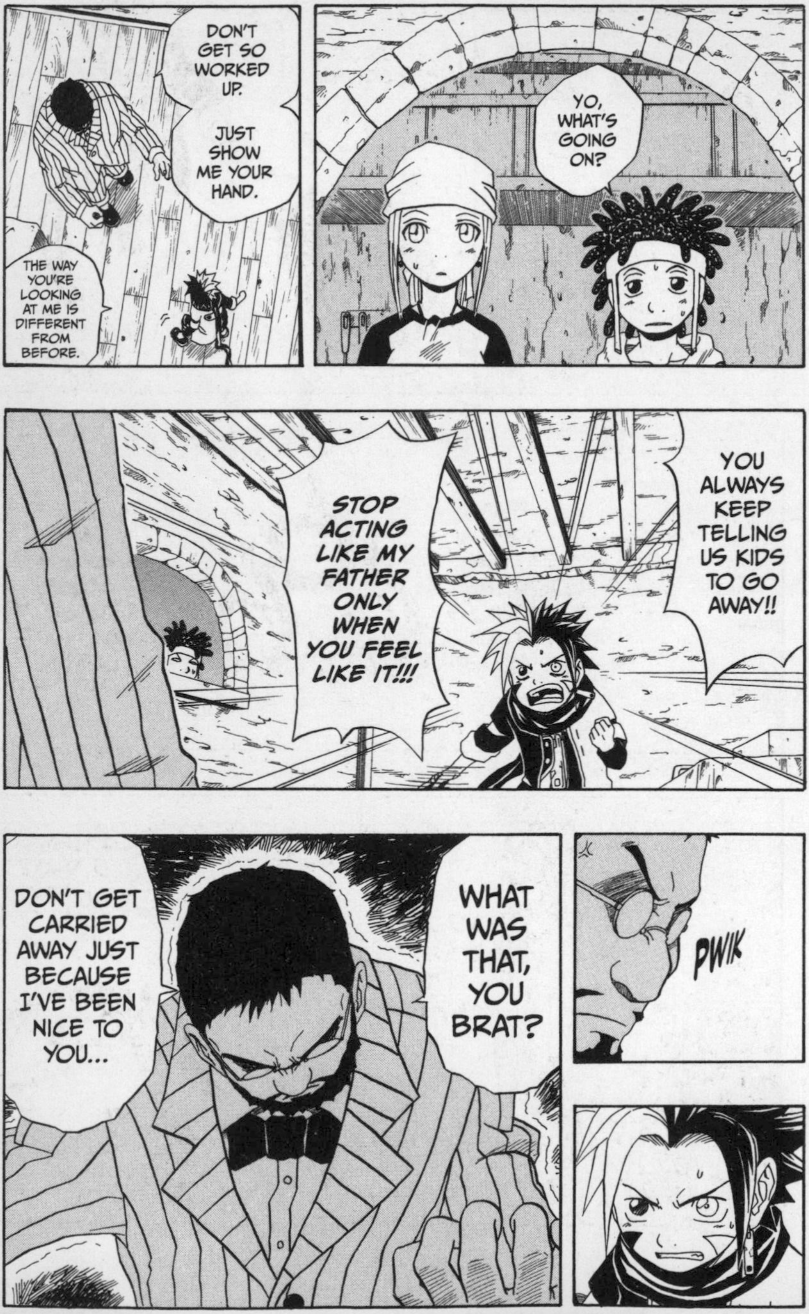
YO, WHAT'S GOING ON?
DON'T GET SO WORKED UP.
JUST SHOW ME YOUR HAND.
THE WAY YOU'RE LOOKING AT ME IS DIFFERENT FROM BEFORE.
YOU ALWAYS KEEP TELLING US KIDS TO GO AWAY!!
STOP ACTING LIKE MY FATHER ONLY WHEN YOU FEEL LIKE IT!!!
PWIK
WHAT WAS THAT, YOU BRAT?
DON'T GET CARRIED AWAY JUST BECAUSE I'VE BEEN NICE TO YOU...

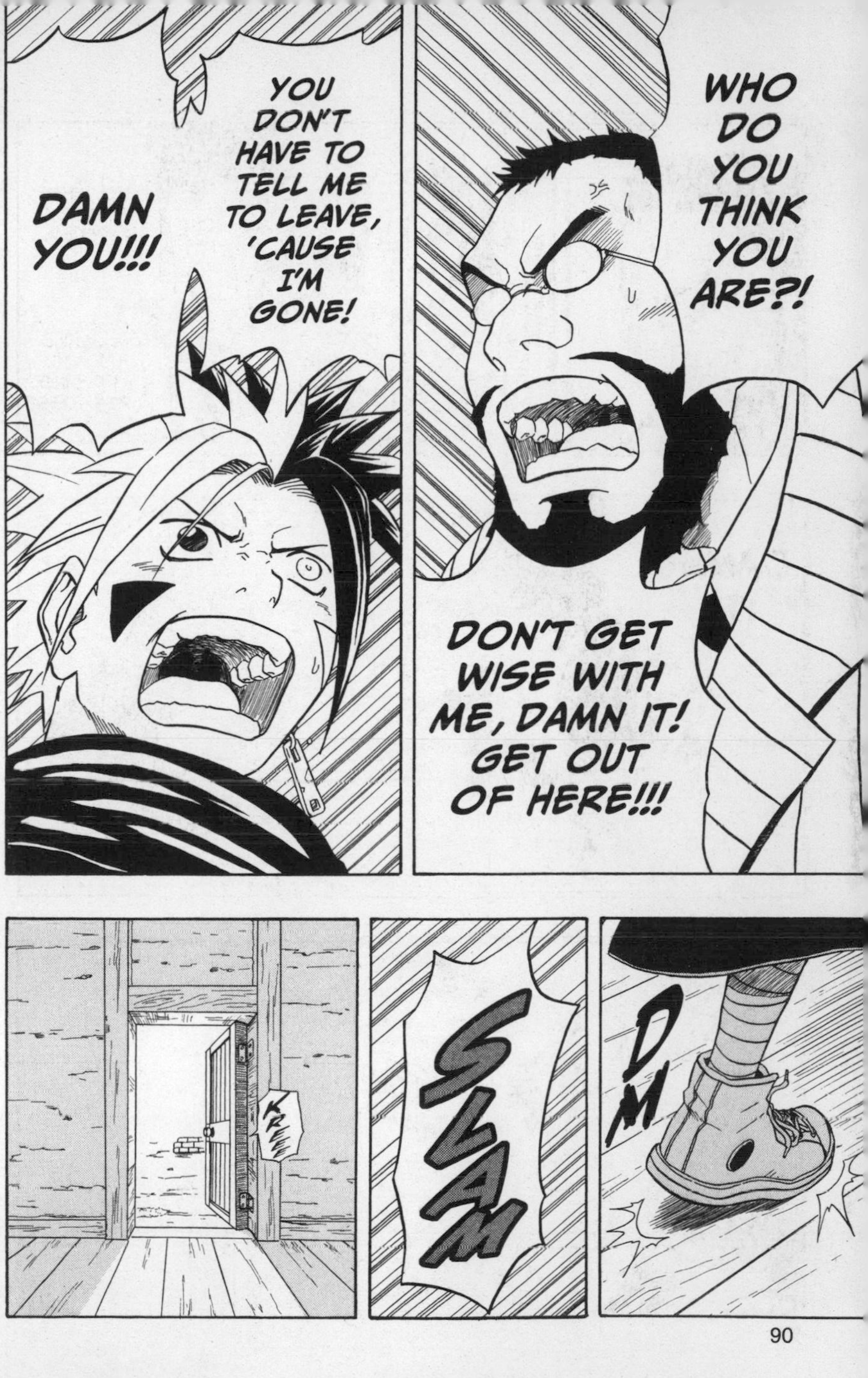
WHO DO YOU THINK YOU ARE?!
DON'T GET WISE WITH ME, DAMN IT! GET OUT OF HERE!!!
YOU DON'T HAVE TO TELL ME TO LEAVE, 'CAUSE I'M GONE!
DAMN YOU!!!
DM
SLAM
KREE

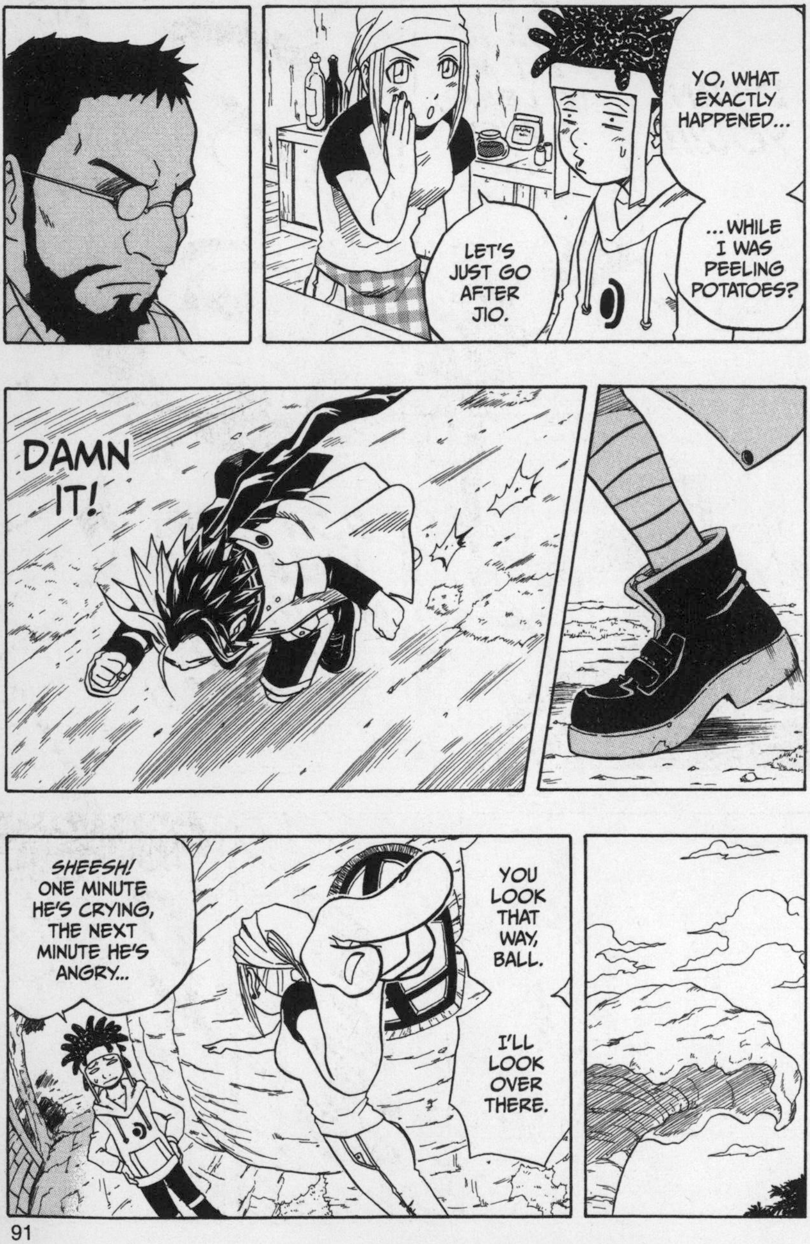
YO, WHAT EXACTLY HAPPENED...
...WHILE I WAS PEELING POTATOES?
LET'S JUST GO AFTER JIO.
DAMN IT!
YOU LOOK THAT WAY, BALL.
I'LL LOOK OVER THERE.
SHEESH! ONE MINUTE HE'S CRYING, THE NEXT MINUTE HE'S ANGRY...

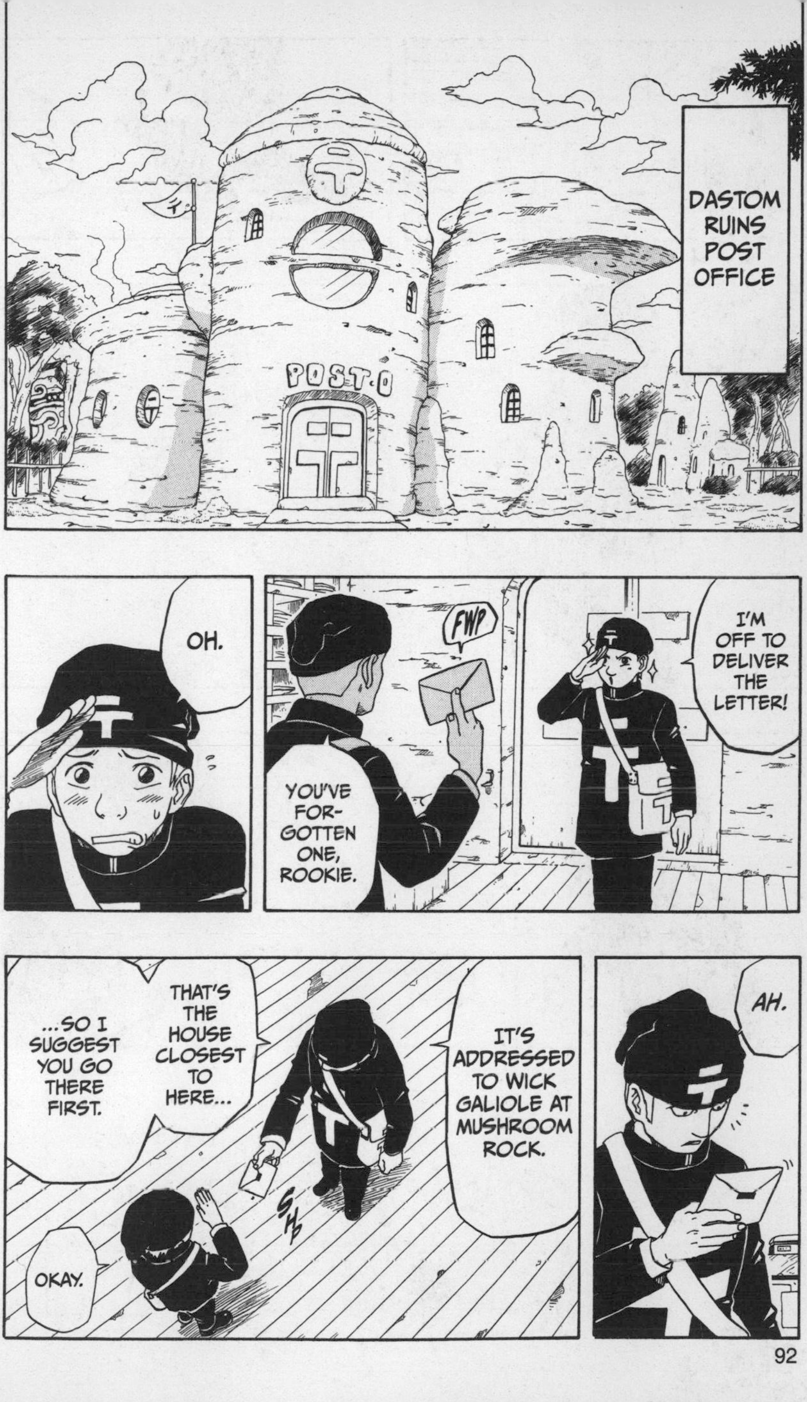
DASTOM RUINS POST OFFICE
POST-O
I'M OFF TO DELIVER THE LETTER!
FWP
YOU'VE FOR-GOTTEN ONE, ROOKIE.
OH.
AH.
IT'S ADDRESSED TO WICK GALIOLE AT MUSHROOM ROCK.
THAT'S THE HOUSE CLOSEST TO HERE...
...SO I SUGGEST YOU GO THERE FIRST.
SHP
OKAY.

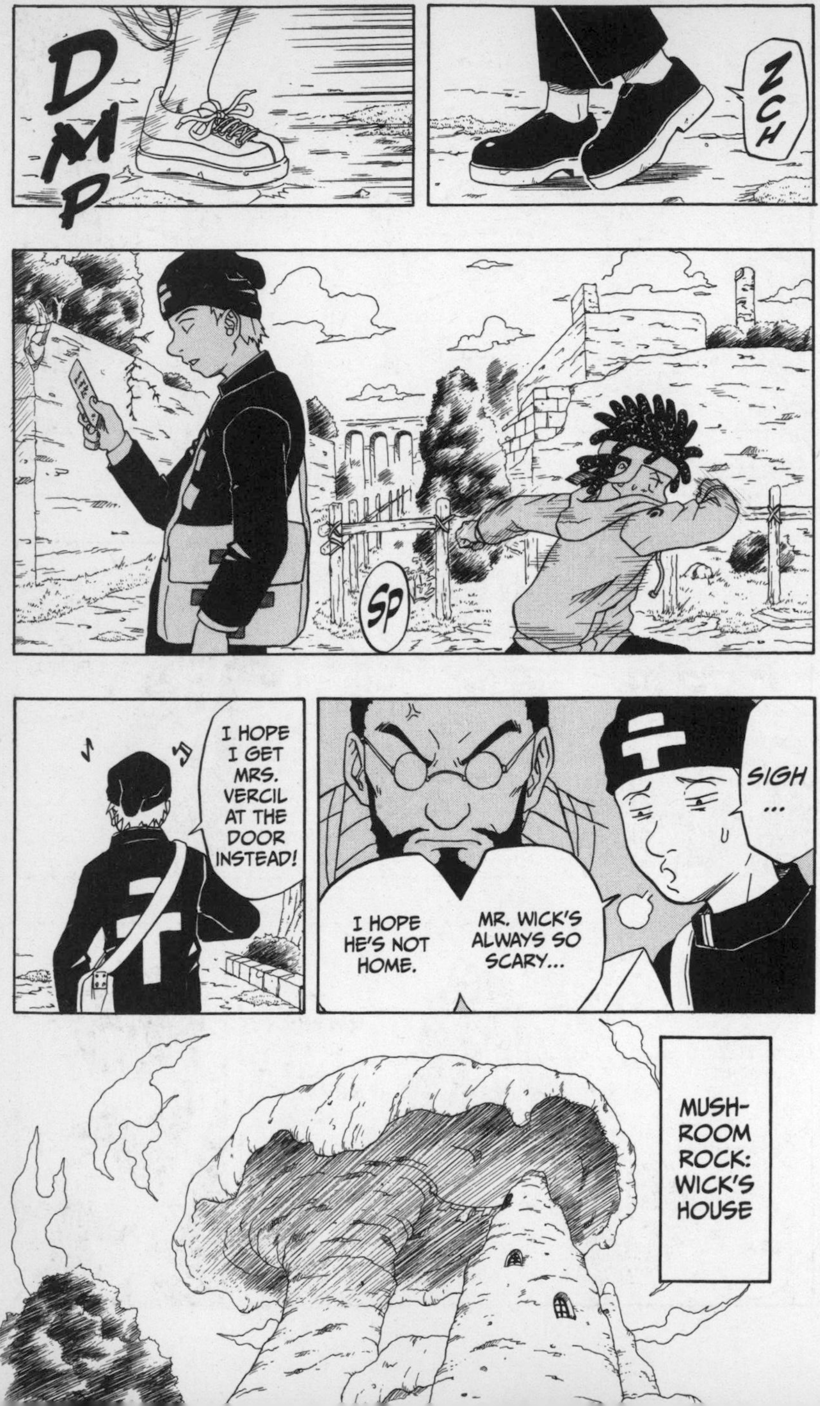
ZCH
DMP
SP
SIGH ...
MR. WICK'S ALWAYS SO SCARY...
I HOPE HE'S NOT HOME.
I HOPE I GET MRS. VERCIL AT THE DOOR INSTEAD!
MUSH-ROOM ROCK: WICK'S HOUSE

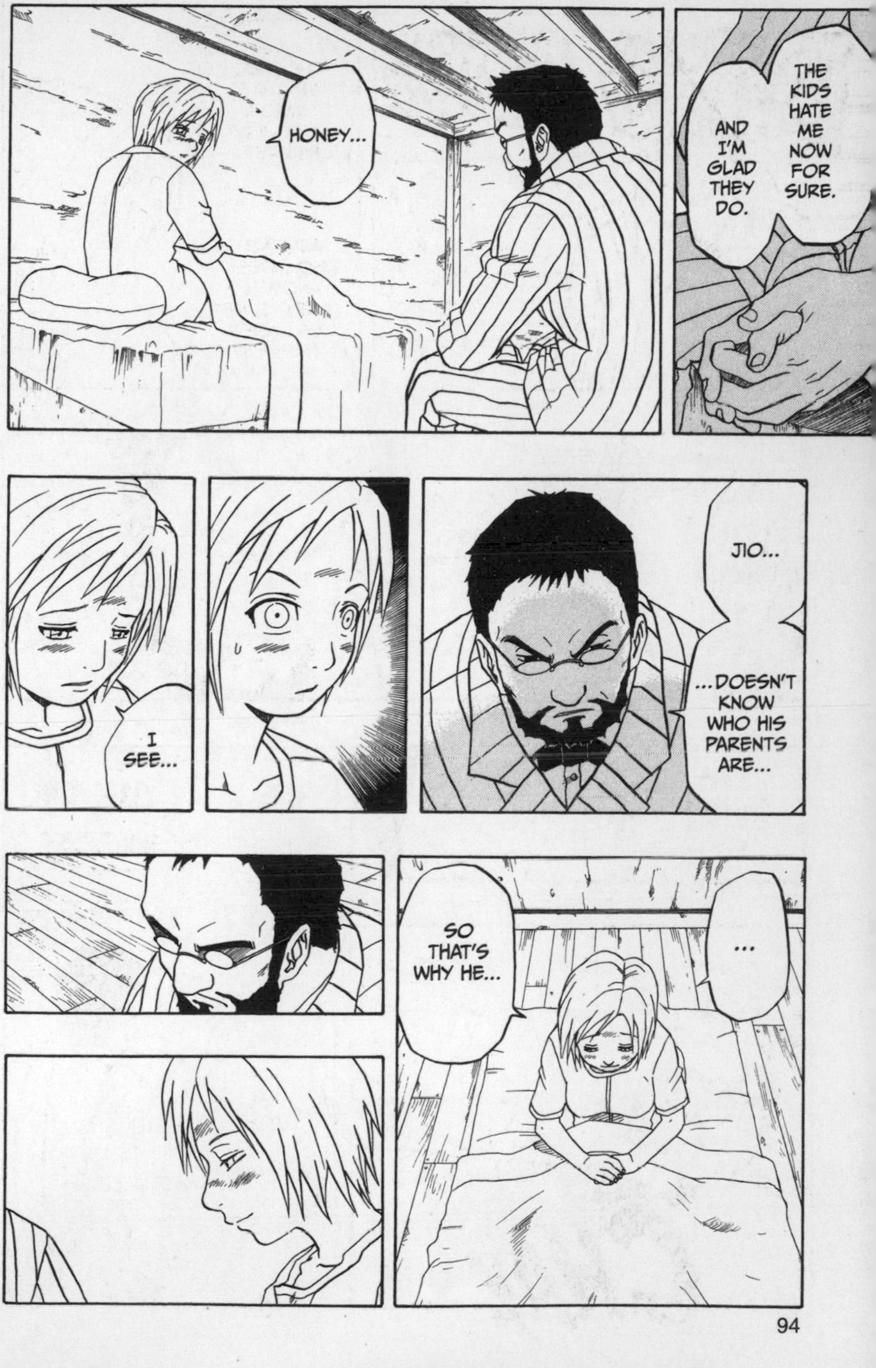
THE KIDS HATE ME NOW FOR SURE.
AND I'M GLAD THEY DO.
HONEY...
JIO...
...DOESN'T KNOW WHO HIS PARENTS ARE...
I SEE...
...
SO THAT'S WHY HE...

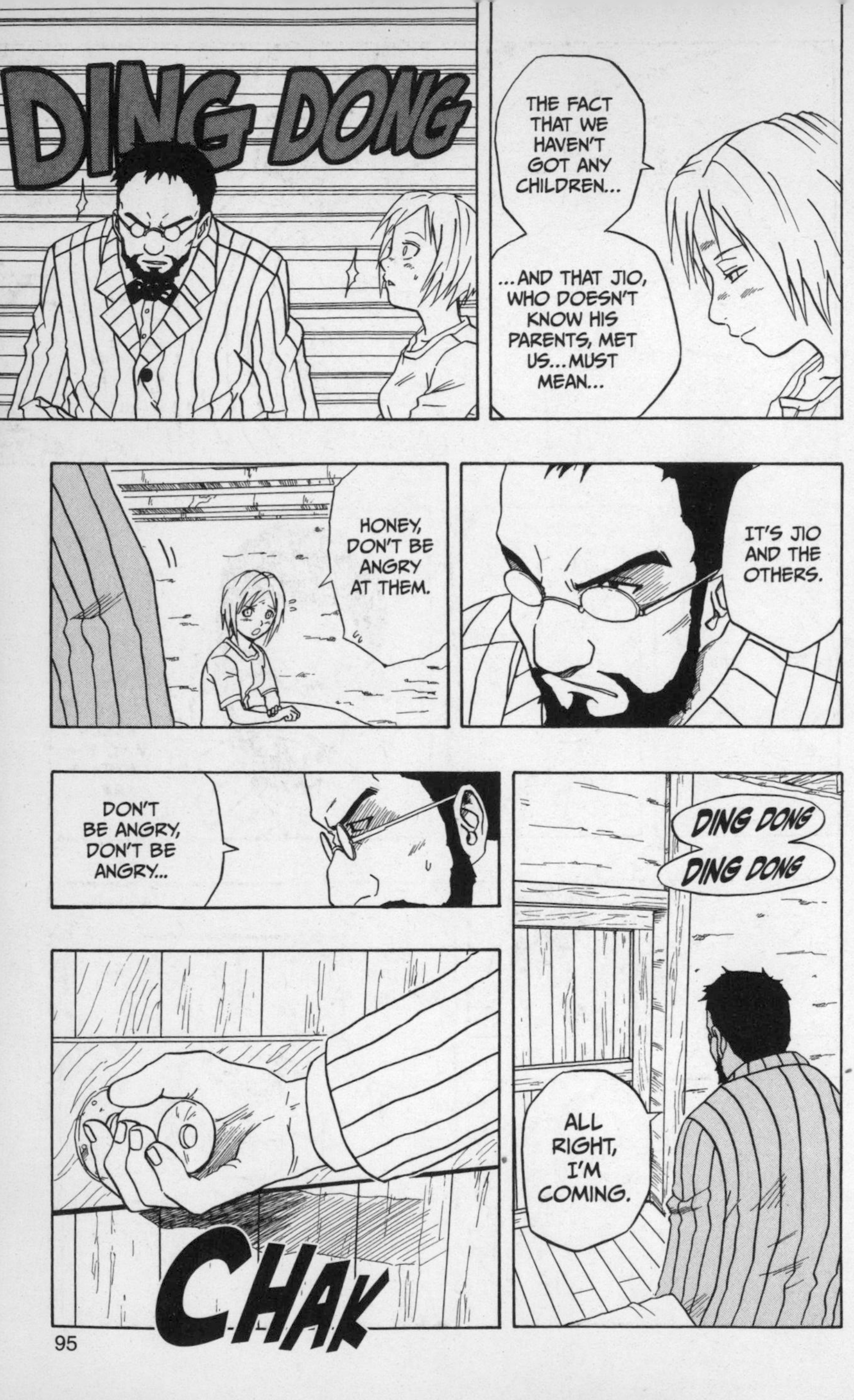
THE FACT THAT WE HAVEN'T GOT ANY CHILDREN...
...AND THAT JIO, WHO DOESN'T KNOW HIS PARENTS, MET US...MUST MEAN...
DING DONG
IT'S JIO AND THE OTHERS.
HONEY, DON'T BE ANGRY AT THEM.
DING DONG
DING DONG
ALL RIGHT, I'M COMING.
DON'T BE ANGRY, DON'T BE ANGRY...
CHAK

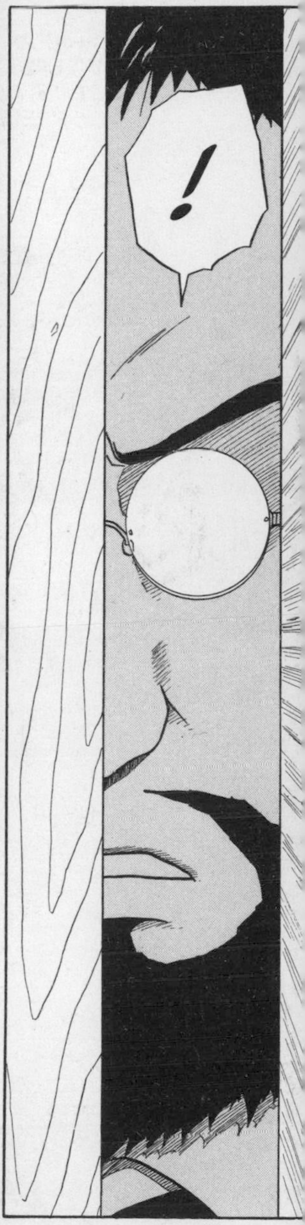
!
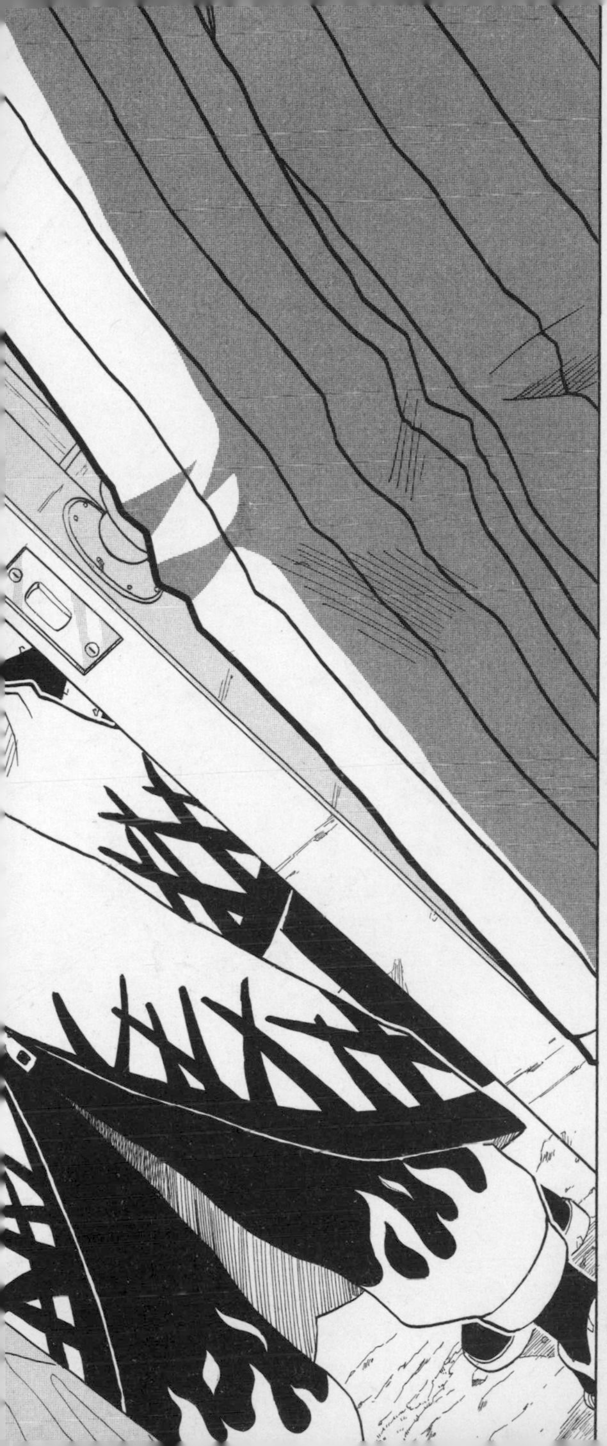

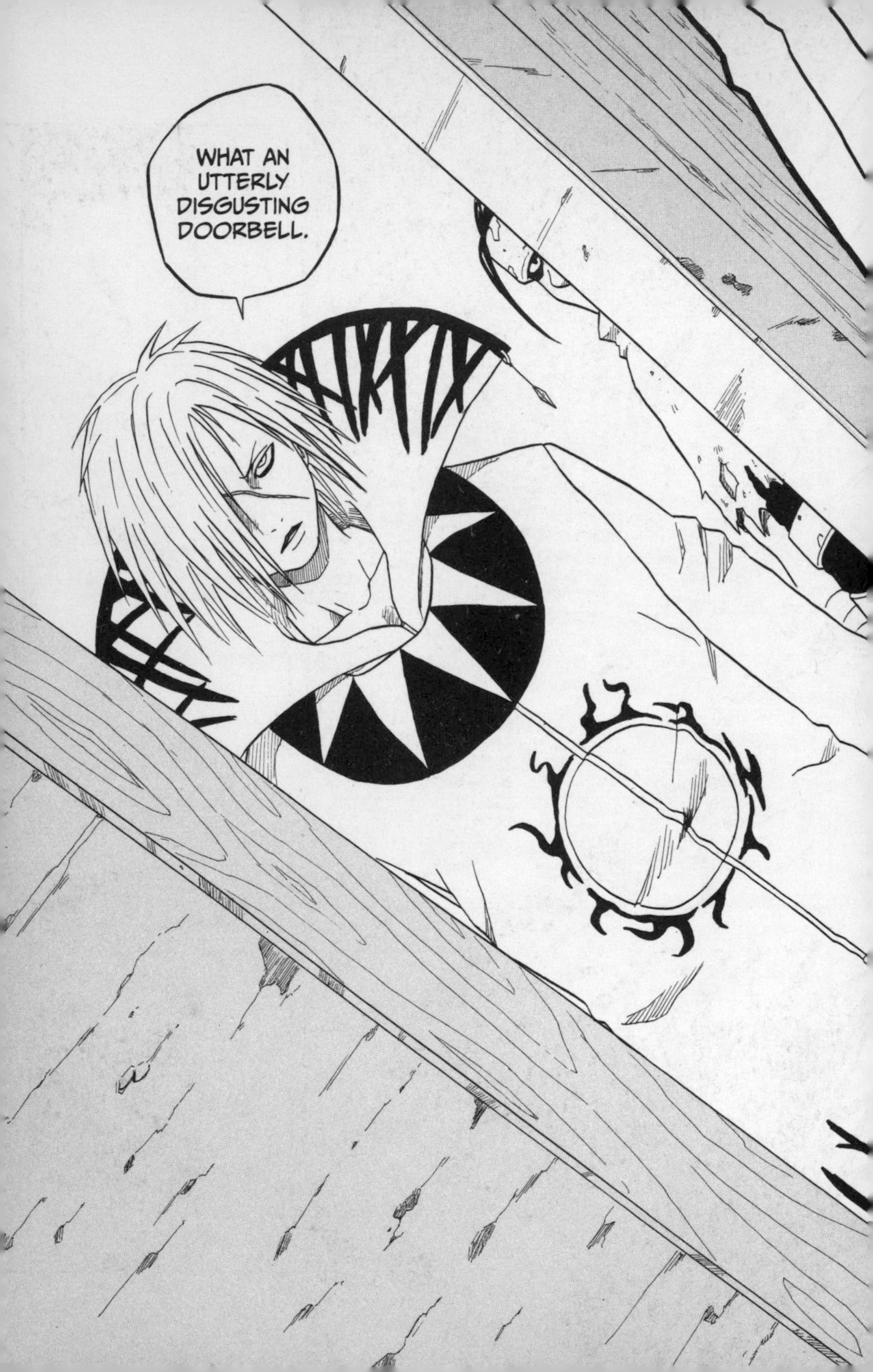
WHAT AN UTTERLY DISGUSTING DOORBELL.

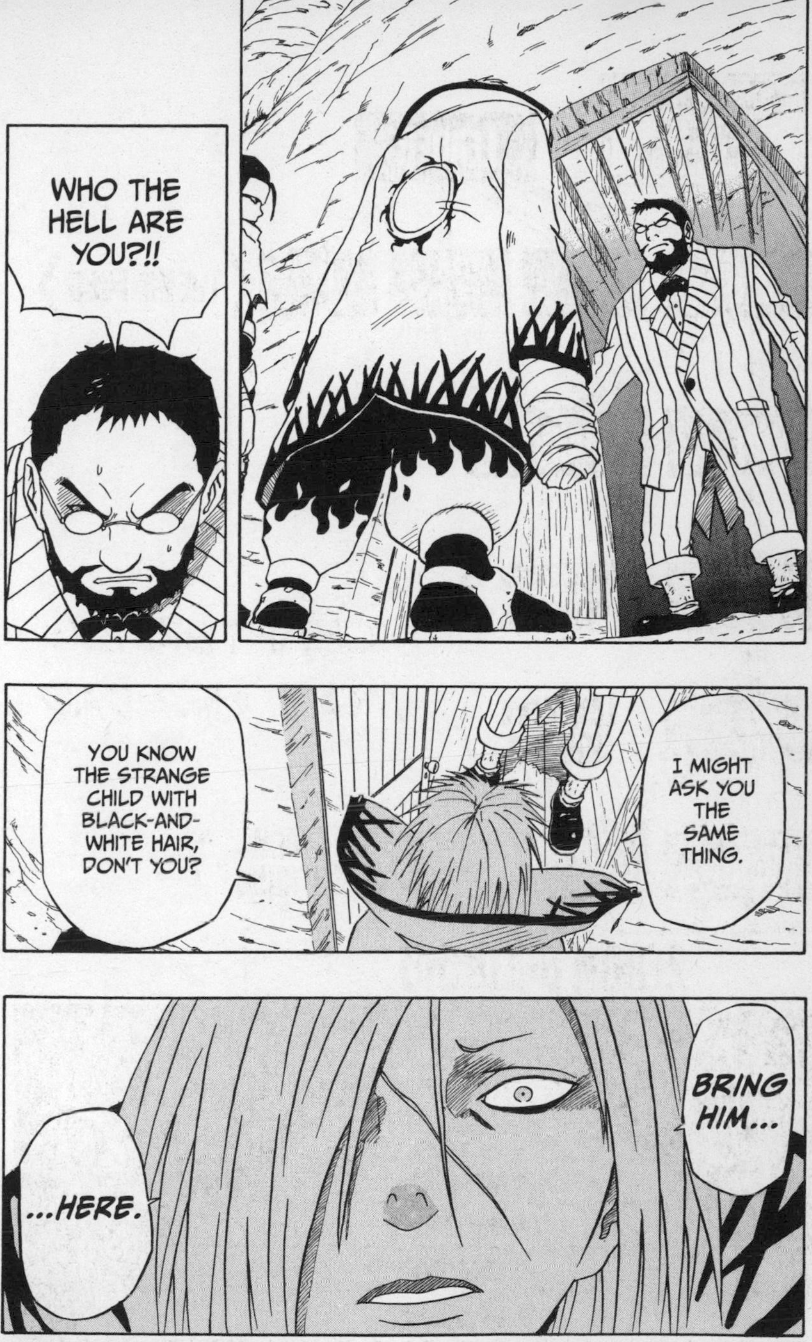
WHO THE HELL ARE YOU?!!
I MIGHT ASK YOU THE SAME THING.
YOU KNOW THE STRANGE CHILD WITH BLACK-AND-WHITE HAIR, DON'T YOU?
BRING HIM...
...HERE.

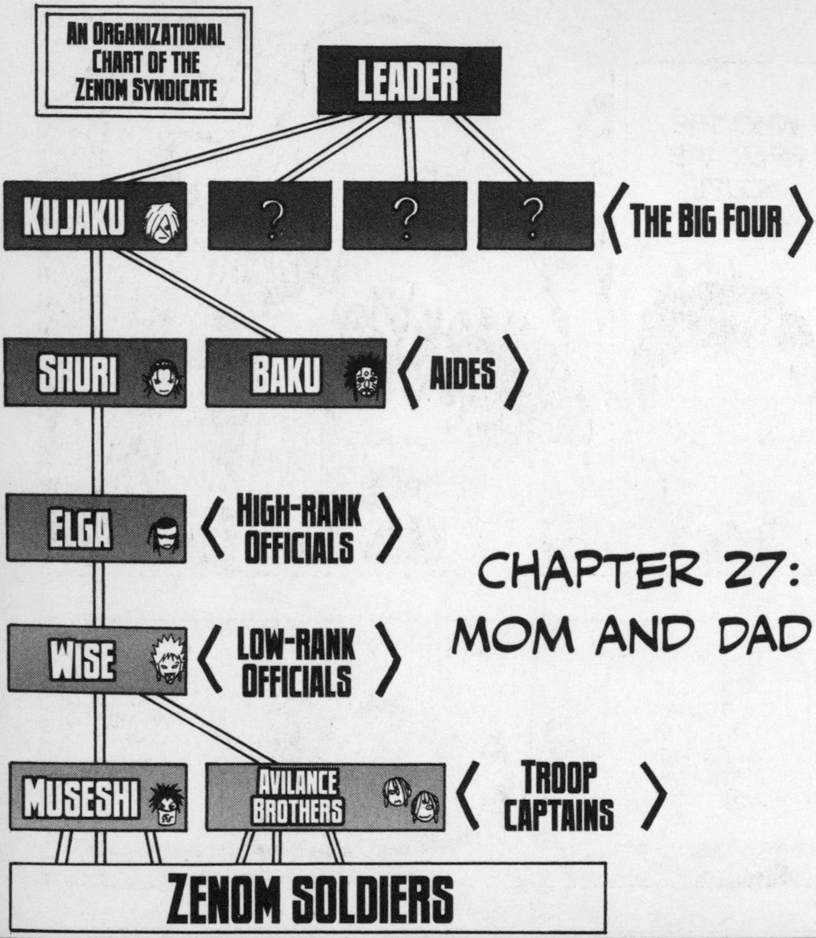
AN ORGANIZATIONAL CHART OF THE ZENOM SYNDICATE
LEADER
KUJAKU
?
?
?
THE BIG FOUR
SHURI
BAKU
AIDES
ELGA
HIGH-RANK OFFICIALS
WISE
LOW-RANK OFFICIALS
MUSESHI
AVILANCE BROTHERS
TROOP CAPTAINS
ZENOM SOLDIERS

CHAPTER 27: MOM AND DAD

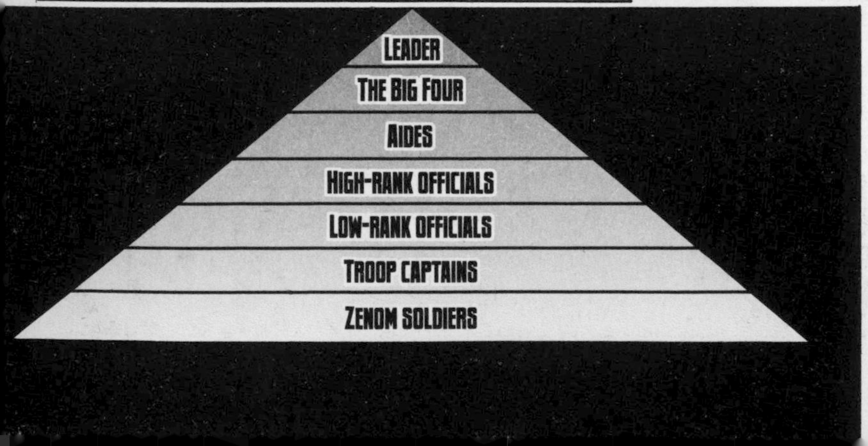
LEADER
THE BIG FOUR
AIDES
HIGH-RANK OFFICIALS
LOW-RANK OFFICIALS
TROOP CAPTAINS
ZENOM SOLDIERS

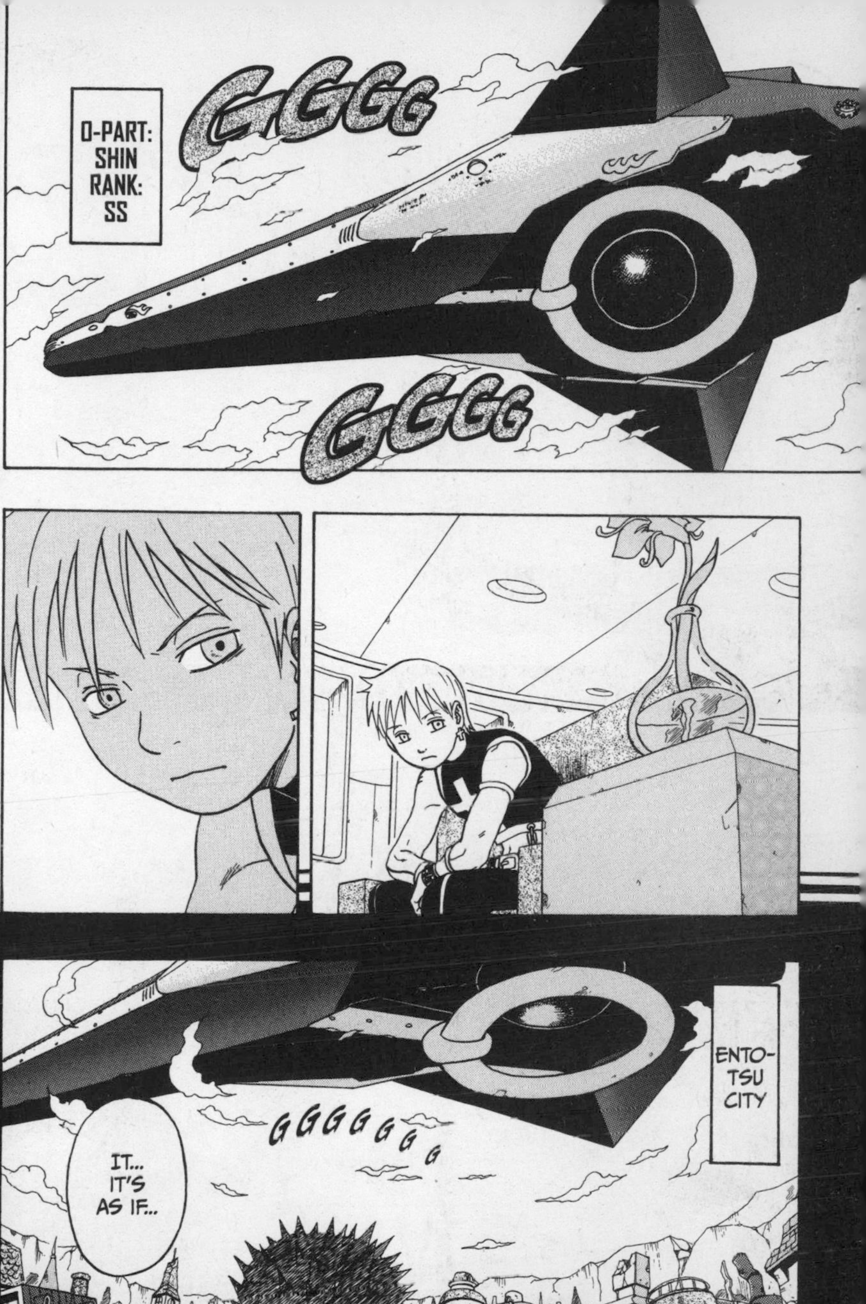
O-PART: SHIN RANK: SS
GGGG
GGGG
ENTO-TSU CITY
GGGGGGGG
IT... IT'S AS IF...

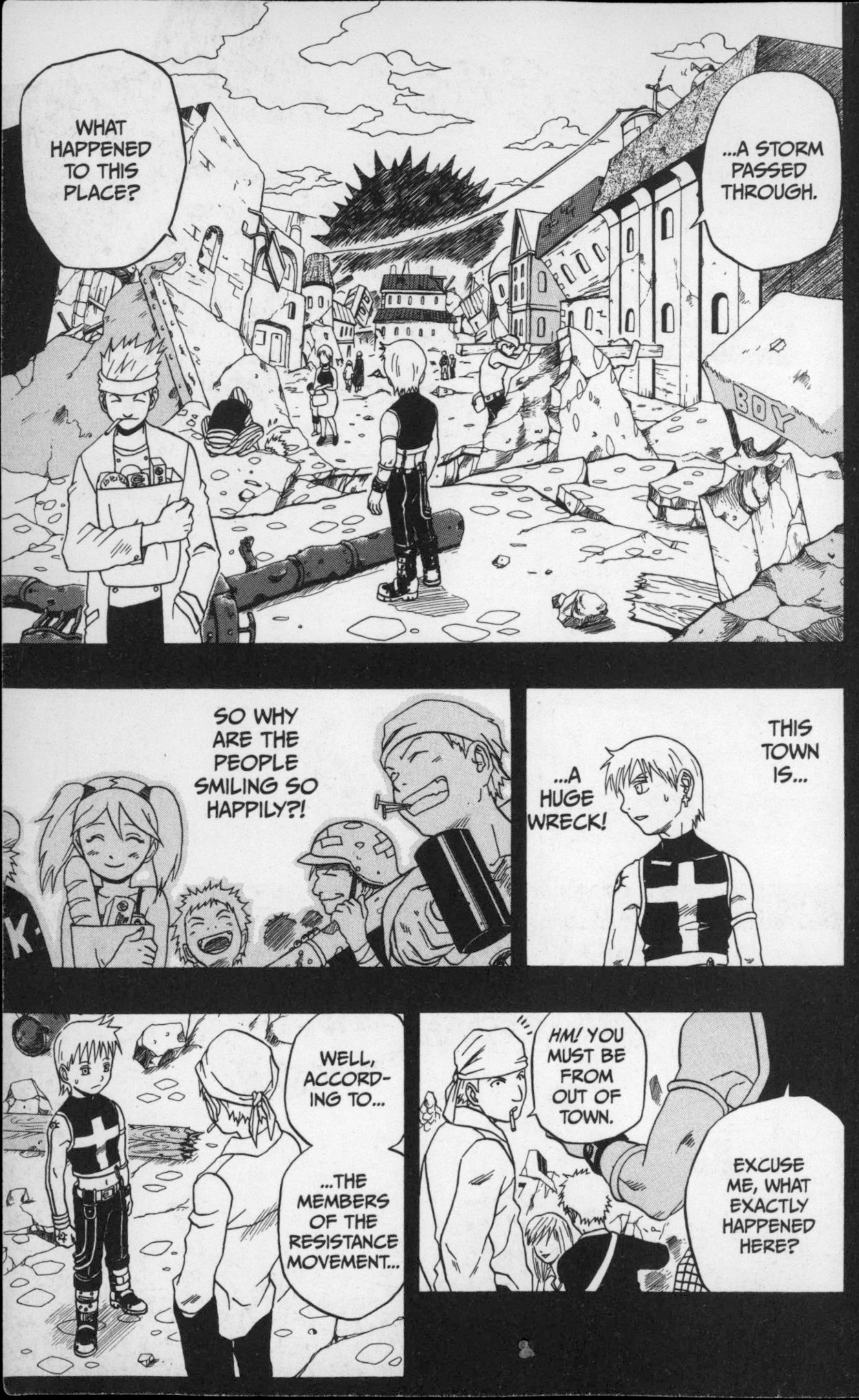
WHAT HAPPENED TO THIS PLACE?
...A STORM PASSED THROUGH.
BOY
THIS TOWN IS...
...A HUGE WRECK!
SO WHY ARE THE PEOPLE SMILING SO HAPPILY?!
EXCUSE ME, WHAT EXACTLY HAPPENED HERE?
HM! YOU MUST BE FROM OUT OF TOWN.
WELL, ACCORD-ING TO...
...THE MEMBERS OF THE RESISTANCE MOVEMENT...

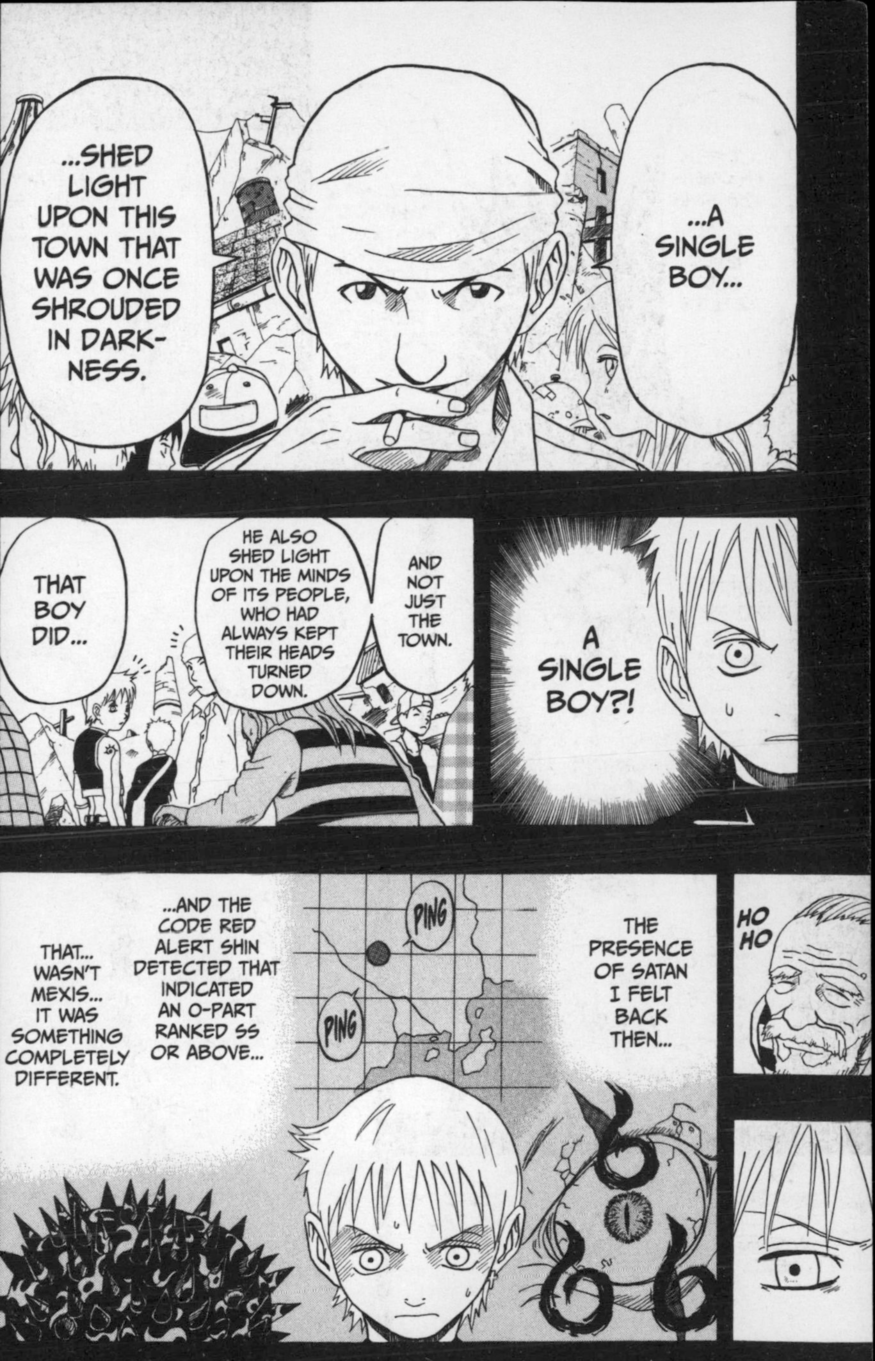
...A SINGLE BOY...
...SHED LIGHT UPON THIS TOWN THAT WAS ONCE SHROUDED IN DARK-NESS.
A SINGLE BOY?!
AND NOT JUST THE TOWN.
HE ALSO SHED LIGHT UPON THE MINDS OF ITS PEOPLE, WHO HAD ALWAYS KEPT THEIR HEADS TURNED DOWN.
THAT BOY DID...
HO HO
THE PRESENCE OF SATAN I FELT BACK THEN...
PING
PING
...AND THE CODE RED ALERT SHIN DETECTED THAT INDICATED AN O-PART RANKED SS OR ABOVE...
THAT... WASN'T MEXIS... IT WAS SOMETHING COMPLETELY DIFFERENT.

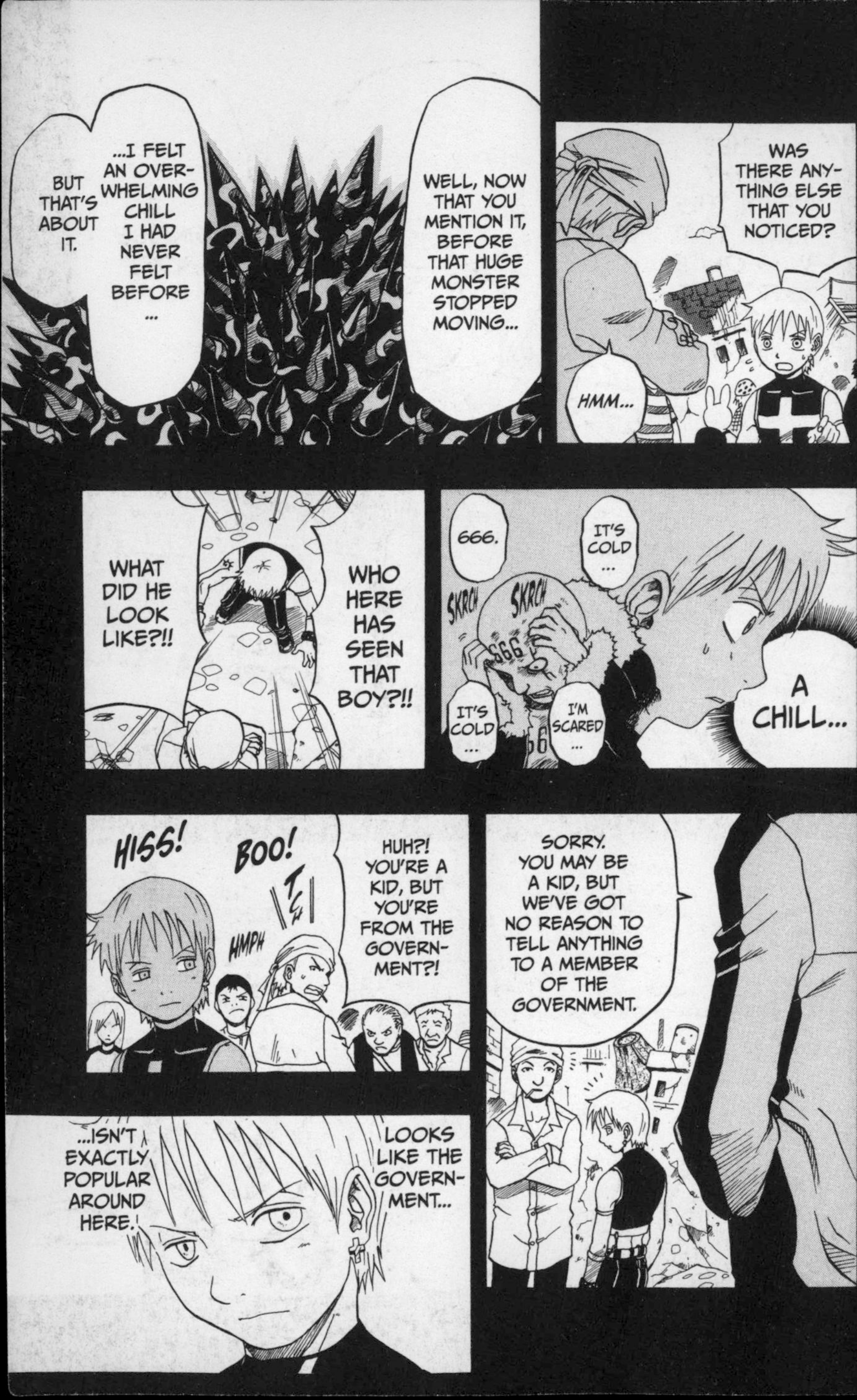
WAS THERE ANYTHING ELSE THAT YOU NOTICED?
HMM...
WELL, NOW THAT YOU MENTION IT, BEFORE THAT HUGE MONSTER STOPPED MOVING...
...I FELT AN OVERWHELMING CHILL I HAD NEVER FELT BEFORE...
BUT THAT'S ABOUT IT.
A CHILL...
IT'S COLD...
666.
SKRCH
SKRCH
I'M SCARED...
IT'S COLD...
WHO HERE HAS SEEN THAT BOY?!!
WHAT DID HE LOOK LIKE?!!
SORRY. YOU MAY BE A KID, BUT WE'VE GOT NO REASON TO TELL ANYTHING TO A MEMBER OF THE GOVERNMENT.
HUH?! YOU'RE A KID, BUT YOU'RE FROM THE GOVERNMENT?!
BOO!
HISS!
HMPH
LOOKS LIKE THE GOVERNMENT...
...ISN'T EXACTLY POPULAR AROUND HERE.

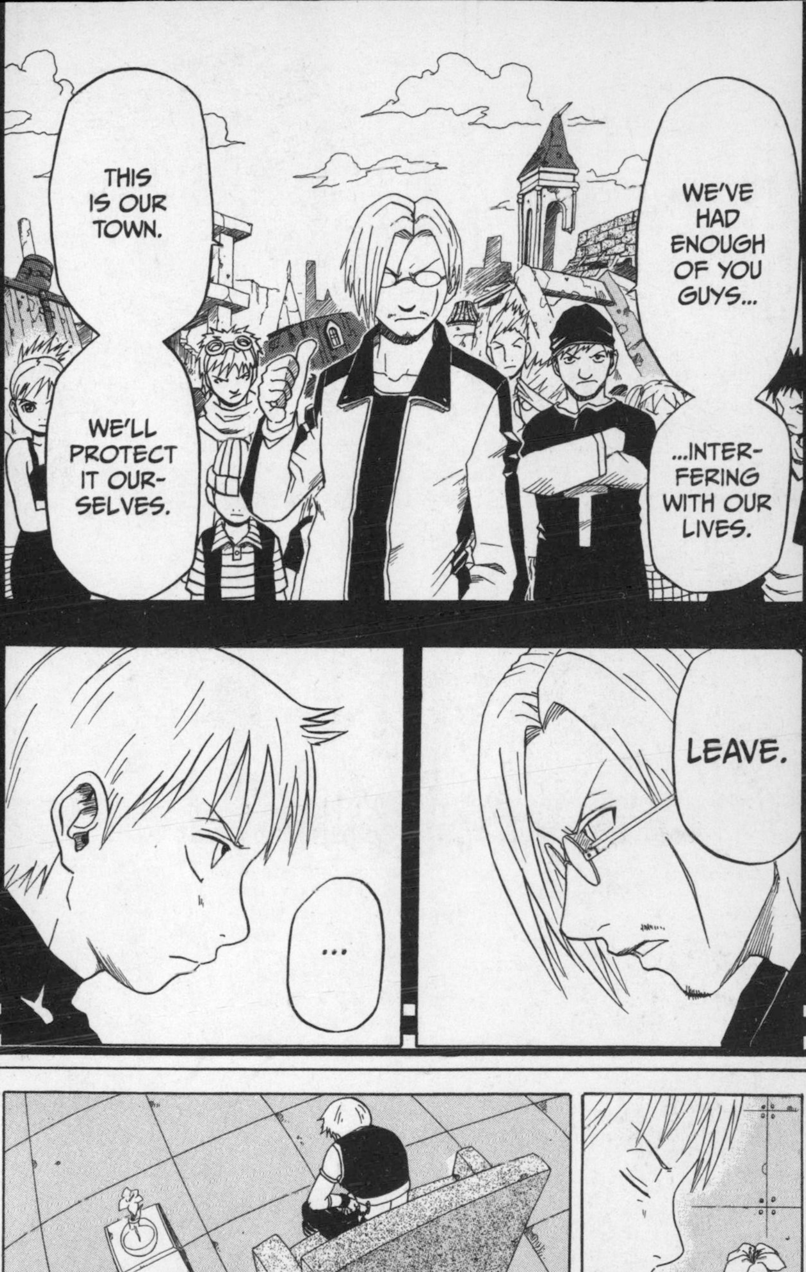
WE'VE HAD ENOUGH OF YOU GUYS...
...INTERFERING WITH OUR LIVES.
THIS IS OUR TOWN.
WE'LL PROTECT IT OURSELVES.
LEAVE.
...

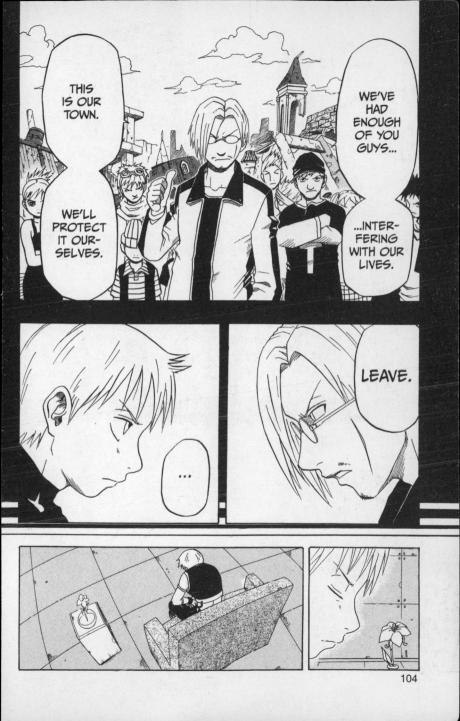

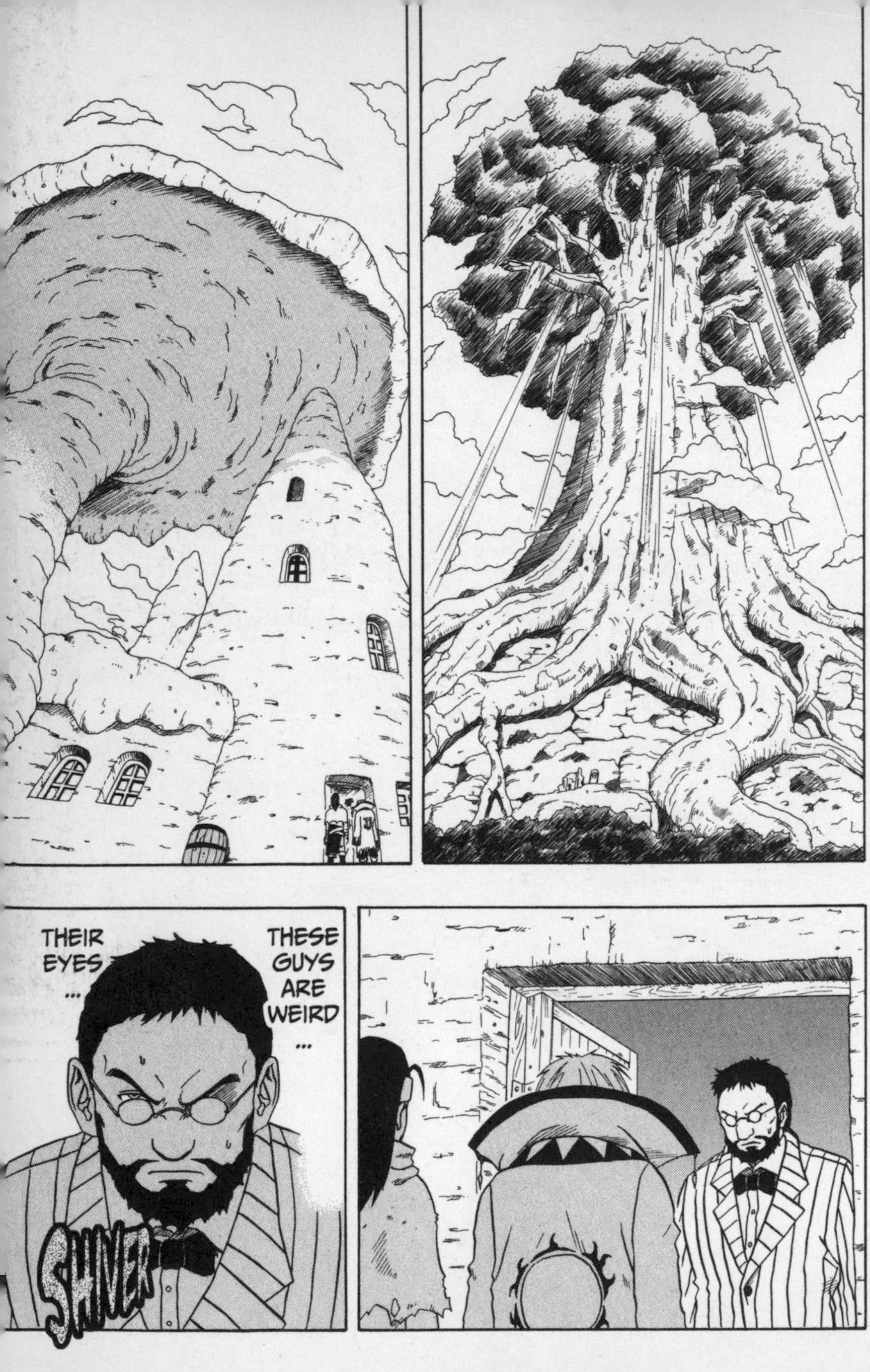
THESE GUYS ARE WEIRD ...
THEIR EYES ...
SHIVER

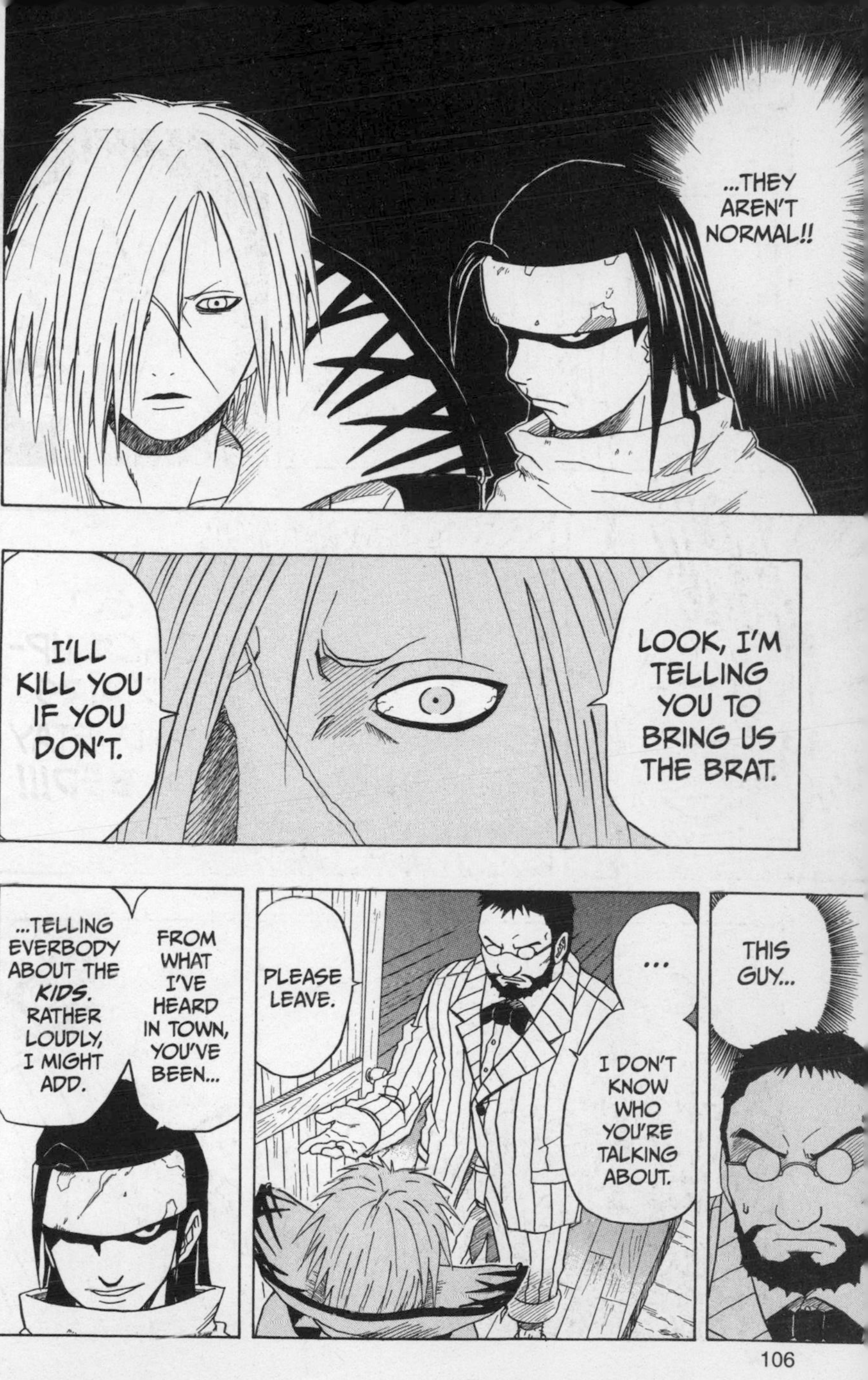
...THEY AREN'T NORMAL!!
LOOK, I'M TELLING YOU TO BRING US THE BRAT.
I'LL KILL YOU IF YOU DON'T.
THIS GUY...
...
I DON'T KNOW WHO YOU'RE TALKING ABOUT.
PLEASE LEAVE.
FROM WHAT I'VE HEARD IN TOWN, YOU'VE BEEN...
...TELLING EVERBODY ABOUT THE *KIDS*. RATHER LOUDLY, I MIGHT ADD.

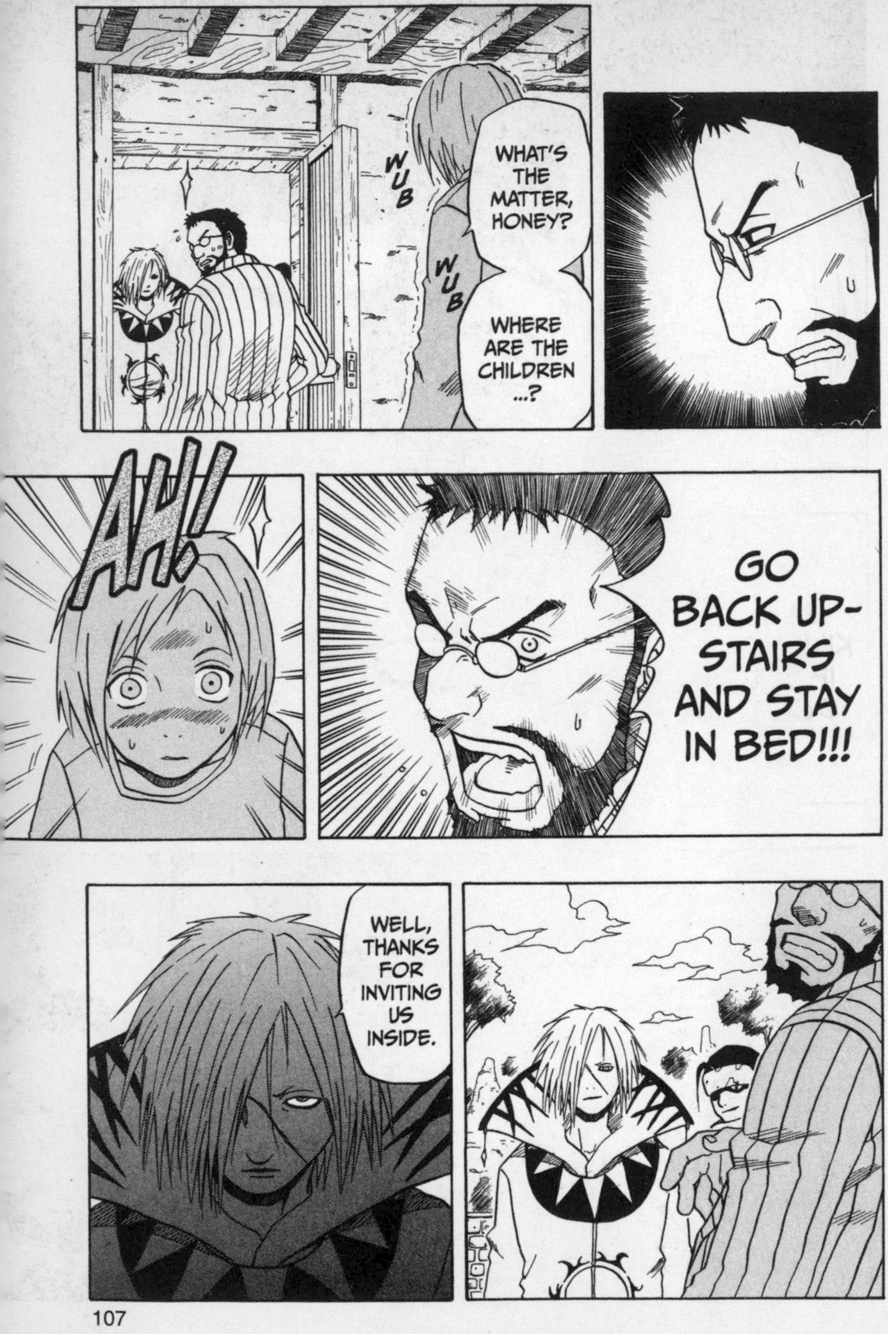
WUB
WUB
WHAT'S THE MATTER, HONEY?
WHERE ARE THE CHILDREN ...?
GO BACK UP-STAIRS AND STAY IN BED!!!
AH!
WELL, THANKS FOR INVITING US INSIDE.

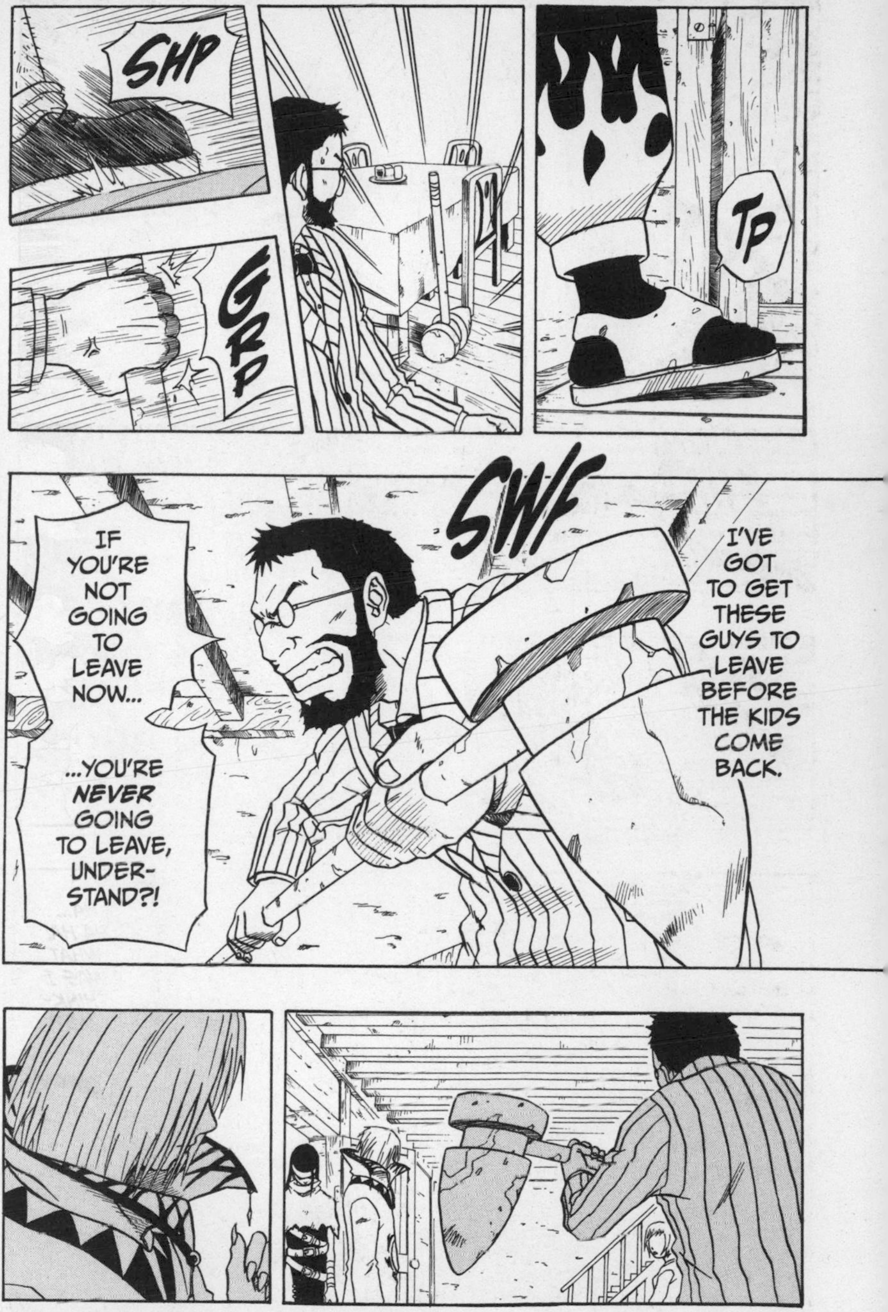
TP
SHP
GRP
SWF
I'VE GOT TO GET THESE GUYS TO LEAVE BEFORE THE KIDS COME BACK.
IF YOU'RE NOT GOING TO LEAVE NOW...
...YOU'RE *NEVER* GOING TO LEAVE, UNDER-STAND?!

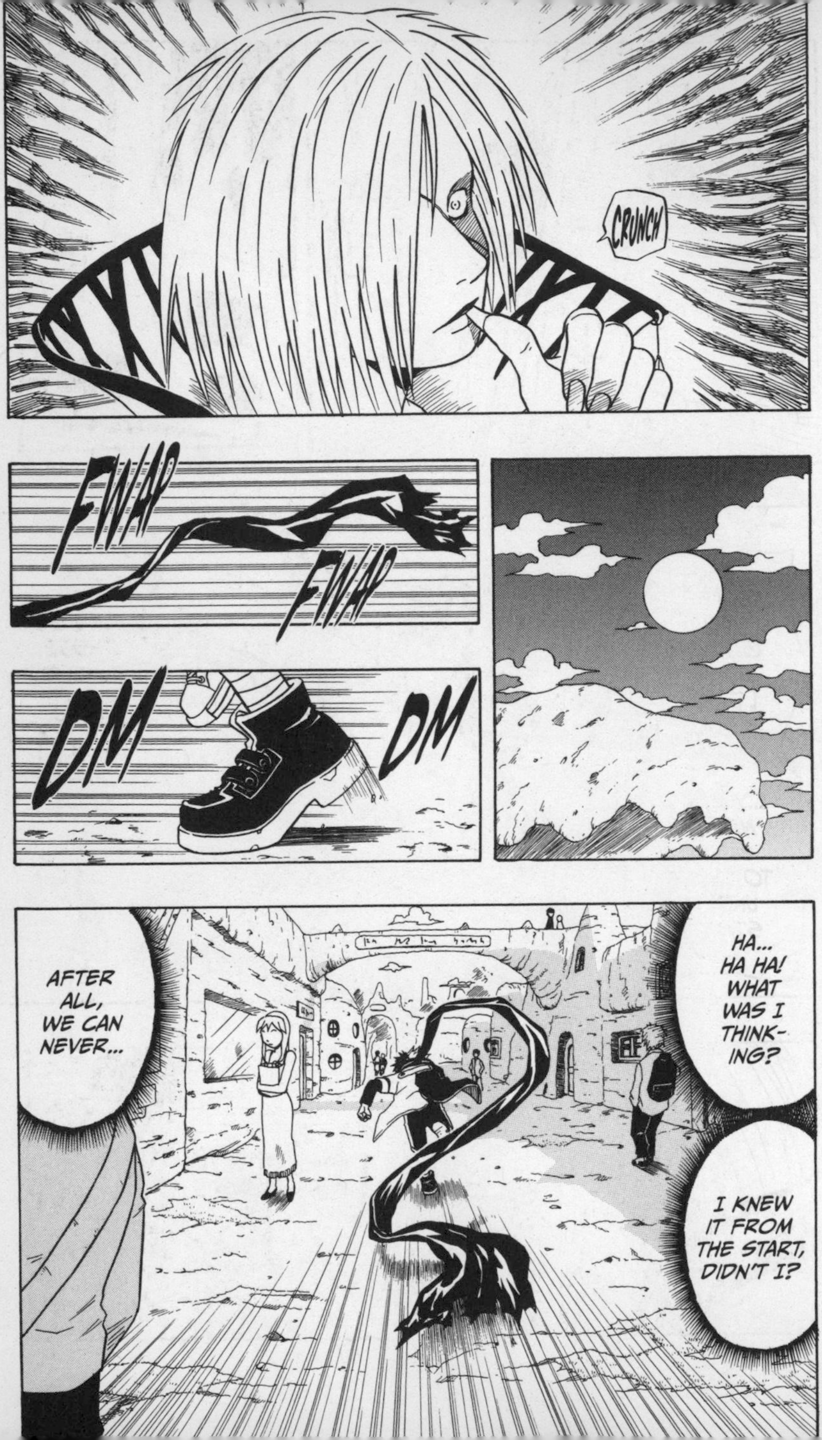
CRUNCH
FWAP
FWAP
DM
DM
HA... HA HA! WHAT WAS I THINKING-ING?
I KNEW IT FROM THE START, DIDN'T I?
AFTER ALL, WE CAN NEVER...

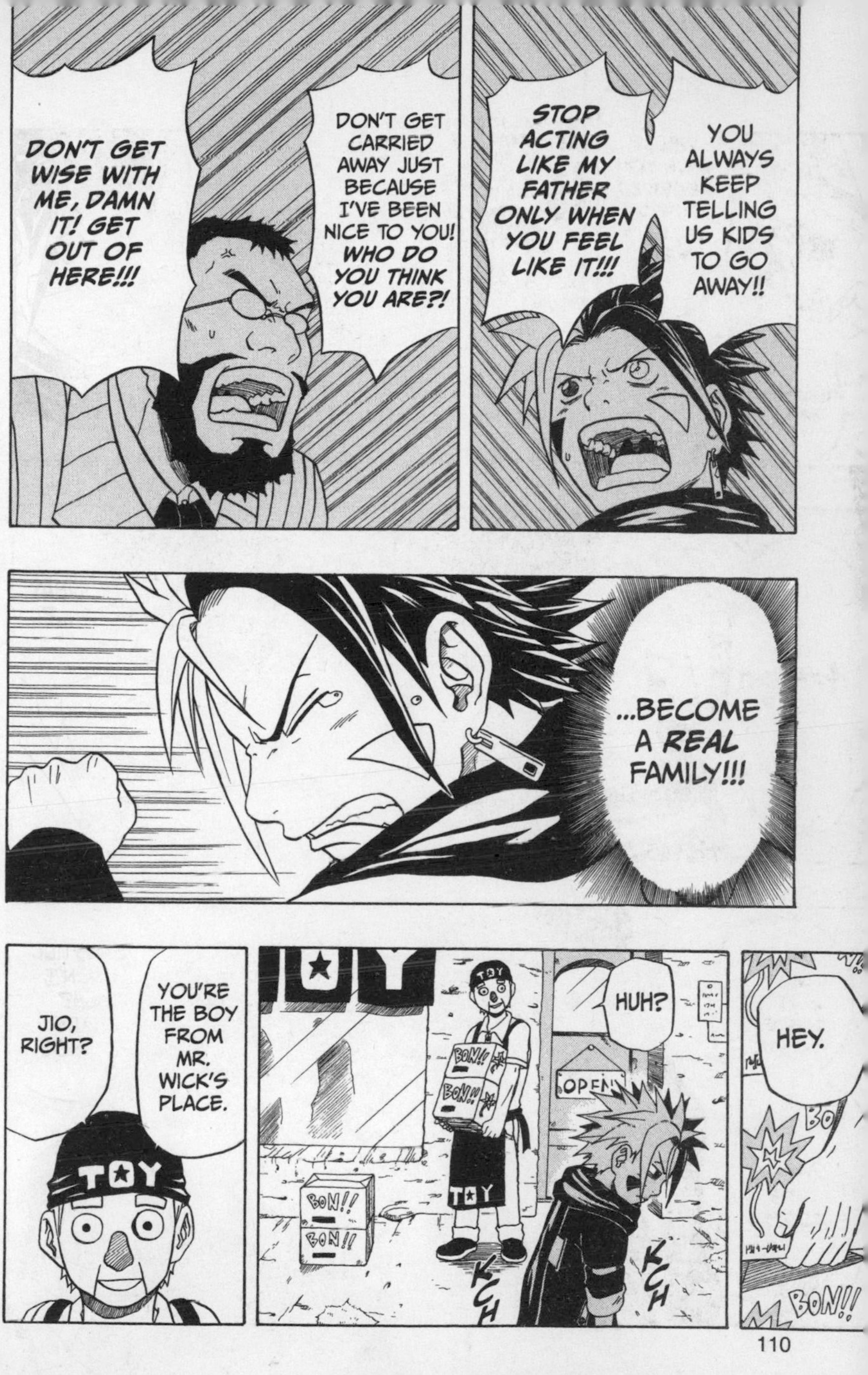
YOU ALWAYS KEEP TELLING US KIDS TO GO AWAY!!
STOP ACTING LIKE MY FATHER ONLY WHEN YOU FEEL LIKE IT!!!
DON'T GET CARRIED AWAY JUST BECAUSE I'VE BEEN NICE TO YOU! WHO DO YOU THINK YOU ARE?!
DON'T GET WISE WITH ME, DAMN IT! GET OUT OF HERE!!!
...BECOME A REAL FAMILY!!!
HEY.
BON!!
HUH?
OPEN
KCH
KCH
YOU'RE THE BOY FROM MR. WICK'S PLACE.
JIO, RIGHT?
TOY

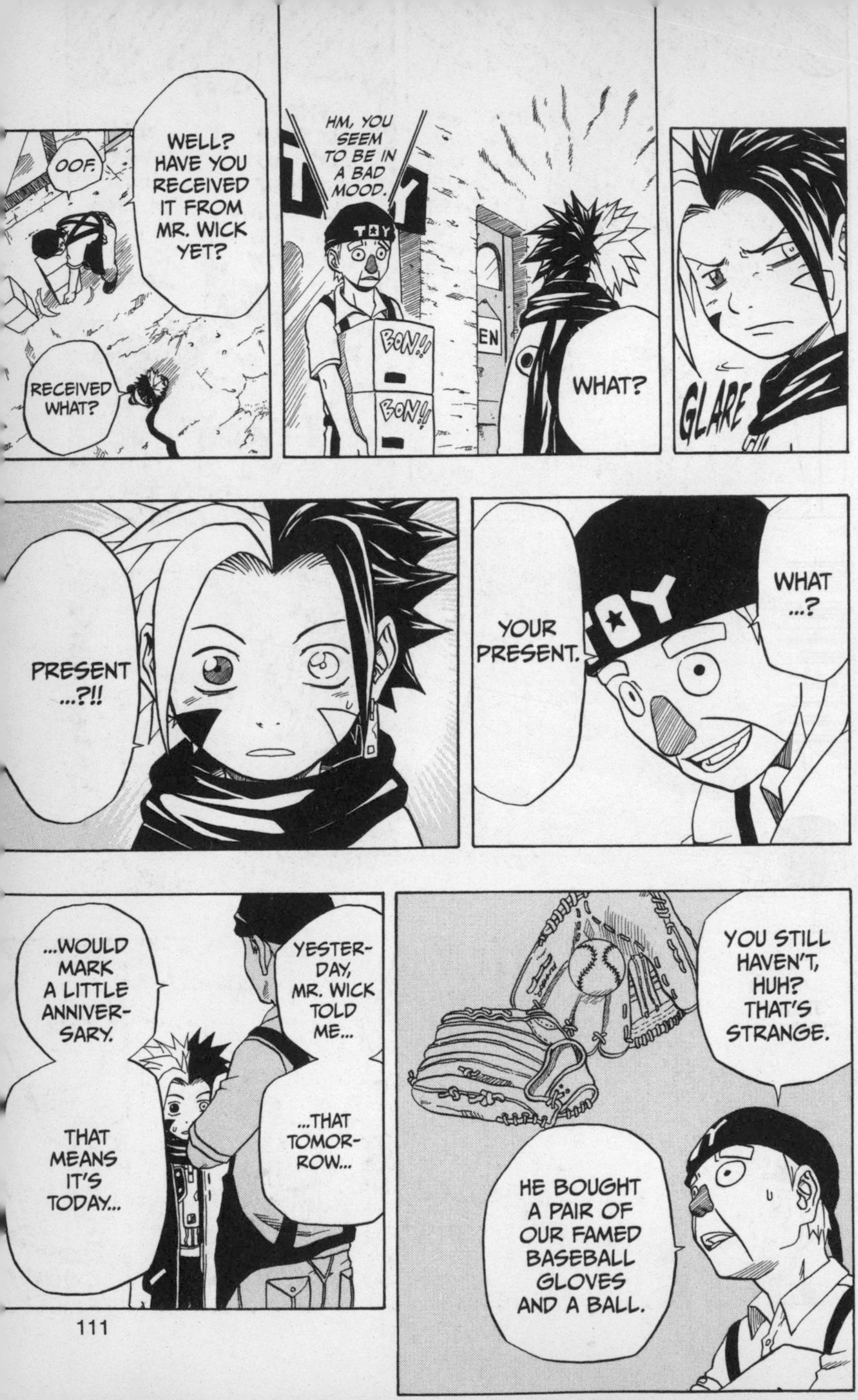
GLARE
WHAT?
HM, YOU SEEM TO BE IN A BAD MOOD.
BON!!
BON!!
WELL? HAVE YOU RECEIVED IT FROM MR. WICK YET?
OOF.
RECEIVED WHAT?
WHAT ...?
YOUR PRESENT.
PRESENT ...?!!
YOU STILL HAVEN'T, HUH? THAT'S STRANGE.
HE BOUGHT A PAIR OF OUR FAMED BASEBALL GLOVES AND A BALL.
YESTER-DAY, MR. WICK TOLD ME...
...THAT TOMOR-ROW...
...WOULD MARK A LITTLE ANNIVER-SARY.
THAT MEANS IT'S TODAY...

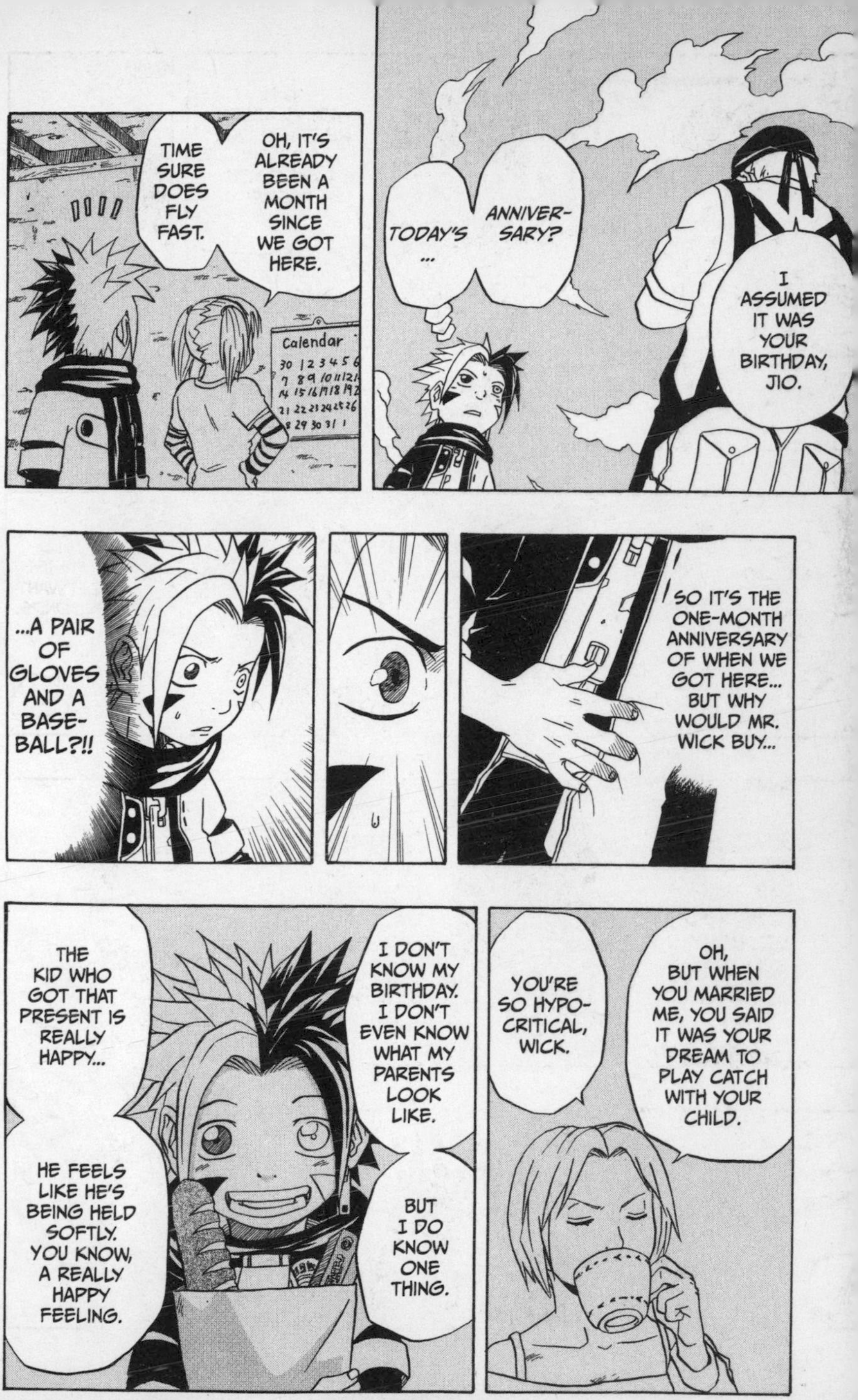
TODAY'S ...
ANNIVER-SARY?
I ASSUMED IT WAS YOUR BIRTHDAY, JIO.
OH, IT'S ALREADY BEEN A MONTH SINCE WE GOT HERE.
TIME SURE DOES FLY FAST.
Calendar
SO IT'S THE ONE-MONTH ANNIVERSARY OF WHEN WE GOT HERE... BUT WHY WOULD MR. WICK BUY...
...A PAIR OF GLOVES AND A BASE-BALL?!!
OH, BUT WHEN YOU MARRIED ME, YOU SAID IT WAS YOUR DREAM TO PLAY CATCH WITH YOUR CHILD.
YOU'RE SO HYPO-CRITICAL, WICK.
I DON'T KNOW MY BIRTHDAY. I DON'T EVEN KNOW WHAT MY PARENTS LOOK LIKE.
THE KID WHO GOT THAT PRESENT IS REALLY HAPPY...
BUT I DO KNOW ONE THING.
HE FEELS LIKE HE'S BEING HELD SOFTLY. YOU KNOW, A REALLY HAPPY FEELING.

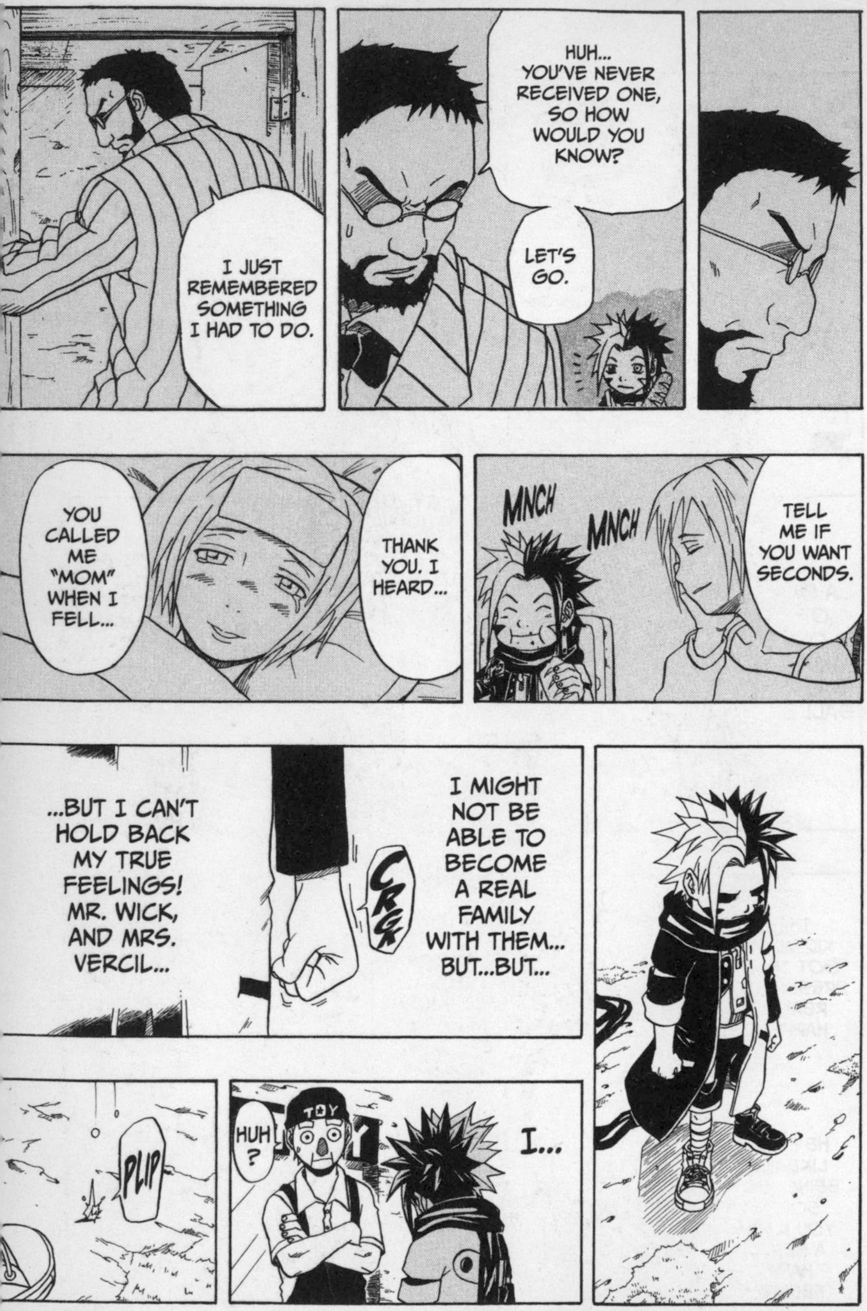
HUH... YOU'VE NEVER RECEIVED ONE, SO HOW WOULD YOU KNOW?
LET'S GO.
I JUST REMEMBERED SOMETHING I HAD TO DO.
TELL ME IF YOU WANT SECONDS.
MNCH
MNCH
THANK YOU. I HEARD...
YOU CALLED ME "MOM" WHEN I FELL...
I MIGHT NOT BE ABLE TO BECOME A REAL FAMILY WITH THEM... BUT...BUT...
CRCK
...BUT I CAN'T HOLD BACK MY TRUE FEELINGS! MR. WICK, AND MRS. VERCIL...
I...
HUH?
TOY
PLIP

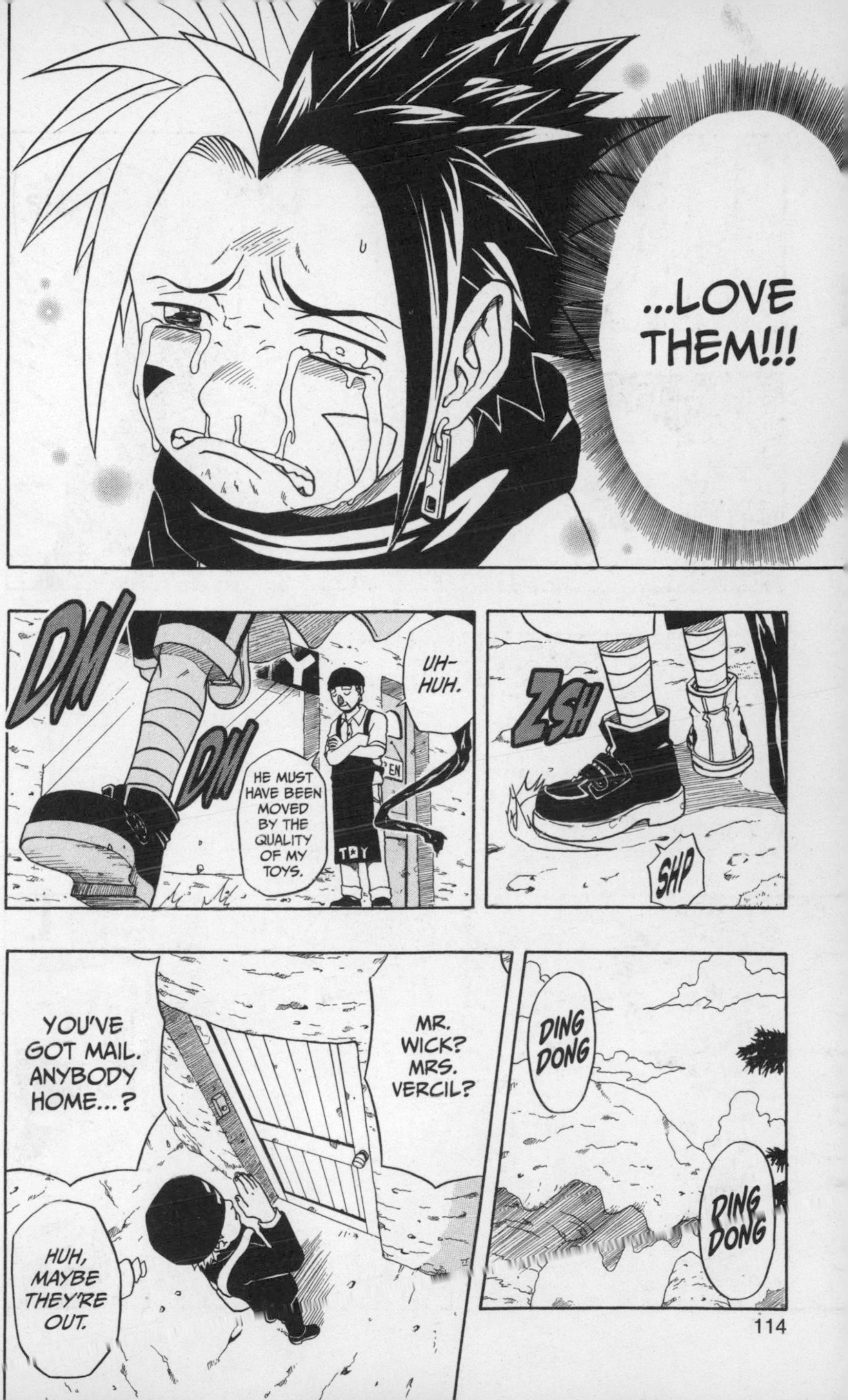
...LOVE THEM!!!
ZSH
SHP
UH-HUH.
DM
DM
HE MUST HAVE BEEN MOVED BY THE QUALITY OF MY TOYS.
TOY
DING DONG
DING DONG
MR. WICK? MRS. VERCIL?
YOU'VE GOT MAIL. ANYBODY HOME...?
HUH, MAYBE THEY'RE OUT.

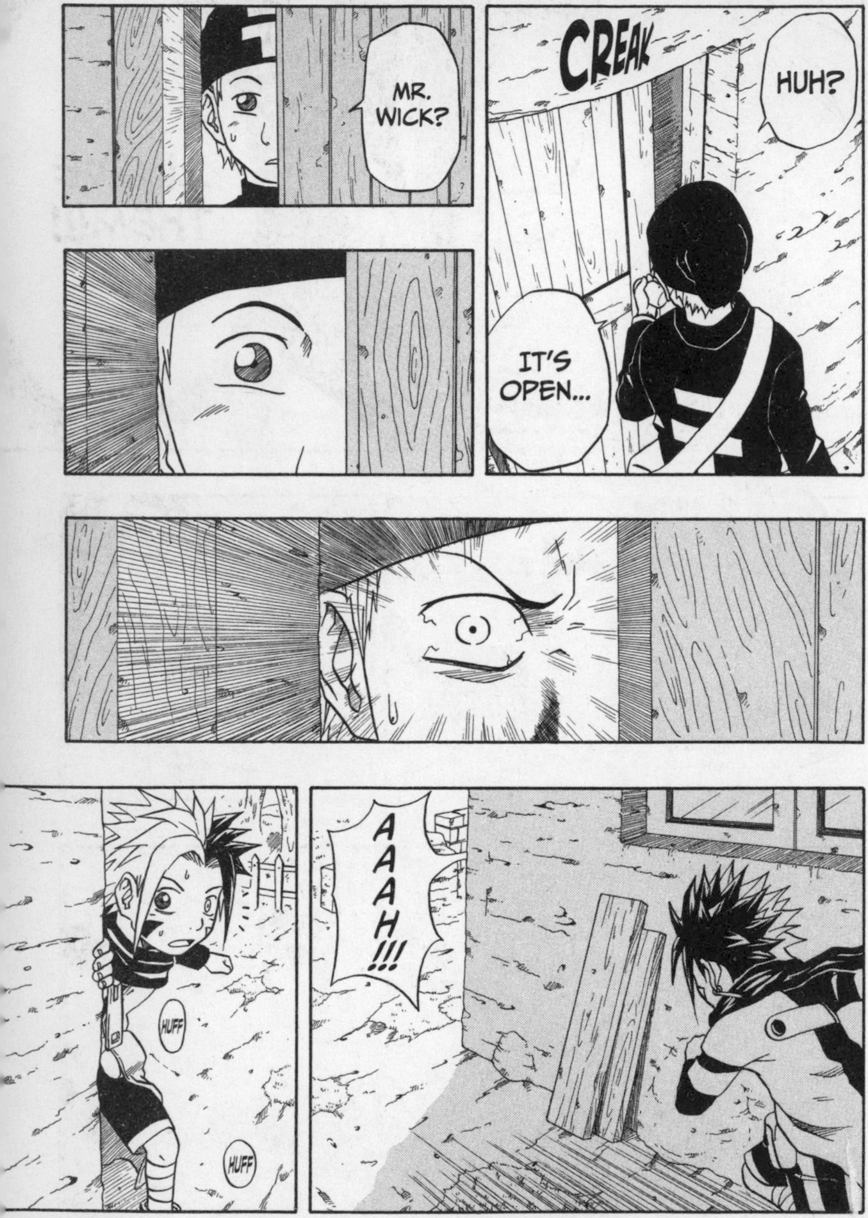
CREAK
HUH?
IT'S OPEN...
MR. WICK?
AAAAH!!!
HUFF
HUFF

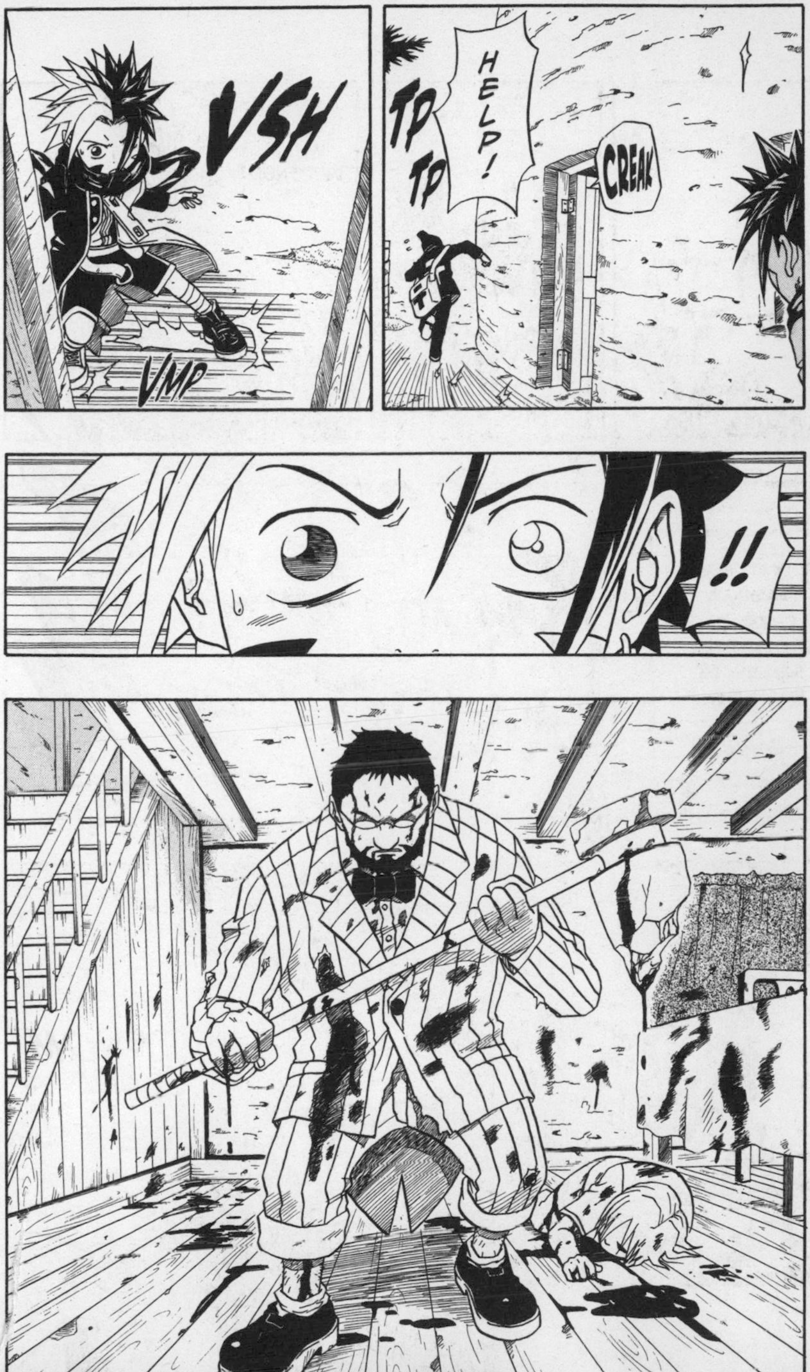
CREAK
HELP!
TP TP
VSH
VMP
!!

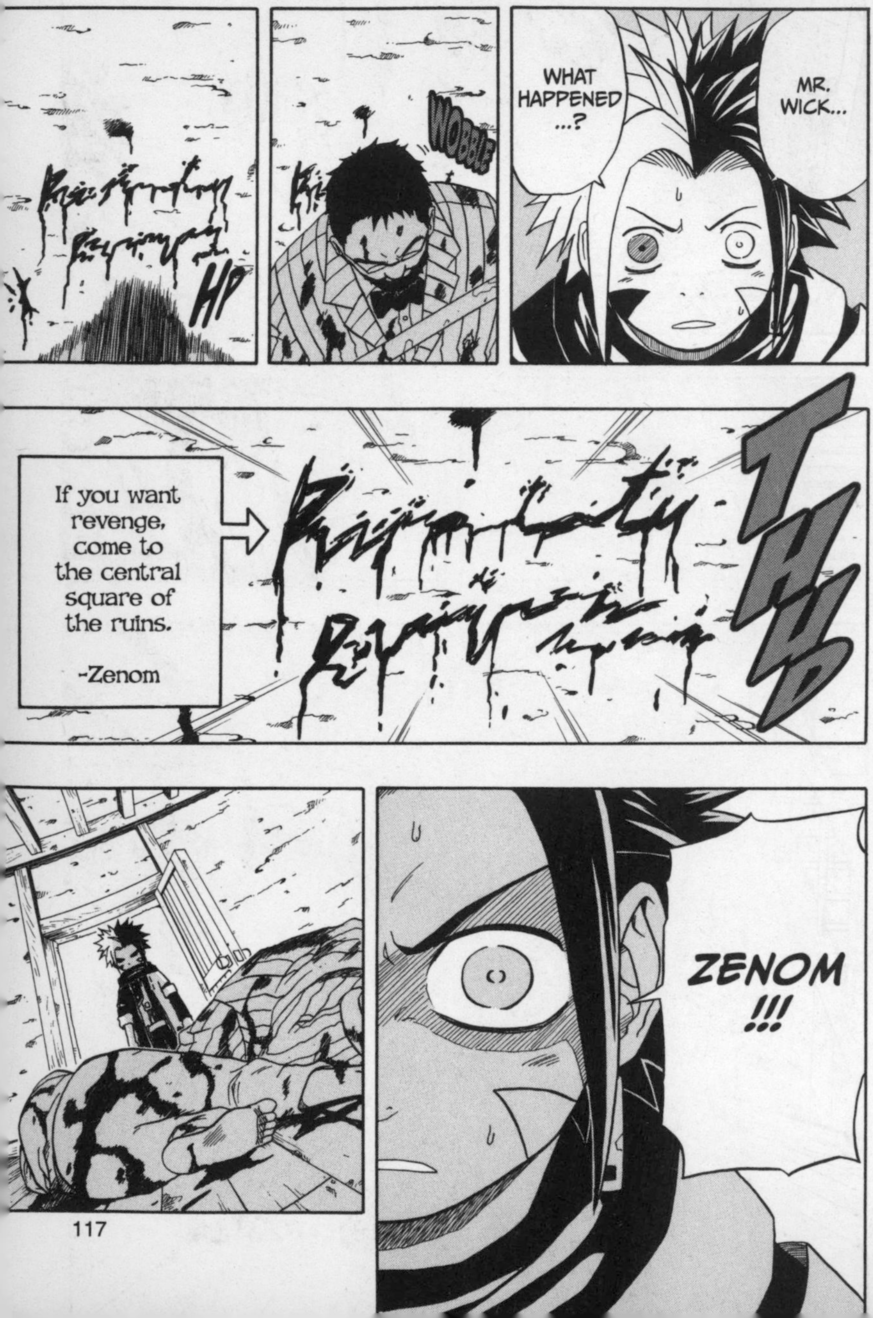
MR. WICK...
WHAT HAPPENED ...?
WOBBLE
HP
THUD
If you want revenge, come to the central square of the ruins.
-Zenom
ZENOM !!!

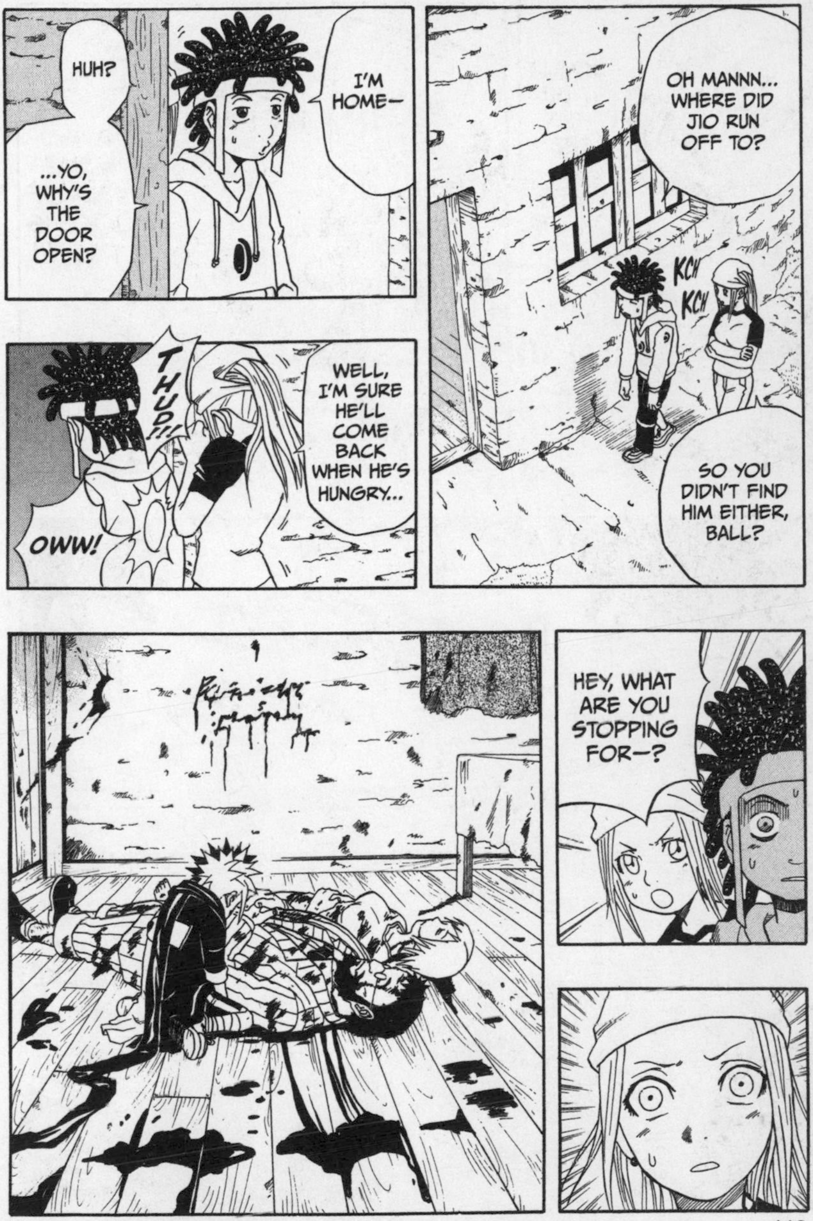
OH MANNN... WHERE DID JIO RUN OFF TO?
KCH
KCH
SO YOU DIDN'T FIND HIM EITHER, BALL?
I'M HOME—
HUH?
...YO, WHY'S THE DOOR OPEN?
WELL, I'M SURE HE'LL COME BACK WHEN HE'S HUNGRY...
THUD!!!
OWW!
HEY, WHAT ARE YOU STOPPING FOR—?

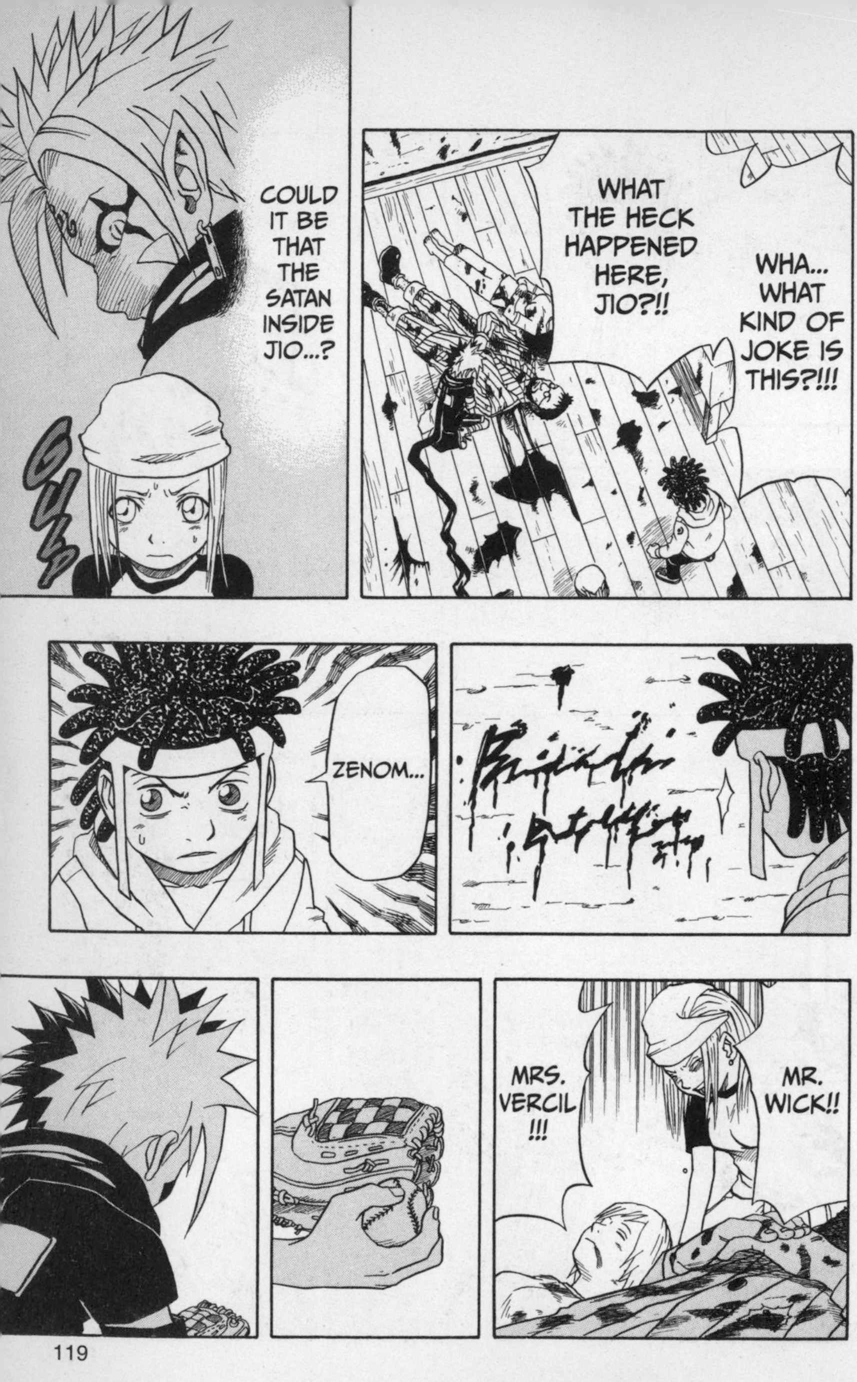
WHA... WHAT KIND OF JOKE IS THIS?!!!
WHAT THE HECK HAPPENED HERE, JIO?!!
COULD IT BE THAT THE SATAN INSIDE JIO...?
GULP
ZENOM...
MR. WICK!!
MRS. VERCIL!!!

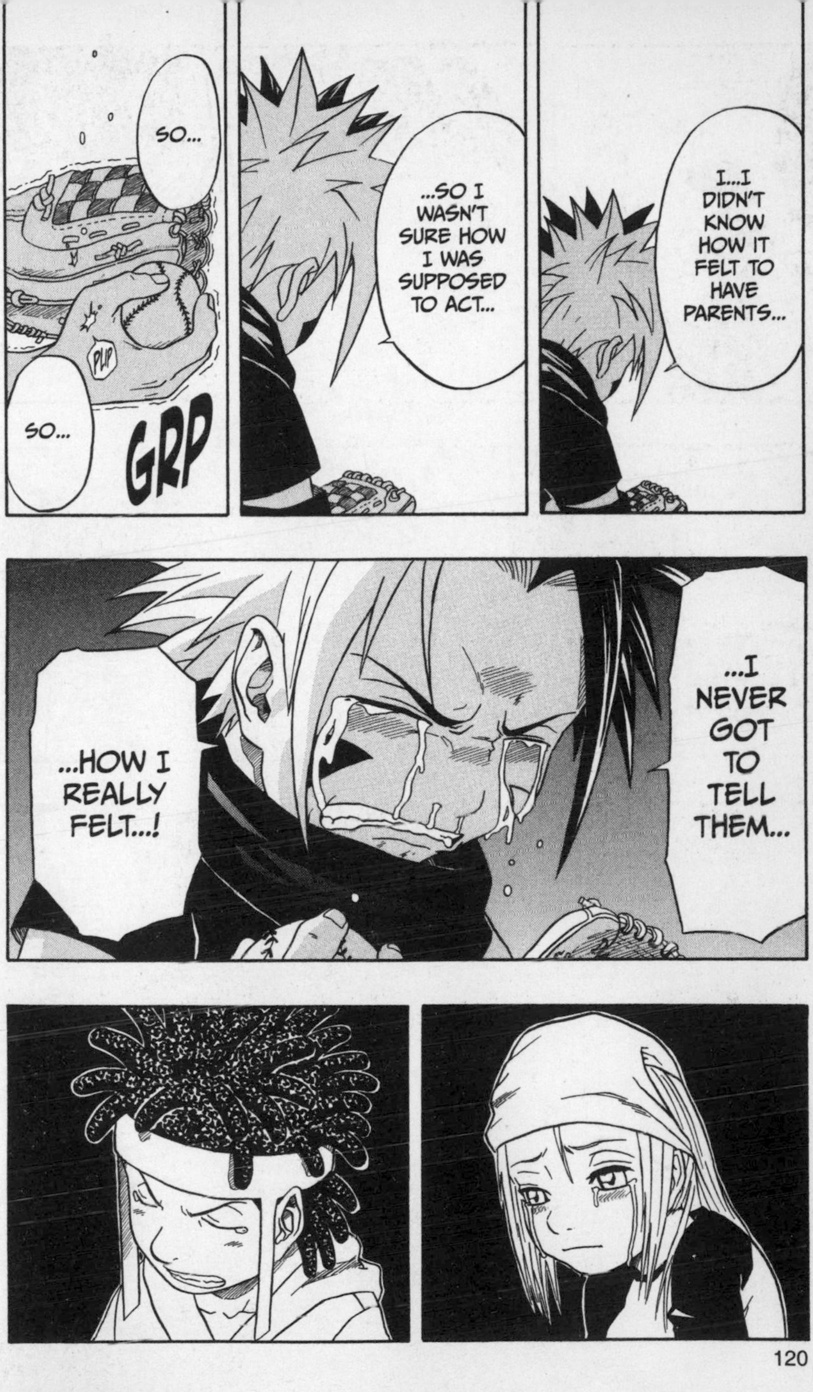
I...I DIDN'T KNOW HOW IT FELT TO HAVE PARENTS...
...SO I WASN'T SURE HOW I WAS SUPPOSED TO ACT...
SO...
PLIP
SO...
GRP
...I NEVER GOT TO TELL THEM...
...HOW I REALLY FELT...!

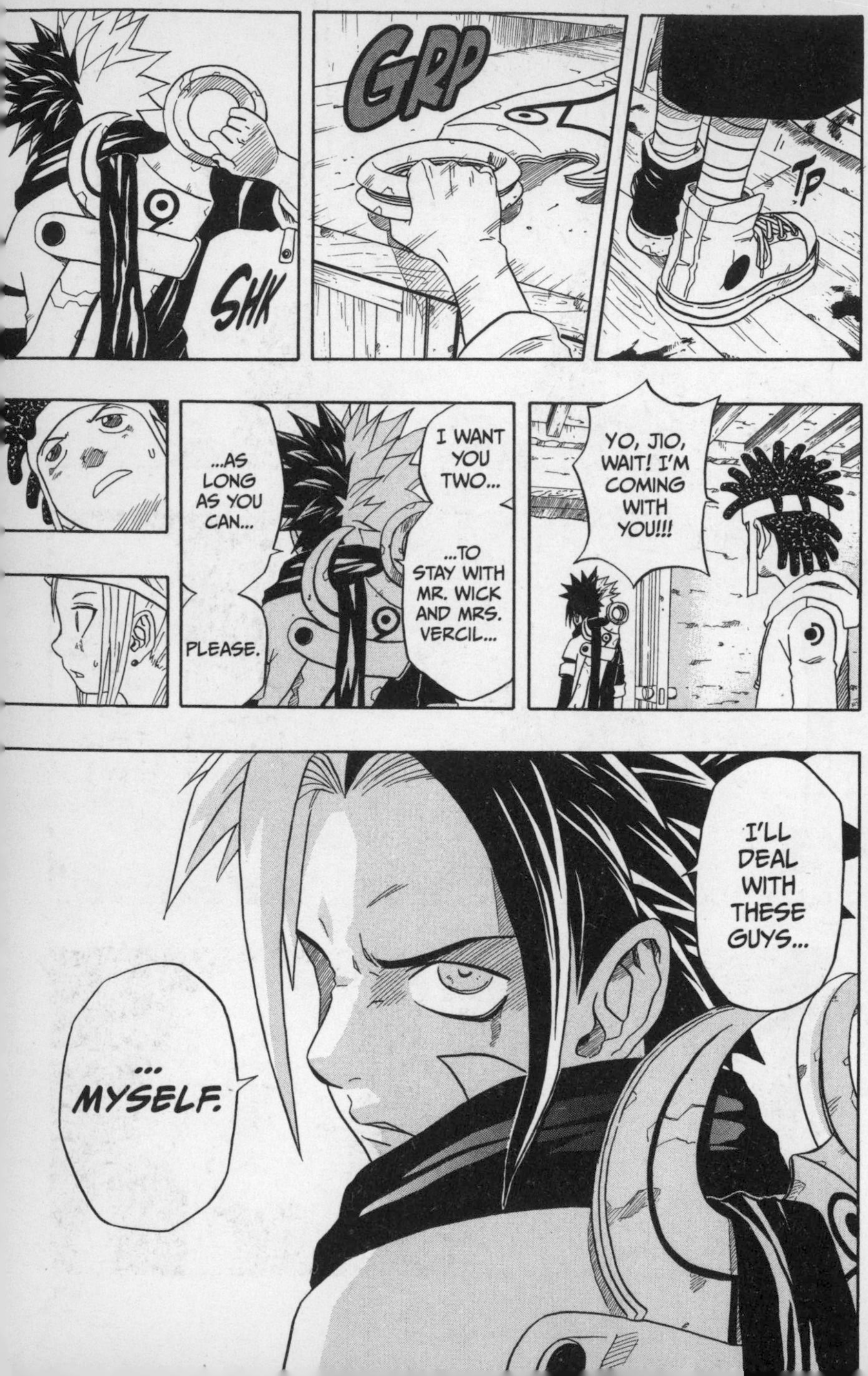
TP
GRP
SHK
YO, JIO, WAIT! I'M COMING WITH YOU!!!
I WANT YOU TWO...
...TO STAY WITH MR. WICK AND MRS. VERCIL...
...AS LONG AS YOU CAN...
PLEASE.
I'LL DEAL WITH THESE GUYS...
... MYSELF.

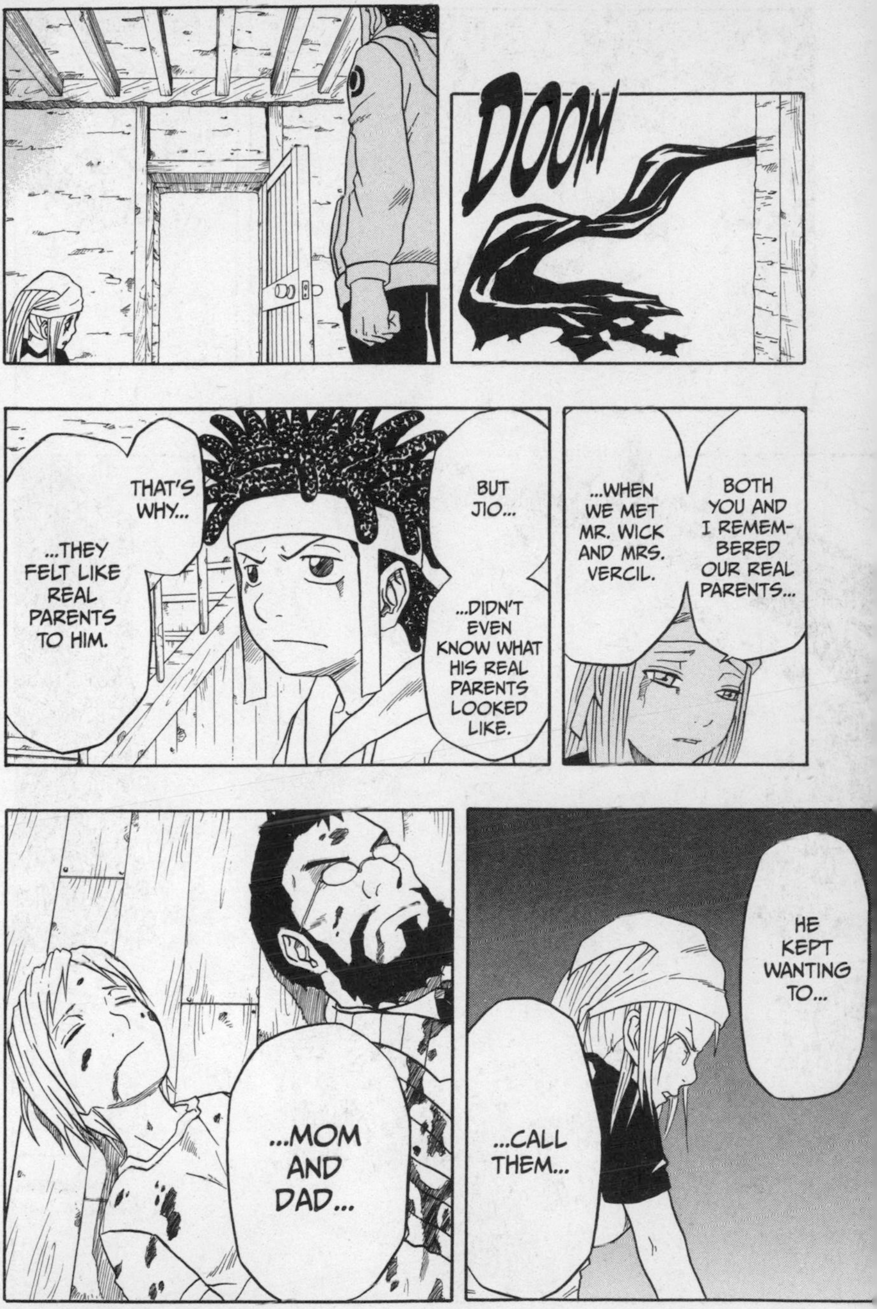
DOOM
BOTH YOU AND I REMEMBERED OUR REAL PARENTS...
...WHEN WE MET MR. WICK AND MRS. VERCIL.
BUT JIO...
...DIDN'T EVEN KNOW WHAT HIS REAL PARENTS LOOKED LIKE.
THAT'S WHY...
...THEY FELT LIKE REAL PARENTS TO HIM.
HE KEPT WANTING TO...
...CALL THEM...
...MOM AND DAD...

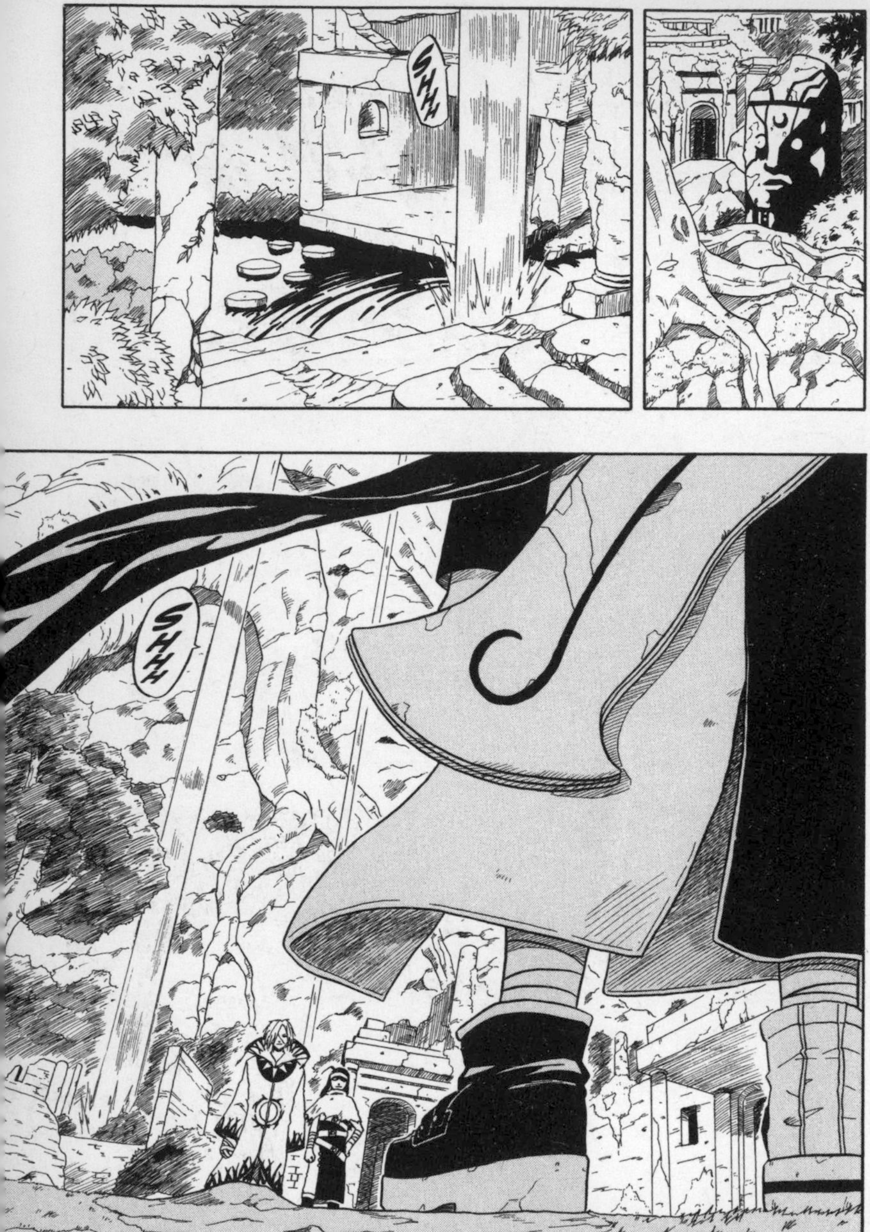
SHHH
SHHH

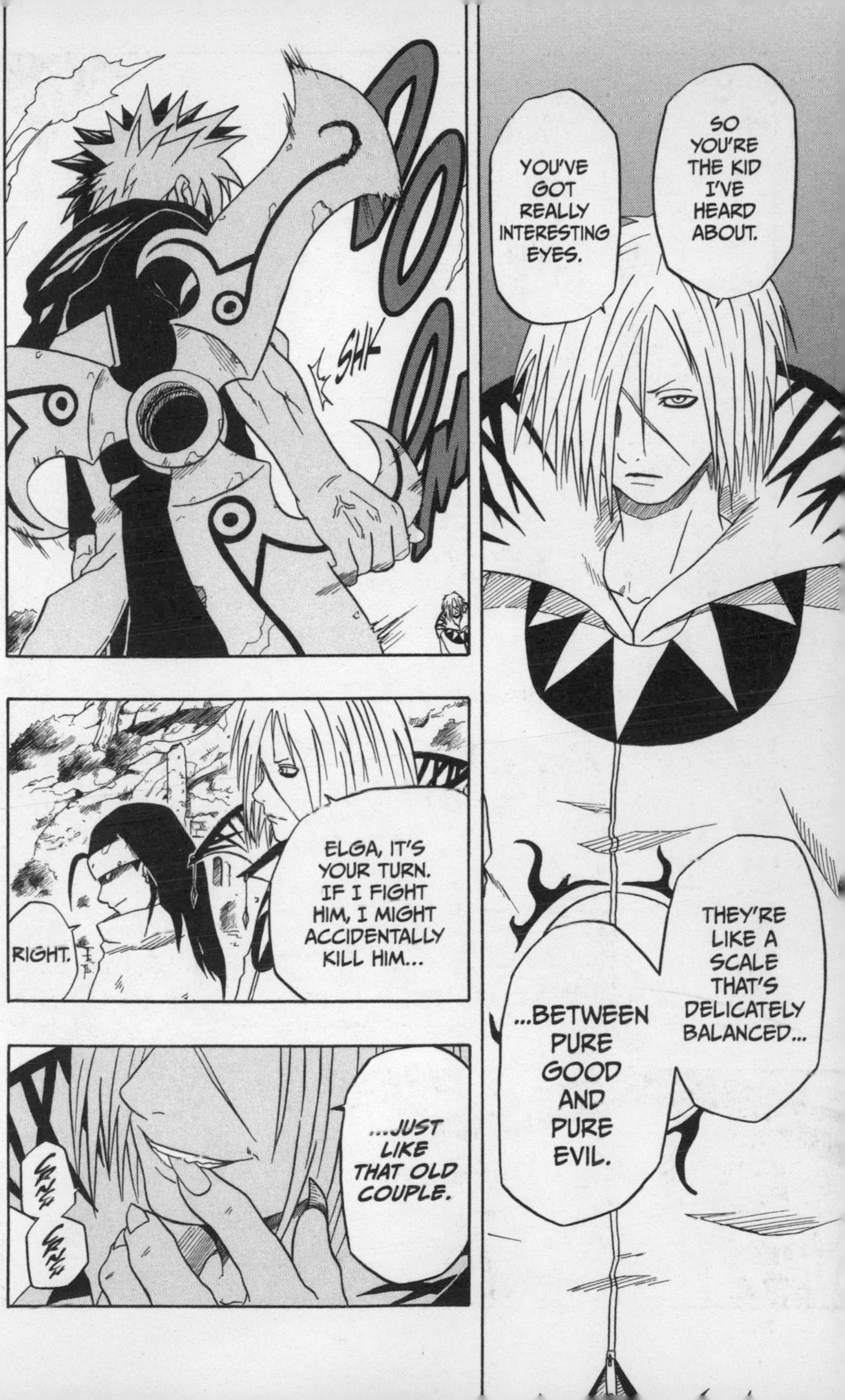
SO YOU'RE THE KID I'VE HEARD ABOUT.
YOU'VE GOT REALLY INTERESTING EYES.
THEY'RE LIKE A SCALE THAT'S DELICATELY BALANCED...
...BETWEEN PURE GOOD AND PURE EVIL.
SHK
ELGA, IT'S YOUR TURN. IF I FIGHT HIM, I MIGHT ACCIDENTALLY KILL HIM...
RIGHT.
...JUST LIKE THAT OLD COUPLE.

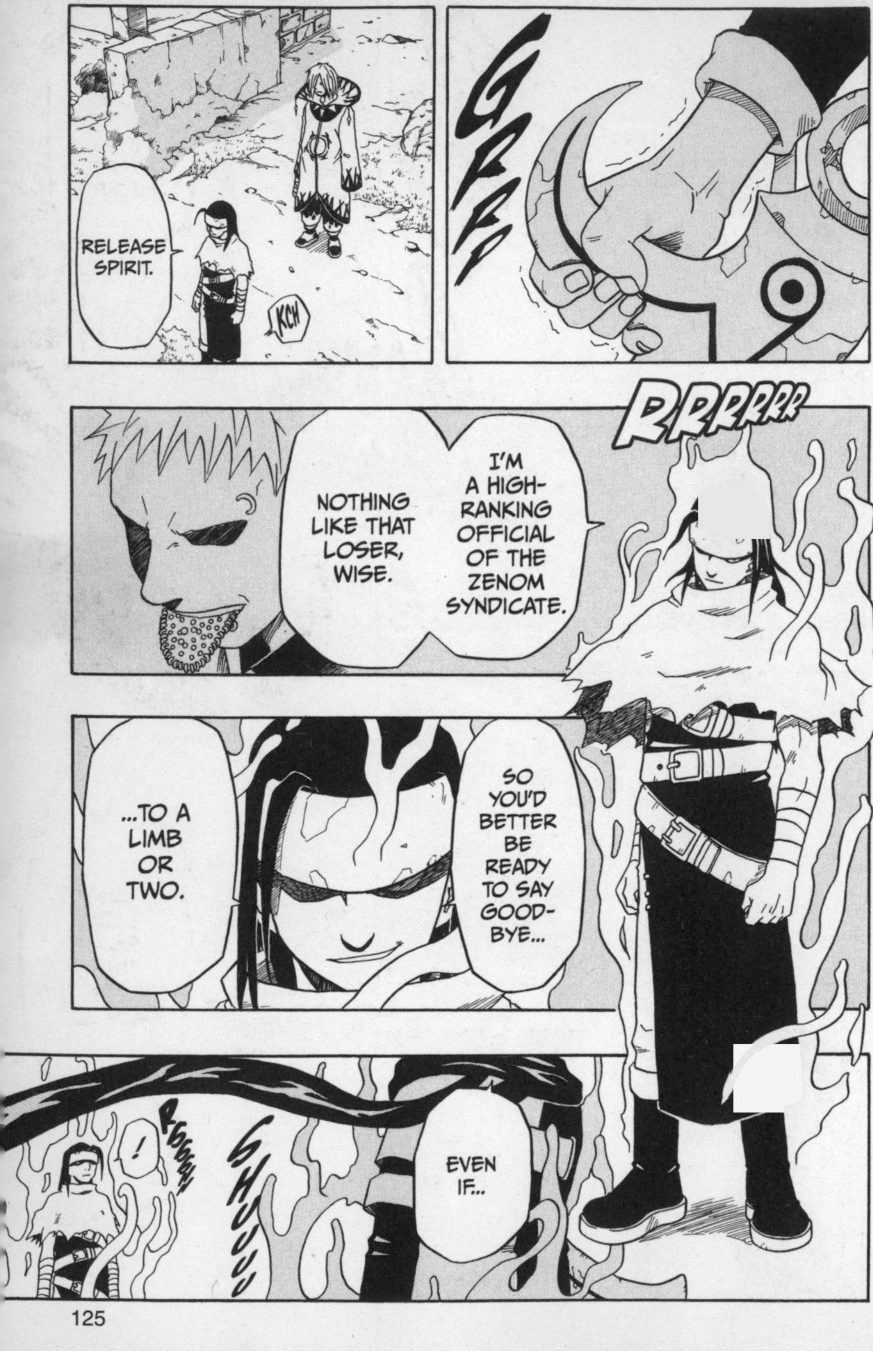
GRPP
RELEASE SPIRIT.
KCH
RRRRRR
I'M A HIGH-RANKING OFFICIAL OF THE ZENOM SYNDICATE.
NOTHING LIKE THAT LOSER, WISE.
SO YOU'D BETTER BE READY TO SAY GOOD-BYE...
...TO A LIMB OR TWO.
EVEN IF...
!

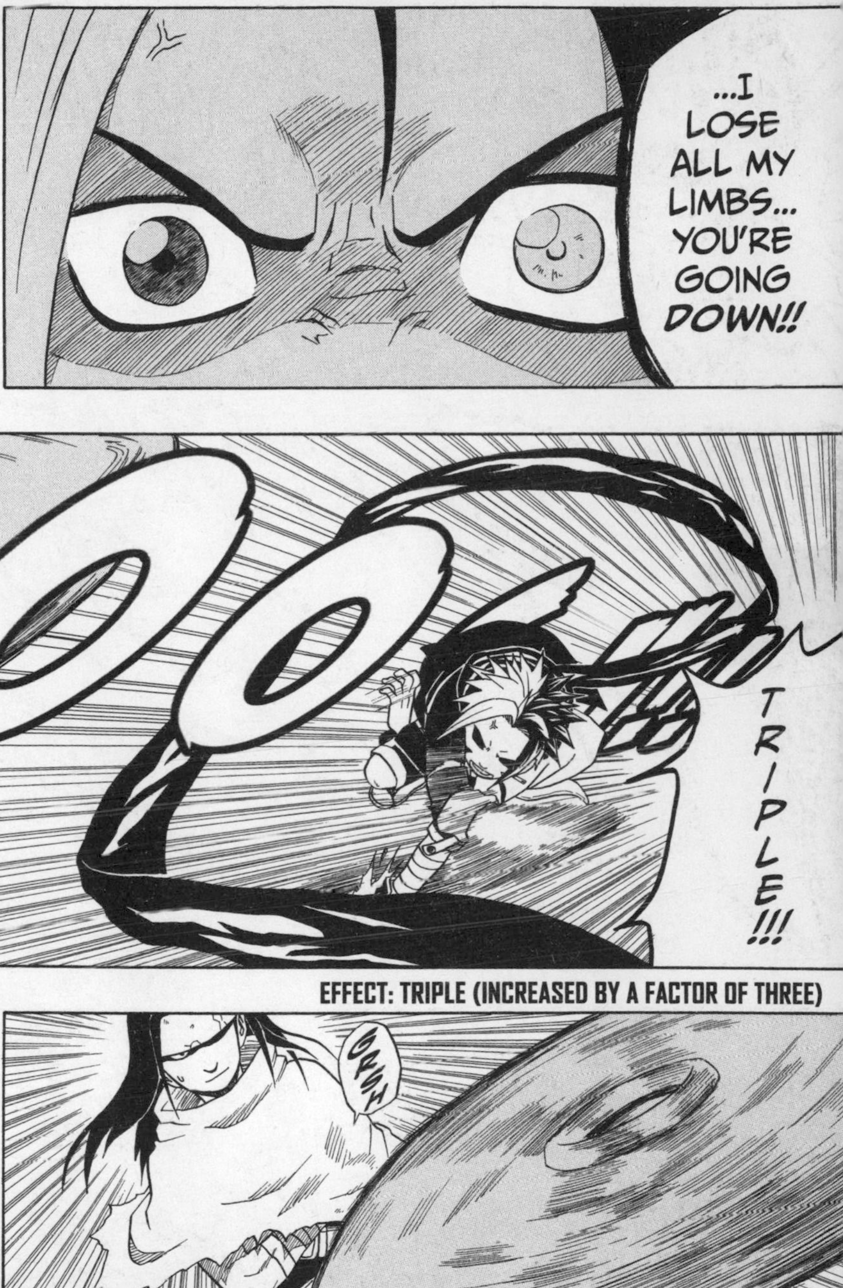
...I LOSE ALL MY LIMBS... YOU'RE GOING DOWN!!
TRIPLE!!!
EFFECT: TRIPLE (INCREASED BY A FACTOR OF THREE)
GRSH

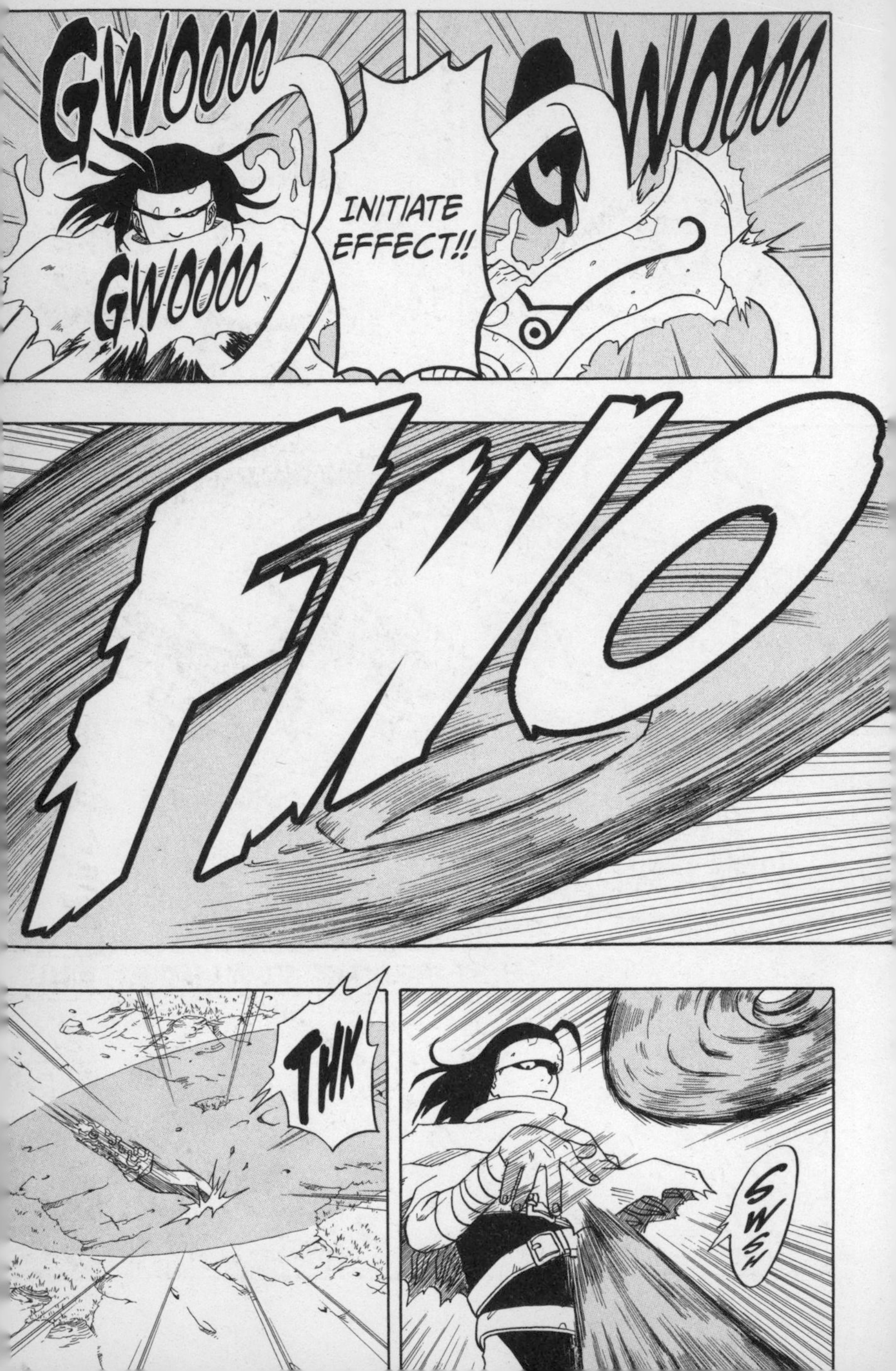
WOOOO
INITIATE EFFECT!!
GWOOOO
GWOOOO
FWO
SWSH
THK

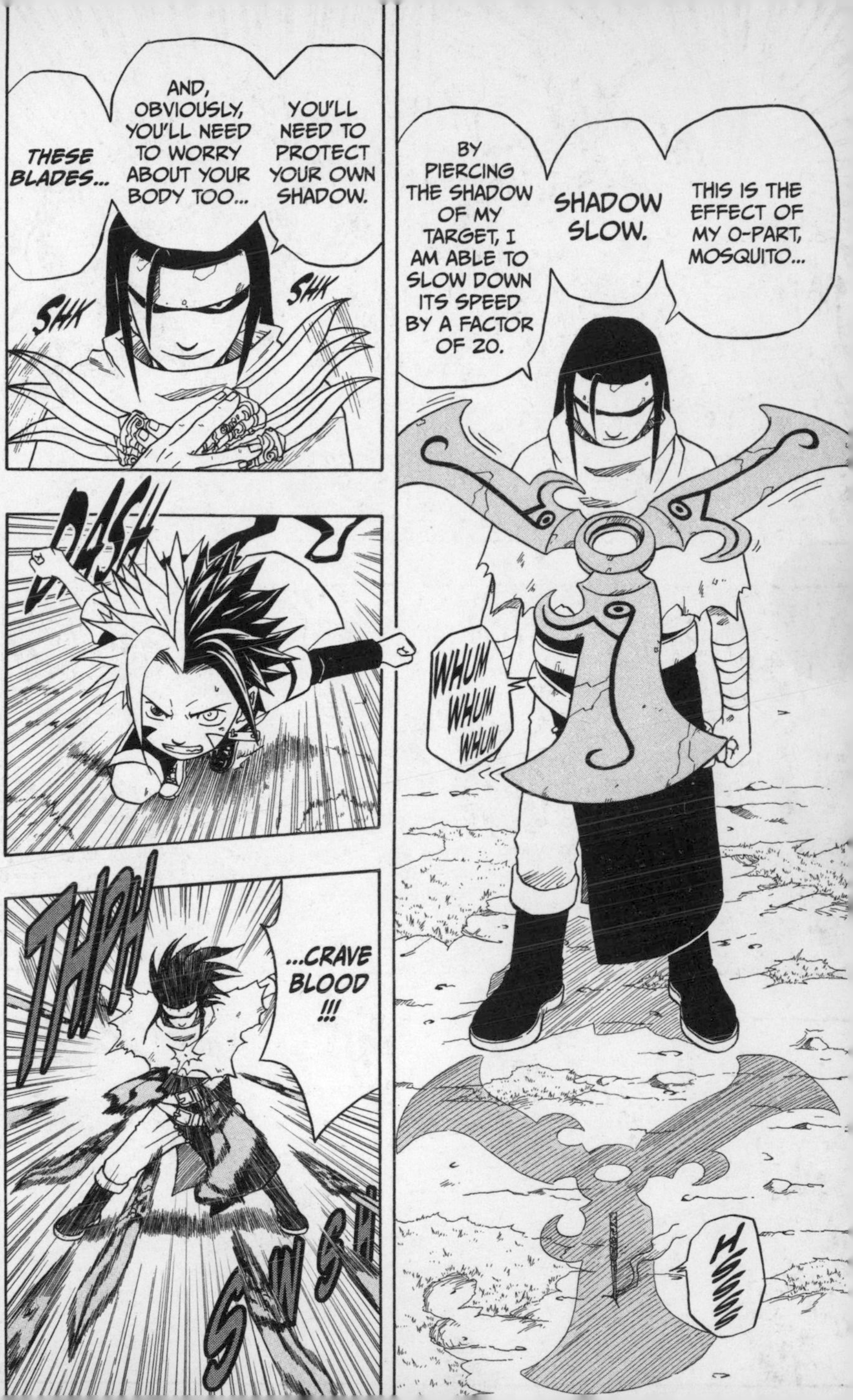
THIS IS THE EFFECT OF MY O-PART, MOSQUITO...
SHADOW SLOW.
BY PIERCING THE SHADOW OF MY TARGET, I AM ABLE TO SLOW DOWN ITS SPEED BY A FACTOR OF 20.
WHUM WHUM WHUM
HSSSSS
YOU'LL NEED TO PROTECT YOUR OWN SHADOW.
AND, OBVIOUSLY, YOU'LL NEED TO WORRY ABOUT YOUR BODY TOO...
THESE BLADES...
SHK
SHK
DASH
...CRAVE BLOOD !!!
THPH

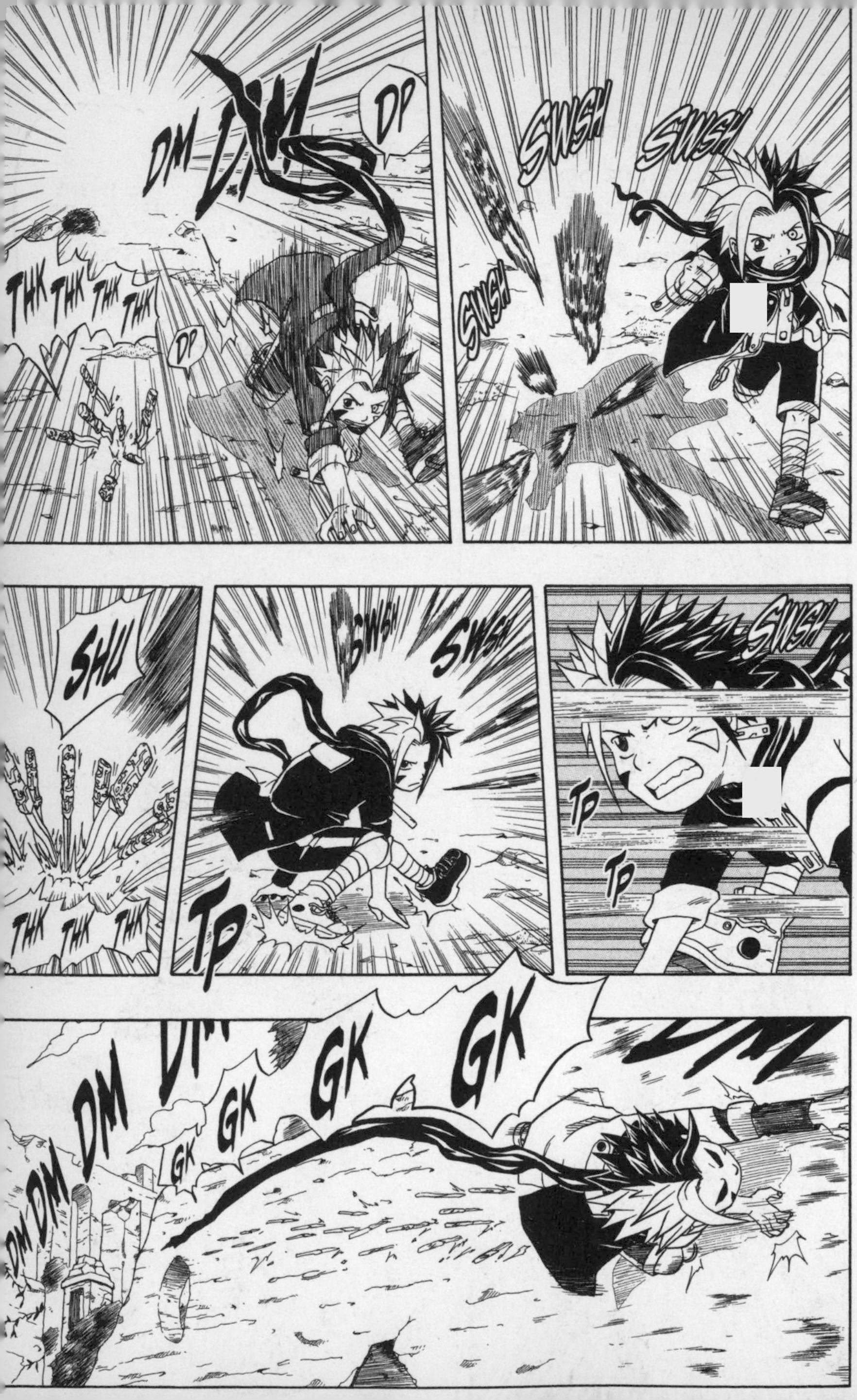
SWSH
SWSH
SWSH
DP
DM DM
THK THK THK THK
DP
SWSH
Tp
Tp
SWSH
SWSH
Tp
SHU
THK THK THK
DM
GK GK GK GK
DM DM DM DM

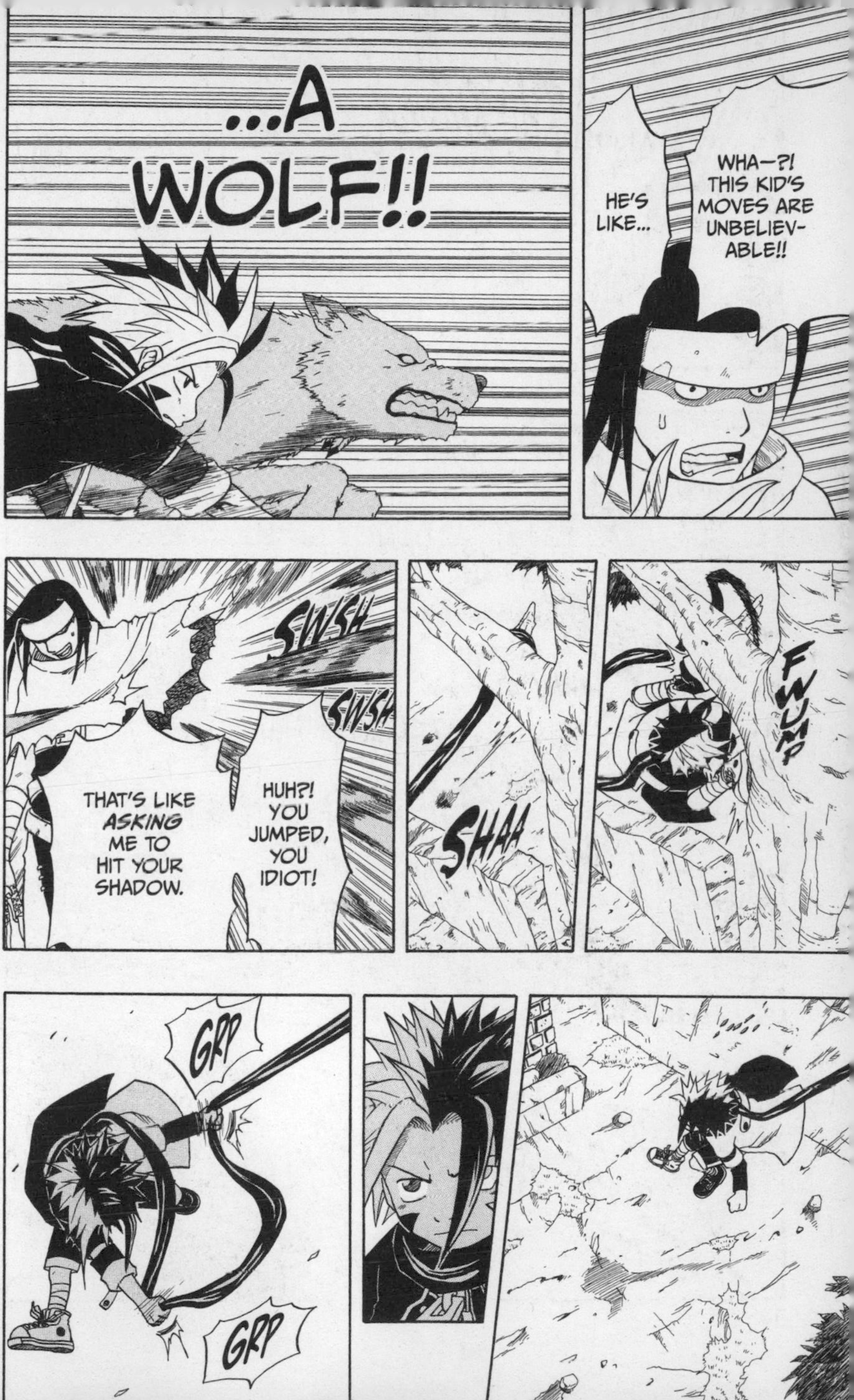
WHA—?! THIS KID'S MOVES ARE UNBELIEV-ABLE!!
HE'S LIKE...
...A WOLF!!
FWUMP
SHAA
SWSH
SWSH
HUH?! YOU JUMPED, YOU IDIOT!
THAT'S LIKE *ASKING* ME TO HIT YOUR SHADOW.
GRP
GRP

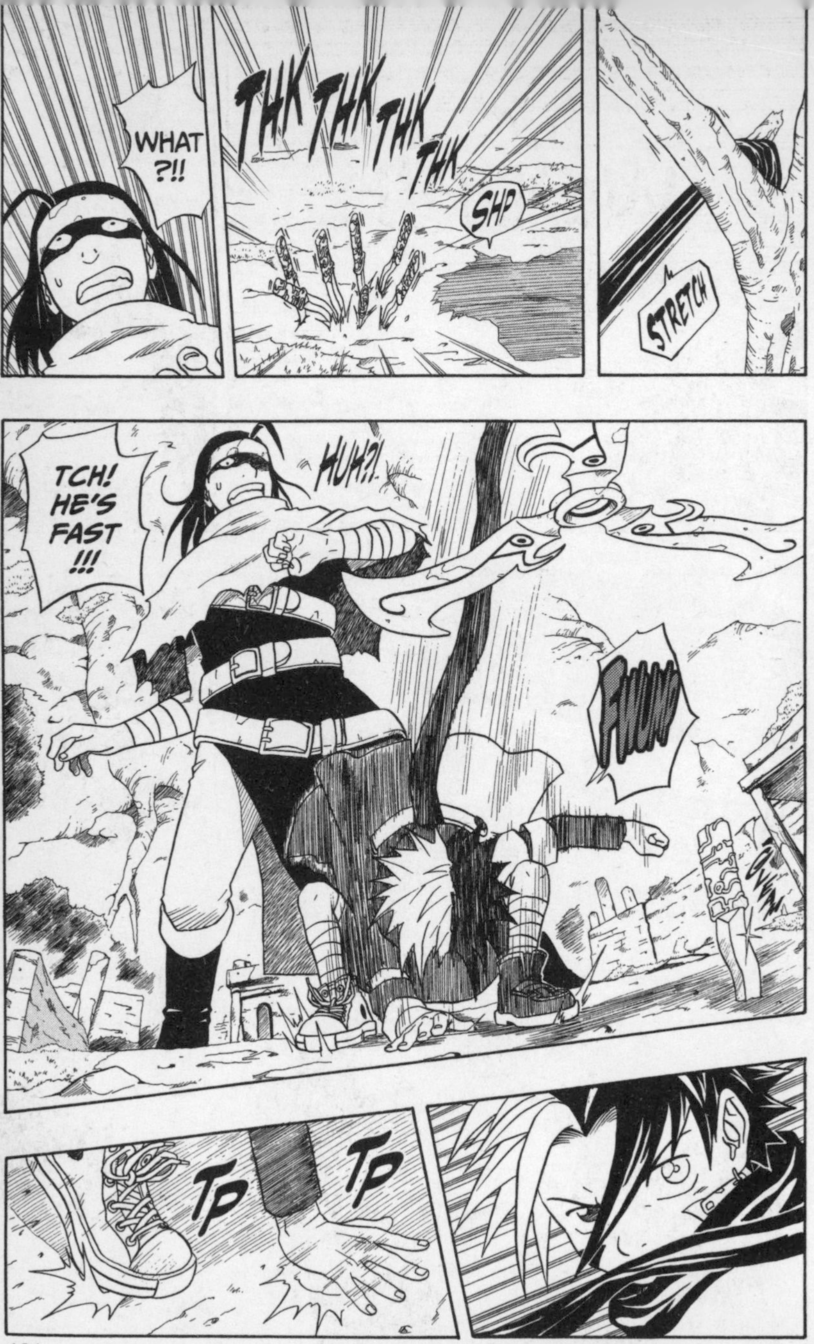
STRETCH
THK THK THK THK
SHP
WHAT ?!!
HUH?!
FWUMP
TCH! HE'S FAST !!!
TP
TP

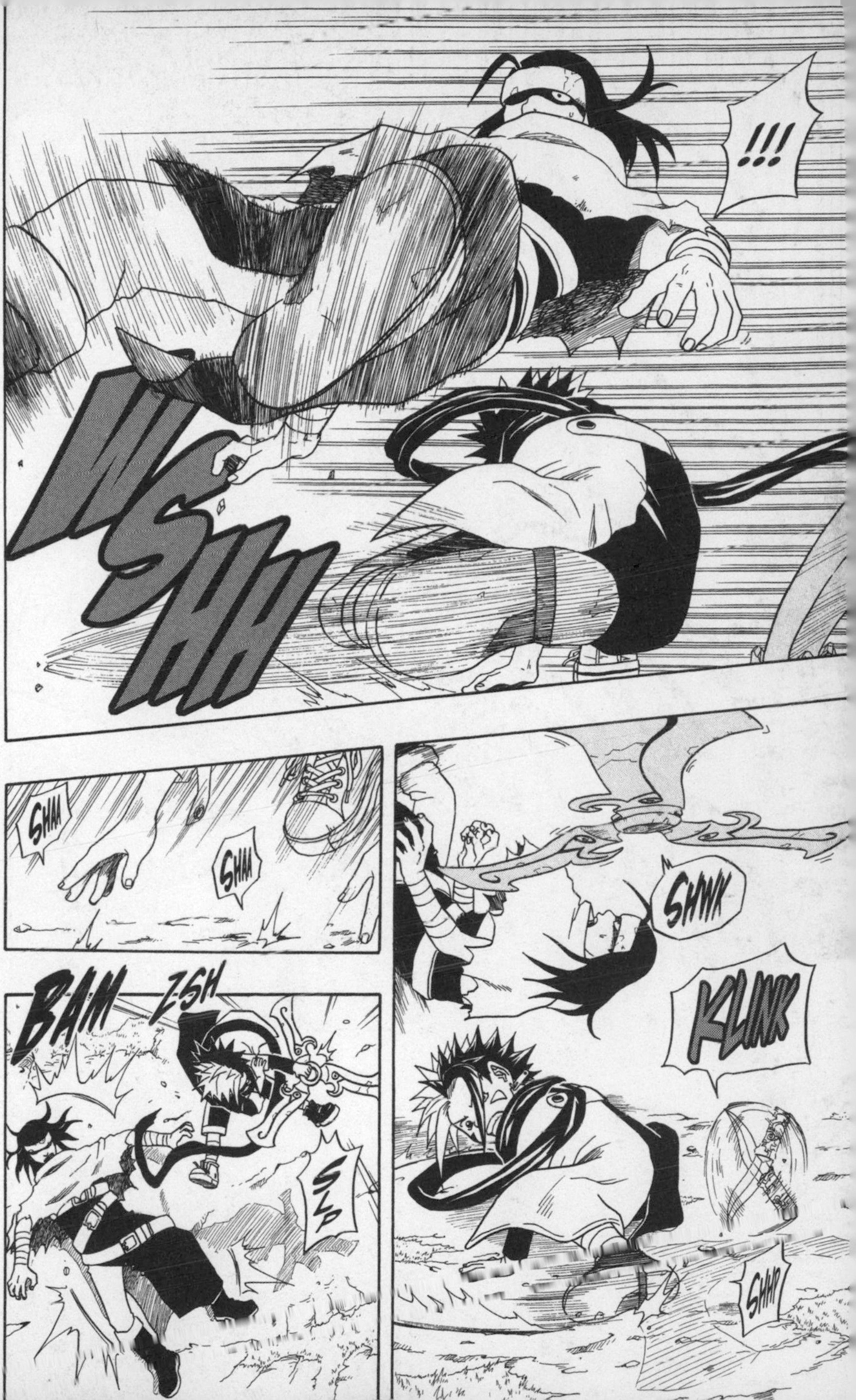
!!!
WSHH
SHWK
KLINK
SHHP
SHAA
SHAA
BAM
Z-SH
SLP

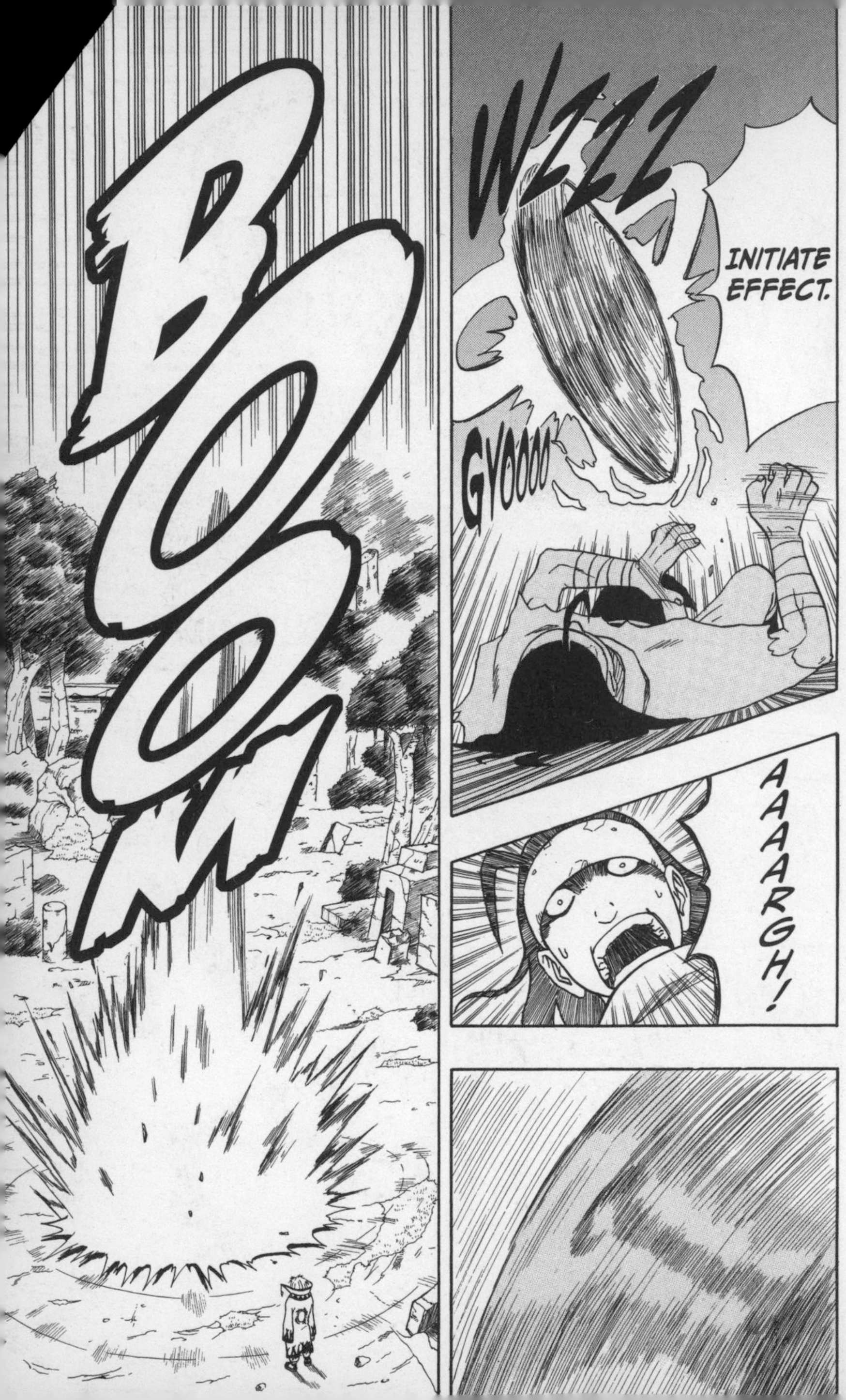
WZZZ
INITIATE EFFECT.
GYOOOO
AAAARGH!
BOOM

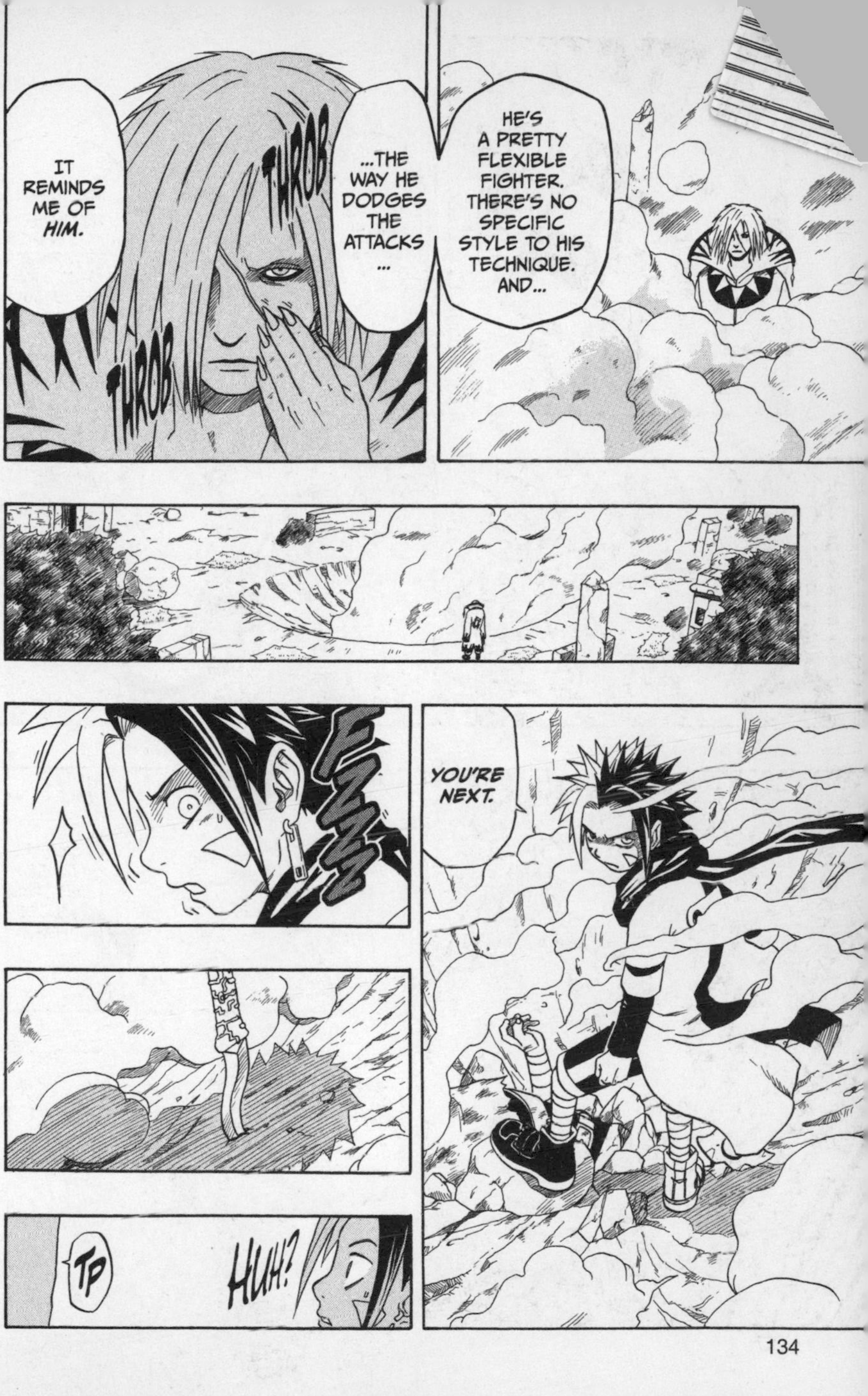
HE'S A PRETTY FLEXIBLE FIGHTER. THERE'S NO SPECIFIC STYLE TO HIS TECHNIQUE. AND...
...THE WAY HE DODGES THE ATTACKS ...
THROB
THROB
IT REMINDS ME OF *HIM.*
YOU'RE NEXT.
FZZZ
TP
HUH?

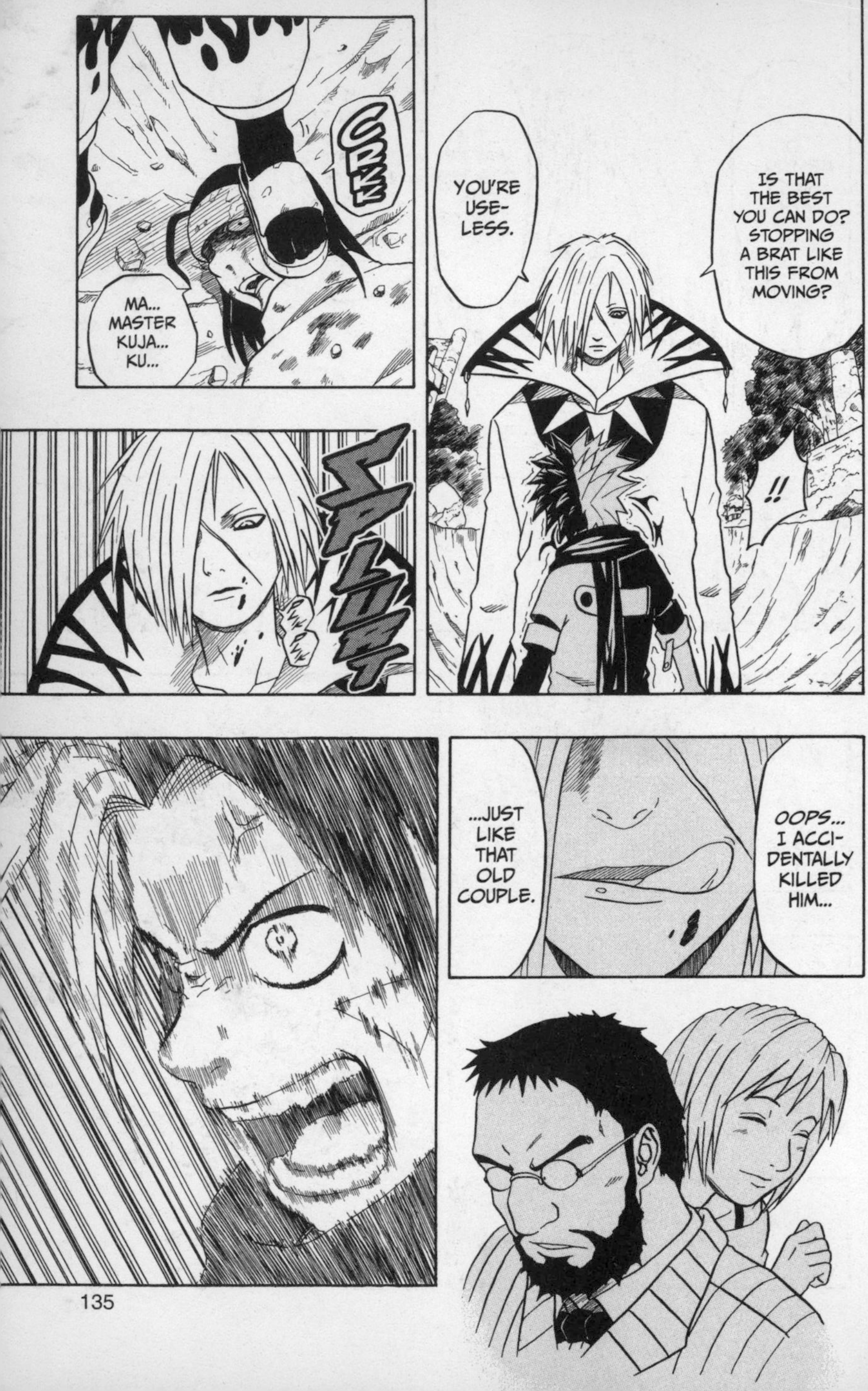
IS THAT THE BEST YOU CAN DO? STOPPING A BRAT LIKE THIS FROM MOVING?
YOU'RE USE-LESS.
!!
MA... MASTER KUJA... KU...
OOPS... I ACCI-DENTALLY KILLED HIM...
...JUST LIKE THAT OLD COUPLE.

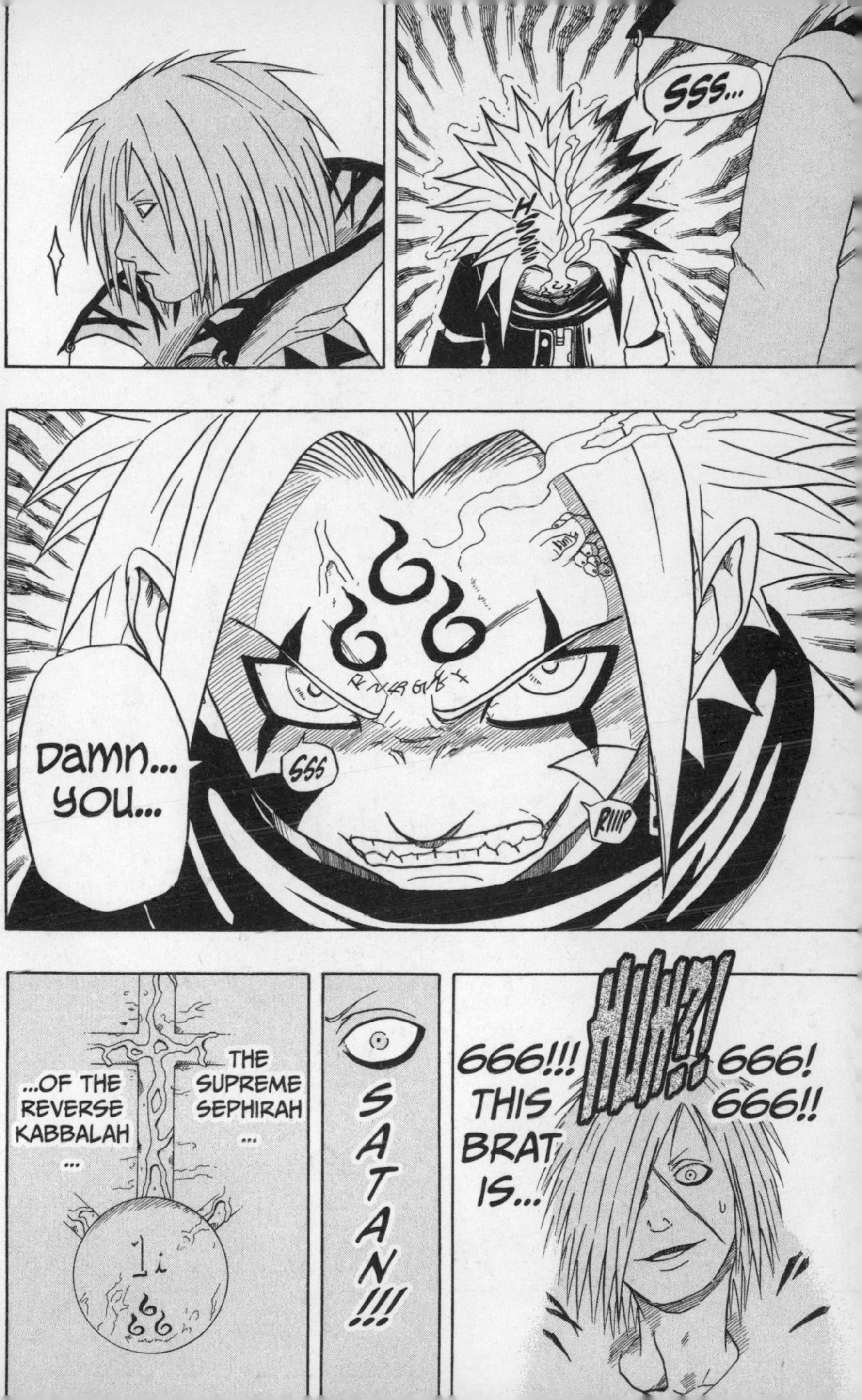

SSS...
HSSSS
SSS
RIIIP
DAMN... YOU...
HUH?!
666!!! THIS BRAT IS...
666! 666!!
SATAN!!!
THE SUPREME SEPHIRAH...
...OF THE REVERSE KABBALAH...

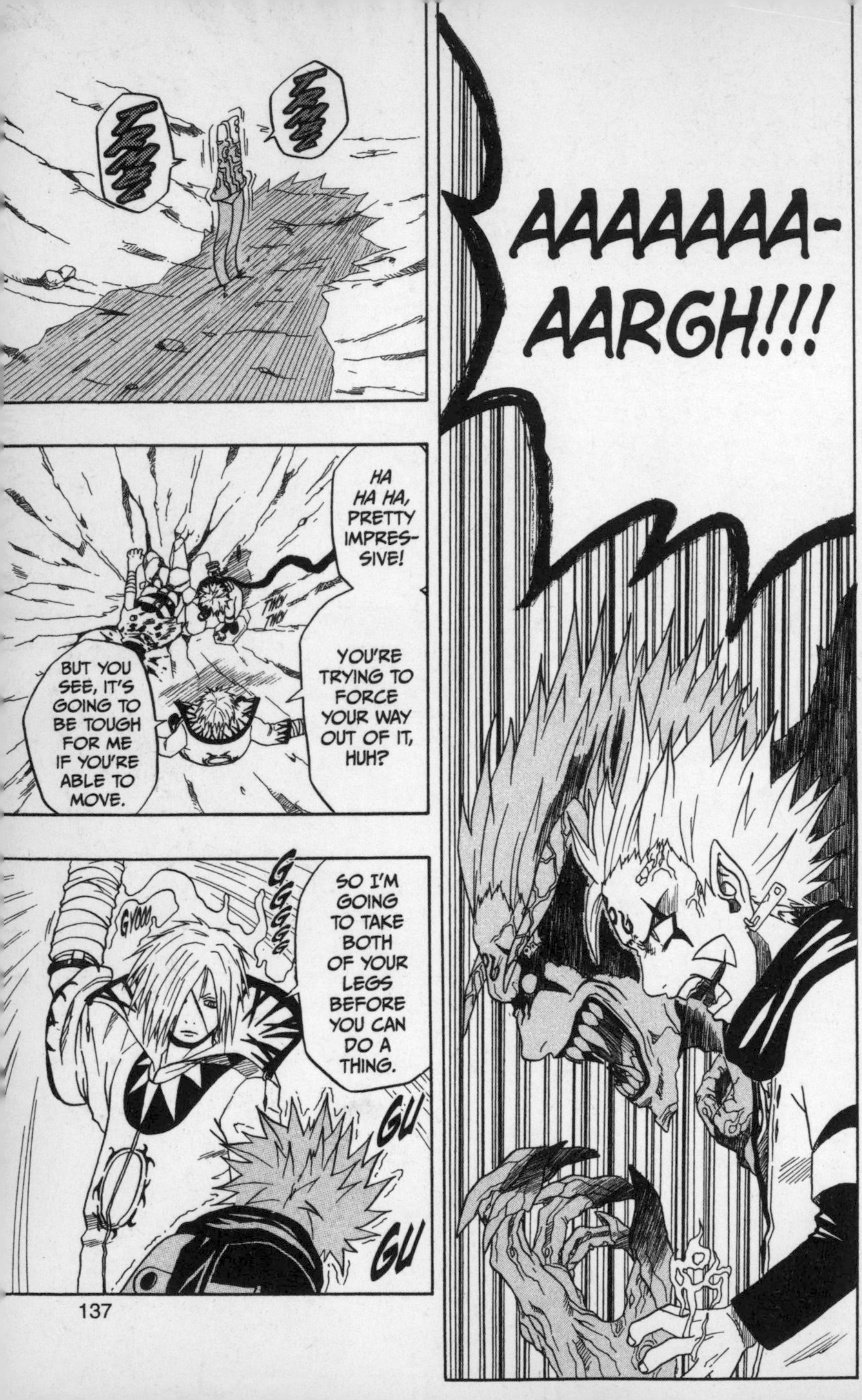
AAAAAAA-AARGH!!!
HA HA HA, PRETTY IMPRES-SIVE!
YOU'RE TRYING TO FORCE YOUR WAY OUT OF IT, HUH?
BUT YOU SEE, IT'S GOING TO BE TOUGH FOR ME IF YOU'RE ABLE TO MOVE.
SO I'M GOING TO TAKE BOTH OF YOUR LEGS BEFORE YOU CAN DO A THING.
GU
GU

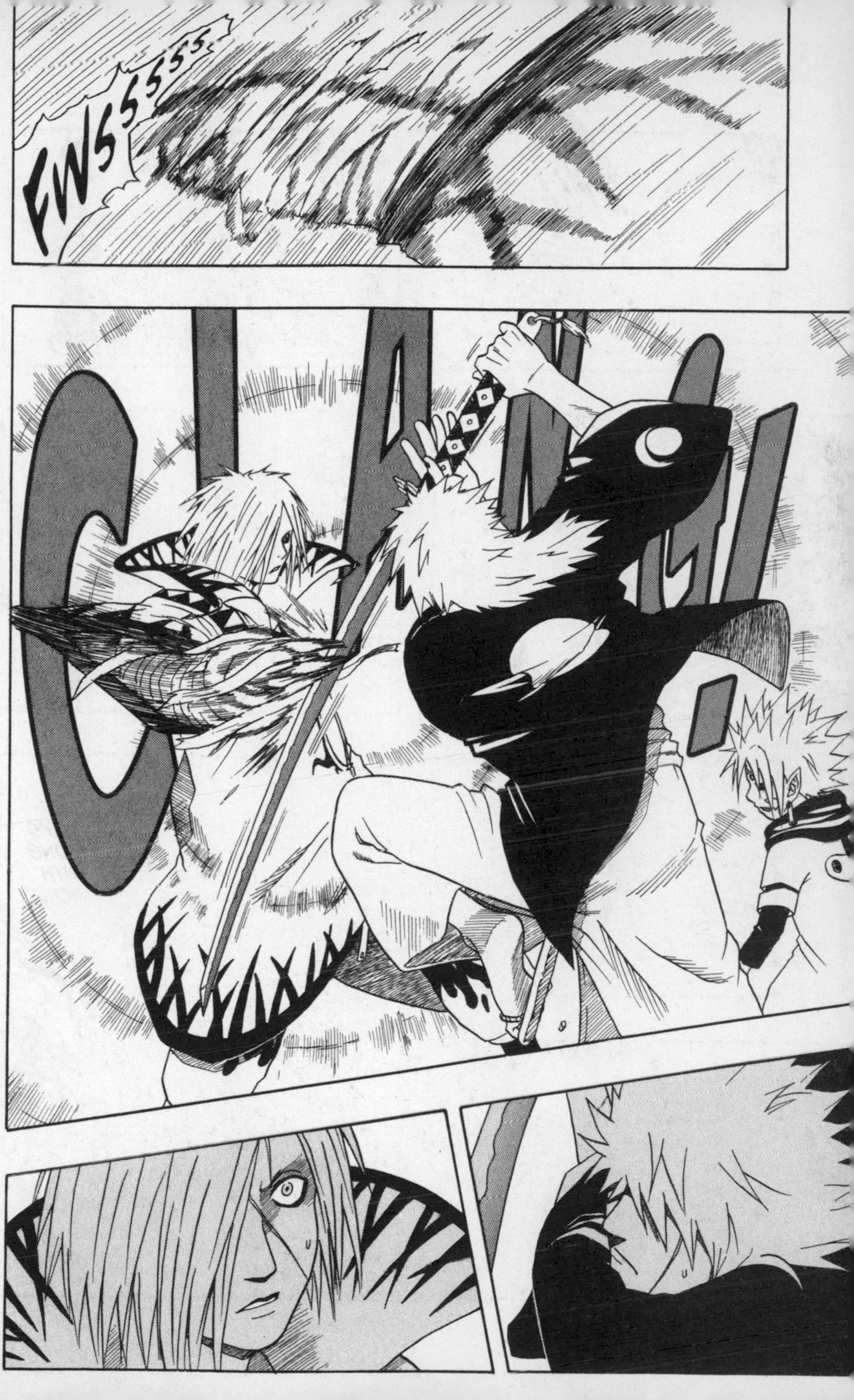
FWSSSSSS
CLANG

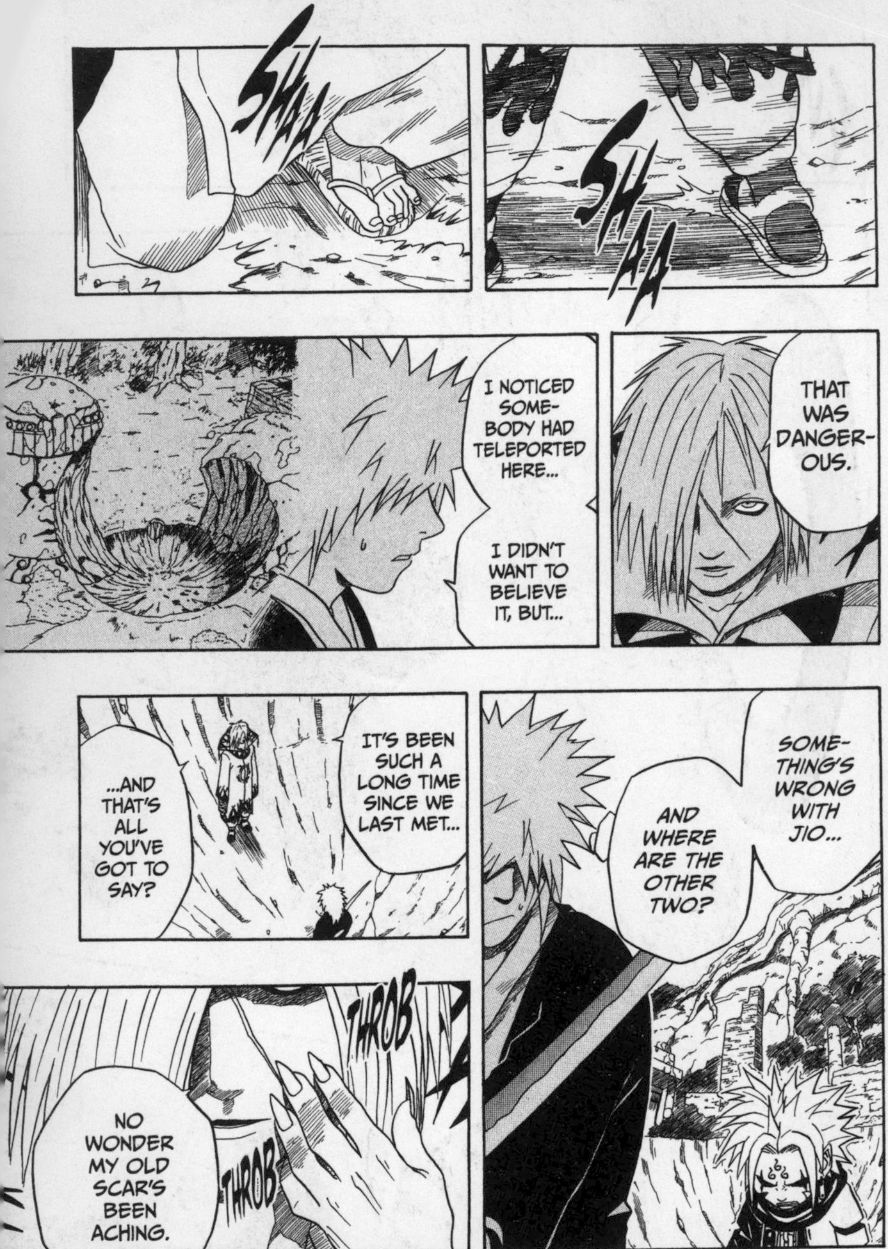
SHAA
SHAA
THAT WAS DANGEROUS.
I NOTICED SOMEBODY HAD TELEPORTED HERE...
I DIDN'T WANT TO BELIEVE IT, BUT...
SOMETHING'S WRONG WITH JIO...
AND WHERE ARE THE OTHER TWO?
IT'S BEEN SUCH A LONG TIME SINCE WE LAST MET...
...AND THAT'S ALL YOU'VE GOT TO SAY?
THROB
THROB
NO WONDER MY OLD SCAR'S BEEN ACHING.

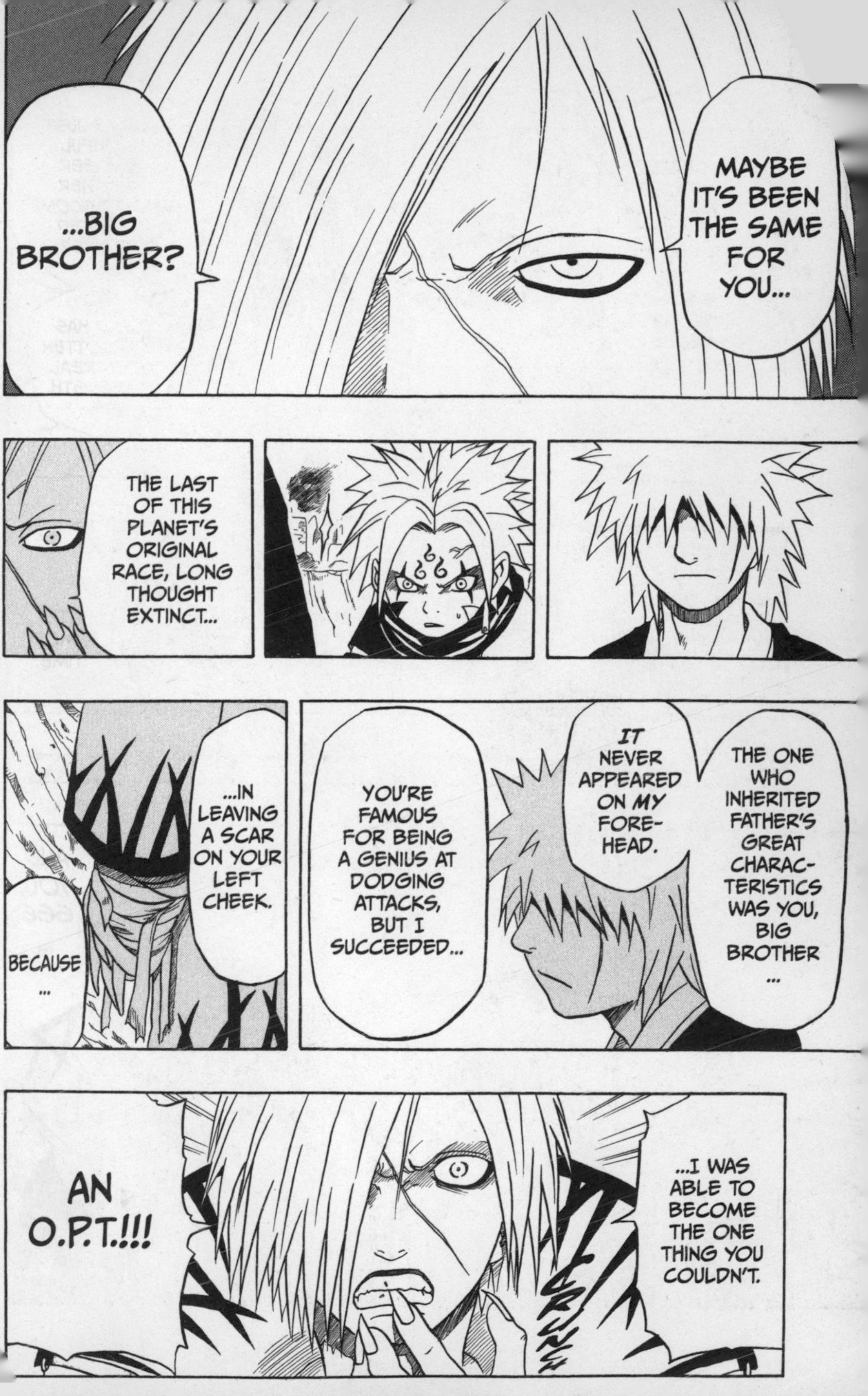
MAYBE IT'S BEEN THE SAME FOR YOU...
...BIG BROTHER?
THE LAST OF THIS PLANET'S ORIGINAL RACE, LONG THOUGHT EXTINCT...
THE ONE WHO INHERITED FATHER'S GREAT CHARAC-TERISTICS WAS YOU, BIG BROTHER...
IT NEVER APPEARED ON MY FORE-HEAD.
YOU'RE FAMOUS FOR BEING A GENIUS AT DODGING ATTACKS, BUT I SUCCEEDED...
...IN LEAVING A SCAR ON YOUR LEFT CHEEK.
BECAUSE...
...I WAS ABLE TO BECOME THE ONE THING YOU COULDN'T.
AN O.P.T.!!!

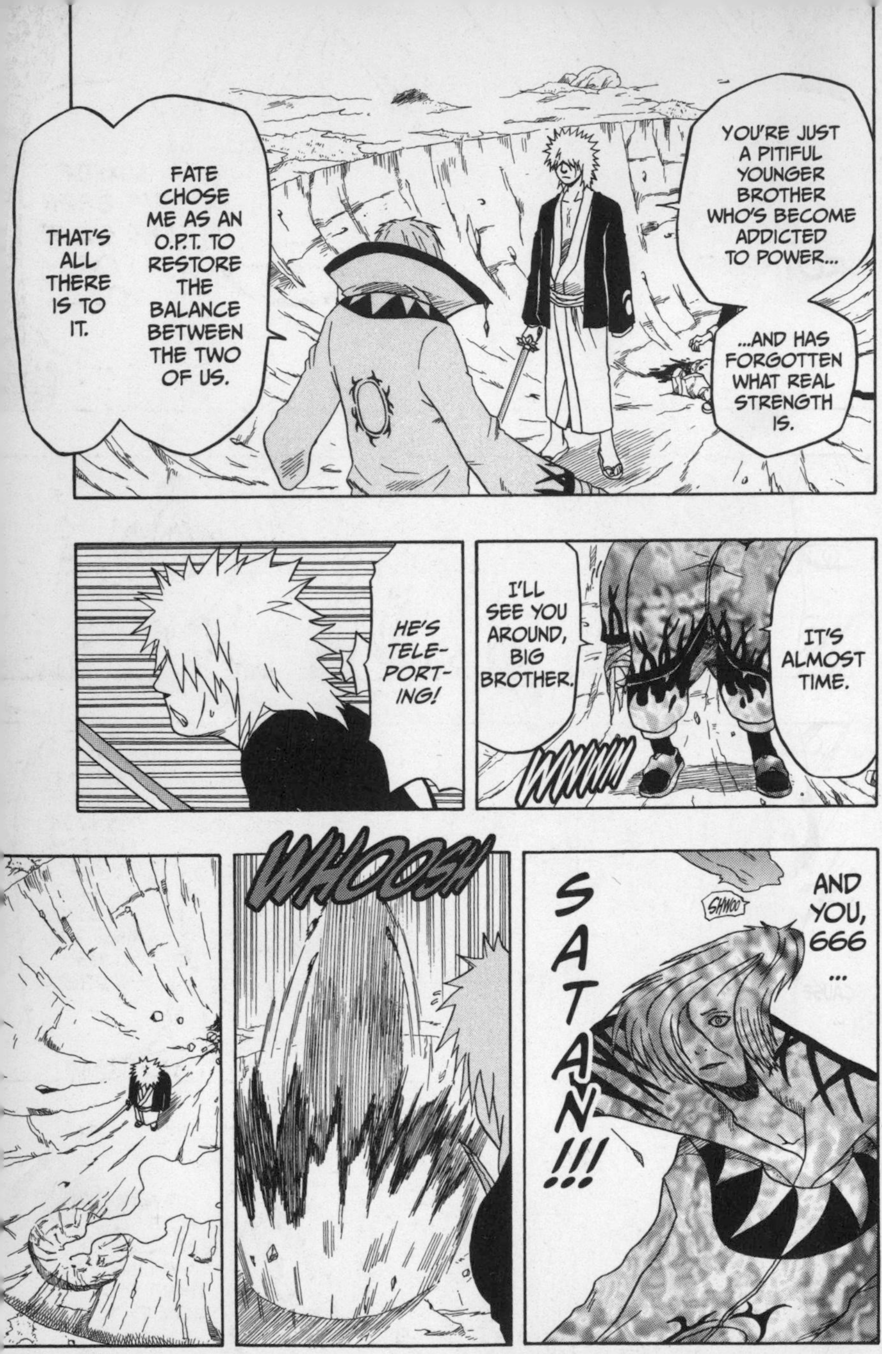
YOU'RE JUST A PITIFUL YOUNGER BROTHER WHO'S BECOME ADDICTED TO POWER...
...AND HAS FORGOTTEN WHAT REAL STRENGTH IS.
FATE CHOSE ME AS AN O.P.T. TO RESTORE THE BALANCE BETWEEN THE TWO OF US.
THAT'S ALL THERE IS TO IT.
IT'S ALMOST TIME.
I'LL SEE YOU AROUND, BIG BROTHER.
HE'S TELE-PORTING!
AND YOU, 666 ...
SHWOO
SATAN!!!
WHOOSH!

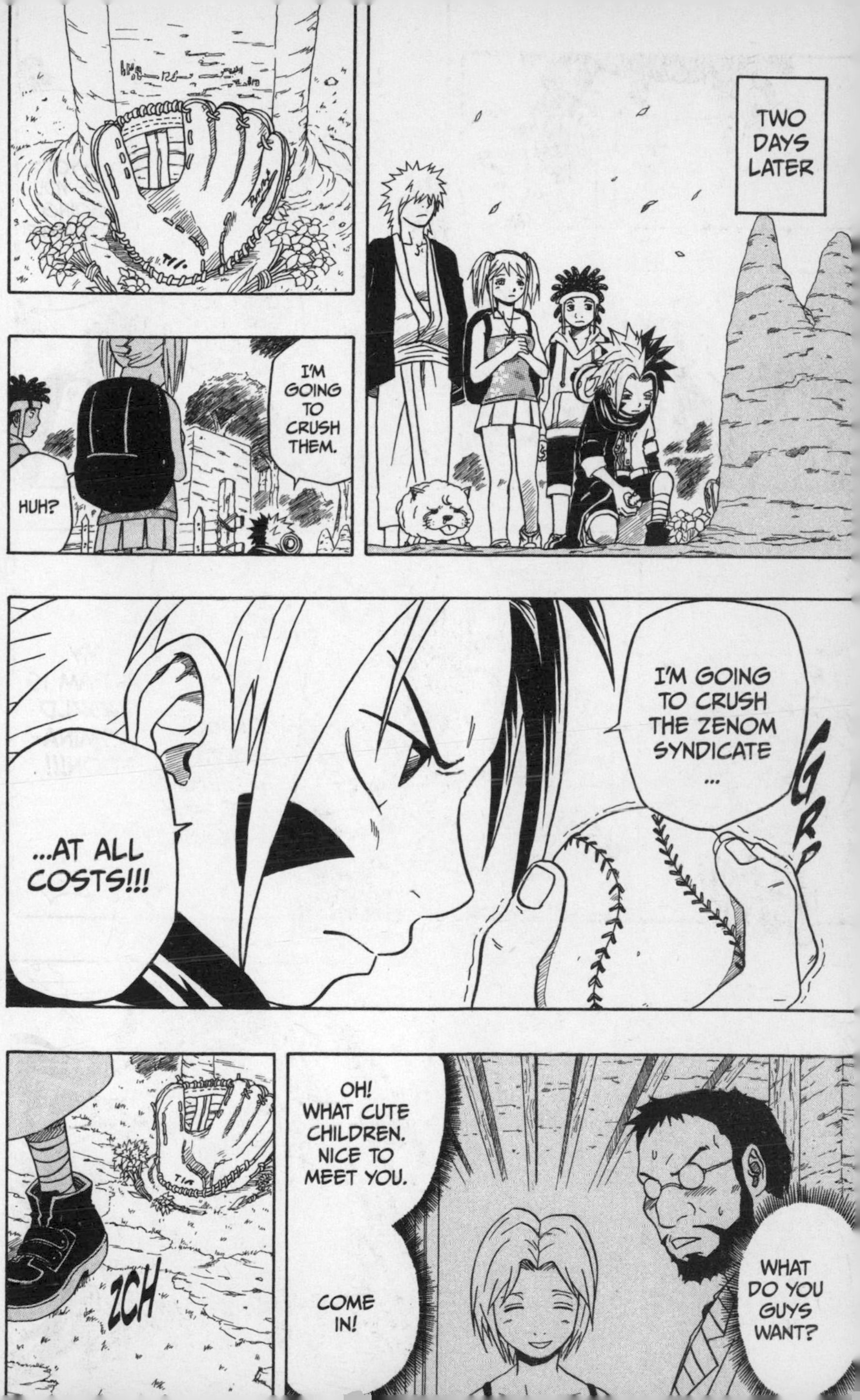
TWO DAYS LATER
I'M GOING TO CRUSH THEM.
HUH?
I'M GOING TO CRUSH THE ZENOM SYNDICATE ...
GRP
...AT ALL COSTS!!!
OH! WHAT CUTE CHILDREN. NICE TO MEET YOU.
WHAT DO YOU GUYS WANT?
COME IN!
ZCH

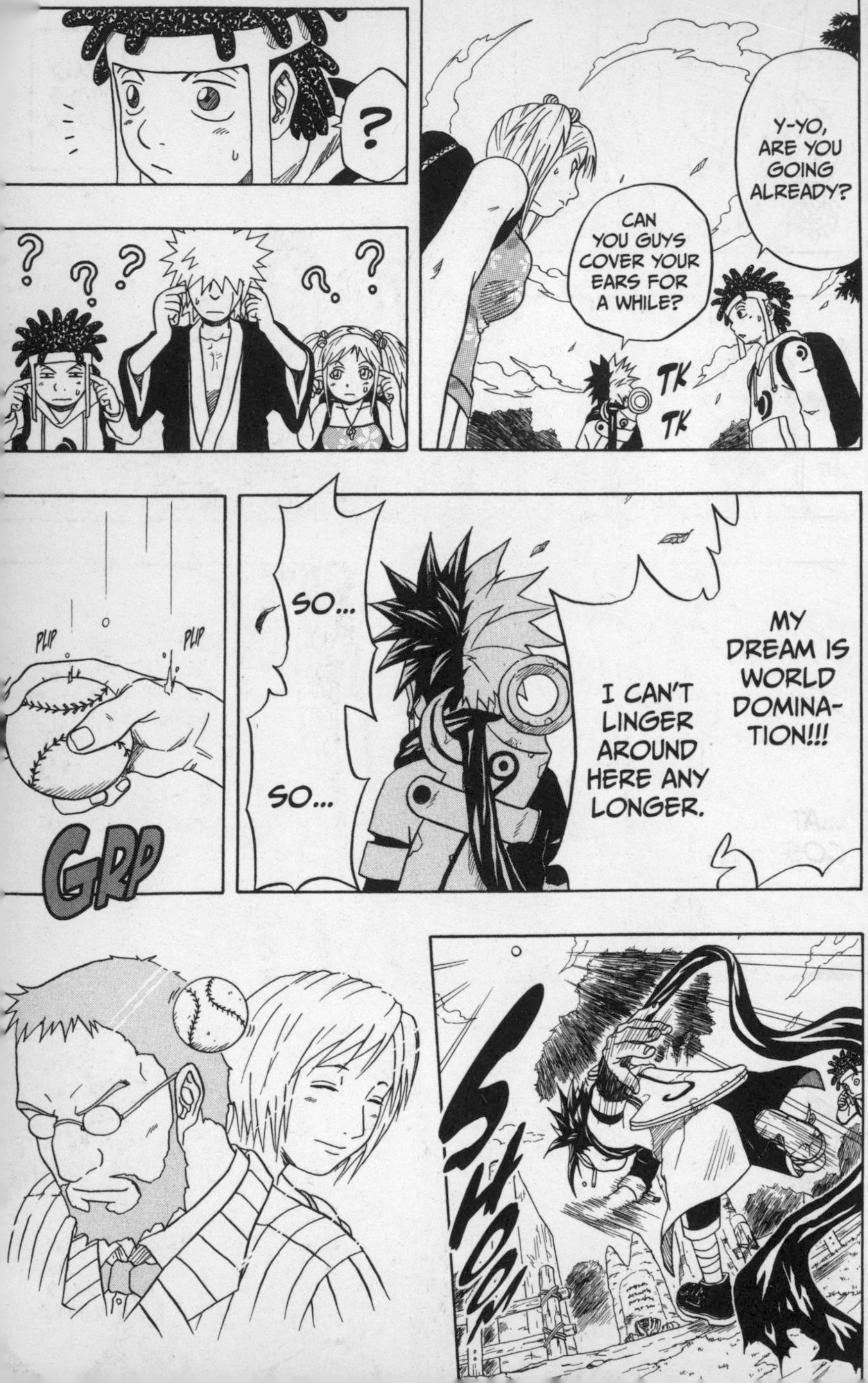
Y-YO, ARE YOU GOING ALREADY?
CAN YOU GUYS COVER YOUR EARS FOR A WHILE?
TK
TK
?
?
?
?
?
MY DREAM IS WORLD DOMINATION!!!
I CAN'T LINGER AROUND HERE ANY LONGER.
SO...
SO...
PLIP
PLIP
GRP

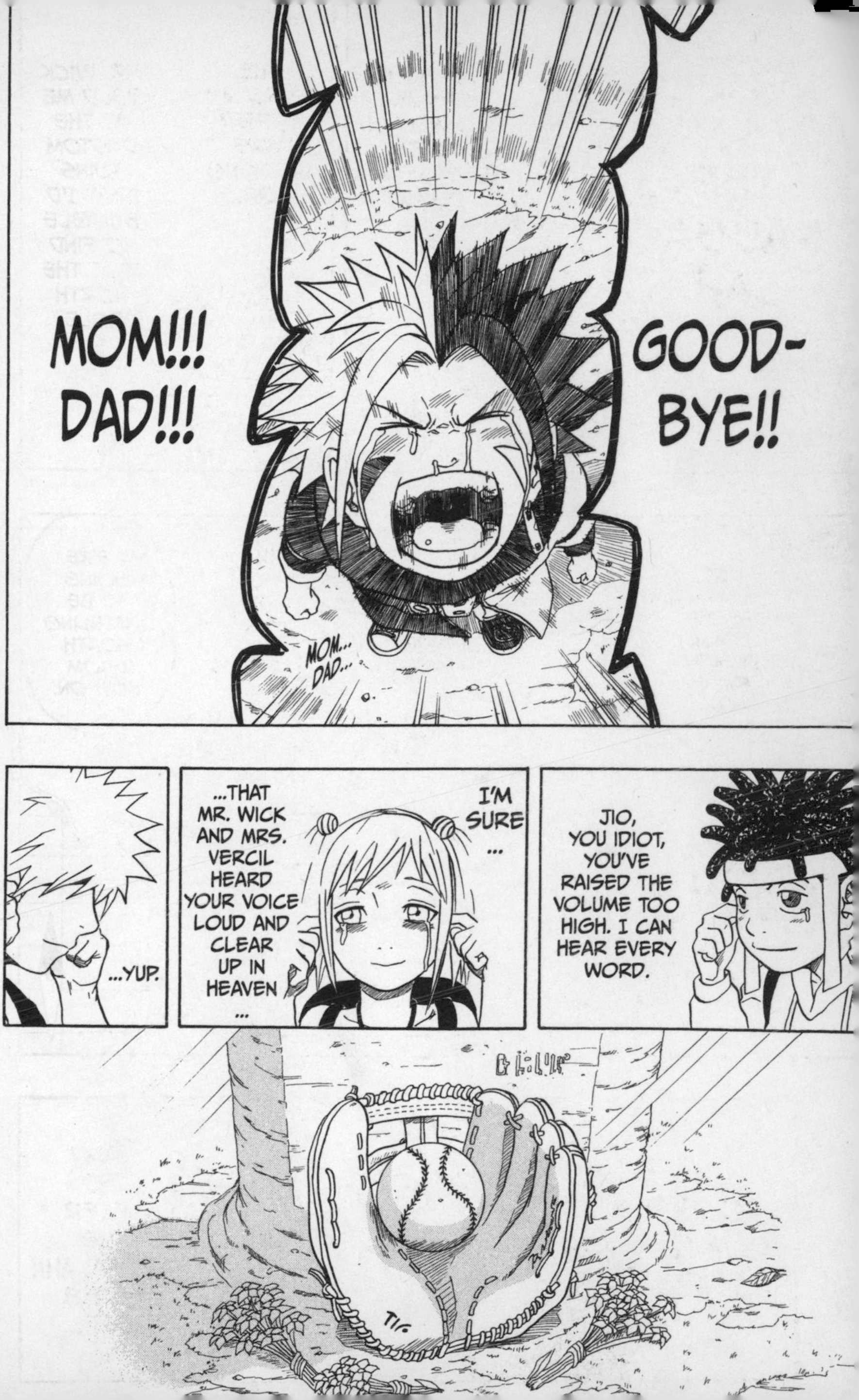
GOOD-BYE!!
MOM!!! DAD!!!
MOM... DAD...
JIO, YOU IDIOT, YOU'VE RAISED THE VOLUME TOO HIGH. I CAN HEAR EVERY WORD.
I'M SURE ...
...THAT MR. WICK AND MRS. VERCIL HEARD YOUR VOICE LOUD AND CLEAR UP IN HEAVEN ...
...YUP.

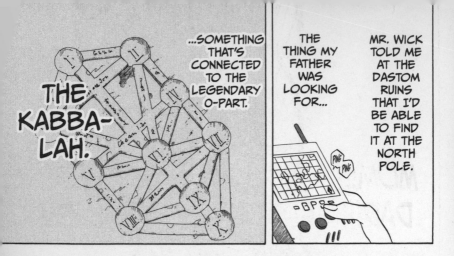

MR. WICK TOLD ME AT THE DASTOM RUINS THAT I'D BE ABLE TO FIND IT AT THE NORTH POLE.
THE THING MY FATHER WAS LOOKING FOR...
PING PING
GPS
...SOMETHING THAT'S CONNECTED TO THE LEGENDARY O-PART.
THE KABBA-LAH.
WE'RE GOING TO BE TRAVELING NORTH FROM NOW ON.
Toom Ruins
Thorny Ruin
Entotsu City
The belly button of the world: Dastom Ruins
AND WE'RE AT THE TRASH DESERT RIGHT NOW...
...SO WE'RE GOING TO GRADUALLY GATHER THE THINGS WE NEED...
PING PING
...AND GO AFTER THE KABBALAH!! WE'RE OFF...
ZIP
...TO THE NORTH POLE!!!

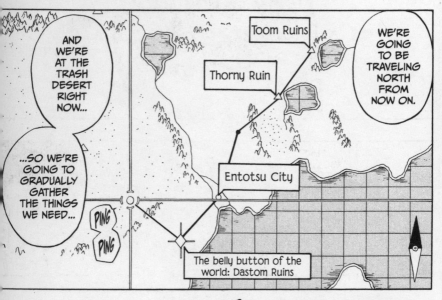

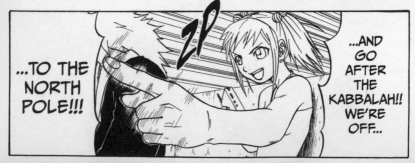

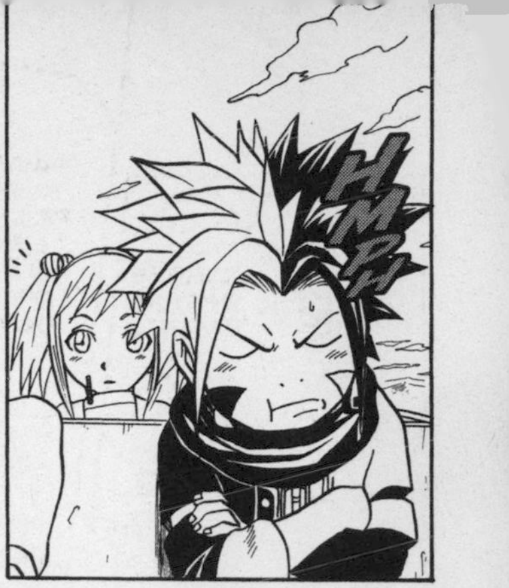
HMPH

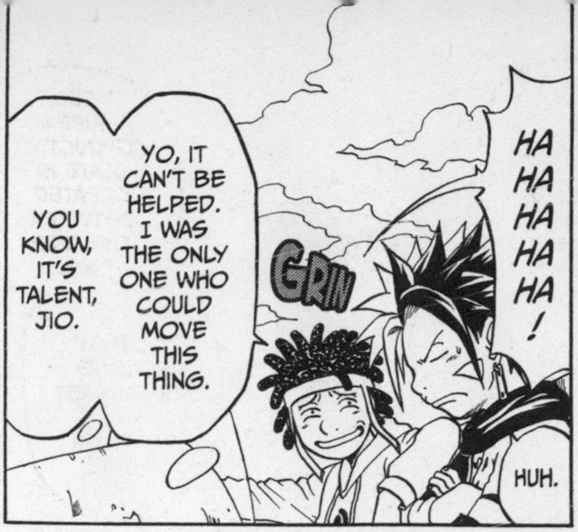
HA HA HA HA HA!
YO, IT CAN'T BE HELPED. I WAS THE ONLY ONE WHO COULD MOVE THIS THING.
YOU KNOW, IT'S TALENT, JIO.
GRIN
HUH.

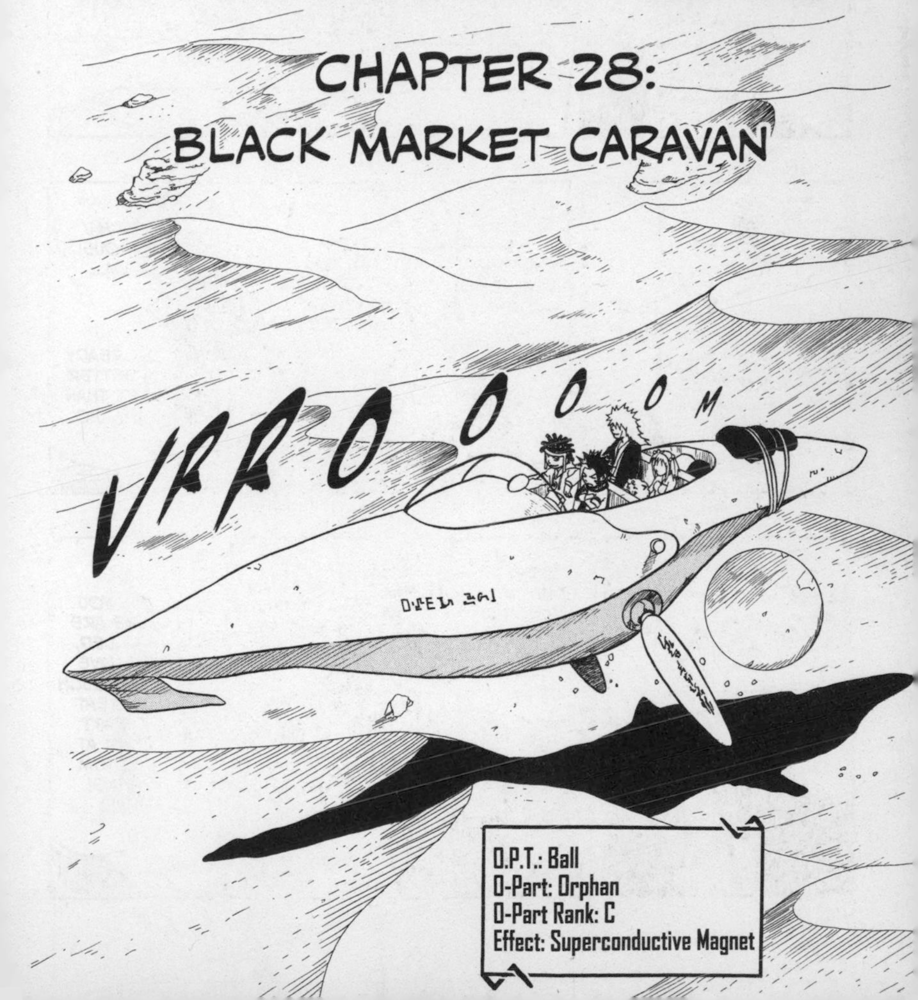
CHAPTER 28:
BLACK MARKET CARAVAN
VRROOOOOM
O.P.T.: Ball
O-Part: Orphan
O-Part Rank: C
Effect: Superconductive Magnet

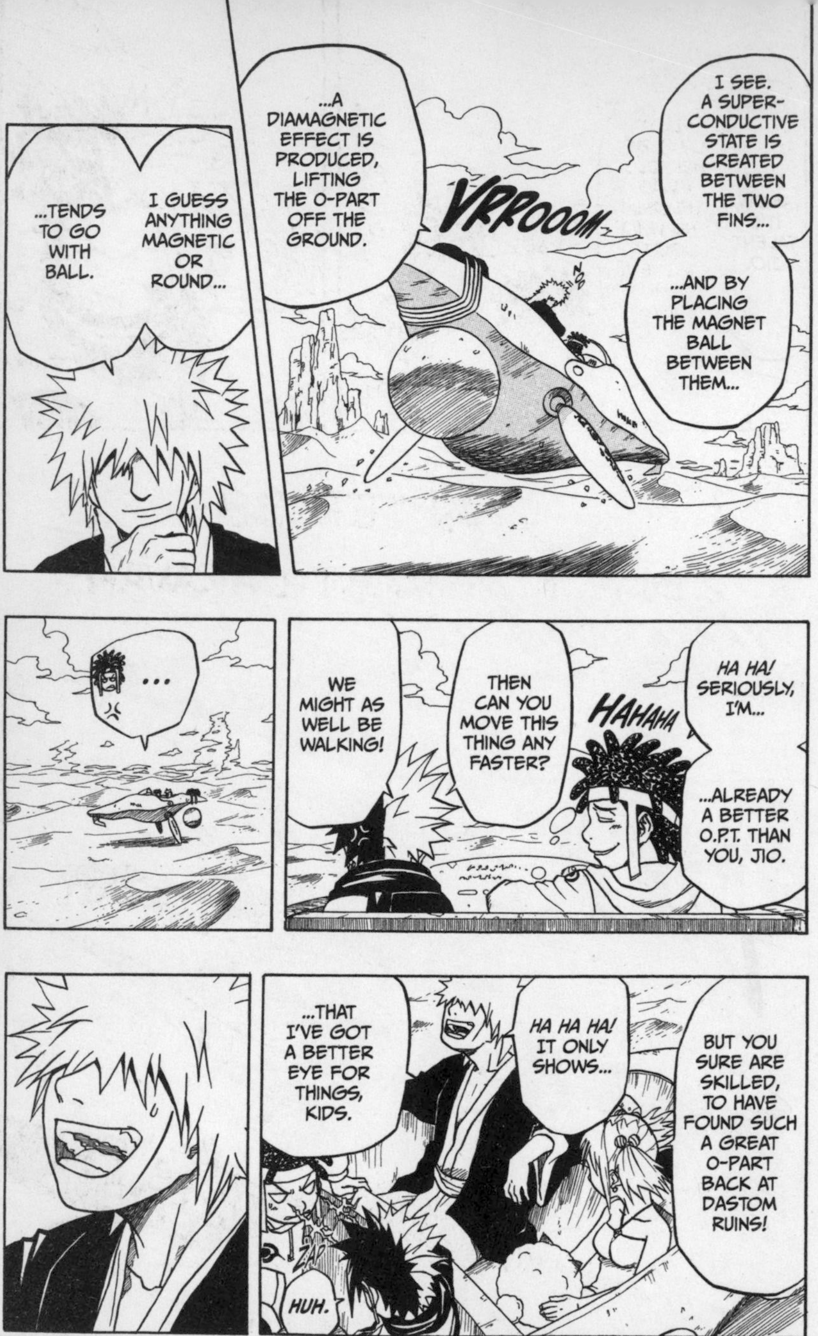
I SEE. A SUPER-CONDUCTIVE STATE IS CREATED BETWEEN THE TWO FINS...
...AND BY PLACING THE MAGNET BALL BETWEEN THEM...
VRROOOM
...A DIAMAGNETIC EFFECT IS PRODUCED, LIFTING THE O-PART OFF THE GROUND.
I GUESS ANYTHING MAGNETIC OR ROUND...
...TENDS TO GO WITH BALL.
HA HA! SERIOUSLY, I'M...
HAHAHA
...ALREADY A BETTER O.P.T. THAN YOU, JIO.
THEN CAN YOU MOVE THIS THING ANY FASTER?
WE MIGHT AS WELL BE WALKING!
...
BUT YOU SURE ARE SKILLED, TO HAVE FOUND SUCH A GREAT O-PART BACK AT DASTOM RUINS!
HA HA HA! IT ONLY SHOWS...
...THAT I'VE GOT A BETTER EYE FOR THINGS, KIDS.
HUH.

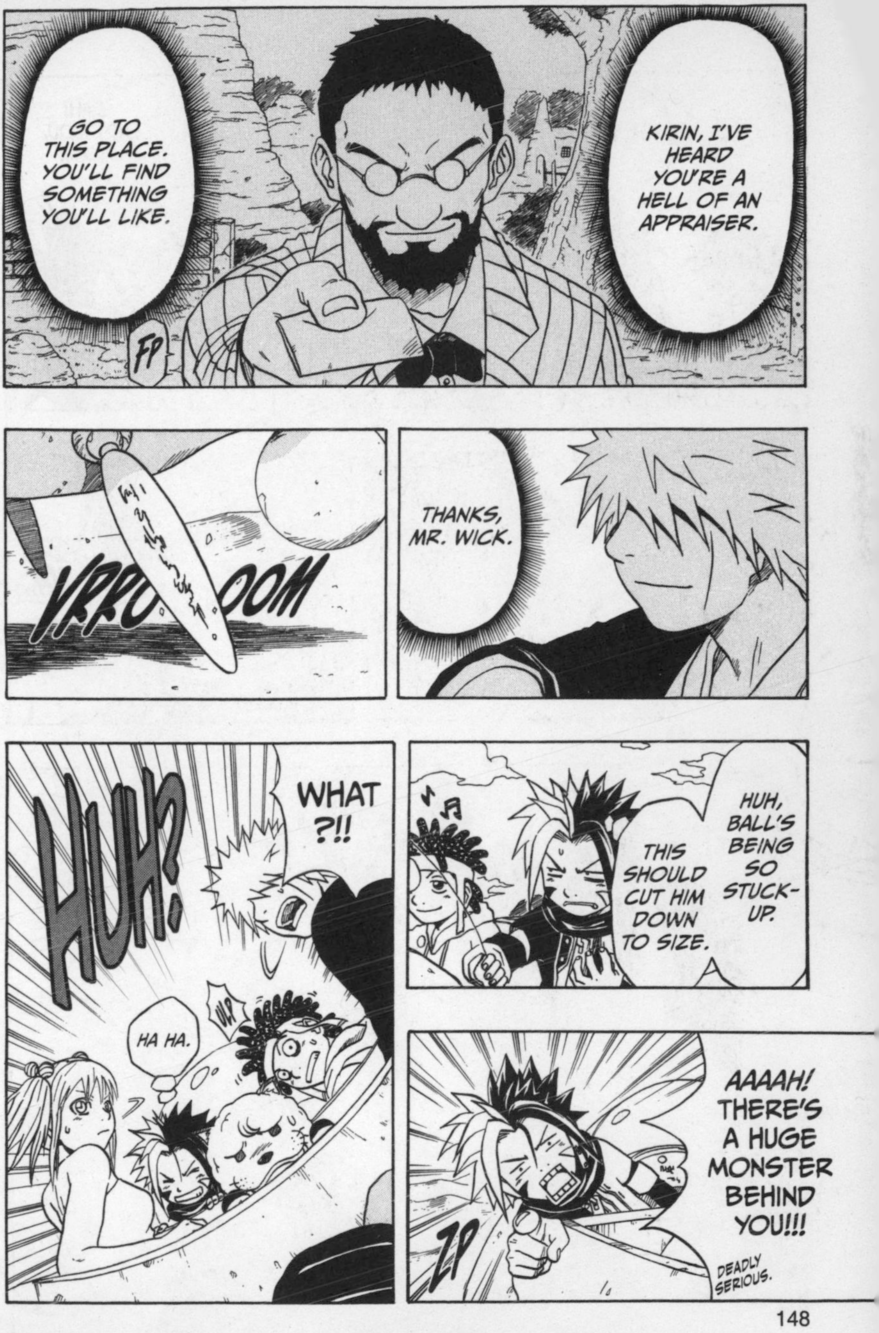
KIRIN, I'VE HEARD YOU'RE A HELL OF AN APPRAISER.
GO TO THIS PLACE. YOU'LL FIND SOMETHING YOU'LL LIKE.
FP
THANKS, MR. WICK.
VRRO OOM
HUH, BALL'S BEING SO STUCK-UP.
THIS SHOULD CUT HIM DOWN TO SIZE.
AAAAH! THERE'S A HUGE MONSTER BEHIND YOU!!!
ZP
DEADLY SERIOUS.
WHAT ?!!
HUH?
HA HA.

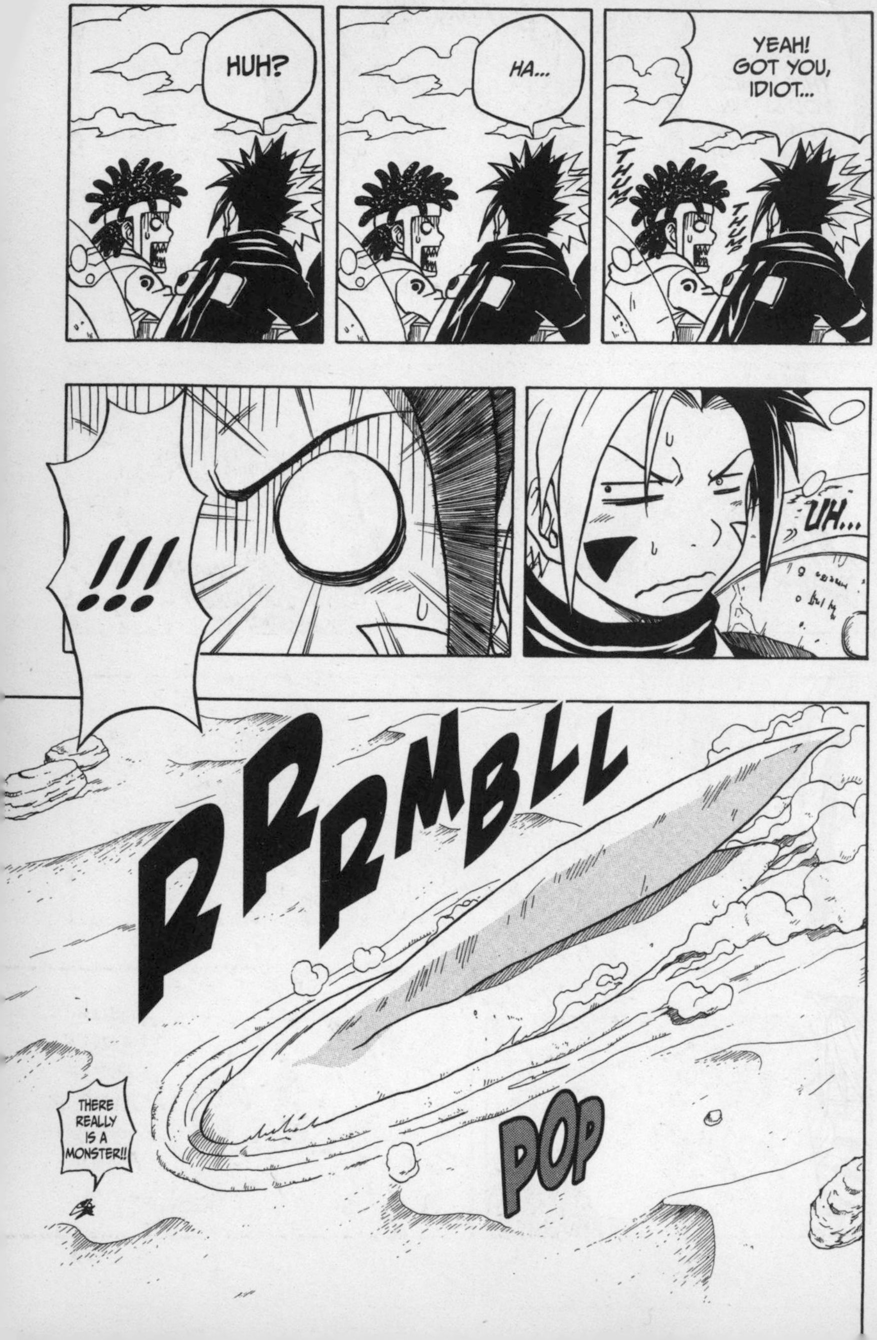
YEAH! GOT YOU, IDIOT...
THUMP
THUMP
HA...
HUH?
UH...
!!!
RRMBLL
POP
THERE REALLY IS A MONSTER!!

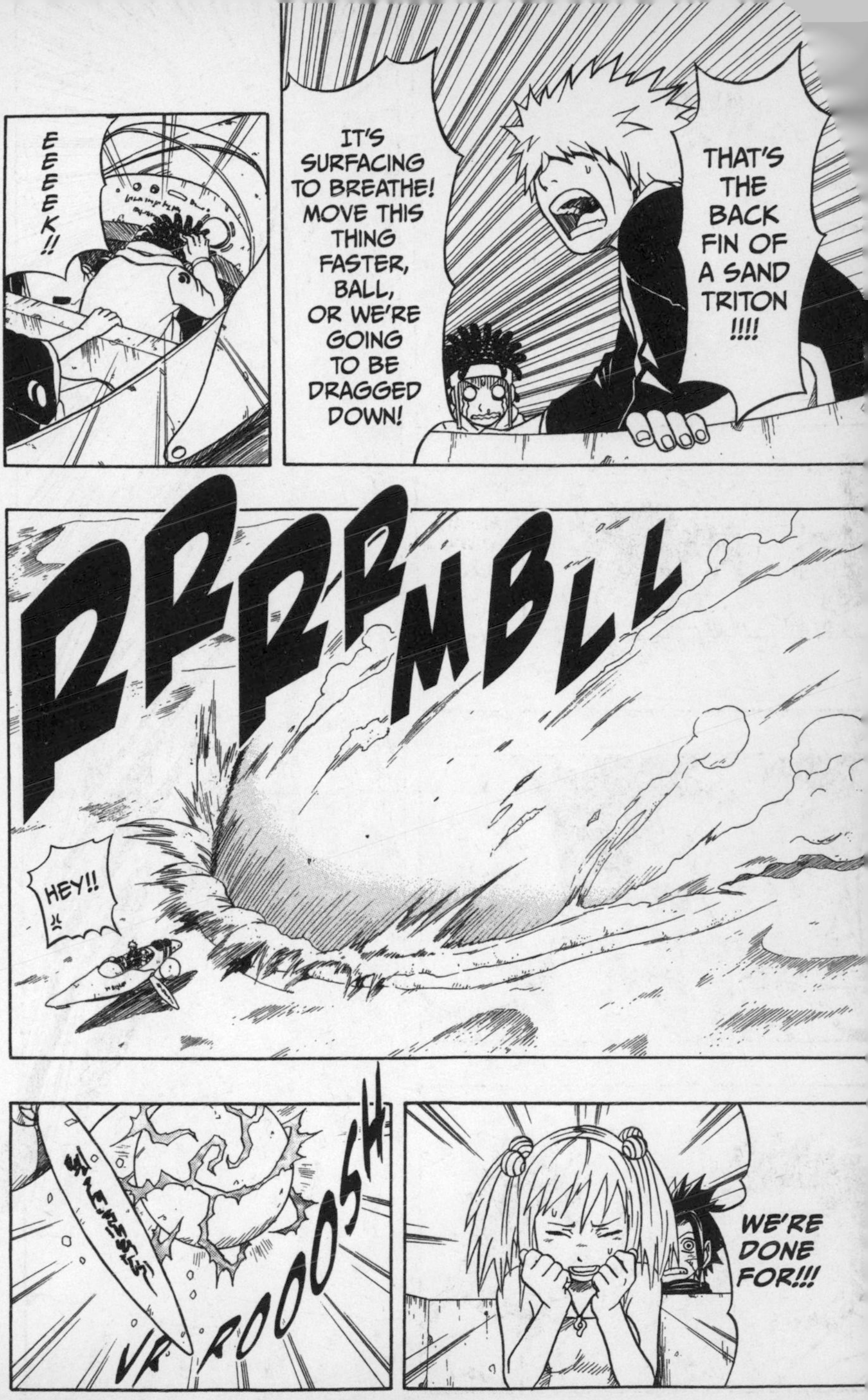
THAT'S THE BACK FIN OF A SAND TRITON !!!!
IT'S SURFACING TO BREATHE! MOVE THIS THING FASTER, BALL, OR WE'RE GOING TO BE DRAGGED DOWN!
EEEEEK!!
RRRRMBLL
HEY!!
WE'RE DONE FOR!!!
VROOOSH

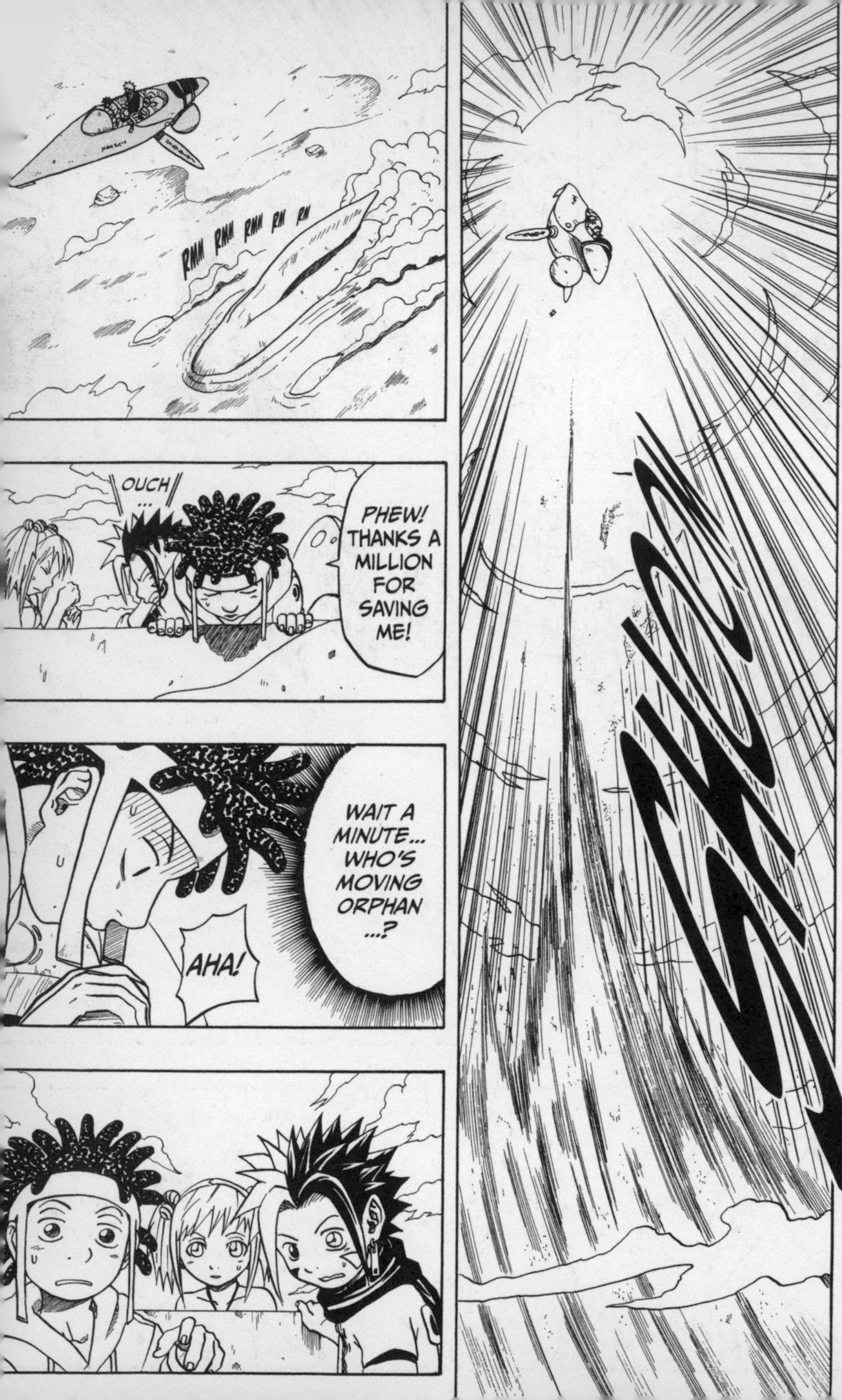
RMM RMM RMM RM RM
PHEW! THANKS A MILLION FOR SAVING ME!
OUCH...
WAIT A MINUTE... WHO'S MOVING ORPHAN ...?
AHA!

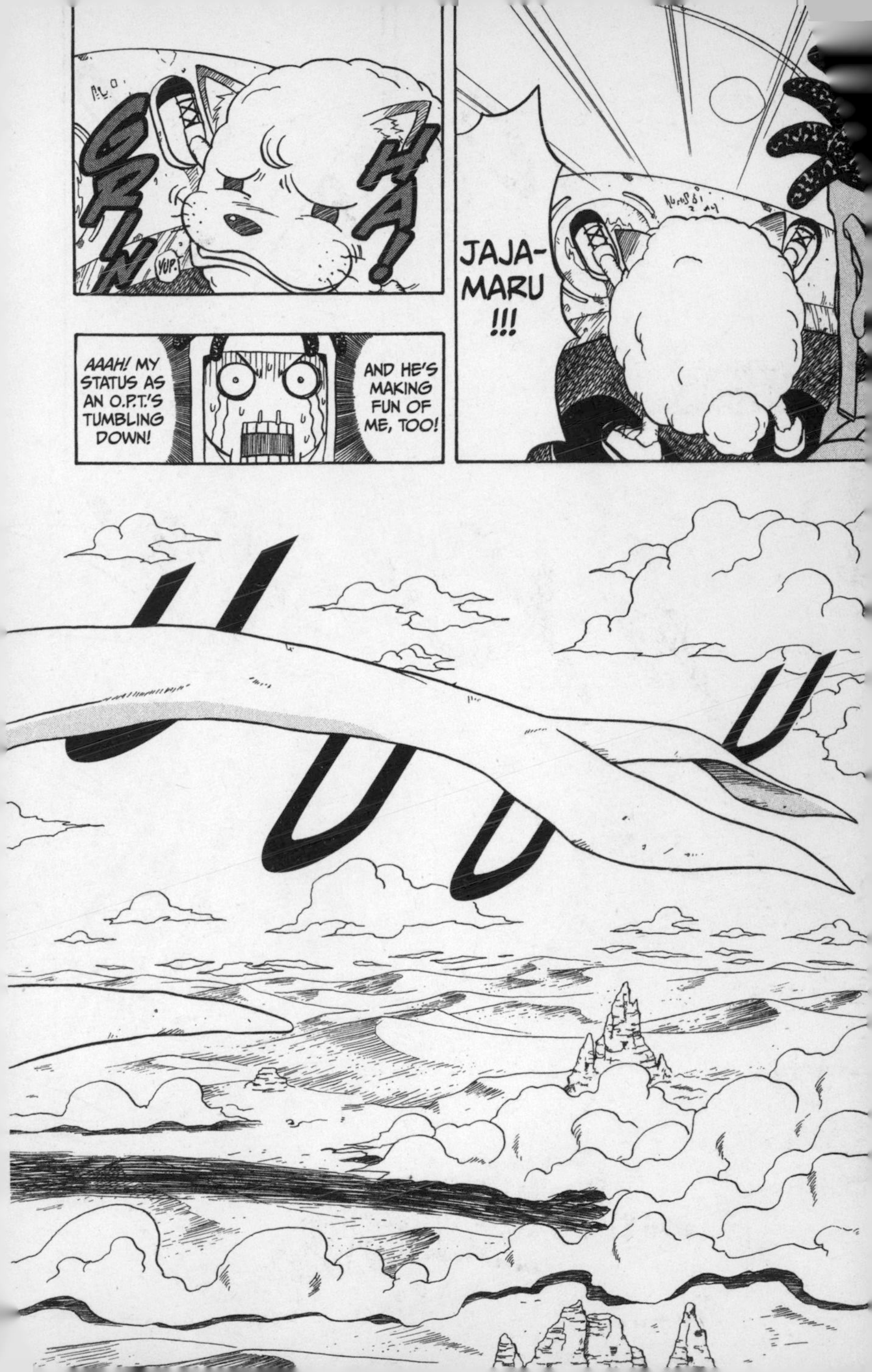
JAJA-MARU !!!
HA!
GRIN
YUP.
AND HE'S MAKING FUN OF ME, TOO!
AAAH! MY STATUS AS AN O.P.T.'S TUMBLING DOWN!

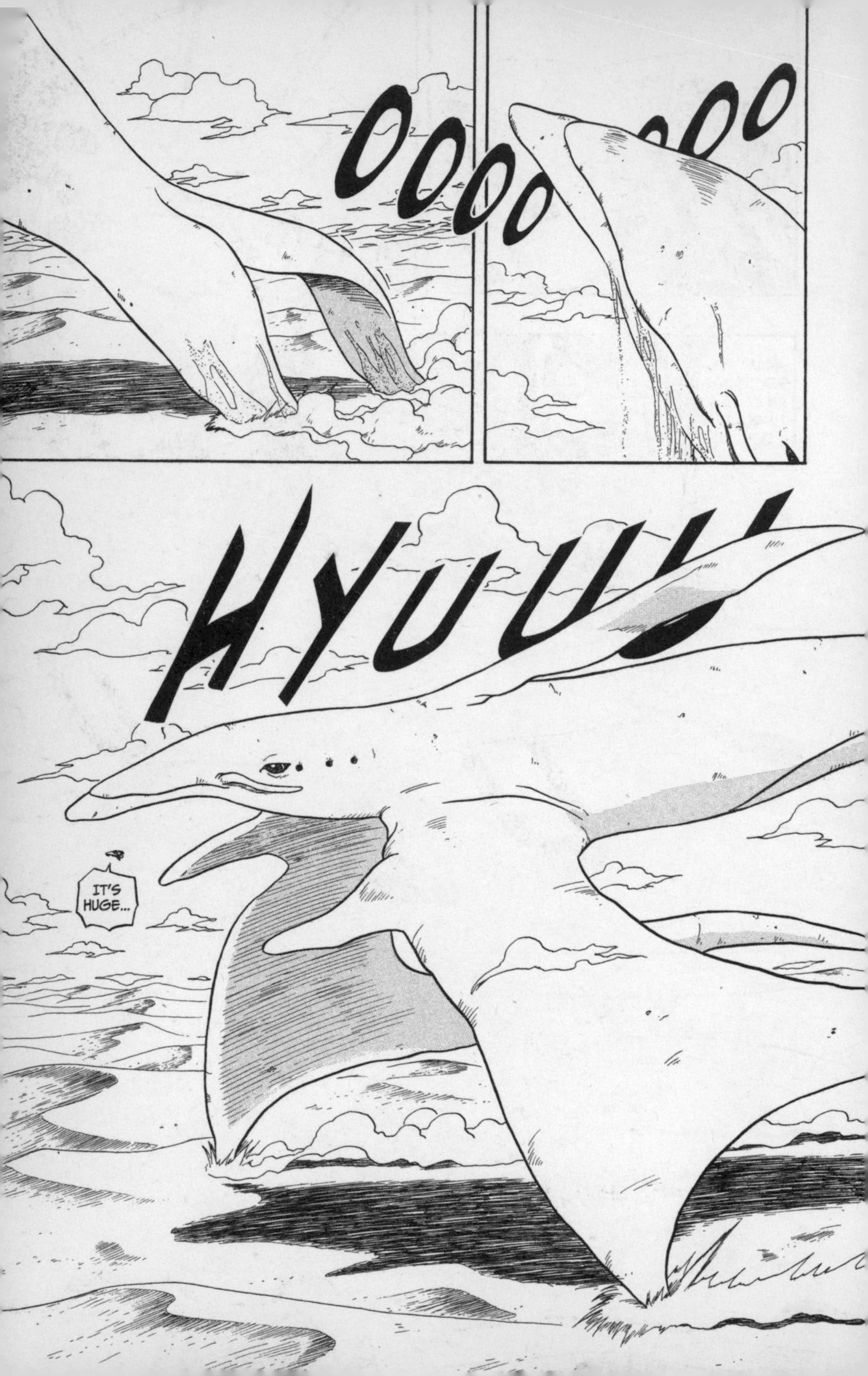
OOOOOOOOOO
HYUUU
IT'S HUGE...

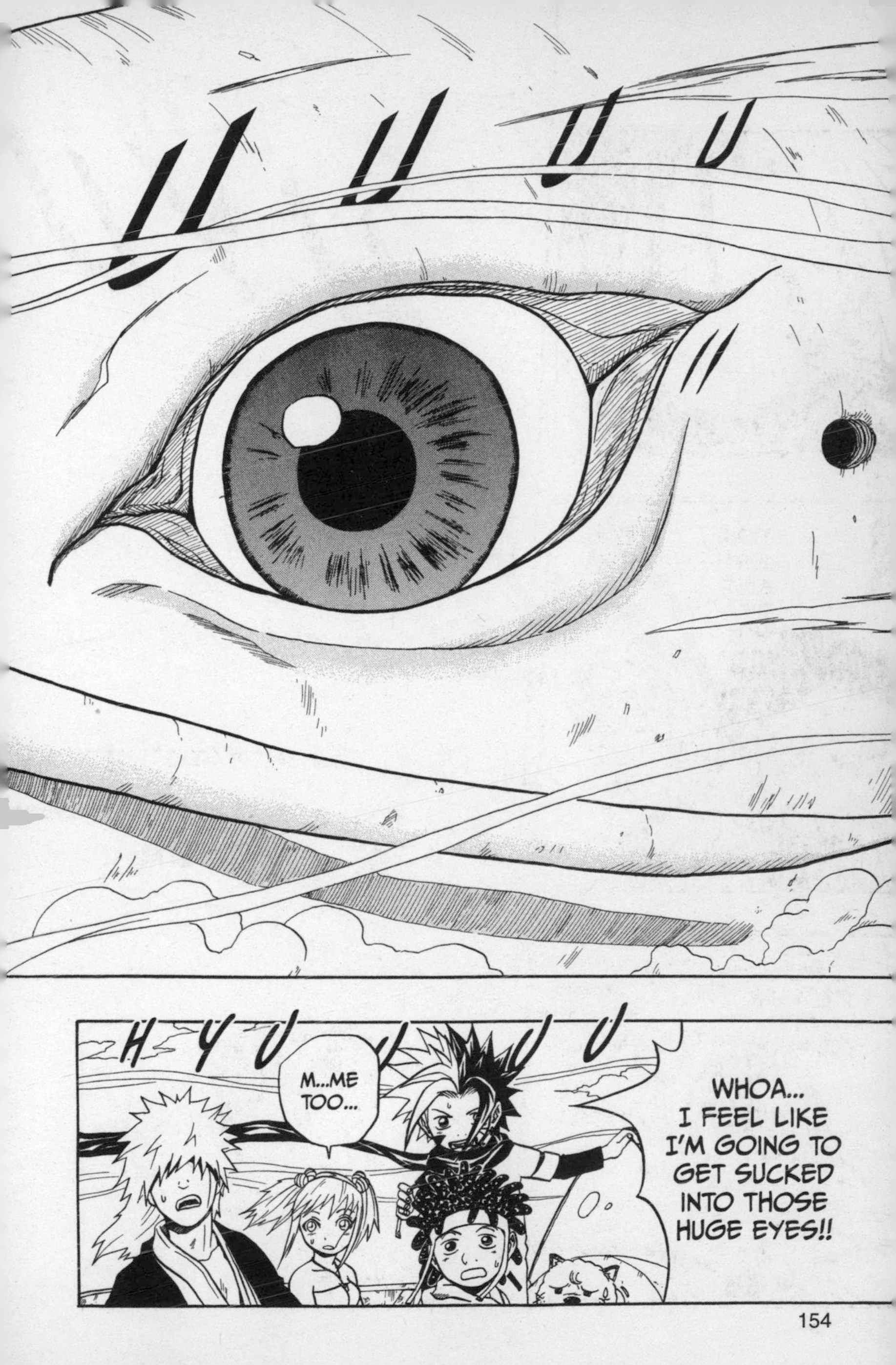
UUUU
HYUUUU
WHOA... I FEEL LIKE I'M GOING TO GET SUCKED INTO THOSE HUGE EYES!!
M...ME TOO...

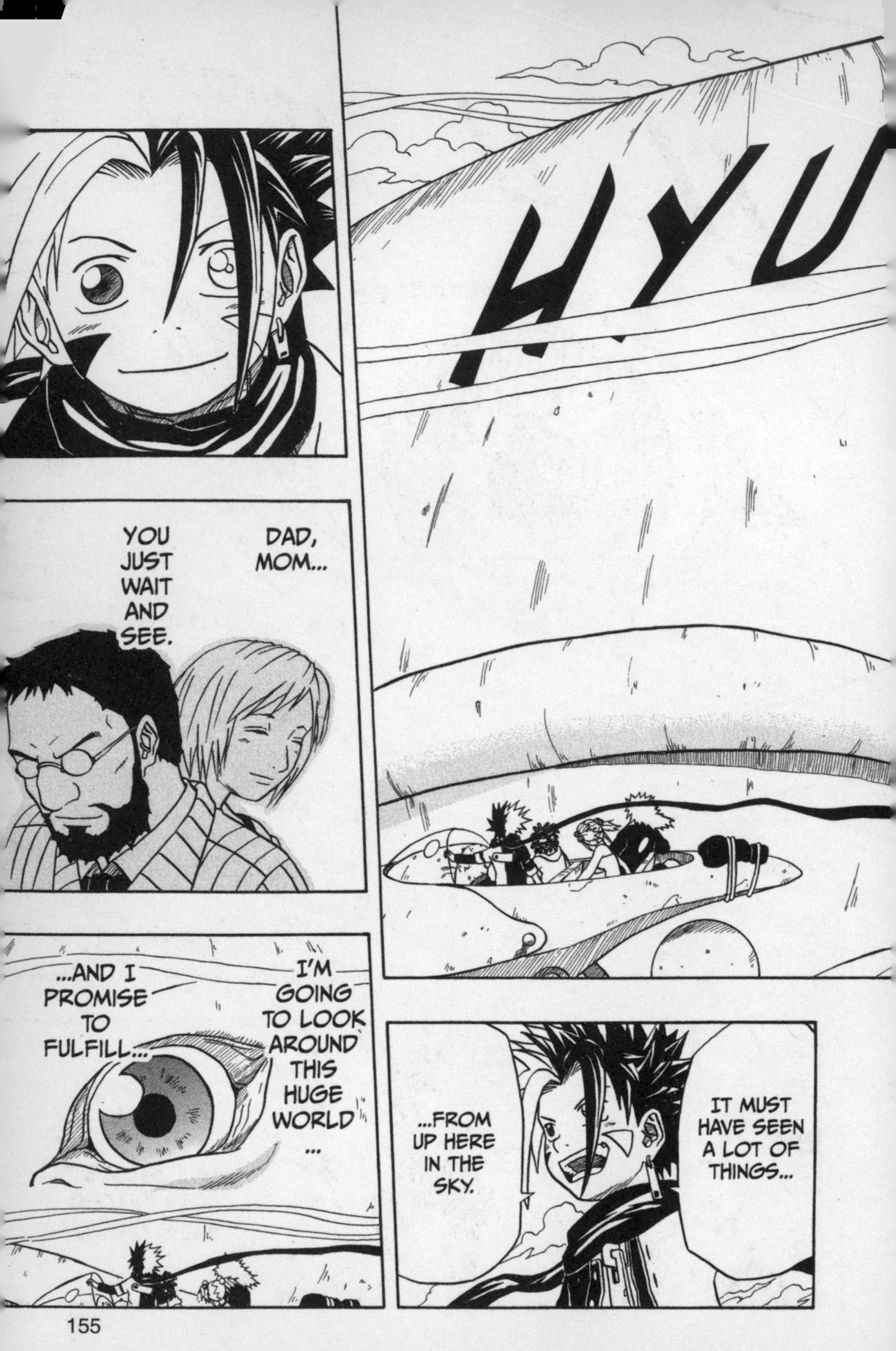
HYU
DAD, MOM...
YOU JUST WAIT AND SEE.
IT MUST HAVE SEEN A LOT OF THINGS...
...FROM UP HERE IN THE SKY.
I'M GOING TO LOOK AROUND THIS HUGE WORLD ...
...AND I PROMISE TO FULFILL...

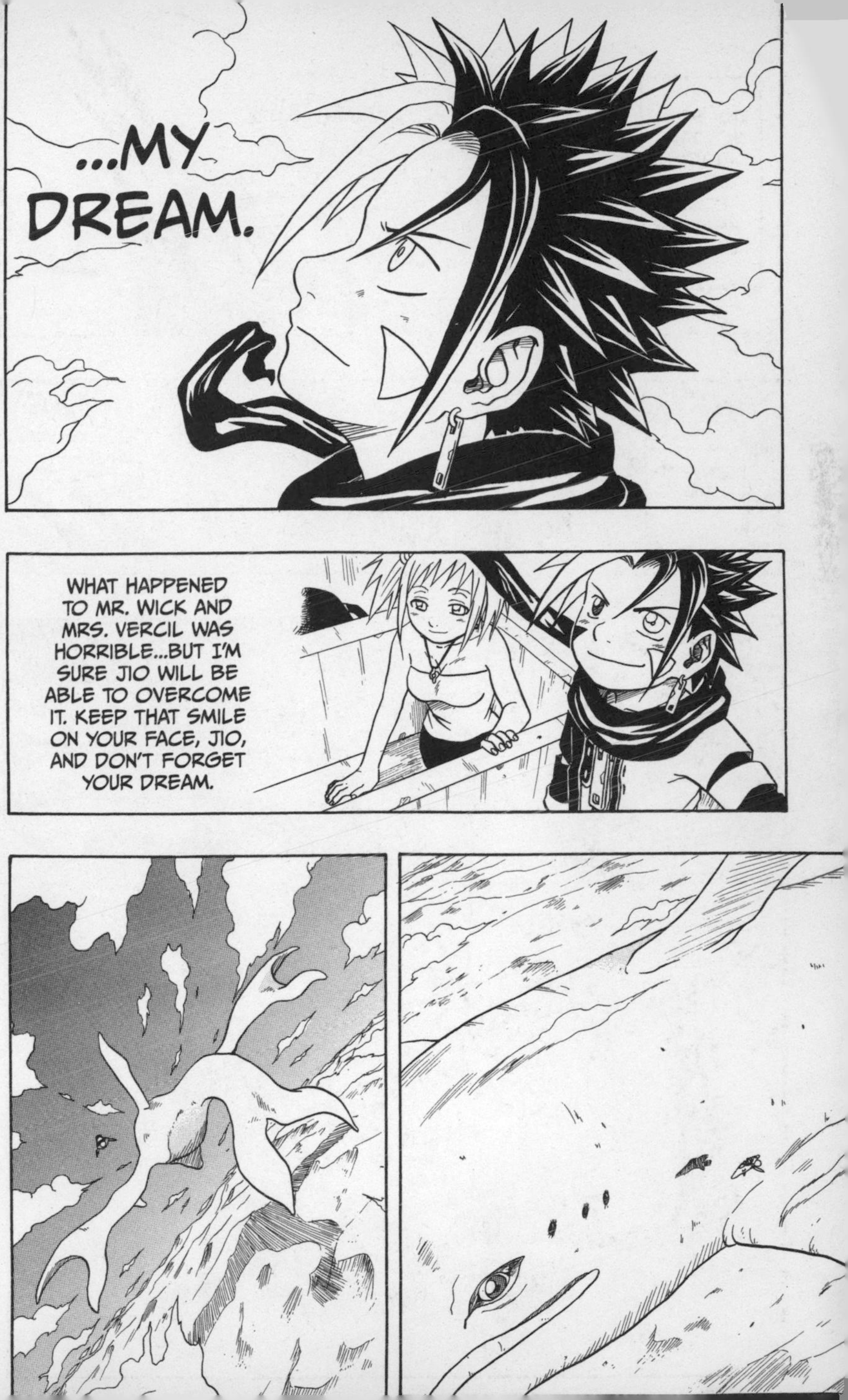
...MY DREAM.
WHAT HAPPENED TO MR. WICK AND MRS. VERCIL WAS HORRIBLE...BUT I'M SURE JIO WILL BE ABLE TO OVERCOME IT. KEEP THAT SMILE ON YOUR FACE, JIO, AND DON'T FORGET YOUR DREAM.

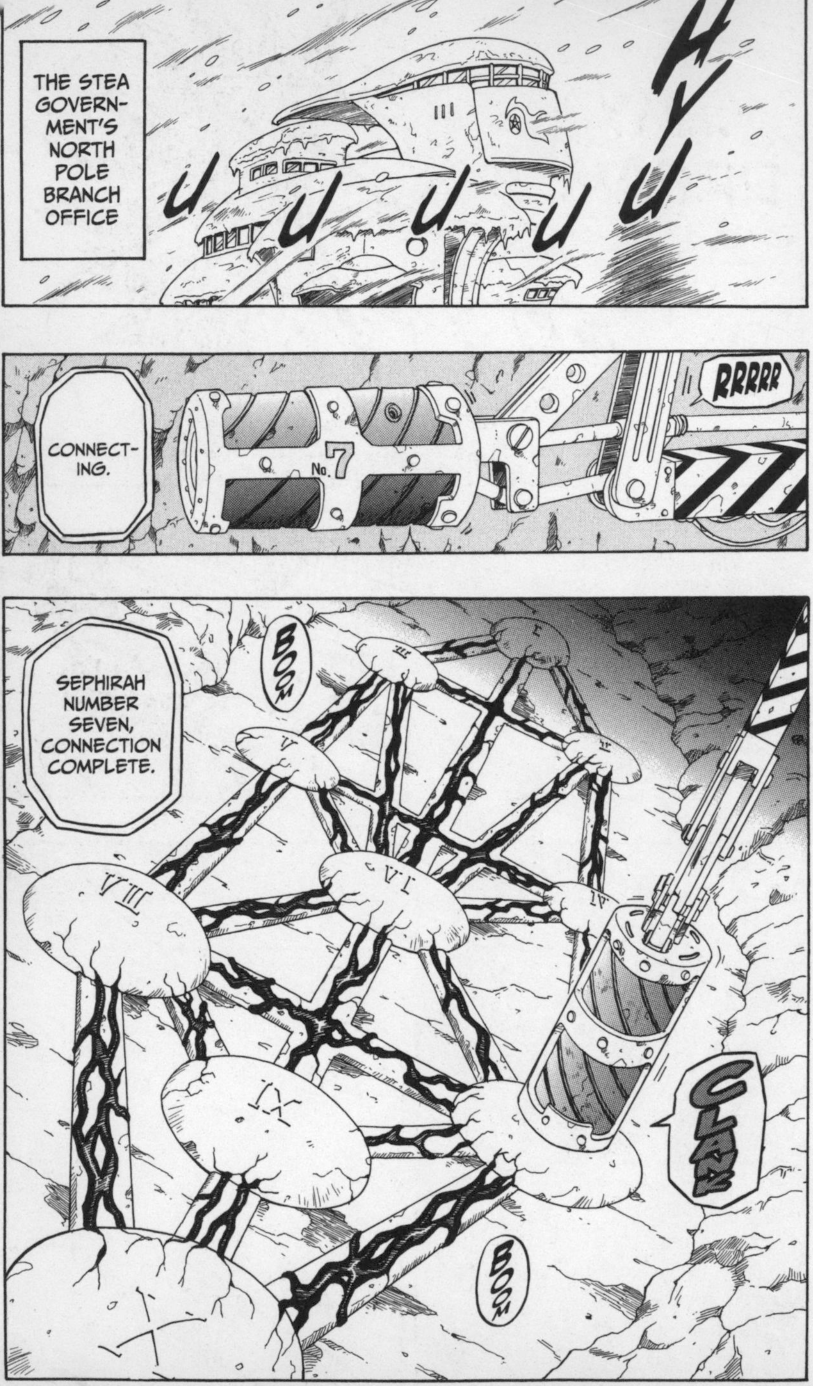
HYUUUUU
THE STEA GOVERNMENT'S NORTH POLE BRANCH OFFICE
RRRRR
No. 7
CONNECTING.
BOOM
SEPHIRAH NUMBER SEVEN, CONNECTION COMPLETE.
CLANK
BOOM

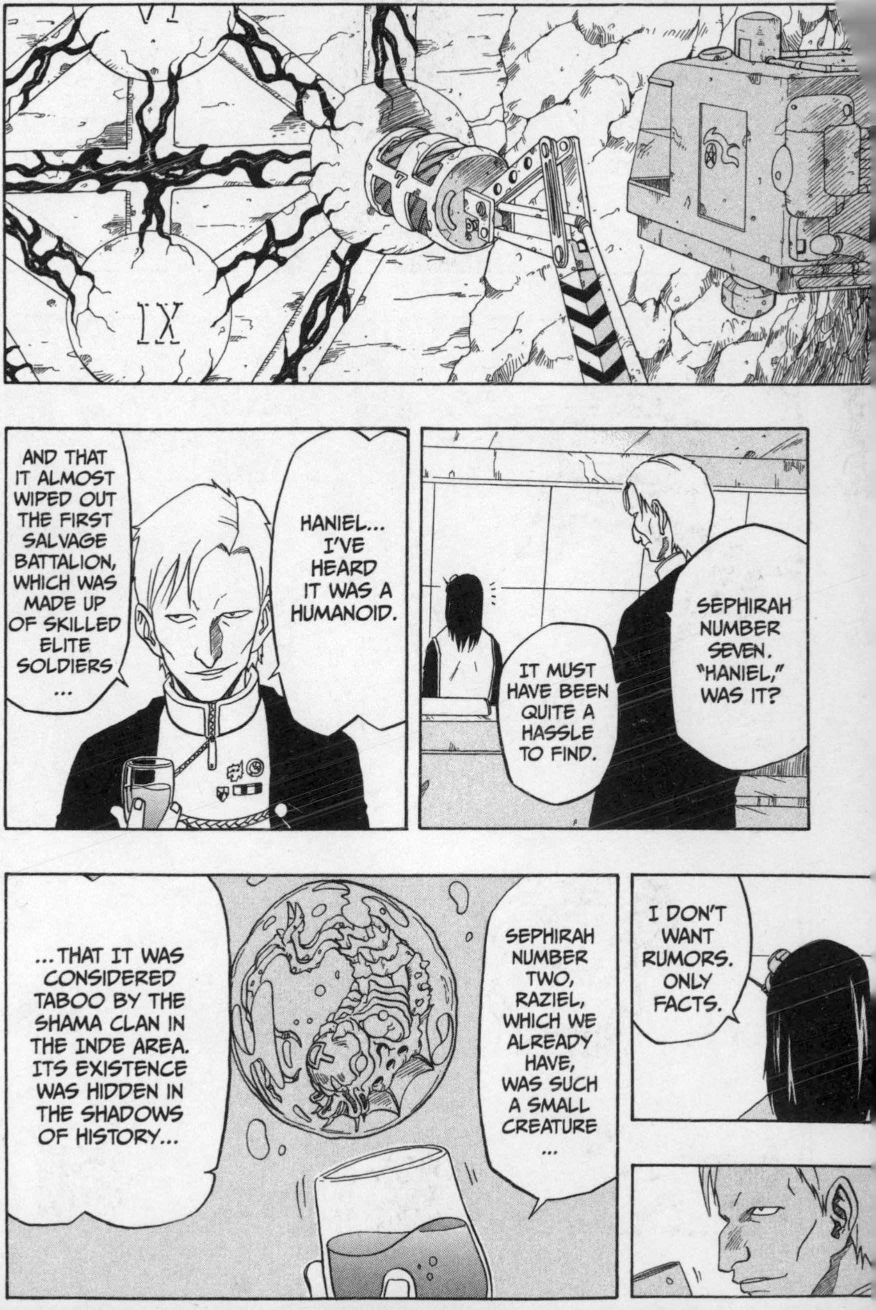
SEPHIRAH NUMBER SEVEN. "HANIEL," WAS IT?
IT MUST HAVE BEEN QUITE A HASSLE TO FIND.
HANIEL... I'VE HEARD IT WAS A HUMANOID.
AND THAT IT ALMOST WIPED OUT THE FIRST SALVAGE BATTALION, WHICH WAS MADE UP OF SKILLED ELITE SOLDIERS ...
I DON'T WANT RUMORS. ONLY FACTS.
SEPHIRAH NUMBER TWO, RAZIEL, WHICH WE ALREADY HAVE, WAS SUCH A SMALL CREATURE ...
...THAT IT WAS CONSIDERED TABOO BY THE SHAMA CLAN IN THE INDE AREA. ITS EXISTENCE WAS HIDDEN IN THE SHADOWS OF HISTORY...

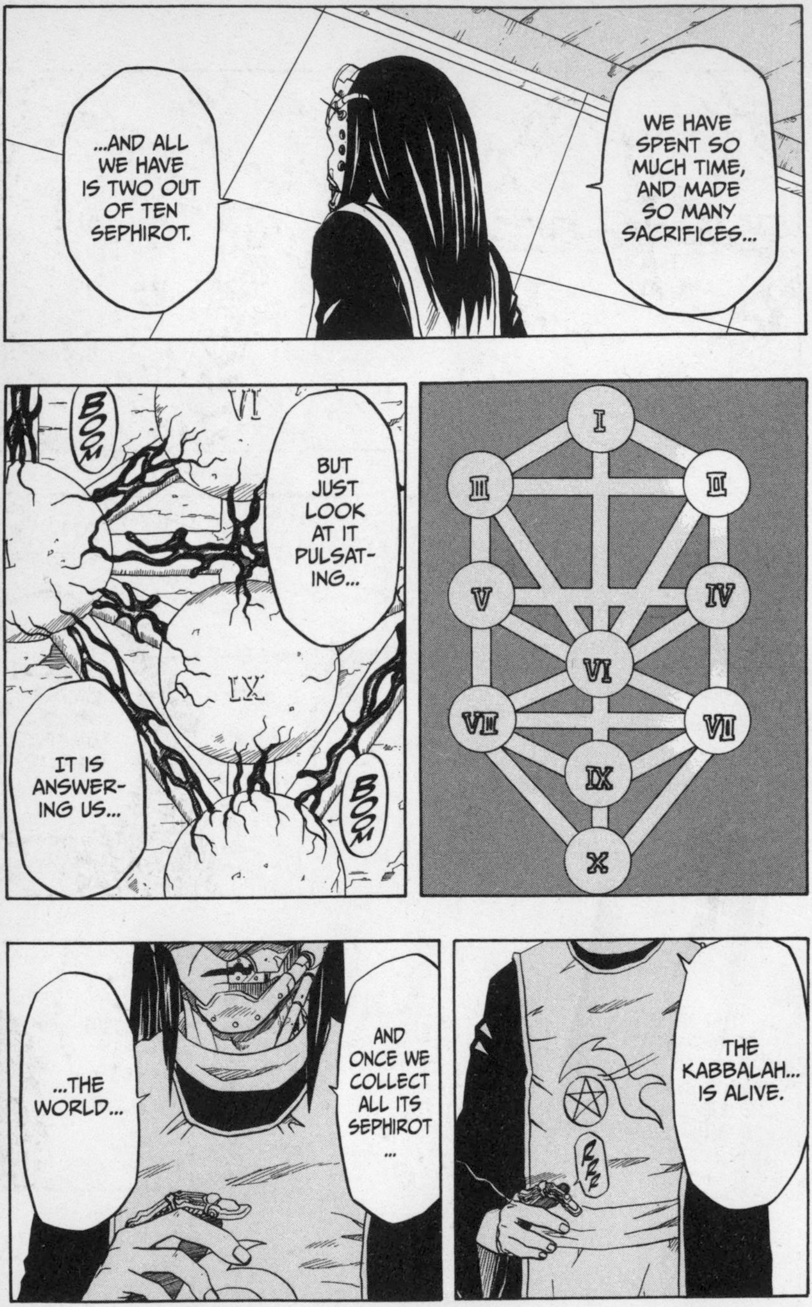
WE HAVE SPENT SO MUCH TIME, AND MADE SO MANY SACRIFICES...
...AND ALL WE HAVE IS TWO OUT OF TEN SEPHIROT.
I
II
III
IV
V
VI
VII
VIII
IX
X
BUT JUST LOOK AT IT PULSATING...
BOOM
IT IS ANSWERING US...
BOOM
THE KABBALAH... IS ALIVE.
AND ONCE WE COLLECT ALL ITS SEPHIROT ...
...THE WORLD...

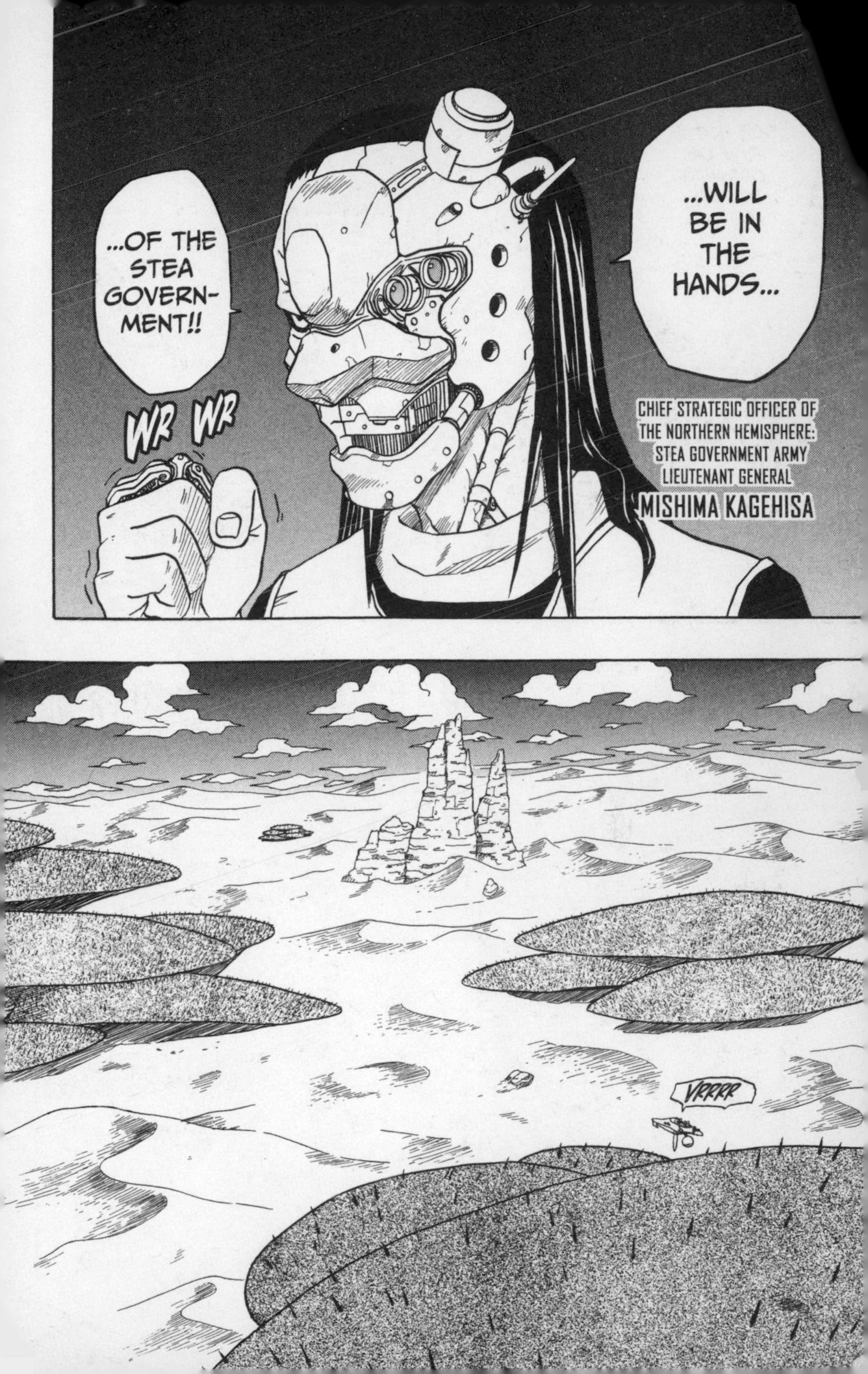
...WILL BE IN THE HANDS...
CHIEF STRATEGIC OFFICER OF THE NORTHERN HEMISPHERE: STEA GOVERNMENT ARMY LIEUTENANT GENERAL MISHIMA KAGEHISA
...OF THE STEA GOVERNMENT!!
WR WR
VRRRR

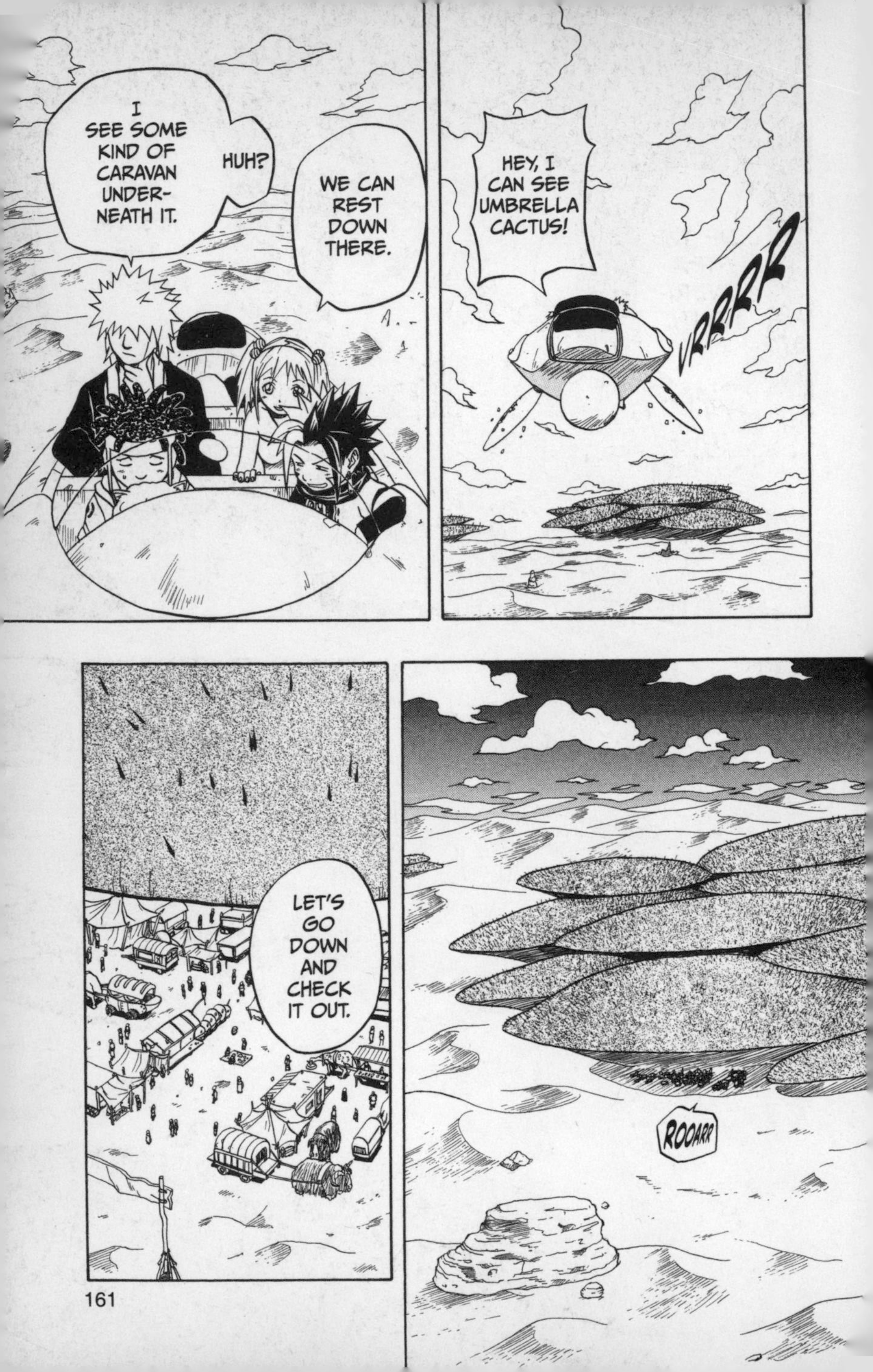
HEY, I CAN SEE UMBRELLA CACTUS!
VRRRR
WE CAN REST DOWN THERE.
HUH?
I SEE SOME KIND OF CARAVAN UNDER-NEATH IT.
ROOARR
LET'S GO DOWN AND CHECK IT OUT.

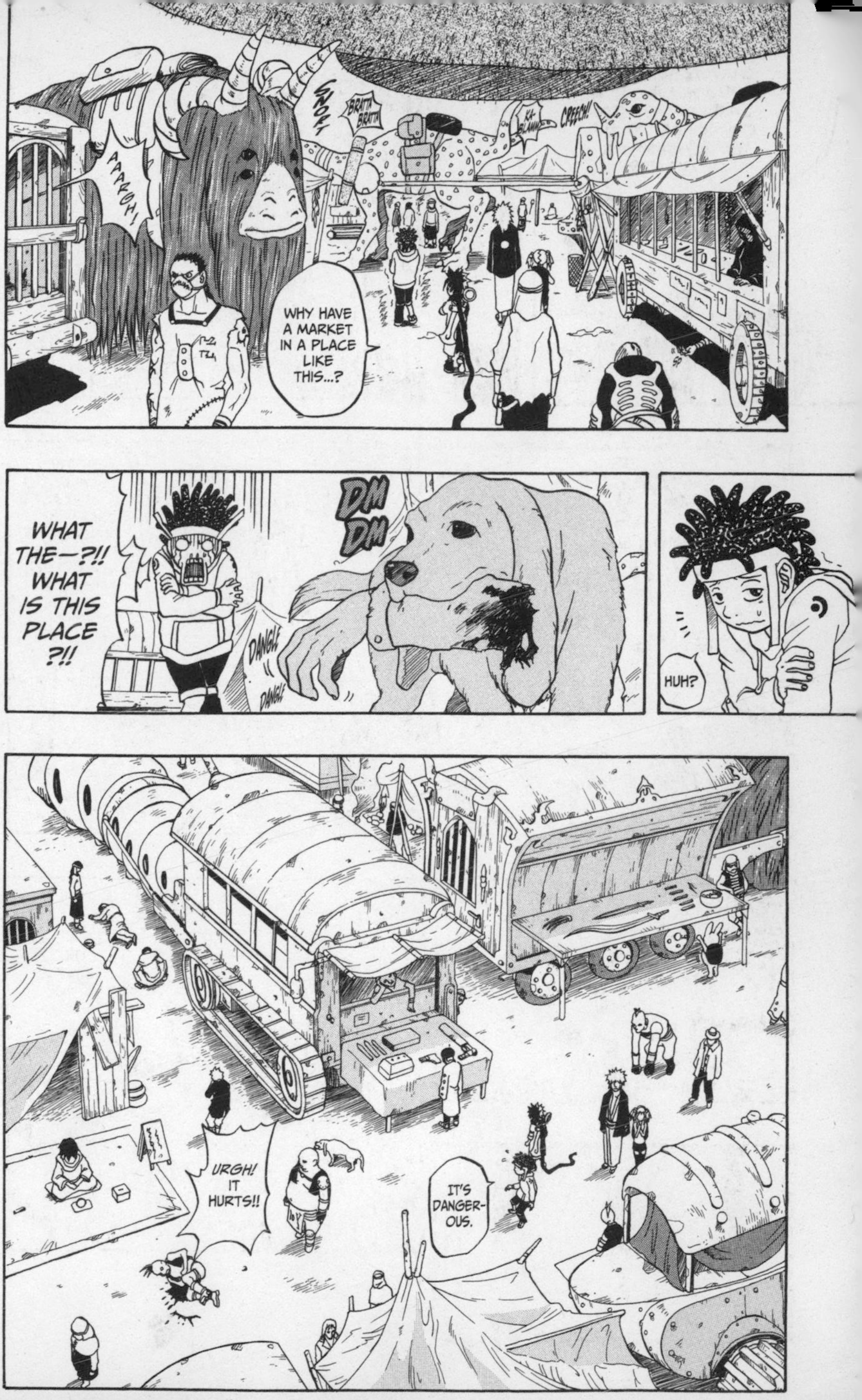
CREECH!
KA-BLAMM
BRATTA BRATTA
SNORT
AAARGH!
WHY HAVE A MARKET IN A PLACE LIKE THIS...?
HUH?
DM DM
WHAT THE—?!! WHAT IS THIS PLACE ?!!
DANGLE DANGLE
IT'S DANGER-OUS.
URGH! IT HURTS!!

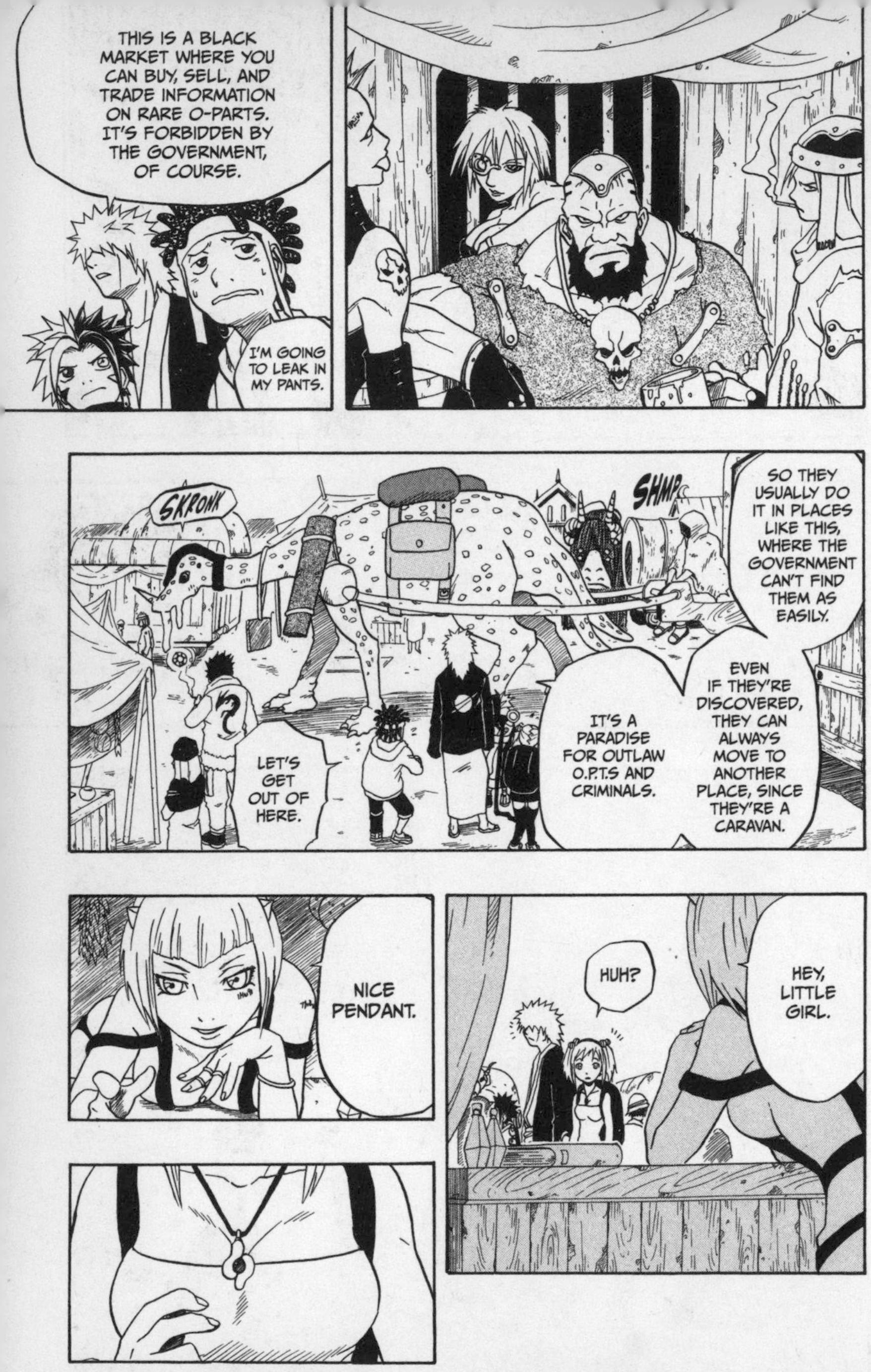
THIS IS A BLACK MARKET WHERE YOU CAN BUY, SELL, AND TRADE INFORMATION ON RARE O-PARTS. IT'S FORBIDDEN BY THE GOVERNMENT, OF COURSE.
I'M GOING TO LEAK IN MY PANTS.
SO THEY USUALLY DO IT IN PLACES LIKE THIS, WHERE THE GOVERNMENT CAN'T FIND THEM AS EASILY.
SHMP
EVEN IF THEY'RE DISCOVERED, THEY CAN ALWAYS MOVE TO ANOTHER PLACE, SINCE THEY'RE A CARAVAN.
IT'S A PARADISE FOR OUTLAW O.P.T.S AND CRIMINALS.
SKRONK
LET'S GET OUT OF HERE.
HEY, LITTLE GIRL.
HUH?
NICE PENDANT.

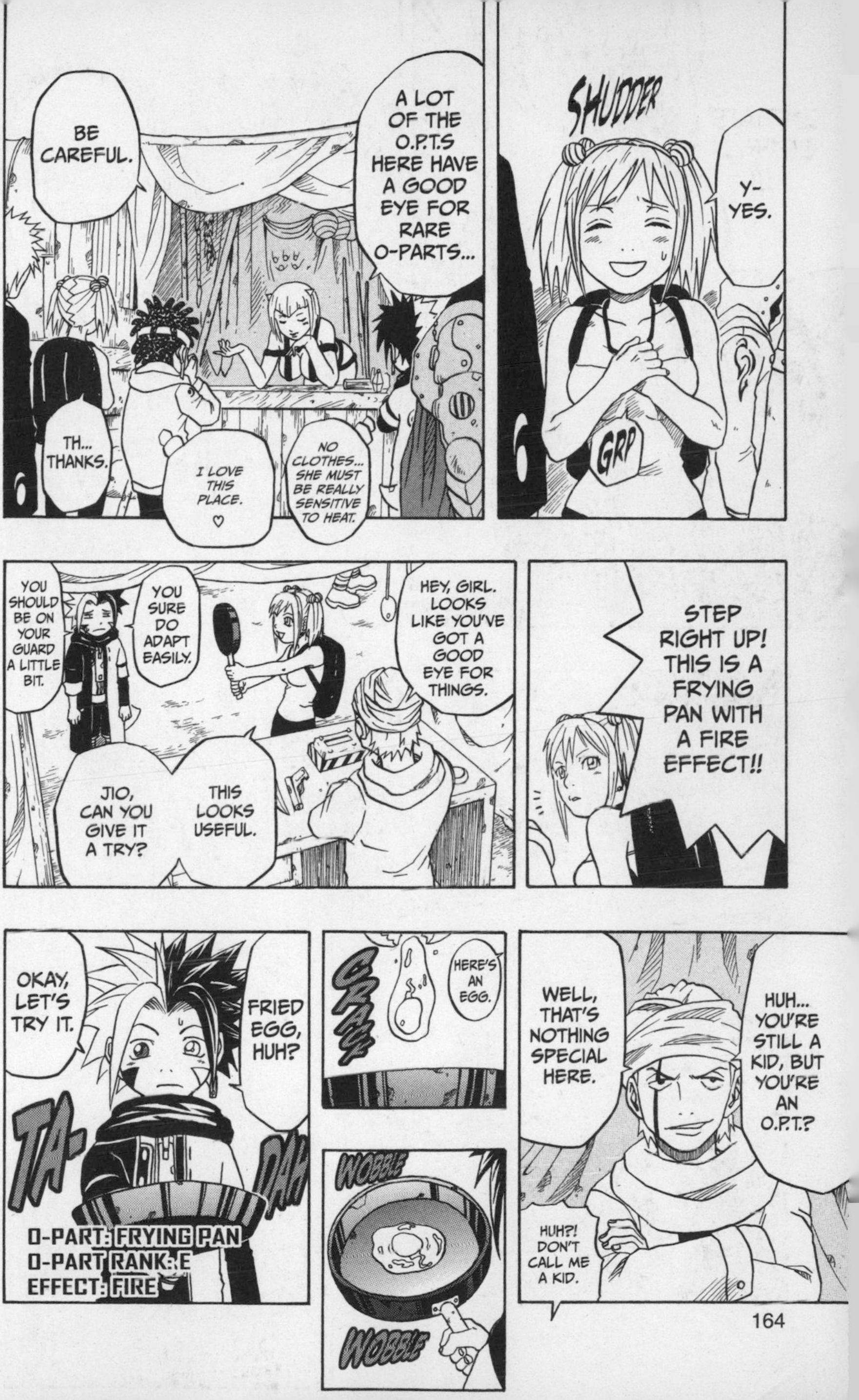
SHUDDER
Y- YES.
GRP
A LOT OF THE O.P.T.S HERE HAVE A GOOD EYE FOR RARE O-PARTS...
BE CAREFUL.
NO CLOTHES... SHE MUST BE REALLY SENSITIVE TO HEAT.
I LOVE THIS PLACE. ♡
TH... THANKS.
STEP RIGHT UP! THIS IS A FRYING PAN WITH A FIRE EFFECT!!
HEY, GIRL. LOOKS LIKE YOU'VE GOT A GOOD EYE FOR THINGS.
YOU SURE DO ADAPT EASILY.
YOU SHOULD BE ON YOUR GUARD A LITTLE BIT.
THIS LOOKS USEFUL.
JIO, CAN YOU GIVE IT A TRY?
HUH... YOU'RE STILL A KID, BUT YOU'RE AN O.P.T.?
WELL, THAT'S NOTHING SPECIAL HERE.
HUH?! DON'T CALL ME A KID.
HERE'S AN EGG.
WOBBLE
WOBBLE
FRIED EGG, HUH?
OKAY, LET'S TRY IT.
TA-
DAH
O-PART: FRYING PAN
O-PART RANK: E
EFFECT: FIRE

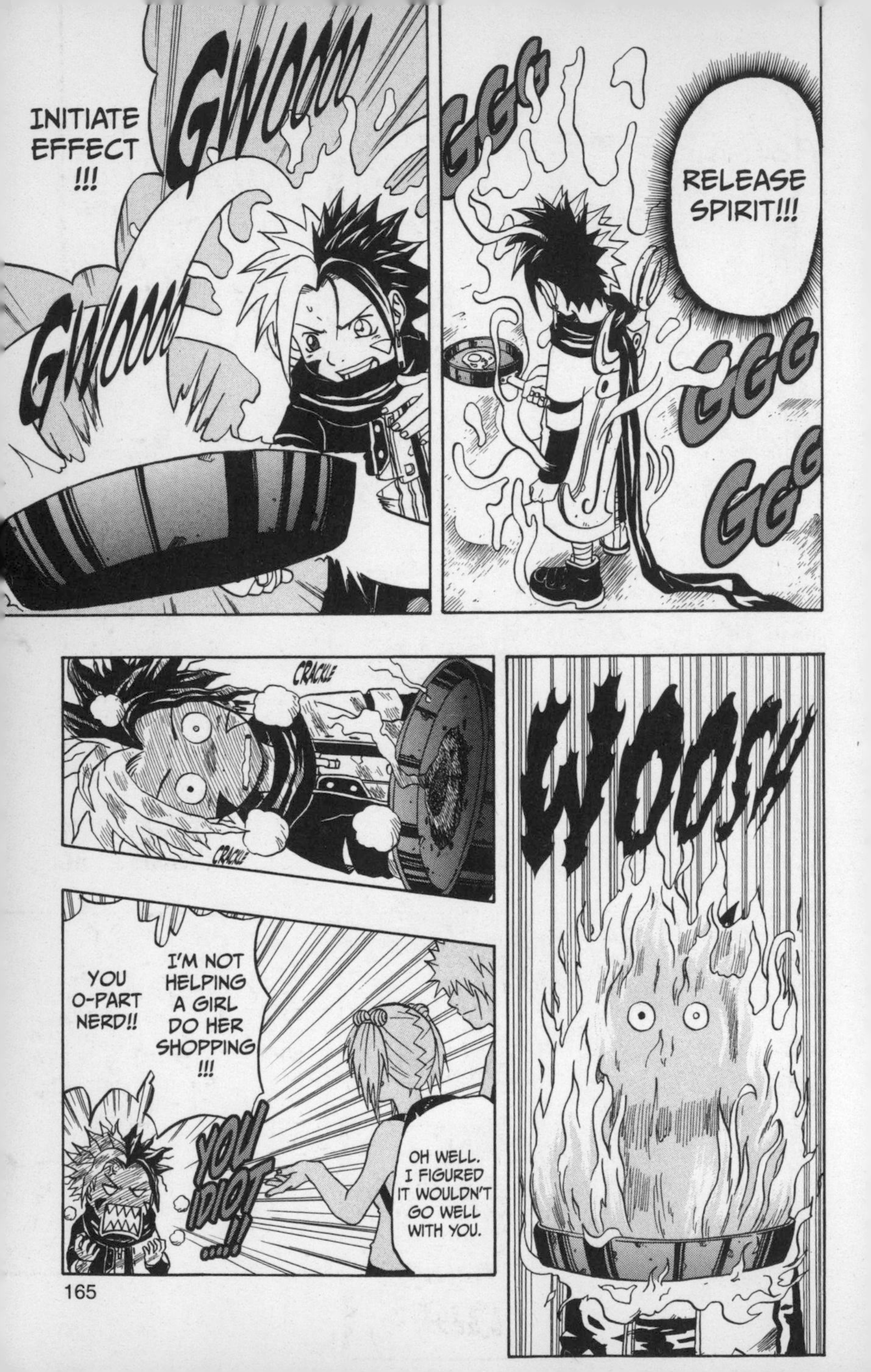
GGG
RELEASE SPIRIT!!!
GGG
GGG
INITIATE EFFECT!!!
GWOOOO
GWOOOO
WOOSH
CRACKLE
CRACKLE
I'M NOT HELPING A GIRL DO HER SHOPPING!!!
YOU O-PART NERD!!
OH WELL. I FIGURED IT WOULDN'T GO WELL WITH YOU.
YOU IDIOT
...!!

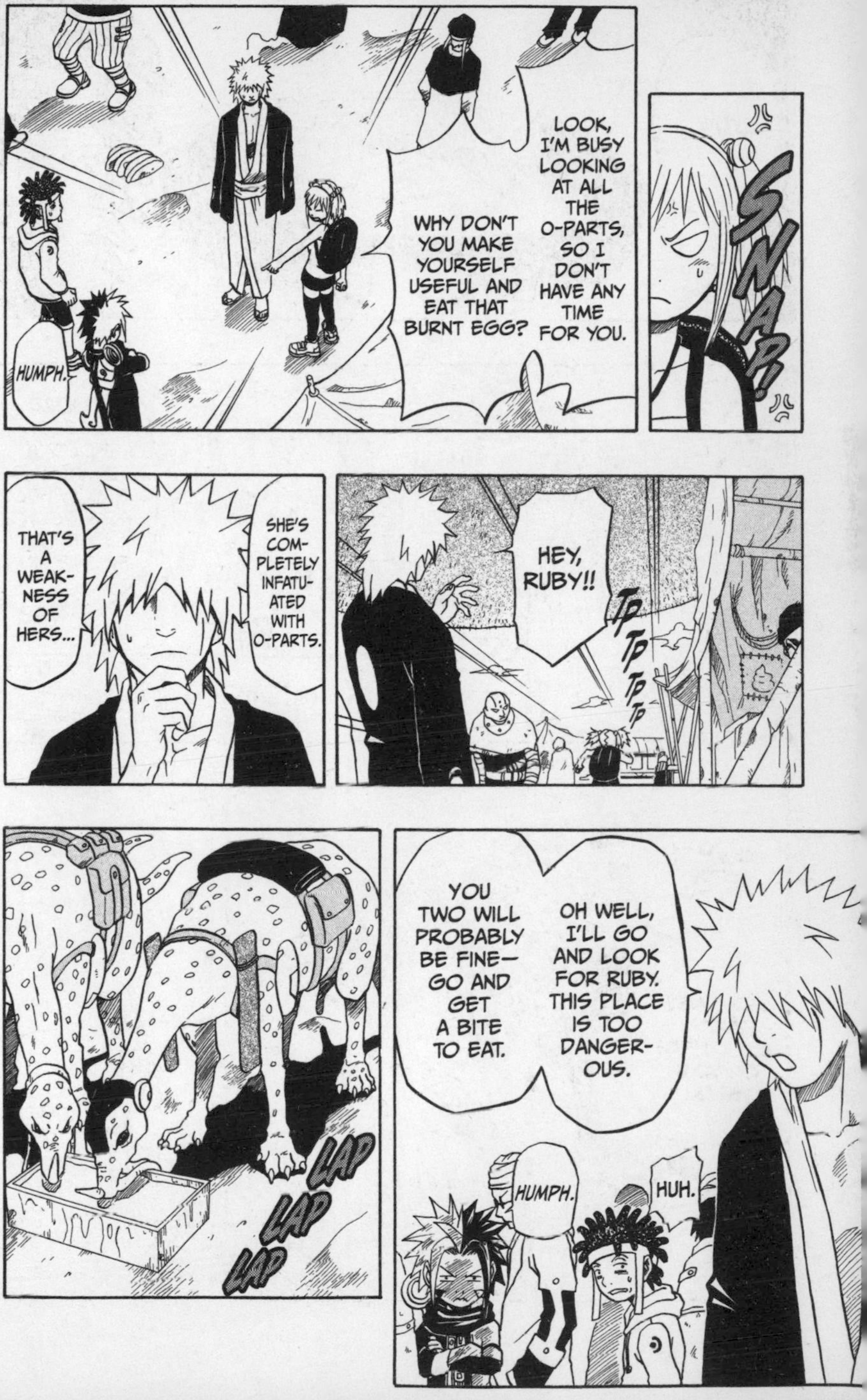
SNAP!
LOOK, I'M BUSY LOOKING AT ALL THE O-PARTS, SO I DON'T HAVE ANY TIME FOR YOU.
WHY DON'T YOU MAKE YOURSELF USEFUL AND EAT THAT BURNT EGG?
HUMPH.
HEY, RUBY!!
TP TP TP TP
SHE'S COMPLETELY INFATUATED WITH O-PARTS.
THAT'S A WEAKNESS OF HERS...
OH WELL, I'LL GO AND LOOK FOR RUBY. THIS PLACE IS TOO DANGEROUS.
YOU TWO WILL PROBABLY BE FINE— GO AND GET A BITE TO EAT.
HUH.
HUMPH.
LAP LAP LAP

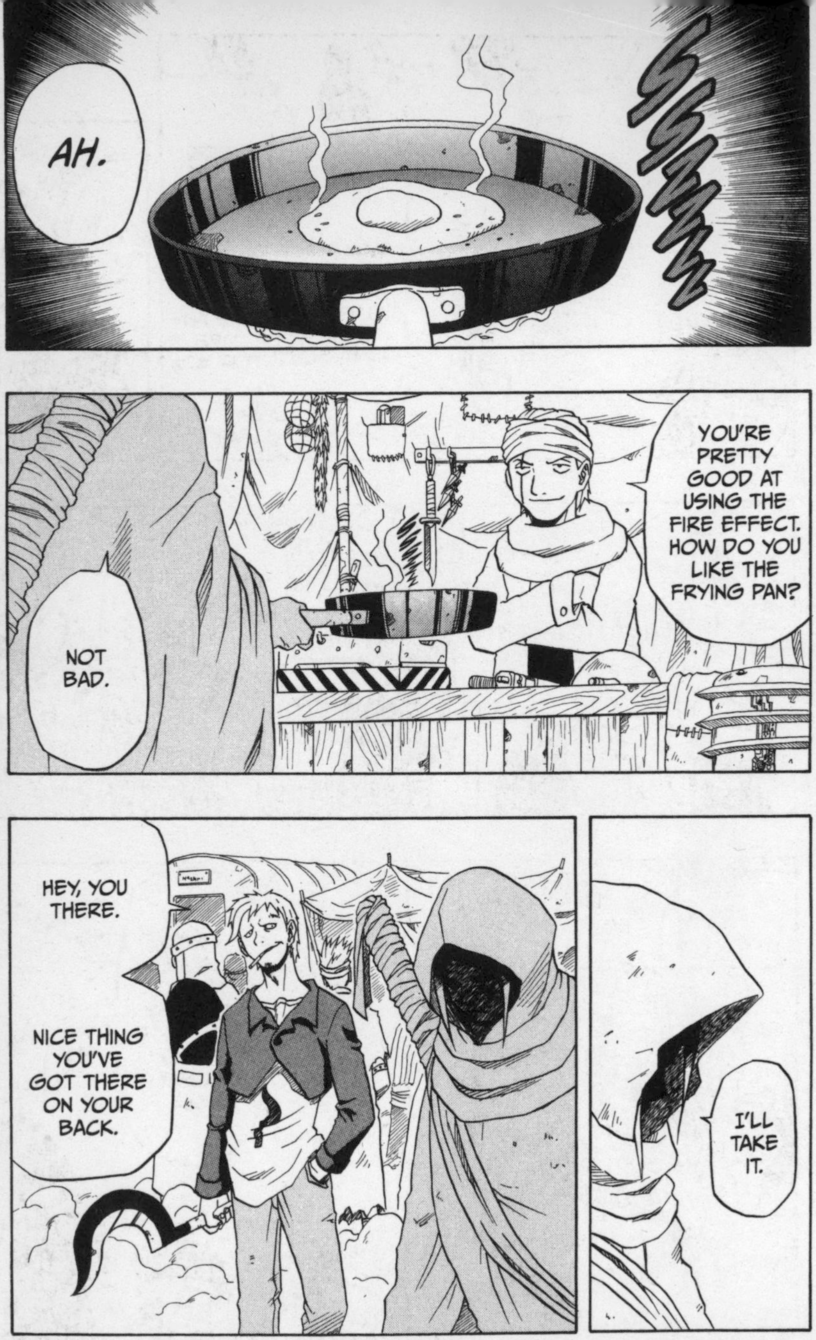
AH.
YOU'RE PRETTY GOOD AT USING THE FIRE EFFECT. HOW DO YOU LIKE THE FRYING PAN?
NOT BAD.
I'LL TAKE IT.
HEY, YOU THERE.
NICE THING YOU'VE GOT THERE ON YOUR BACK.

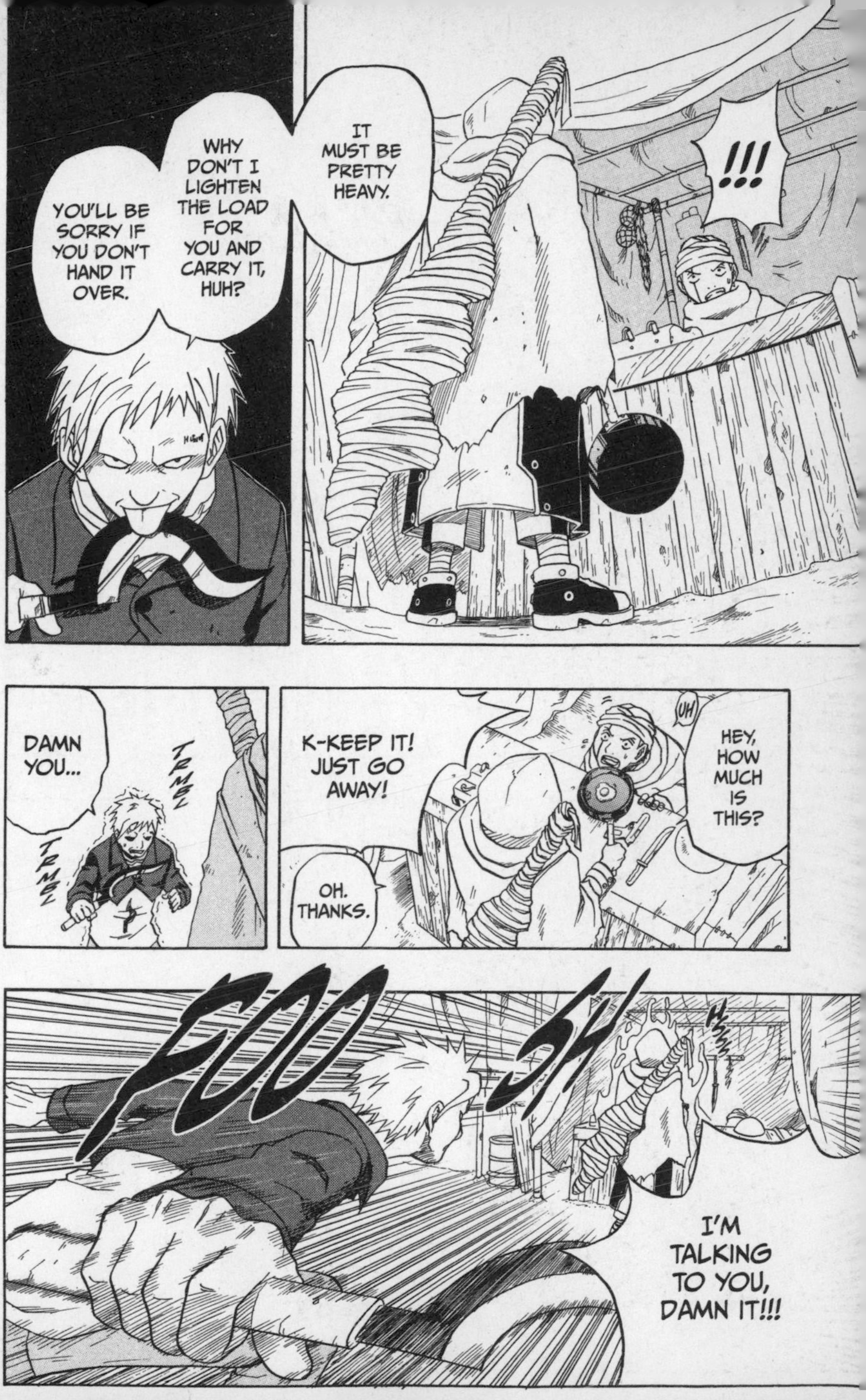
IT MUST BE PRETTY HEAVY.
WHY DON'T I LIGHTEN THE LOAD FOR YOU AND CARRY IT, HUH?
YOU'LL BE SORRY IF YOU DON'T HAND IT OVER.
!!!
HEY, HOW MUCH IS THIS?
UH
K-KEEP IT! JUST GO AWAY!
OH. THANKS.
DAMN YOU...
TRMBL
TRMBL
FOOSH
I'M TALKING TO YOU, DAMN IT!!!

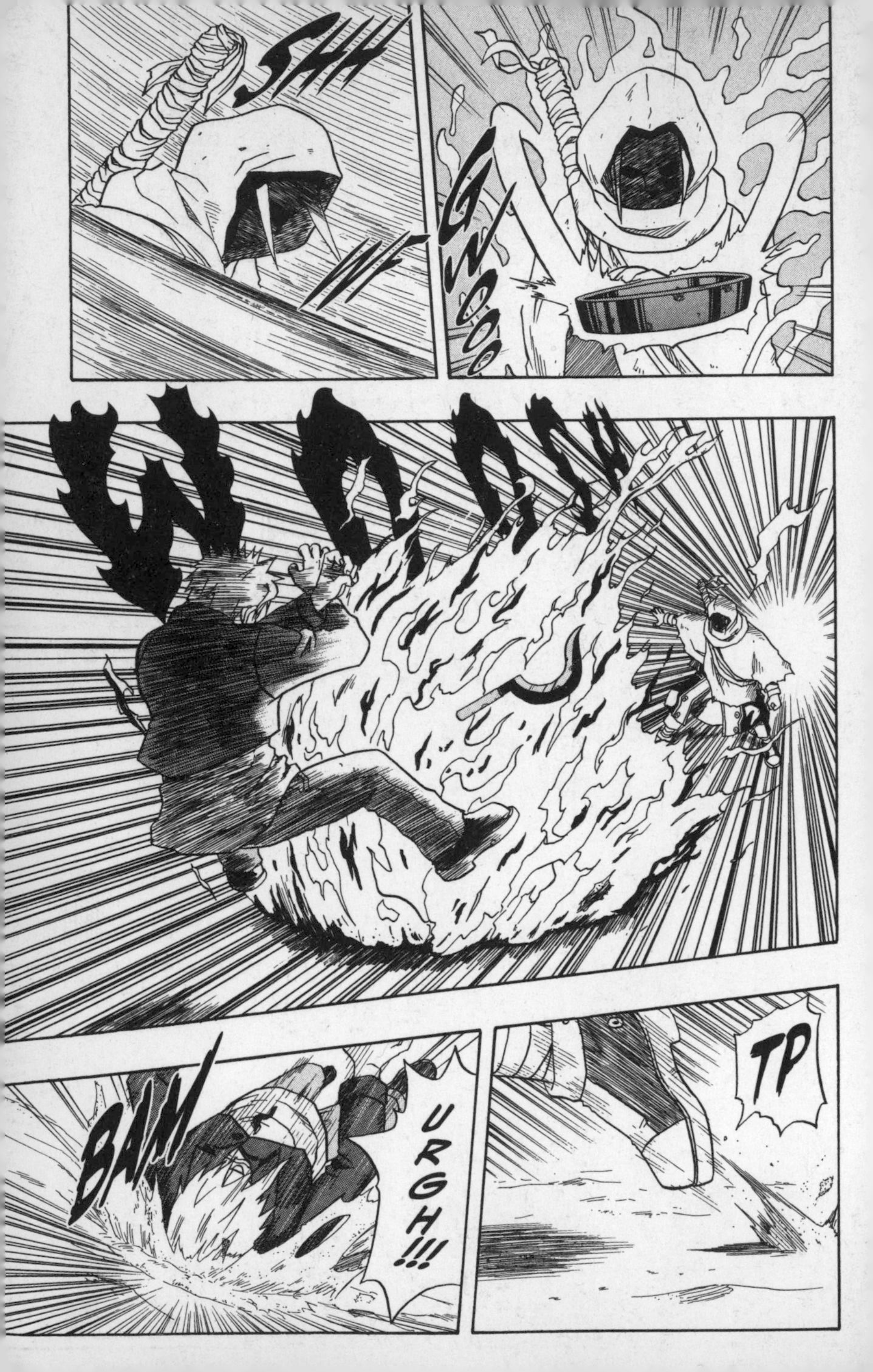
GWOOOO
SHH
TP
BAM
URGH!!!

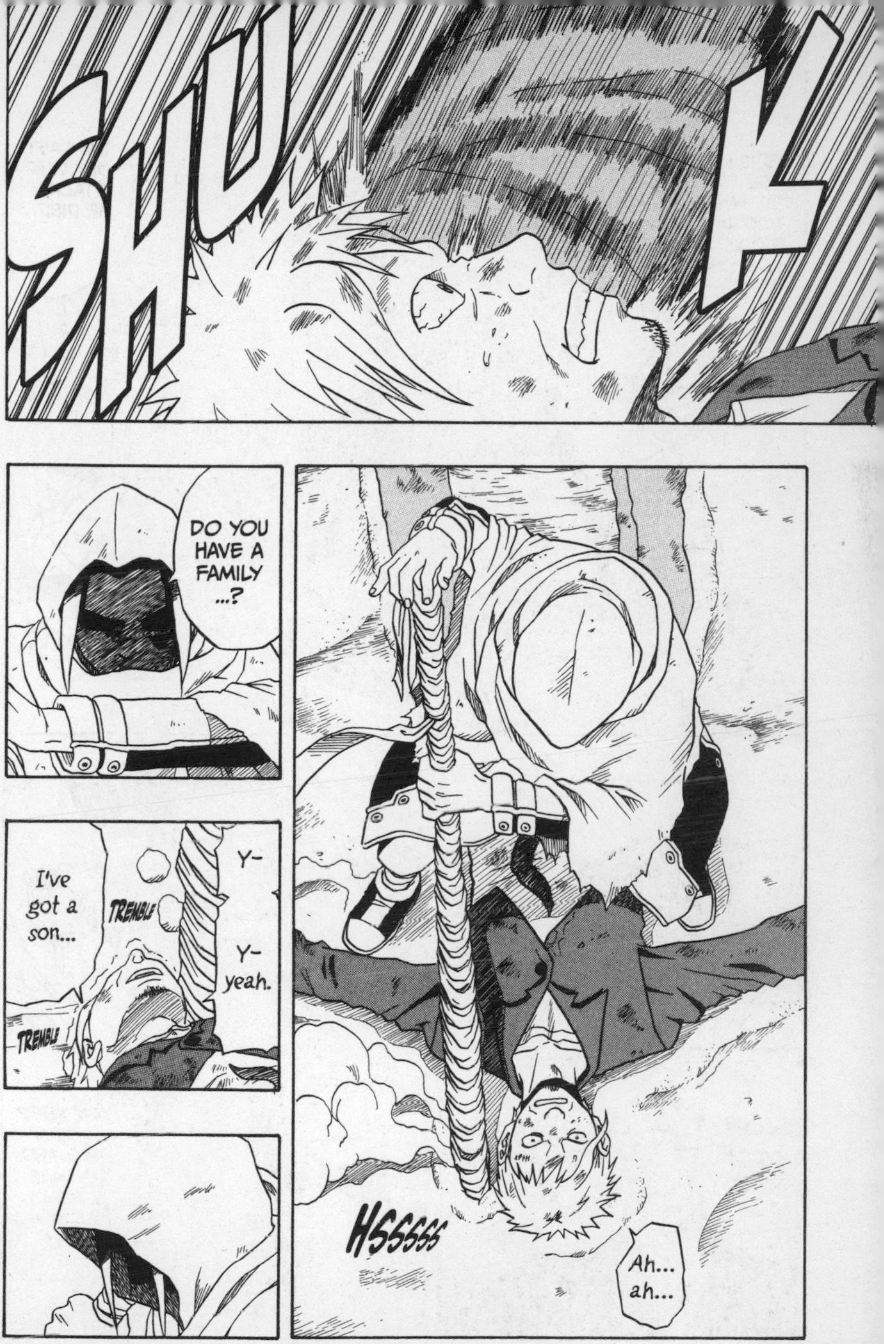
SHUK
HSSSSS
Ah... ah...
DO YOU HAVE A FAMILY ...?
Y-
Y-yeah.
I've got a son...
TREMBLE
TREMBLE

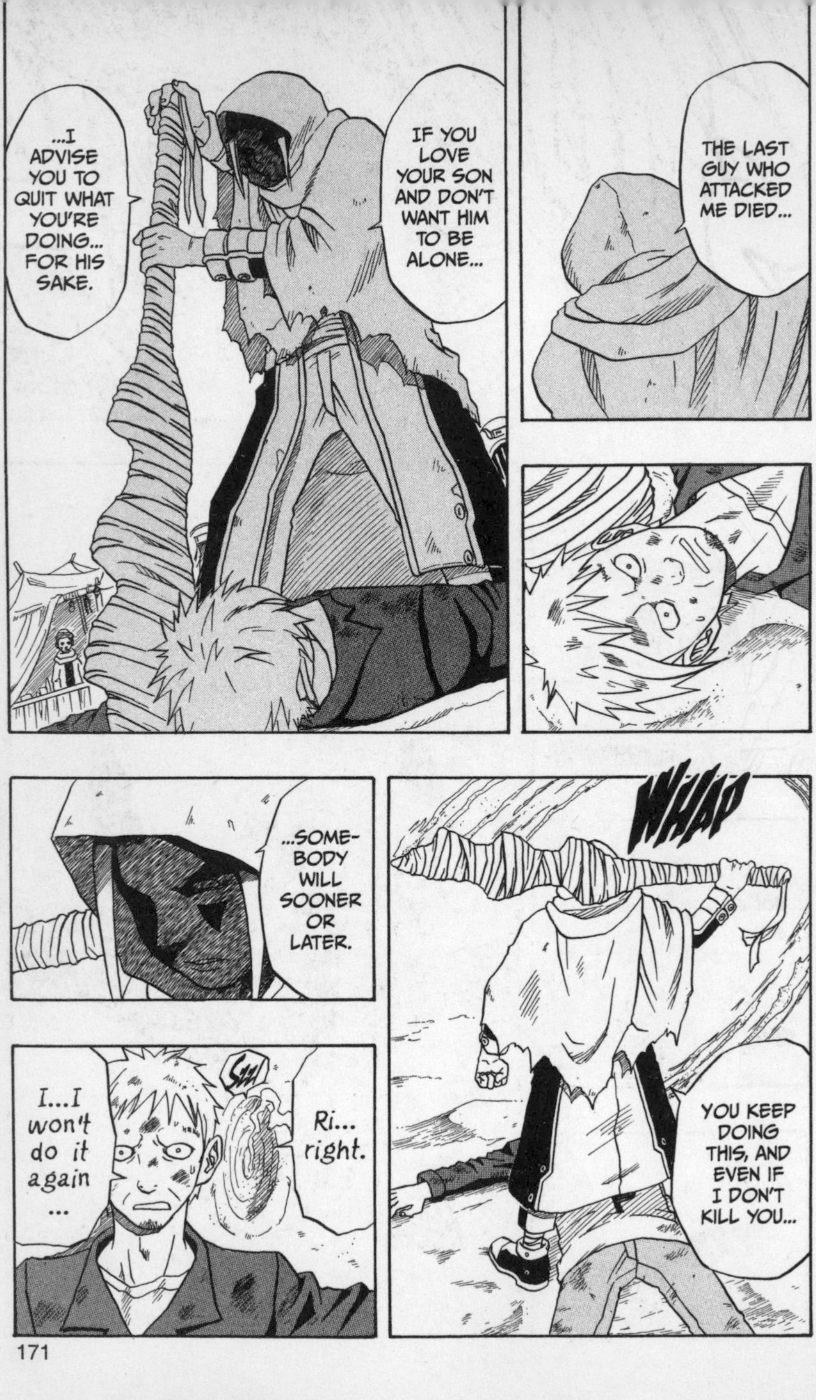
THE LAST GUY WHO ATTACKED ME DIED...
IF YOU LOVE YOUR SON AND DON'T WANT HIM TO BE ALONE...
...I ADVISE YOU TO QUIT WHAT YOU'RE DOING... FOR HIS SAKE.
WHAP
YOU KEEP DOING THIS, AND EVEN IF I DON'T KILL YOU...
...SOME-BODY WILL SOONER OR LATER.
Ri... right.
I...I won't do it again ...

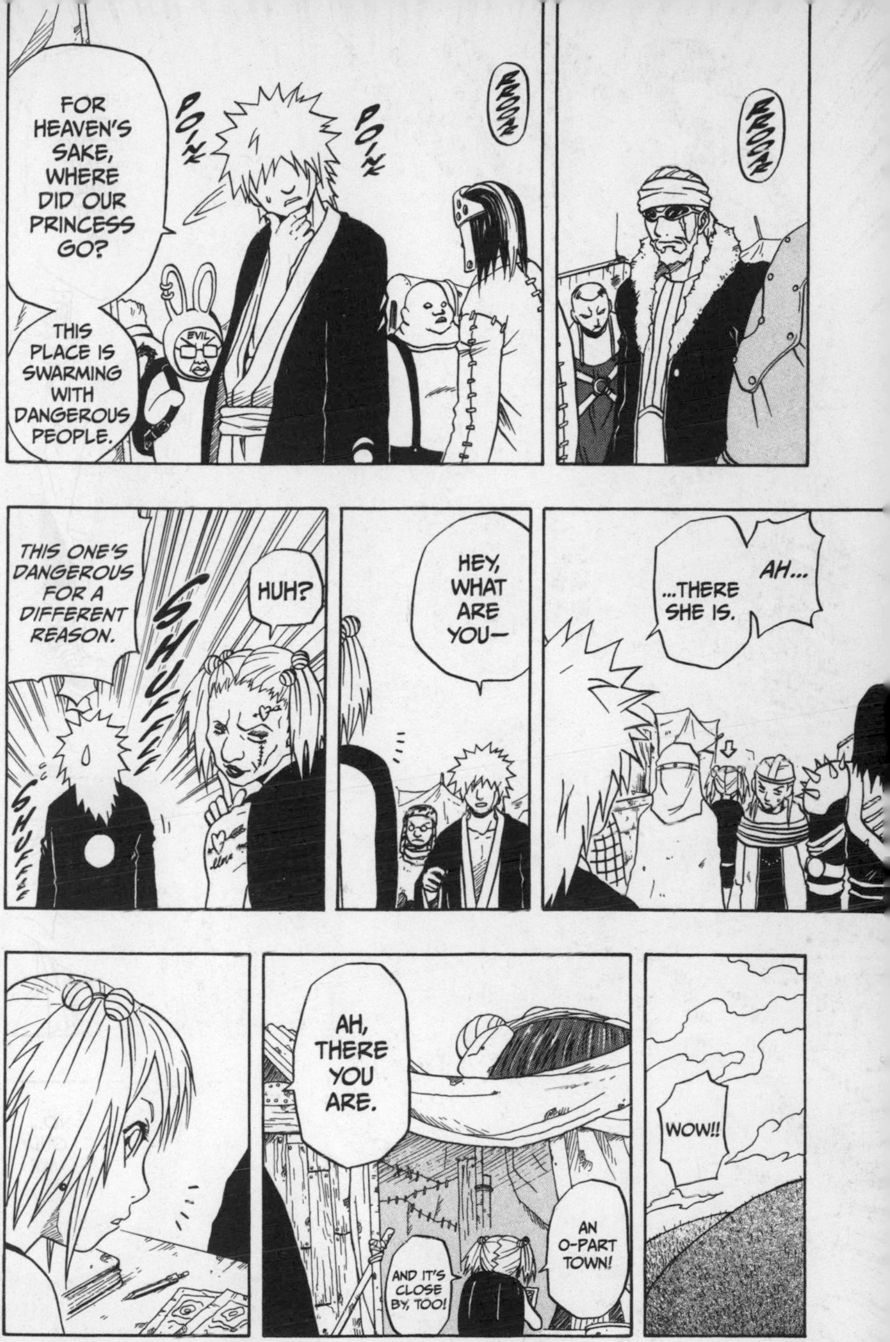
FOR HEAVEN'S SAKE, WHERE DID OUR PRINCESS GO?
EVIL
THIS PLACE IS SWARMING WITH DANGEROUS PEOPLE.
AH...
...THERE SHE IS.
HEY, WHAT ARE YOU—
HUH?
THIS ONE'S DANGEROUS FOR A DIFFERENT REASON.
WOW!!
AH, THERE YOU ARE.
AN O-PART TOWN!
AND IT'S CLOSE BY, TOO!

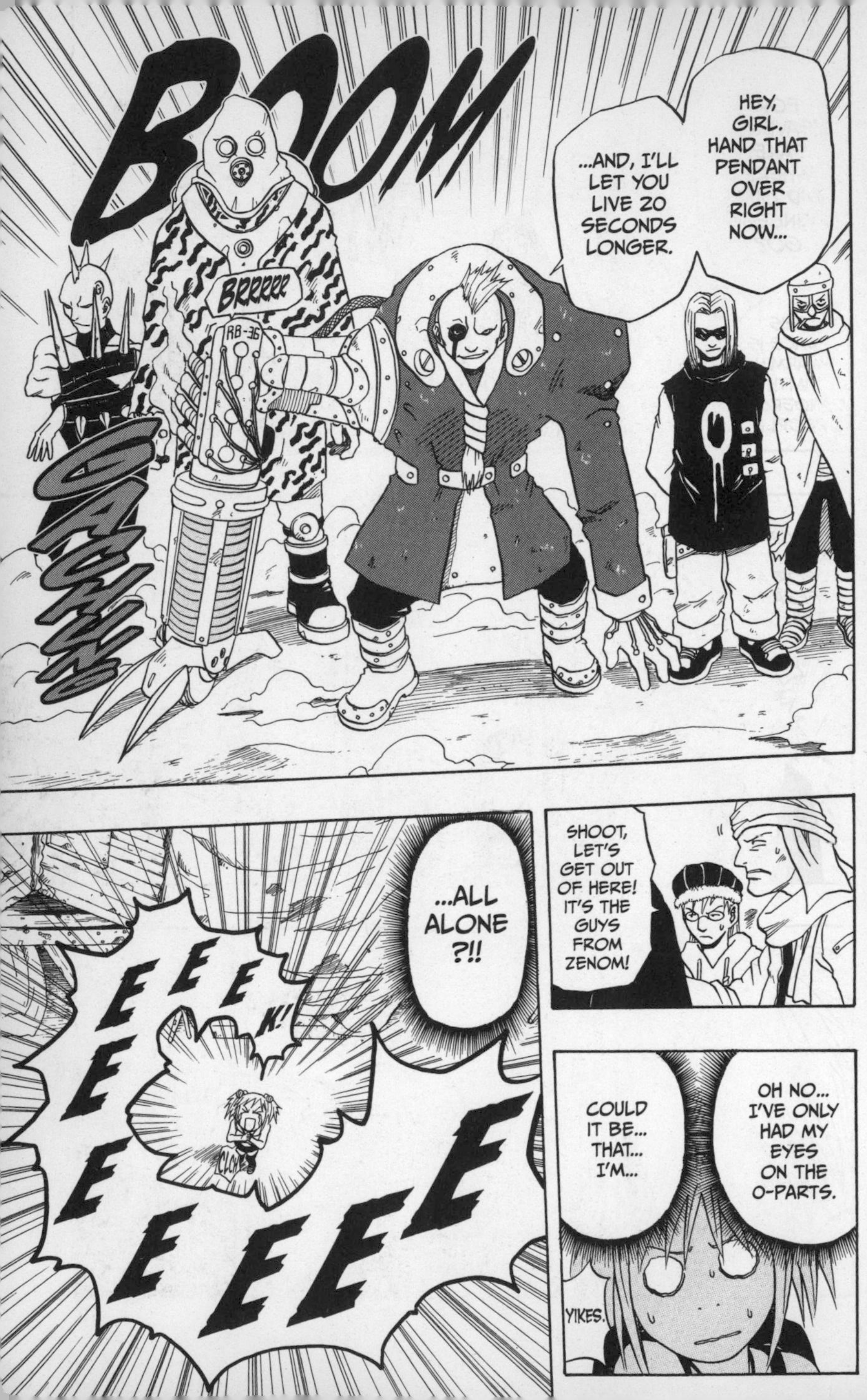
HEY, GIRL. HAND THAT PENDANT OVER RIGHT NOW...
...AND, I'LL LET YOU LIVE 20 SECONDS LONGER.
BOOM
BRRRRR
RB-36
SHOOT, LET'S GET OUT OF HERE! IT'S THE GUYS FROM ZENOM!
OH NO... I'VE ONLY HAD MY EYES ON THE O-PARTS.
COULD IT BE... THAT... I'M...
YIKES.
...ALL ALONE ?!!
EEEEEEEEEEEEEK!

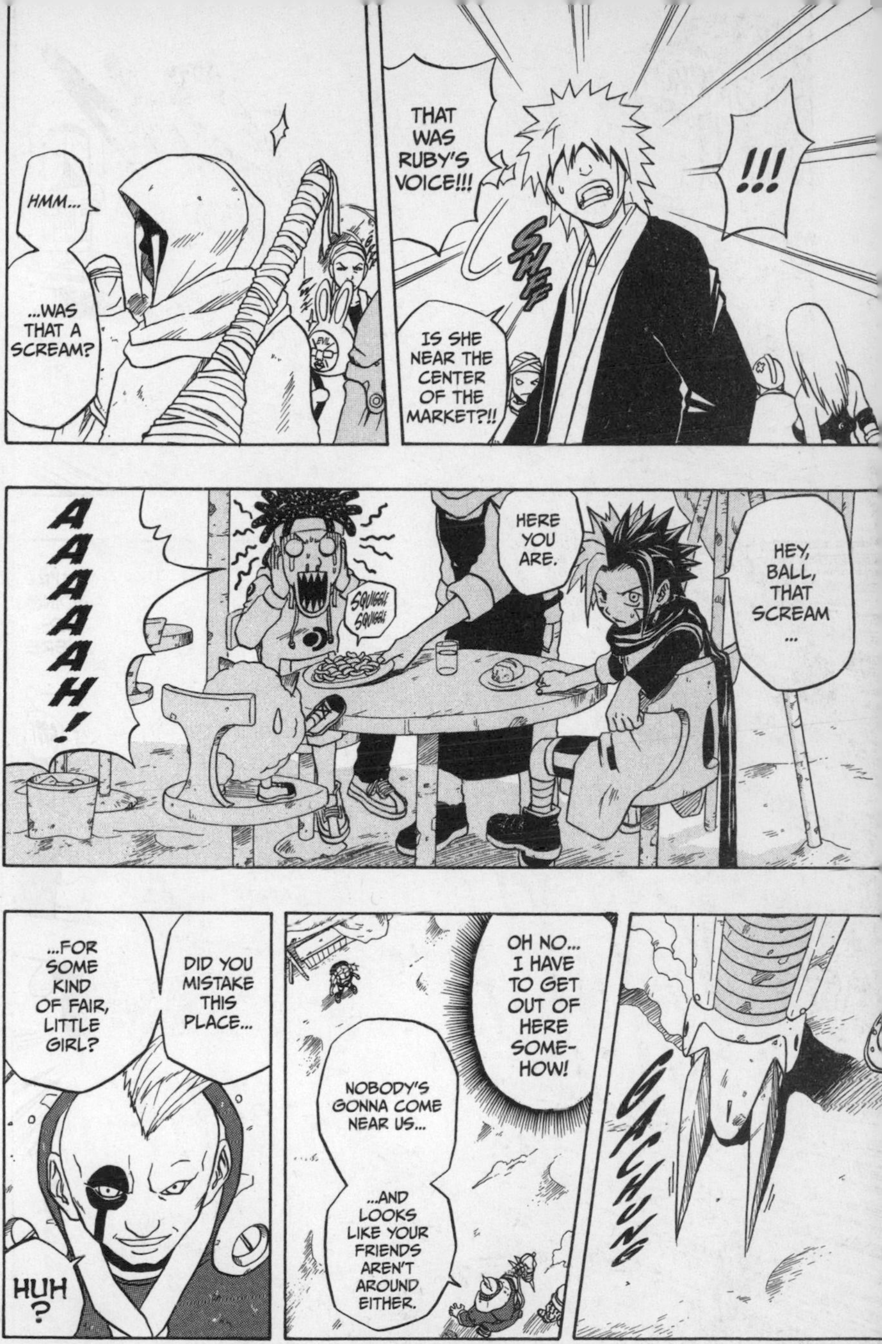
!!!
THAT WAS RUBY'S VOICE!!!
SHFF
IS SHE NEAR THE CENTER OF THE MARKET?!!
HMM...
...WAS THAT A SCREAM?
HEY, BALL, THAT SCREAM ...
HERE YOU ARE.
SQUIGGLE SQUIGGLE
AAAAAAH!
GACHUNG
OH NO... I HAVE TO GET OUT OF HERE SOME-HOW!
NOBODY'S GONNA COME NEAR US...
...AND LOOKS LIKE YOUR FRIENDS AREN'T AROUND EITHER.
DID YOU MISTAKE THIS PLACE...
...FOR SOME KIND OF FAIR, LITTLE GIRL?
HUH?

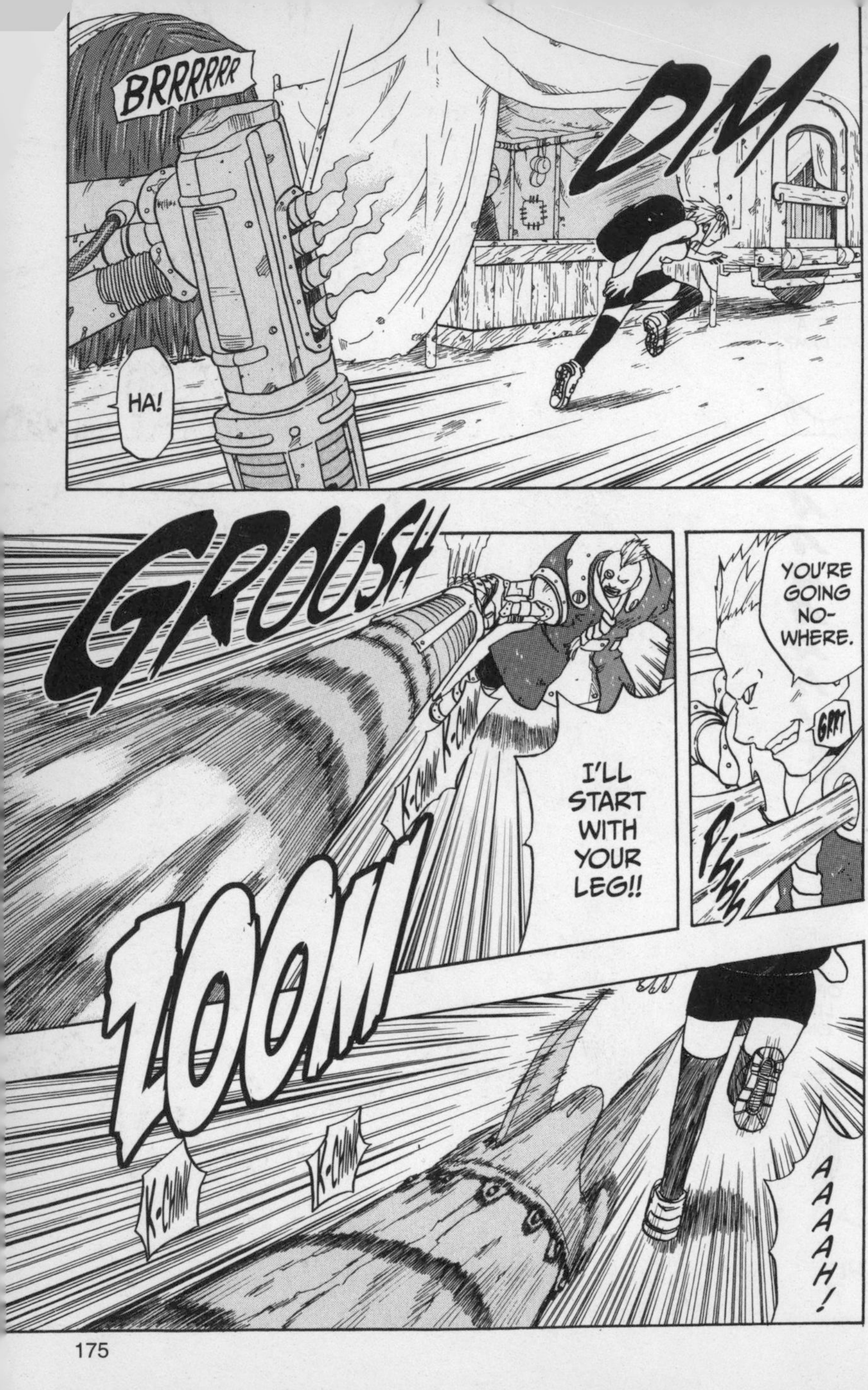
DM
BRRRRRR
HA!
YOU'RE GOING NO-WHERE.
GRRT
GROOSH
I'LL START WITH YOUR LEG!!
AAAAAH!
ZOOM

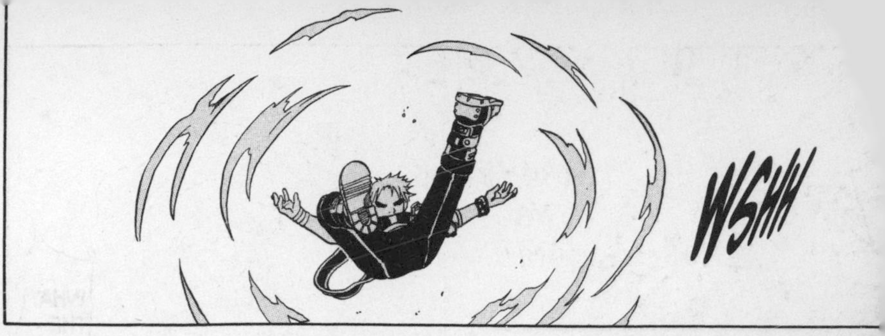
WSHH
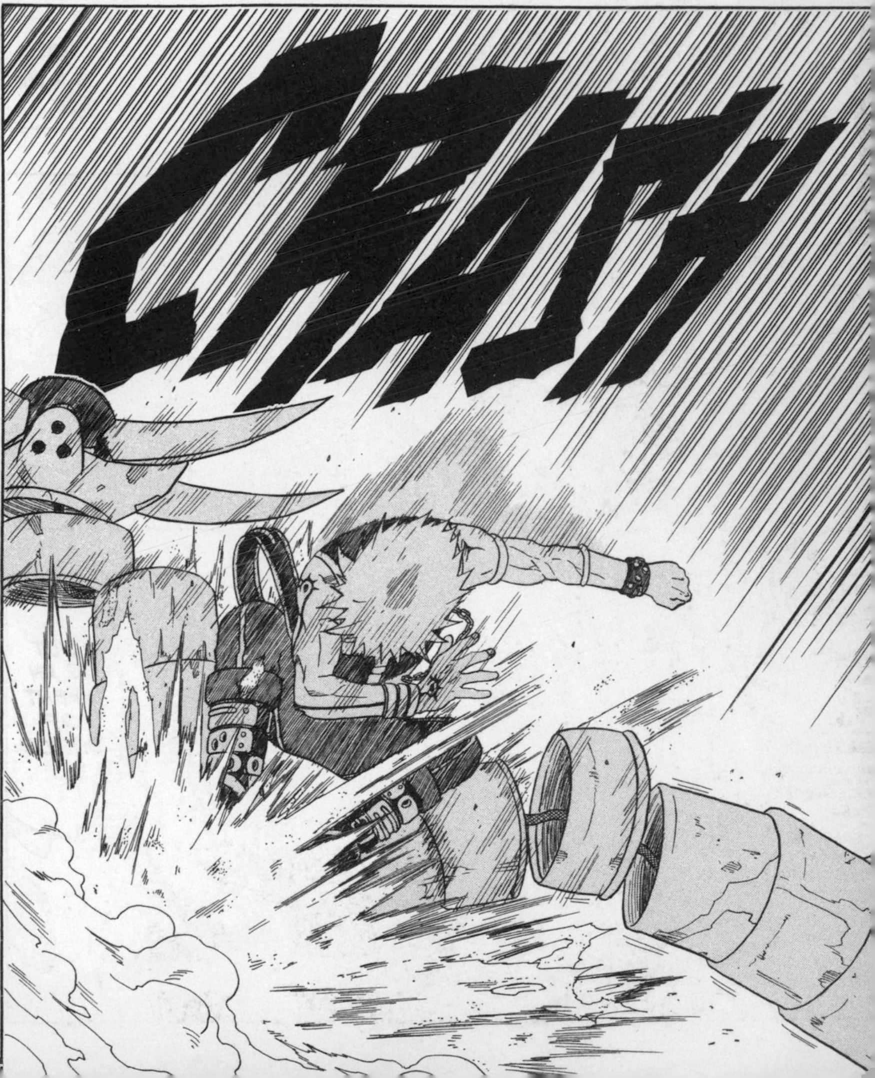
CRASH

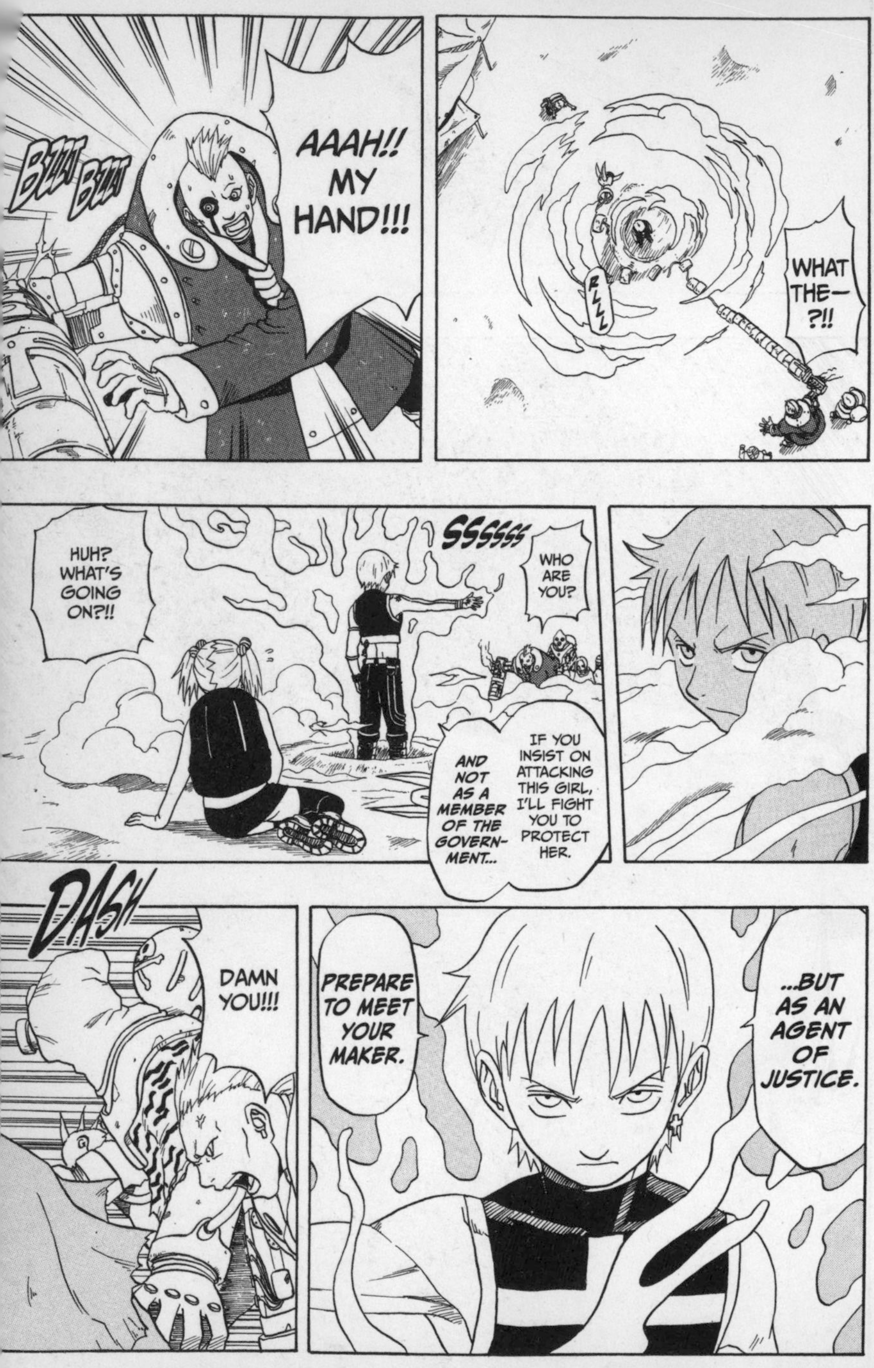
WHAT THE—?!!
RLLL
BZZT BZZT
AAAH!! MY HAND!!!
WHO ARE YOU?
SSSSSS
HUH? WHAT'S GOING ON?!!
IF YOU INSIST ON ATTACKING THIS GIRL, I'LL FIGHT YOU TO PROTECT HER.
AND NOT AS A MEMBER OF THE GOVERNMENT...
...BUT AS AN AGENT OF JUSTICE.
PREPARE TO MEET YOUR MAKER.
DASH
DAMN YOU!!!

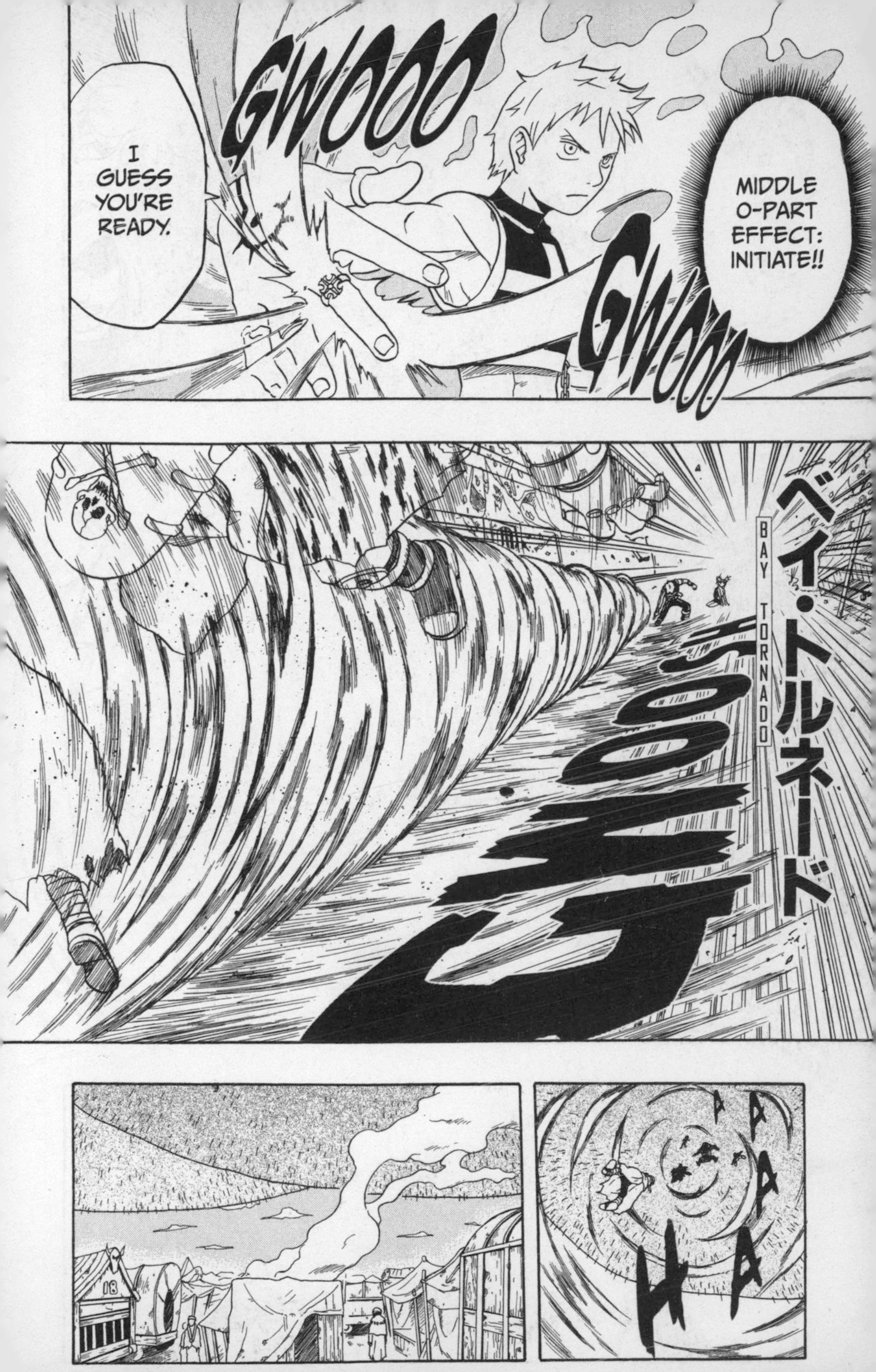
MIDDLE O-PART EFFECT: INITIATE!!
GWOOO
GWOOO
I GUESS YOU'RE READY.
ベイ・トルネード
BAY TORNADO
WHOOSH
HA HA

POK

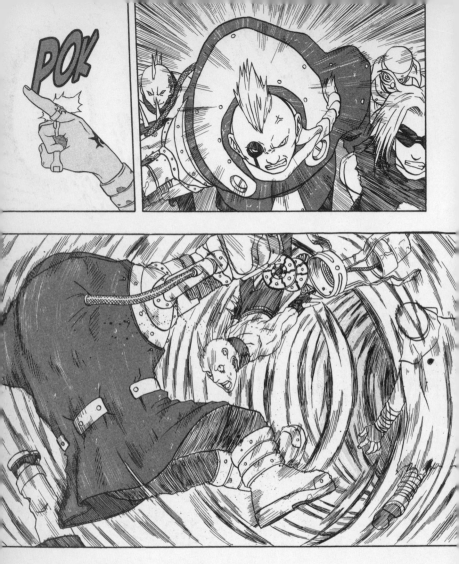

AND GOOD-LOOKING, TOO...

H-HE'S AMAZING.

THUMP

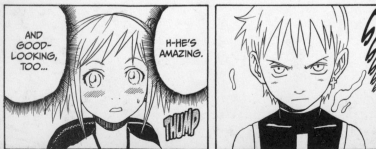

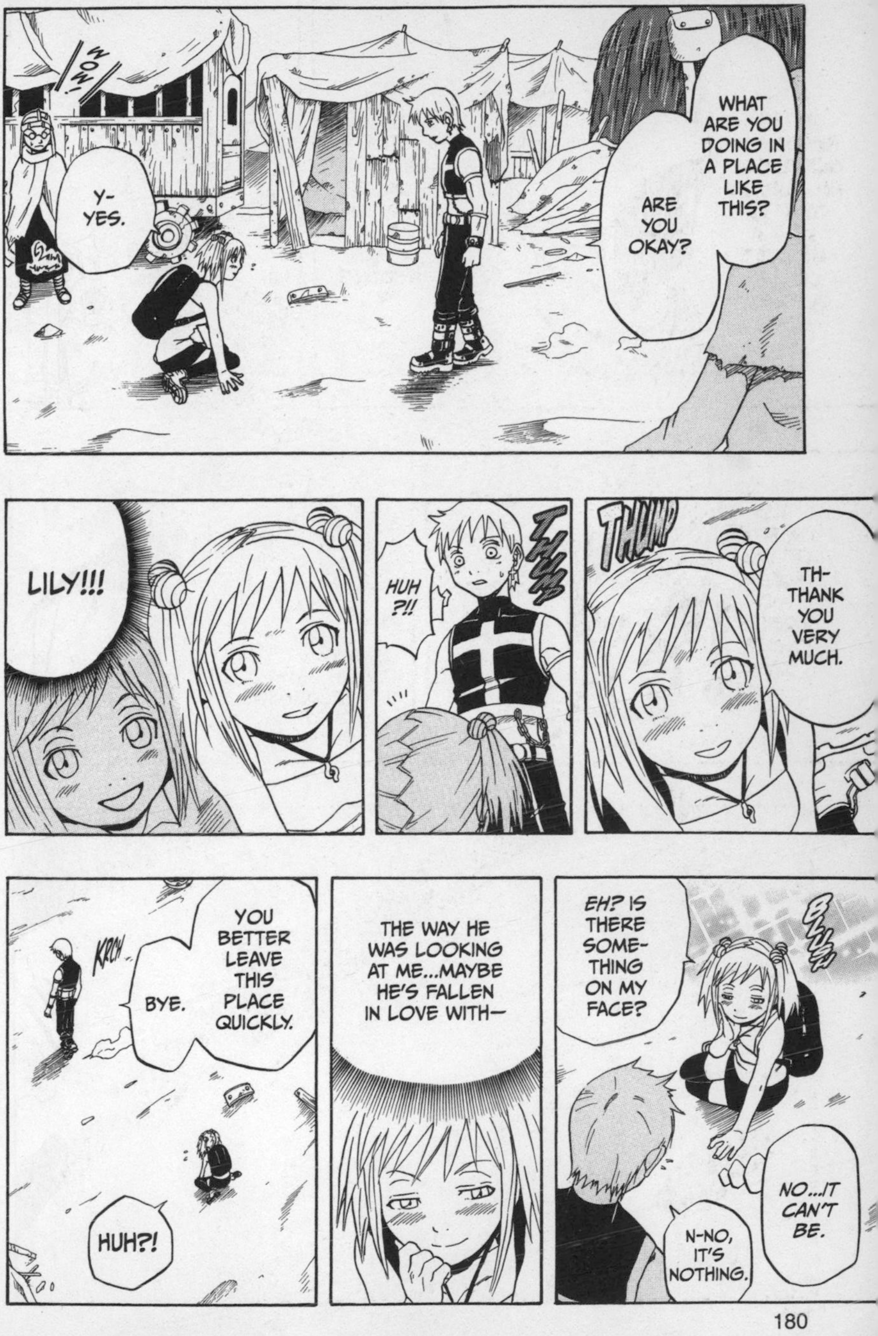
WHAT ARE YOU DOING IN A PLACE LIKE THIS?
ARE YOU OKAY?
WOW!
Y- YES.
THUMP
TH- THANK YOU VERY MUCH.
THMM
HUH ?!!
LILY!!!
EH? IS THERE SOME- THING ON MY FACE?
NO...IT CAN'T BE.
N-NO, IT'S NOTHING.
THE WAY HE WAS LOOKING AT ME...MAYBE HE'S FALLEN IN LOVE WITH—
YOU BETTER LEAVE THIS PLACE QUICKLY.
BYE.
KRCH
HUH?!

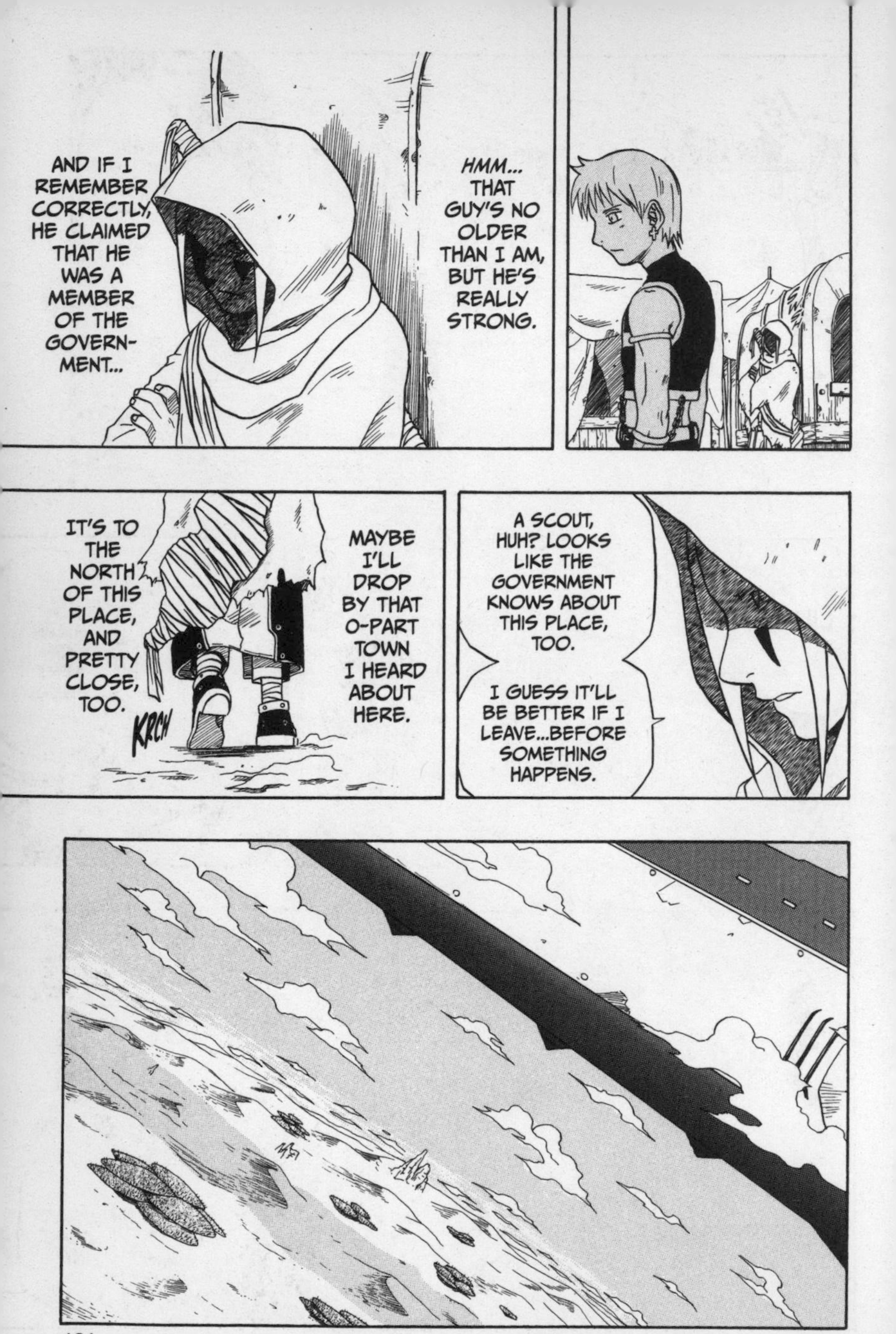
HMM... THAT GUY'S NO OLDER THAN I AM, BUT HE'S REALLY STRONG.
AND IF I REMEMBER CORRECTLY, HE CLAIMED THAT HE WAS A MEMBER OF THE GOVERNMENT...
A SCOUT, HUH? LOOKS LIKE THE GOVERNMENT KNOWS ABOUT THIS PLACE, TOO.
I GUESS IT'LL BE BETTER IF I LEAVE...BEFORE SOMETHING HAPPENS.
MAYBE I'LL DROP BY THAT O-PART TOWN I HEARD ABOUT HERE.
IT'S TO THE NORTH OF THIS PLACE, AND PRETTY CLOSE, TOO.
KRCH

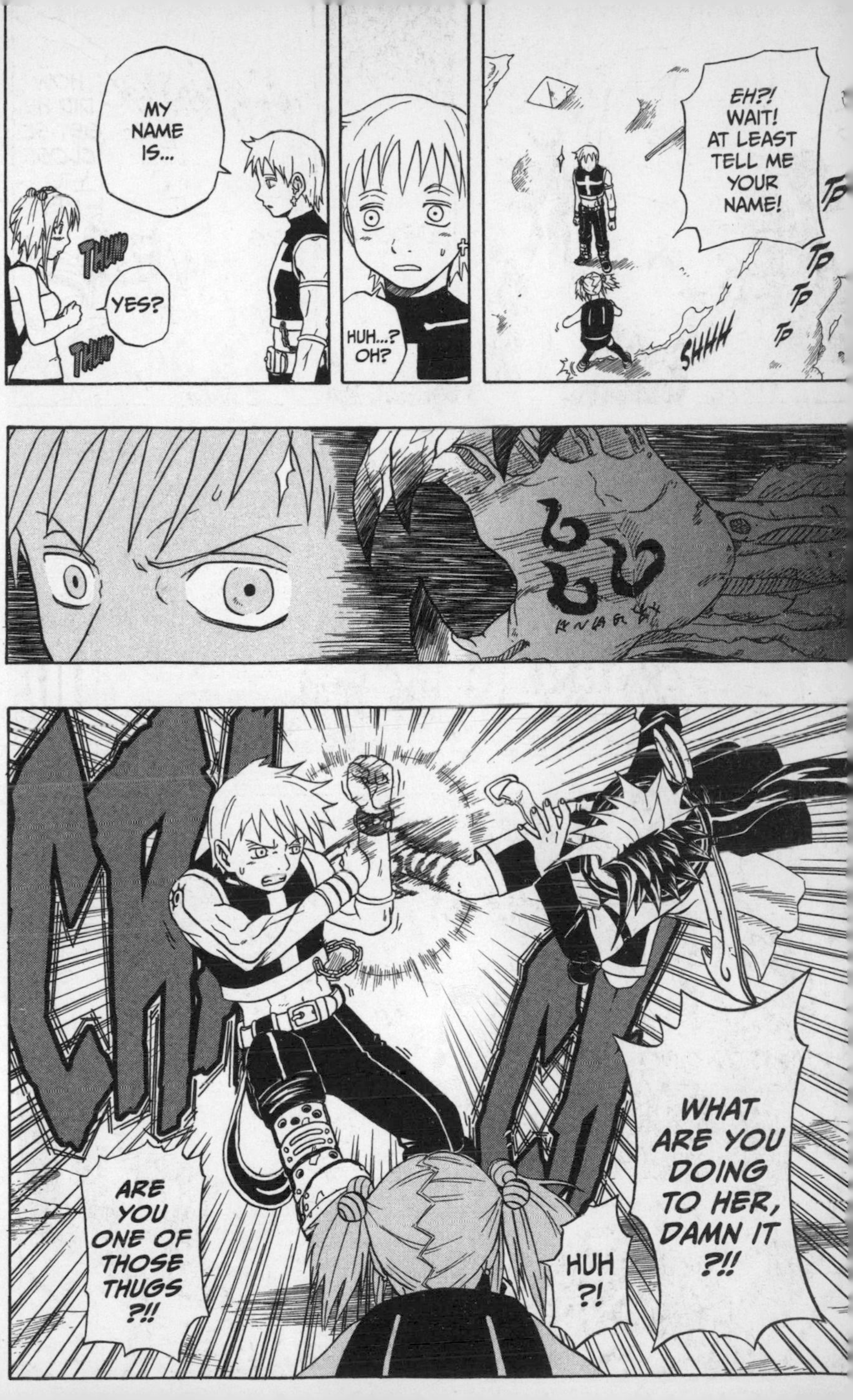
EH?! WAIT! AT LEAST TELL ME YOUR NAME!
TP
TP
TP
TP
SHHH
HUH...? OH?
MY NAME IS...
THUMP
YES?
THUMP
WHAT ARE YOU DOING TO HER, DAMN IT ?!!
HUH ?!
ARE YOU ONE OF THOSE THUGS ?!!

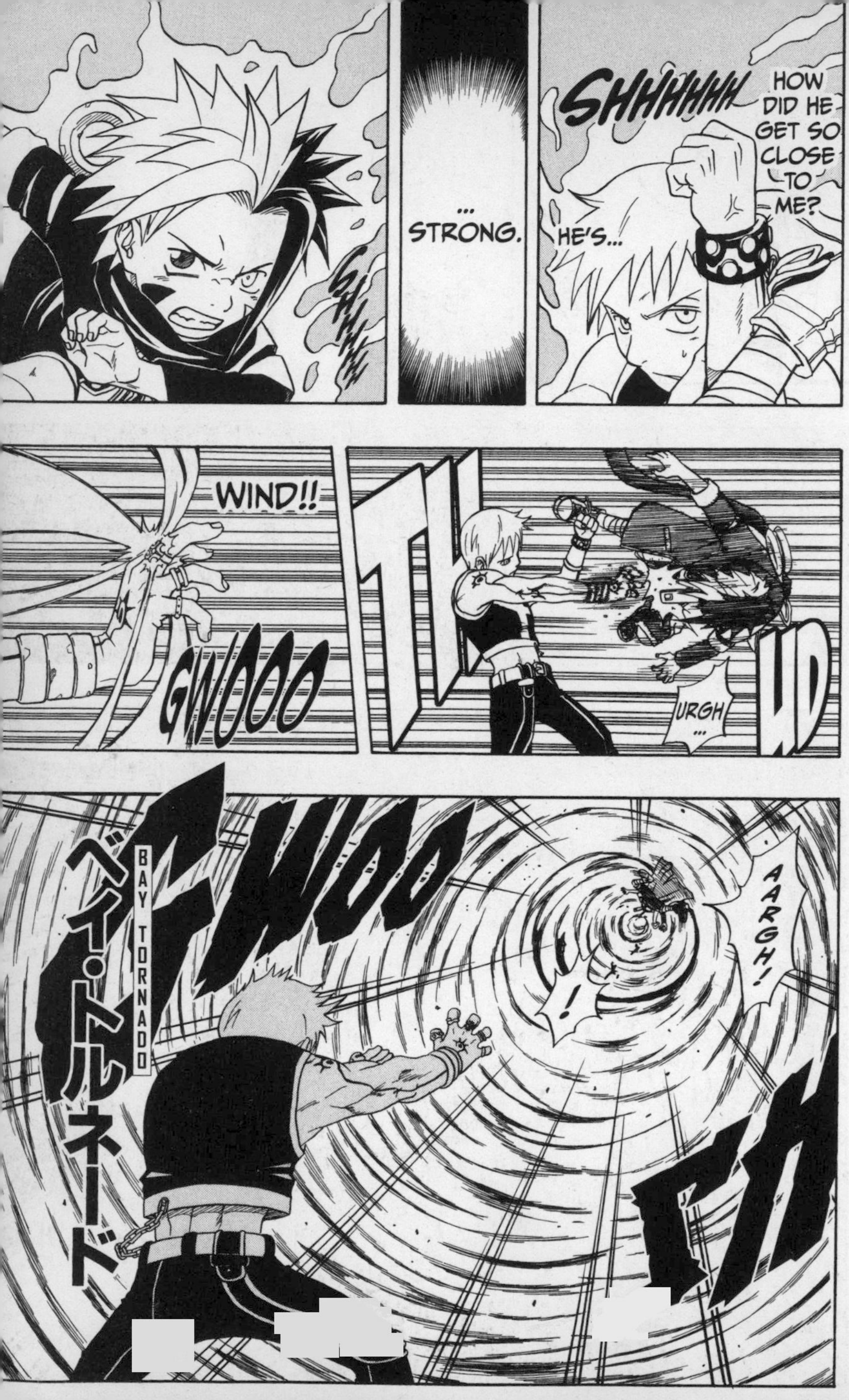
SHHHHHH
HOW DID HE GET SO CLOSE TO ME?
HE'S...
... STRONG.
TH
UD
URGH ...
WIND!!
GWOOO
ベイ・トルネード
BAY TORNADO
FWOO
AARGH!
!

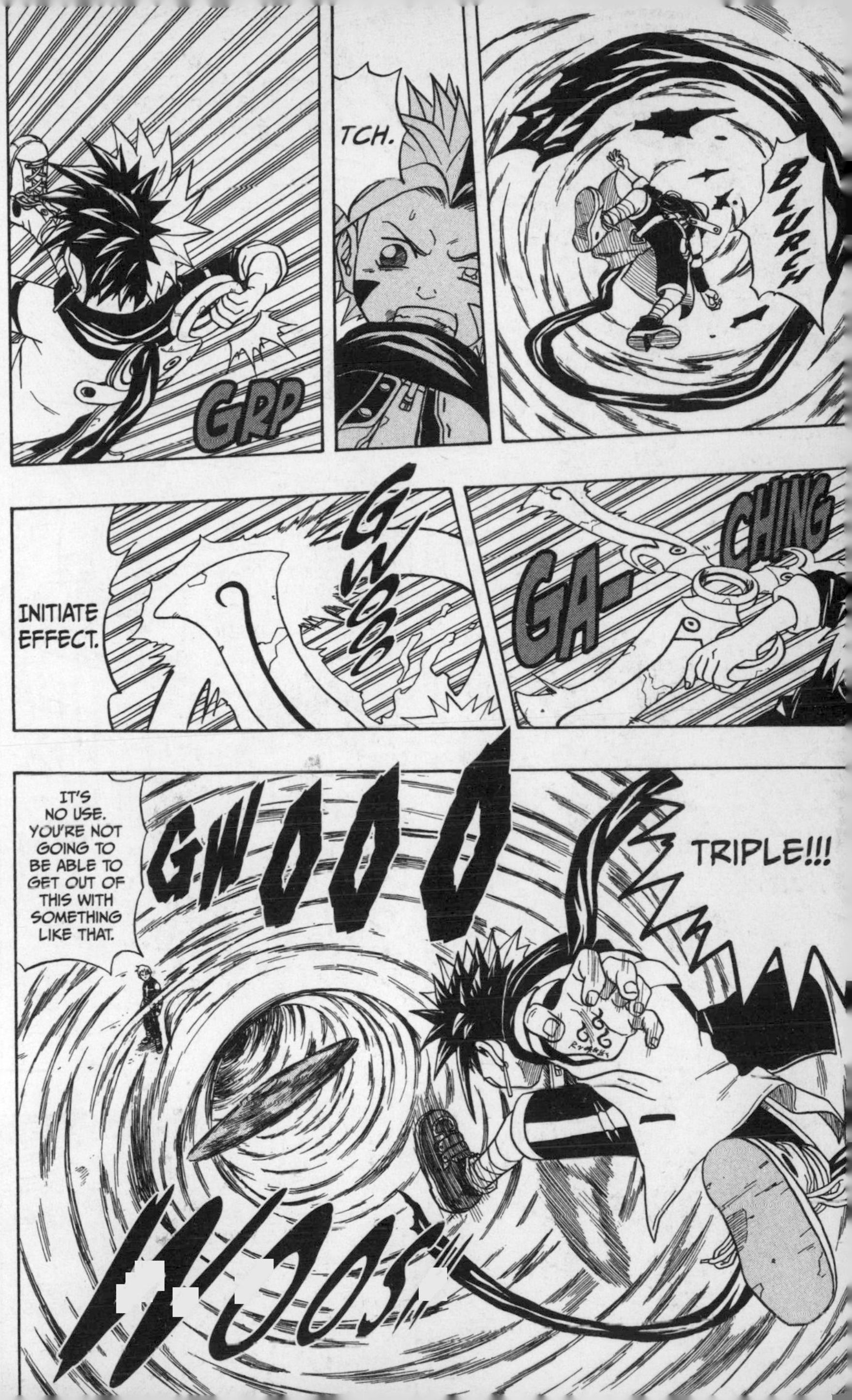
BLURCH
TCH.
GRP
GA- CHING
INITIATE EFFECT.
GWOOOO
TRIPLE!!!
GWOOOO
IT'S NO USE. YOU'RE NOT GOING TO BE ABLE TO GET OUT OF THIS WITH SOMETHING LIKE THAT.

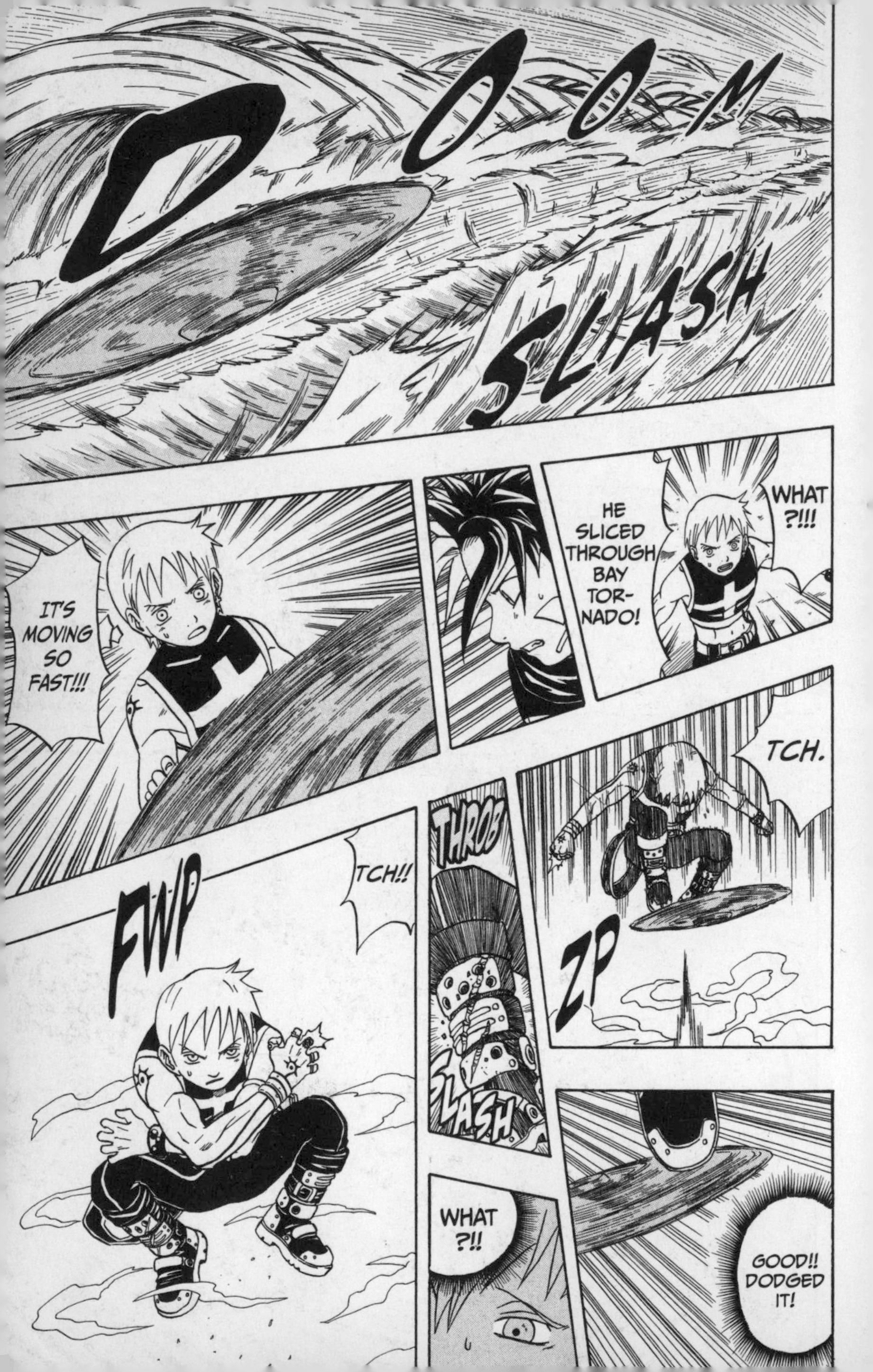
DOOM
SLASH
WHAT ?!!!
HE SLICED THROUGH BAY TOR-NADO!
IT'S MOVING SO FAST!!!
TCH.
ZP
THROB
SLASH
GOOD!! DODGED IT!
WHAT ?!!
TCH!!
FWP

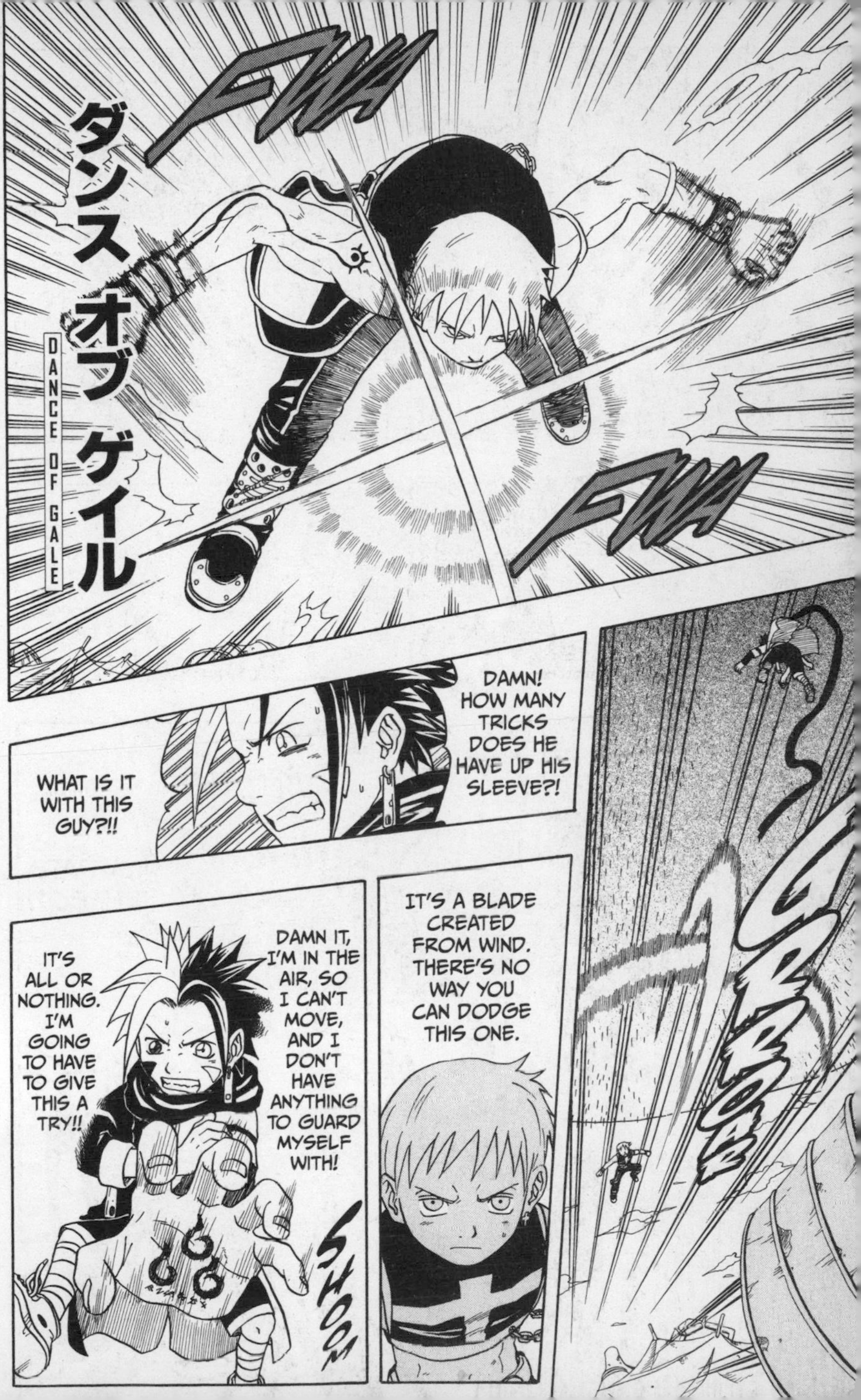
FWA
FWA
ダンス オブ ゲイル
DANCE OF GALE
DAMN! HOW MANY TRICKS DOES HE HAVE UP HIS SLEEVE?!
WHAT IS IT WITH THIS GUY?!!
IT'S A BLADE CREATED FROM WIND. THERE'S NO WAY YOU CAN DODGE THIS ONE.
DAMN IT, I'M IN THE AIR, SO I CAN'T MOVE, AND I DON'T HAVE ANYTHING TO GUARD MYSELF WITH!
IT'S ALL OR NOTHING. I'M GOING TO HAVE TO GIVE THIS A TRY!!
SHOOO!

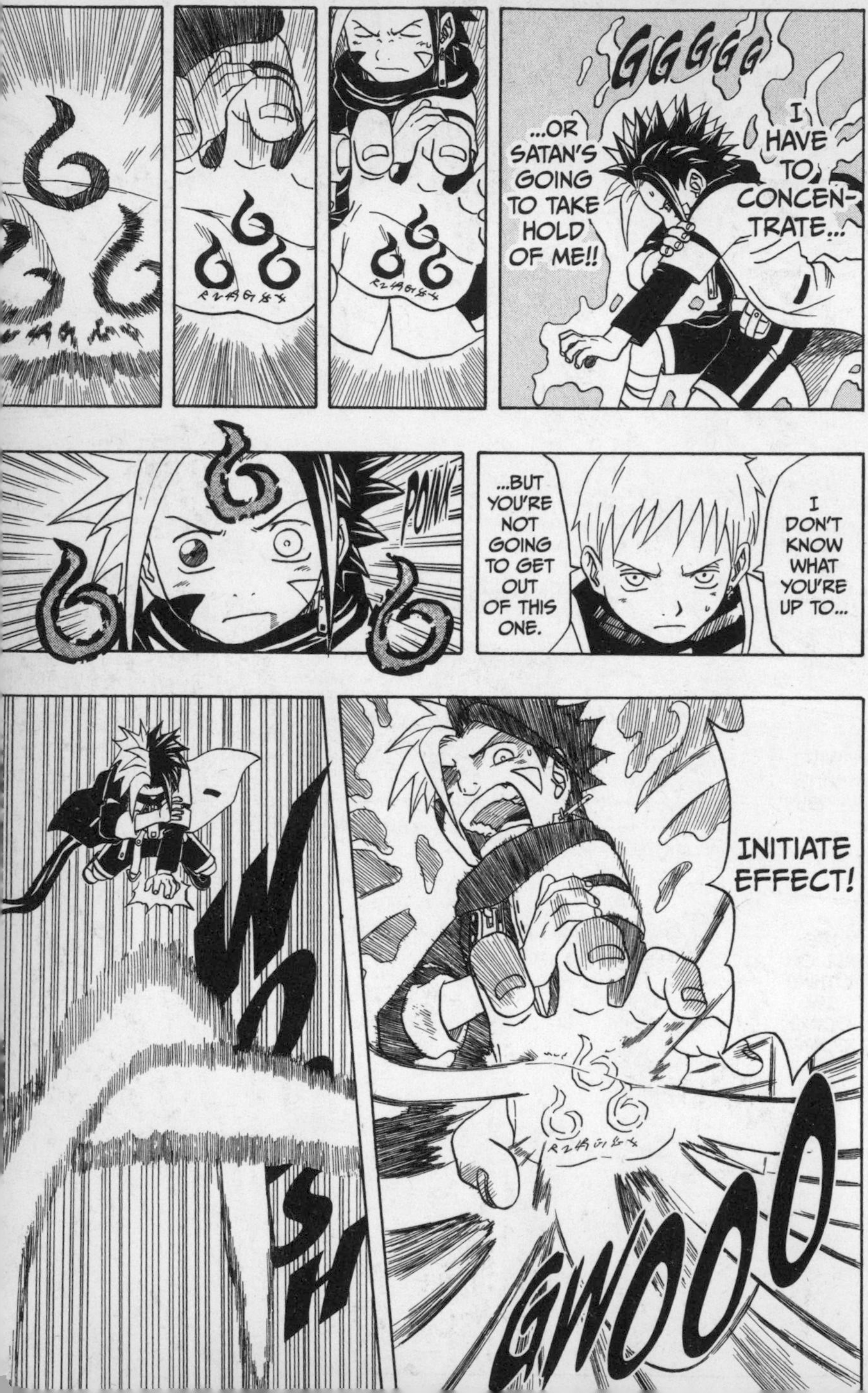
GGGGG
I HAVE TO CONCENTRATE...
...OR SATAN'S GOING TO TAKE HOLD OF ME!!
I DON'T KNOW WHAT YOU'RE UP TO...
...BUT YOU'RE NOT GOING TO GET OUT OF THIS ONE.
POINK
INITIATE EFFECT!
GWOOOO

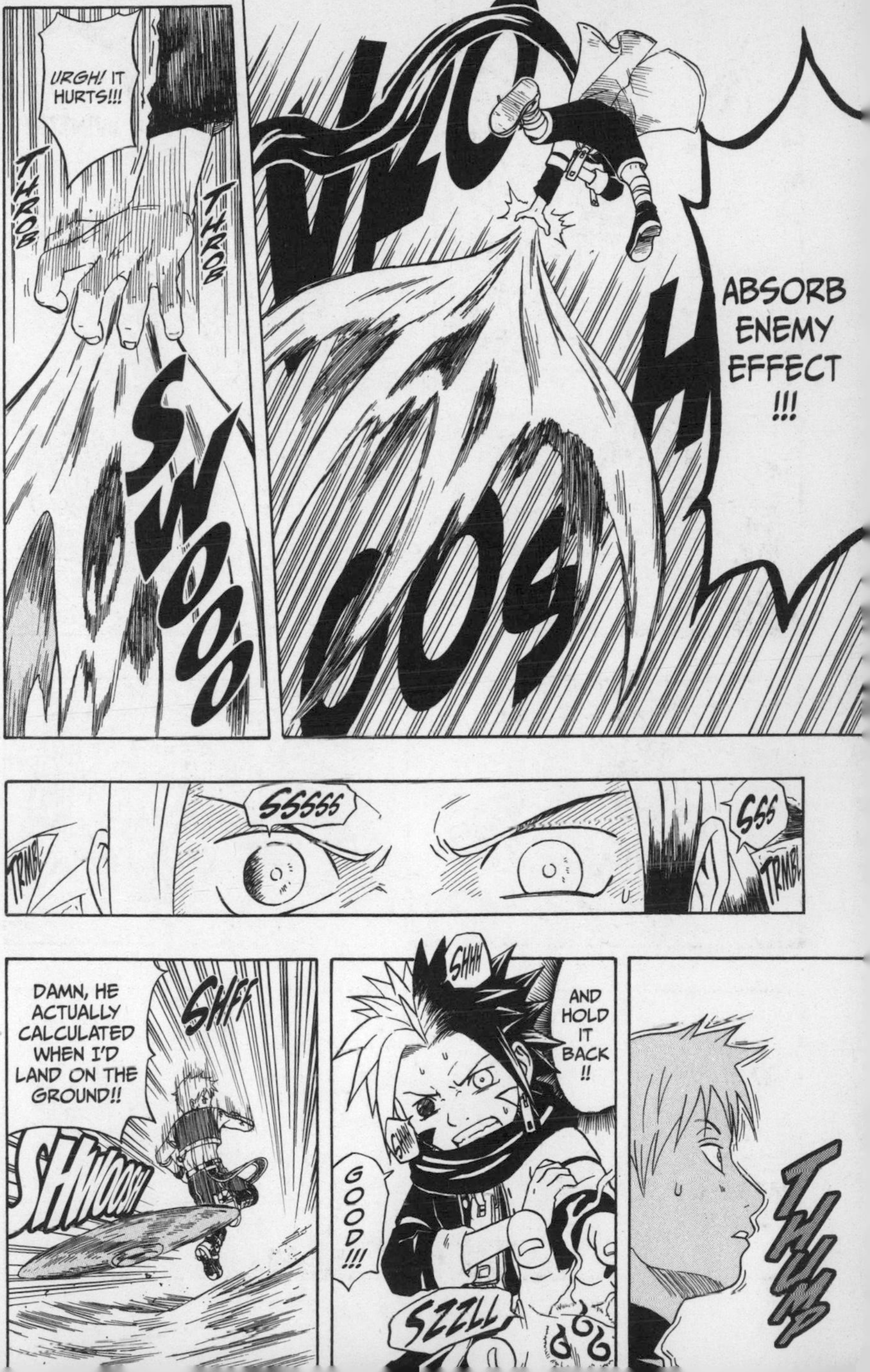
ABSORB ENEMY EFFECT !!!
URGH! IT HURTS!!!
THROB
THROB
SWOOO
SSS
TRMBL
SSSSS
TRMBL
SHHH
AND HOLD IT BACK !!
GOOD!!!
SZZLL
DAMN, HE ACTUALLY CALCULATED WHEN I'D LAND ON THE GROUND!!
SHFF
SHWOOSH

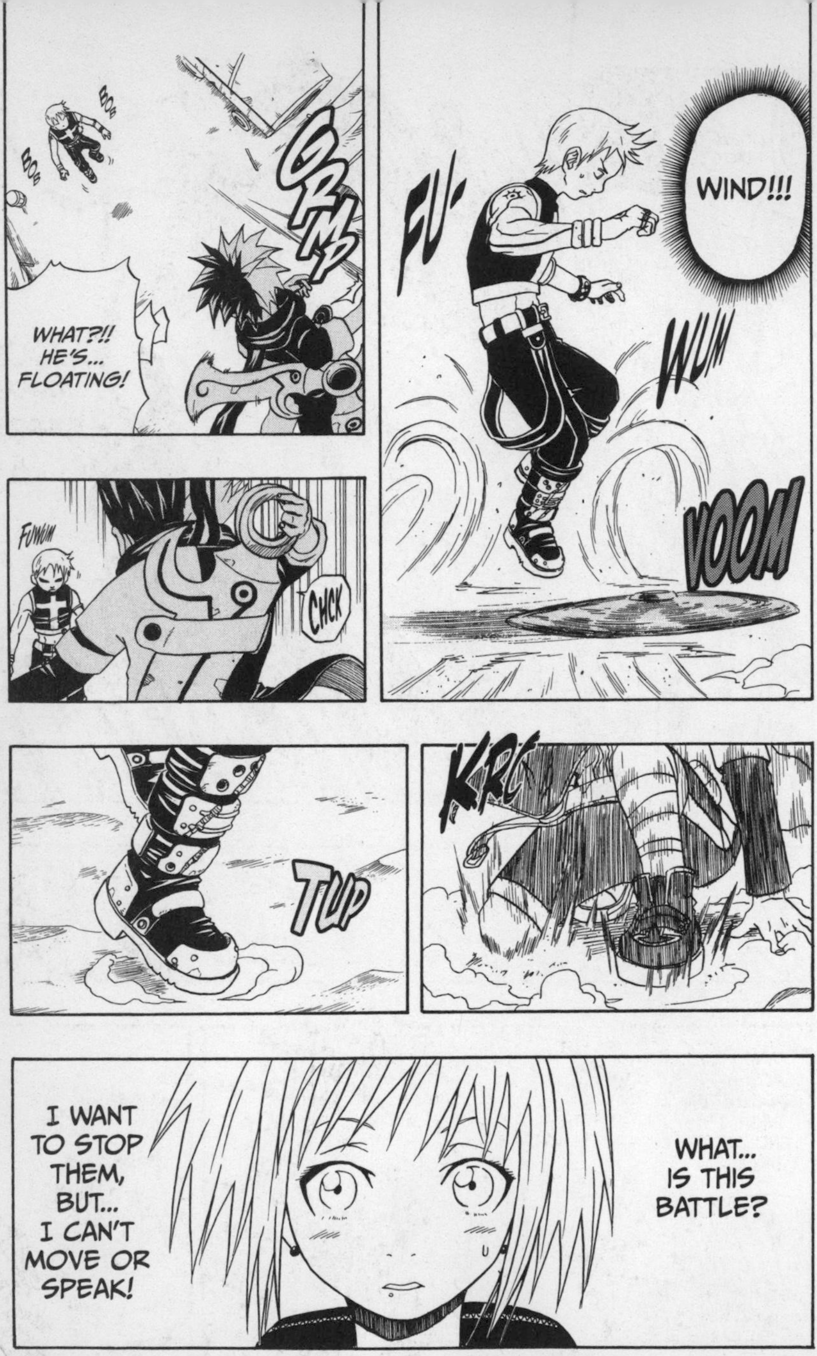
WIND!!!
FU-
WUM
VOOM
BOE
BOE
GRMP
WHAT?!! HE'S... FLOATING!
CHCK
FUWUM
KRC
TUP
WHAT... IS THIS BATTLE?
I WANT TO STOP THEM, BUT... I CAN'T MOVE OR SPEAK!

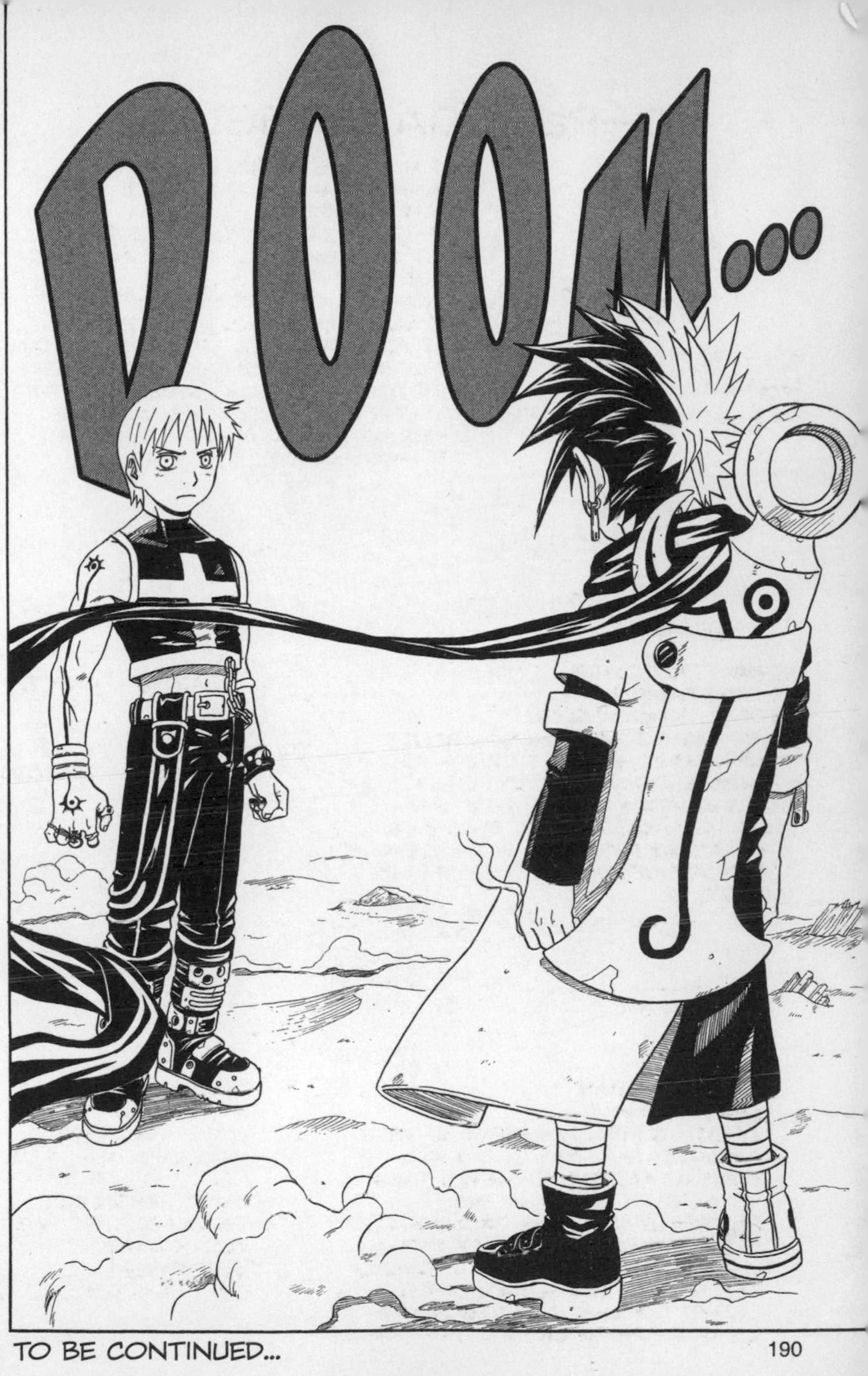
DOOM...

TO BE CONTINUED...

O-Parts CATALOGUE ⑦

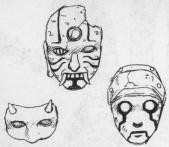

O-PARTS: THE MASKS OF MAGIMA
(HANNYA, MAIHIME, KAGEMARU)
O-PART RANK: C
EFFECT: TELEPATHY, TELEPORTATION
(BUT ONLY WHEN ALL THREE ARE USED
TOGETHER)
MASK-TYPE O-PARTS USED BY BAKU,
HIS SON MU, AND HIS DAUGHTER LEM.
THE TELEPORTATION EFFECT, WHICH CAN
ONLY BE USED WHEN ALL THREE MASKS
ARE TOGETHER, IS SO STRENUOUS THAT
IT SHORTENS THEIR LIVES. MOST OF
THEIR BATTLE MOVES ARE ILLUSION
TECHNIQUES.

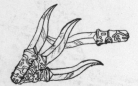

O-PART: MOSQUITO
O-PART RANK: B
EFFECT: SHADOW SLOW
JUST LIKE ITS NAME, MOSQUITO, IT
LIKES SHADOWS AND IS DRAWN TO
HUMAN BLOOD. IT WOULD BE NO
EXAGGERATION TO SAY THAT THE
O.P.T. ELGA WAS ABLE TO BECOME A
HIGH-RANKING OFFICIAL IN THE ZENOM
SYNDICATE SOLELY BECAUSE OF THIS
O-PART.

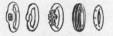

O-PART: JUSTICE
O-PART RANK: C
EFFECT: EARTH, ?, WIND, ?, ?
FIVE O-PARTS BELONGING
TO CROSS. THIS O-PART'S
TRUE ABILITY COMES TO
LIFE WHEN ITS FIVE EFFECTS
ARE COMBINED.

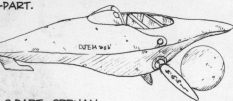

O-PART: ORPHAN
O-PART RANK: C
EFFECT: SUPERCONDUCTIVE MAGNET
A VEHICLE THAT WILL VERY LIKELY
HELP JIO AND THE GANG ON THEIR
JOURNEY. IT SEEMS TO GO
EXTREMELY WELL WITH JAJA-MARU,
WHICH MAKES EVERYBODY A LITTLE
UNEASY. JUDGING FROM ITS DESIGN,
THE ANCIENT PEOPLE MAY HAVE
COPIED THE SHAPE OF THE FLYING
SAND TRITON TO CREATE THIS O-PART.

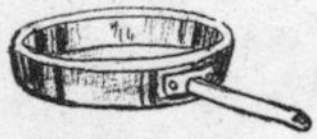

O-PART: FRYING PAN
O-PART RANK: E
EFFECT: FIRE
A MUST-HAVE FOR
ALL TRAVELING O.P.T.S.
YOU CAN'T USE IT
AS A WEAPON, BUT
I'VE HEARD THAT FRIED
RICE COOKED WITH
THIS FRYING
PAN IS THE BEST.

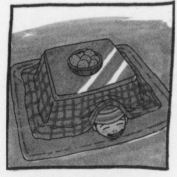

SEISHI KISHIMOTO

To us manga artists, the biggest enemy in winter — stronger than any final boss — is that devilish under-the-table heater: the kotatsu!

It's fused to my body like a tortoise shell...

I...can't...get out...

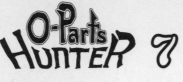

O-Parts HunteR 7

VIZ Media Edition
STORY AND ART BY SEISHI KISHIMOTO

English Adaptation/Tetsuichiro Miyaki
Touch-up Art & Lettering/Gia Cam Luc
Cover Design/Amy Martin
Interior Design/Andrea Rice
Editor/Carol Fox

Editor in Chief, Books/Alvin Lu
Editor in Chief, Magazines/Marc Weidenbaum
VP of Publishing Licensing/Rika Inouye
VP of Sales/Gonzalo Ferreyra
Sr. VP of Marketing/Liza Coppola
Publisher/Hyoe Narita

Printed in the U.S.A.

Published by VIZ Media, LLC
P.O. Box 77010
San Francisco, CA 94107

10 9 8 7 6 5 4 3 2 1
First printing, December 2007

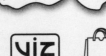

www.viz.com

store.viz.com

tion Goes Public

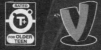

www.viz.com
store.viz.com

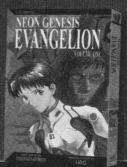

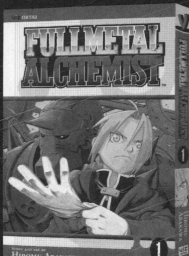
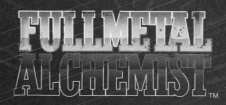

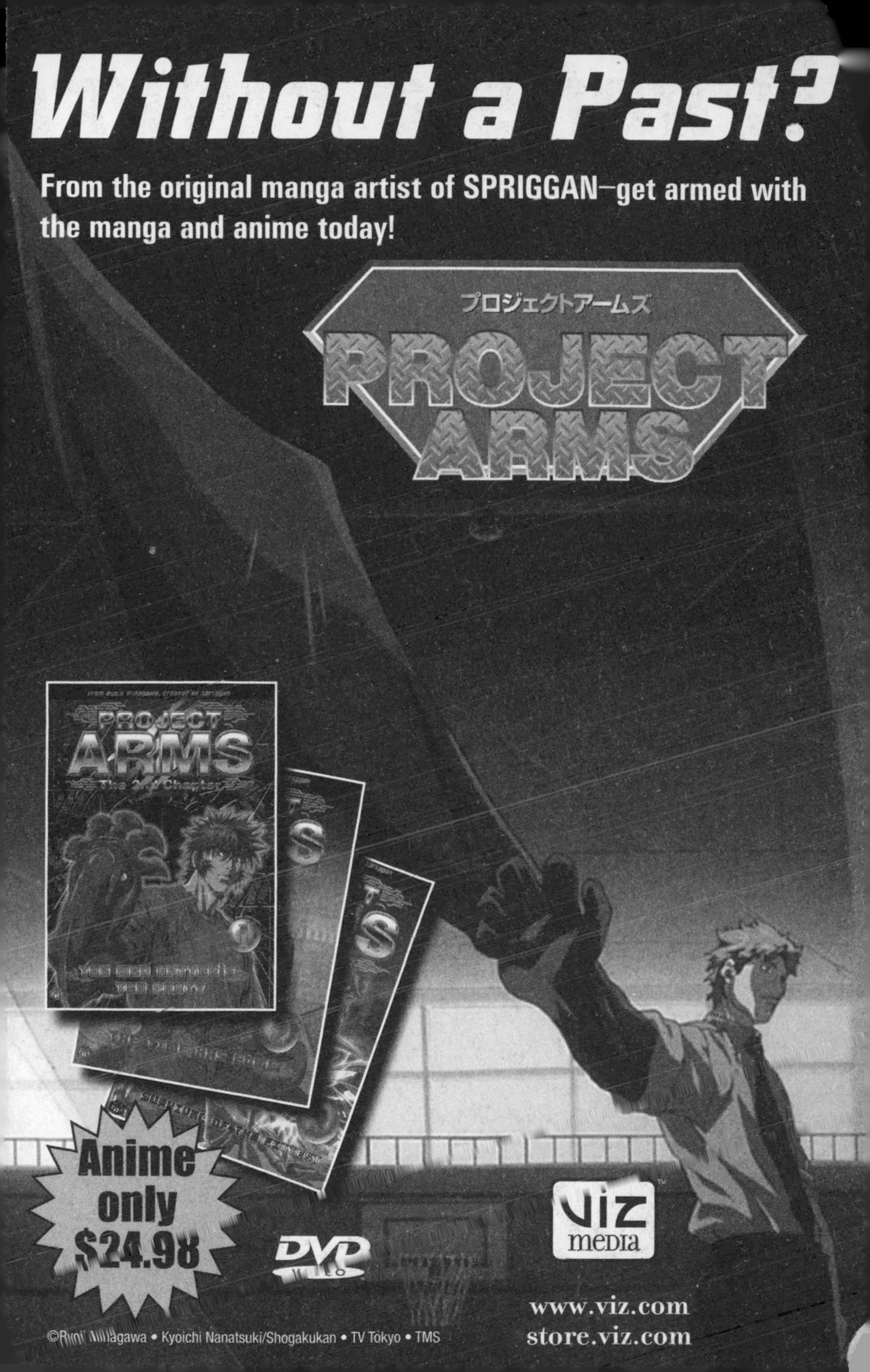
Without a Past?
From the original manga artist of SPRIGGAN—get armed with the manga and anime today!
プロジェクトアームズ
PROJECT ARMS
PROJECT ARMS
The 2nd Chapter
Anime only $24.98
DVD VIDEO
viz media
www.viz.com
store.viz.com
©Ryoji Minagawa • Kyoichi Nanatsuki/Shogakukan • TV Tokyo • TMS

What's a Future

Ryo thought he was normal until he learned his arm was secretly replaced with a powerful weapon. But he soon learns that there are others—teens like him—with mechanical limbs and no idea how the weapons were implanted. Now a secret organization is after the only living samples of this technology and wants to obtain their power by any means possible...

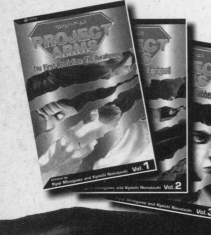

LOVE MANGA?
LET US KNOW WHAT YOU THINK!

OUR MANGA SURVEY IS NOW
AVAILABLE ONLINE. PLEASE VISIT:
VIZ.COM/MANGASURVEY

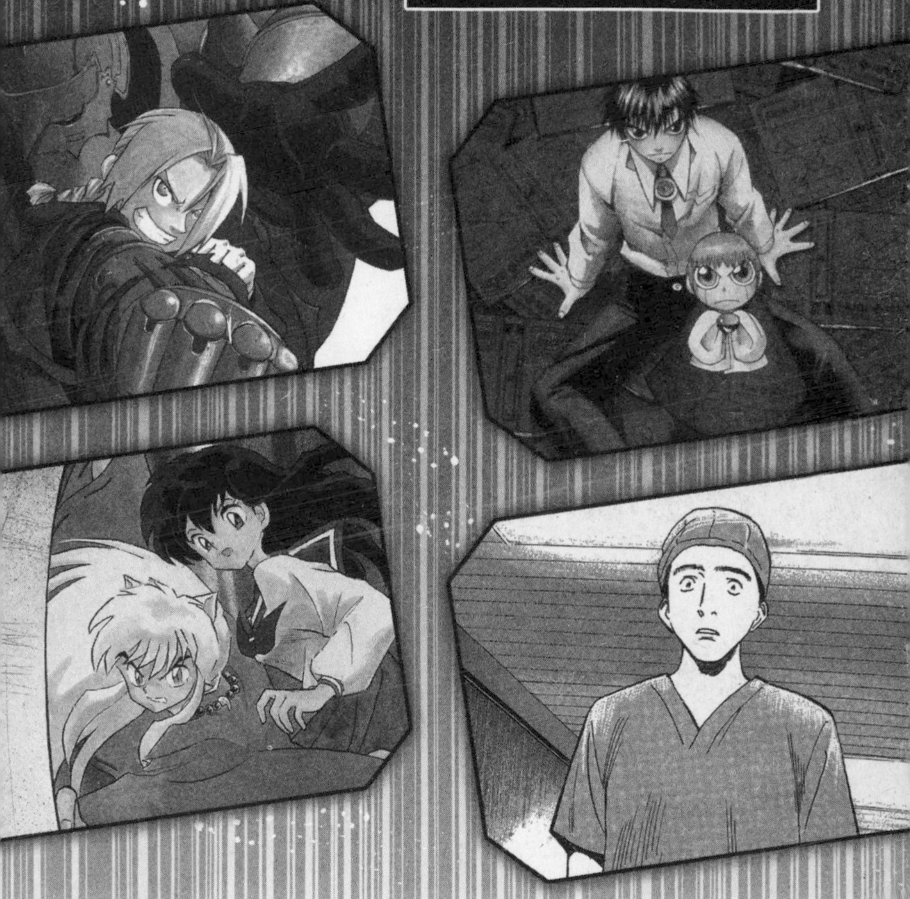

HELP US
YOU LOVE

FULLMETAL ALCHEMIST © Hiromu Arai/ HIRO SQUARE ENIX INUYASHA © 1997 Rumiko TAKAHASHI/Shogakukan Inc.
NAOKI URASAWA/ MONSTER © 1995 Naoki URASAWA Studio Nuts/Shogakukan Inc. ZATCH BELL! © 2001 Makoto RAIKU/Shogakukan Inc.

O-Parts HUNTER